DATE DUE

NOV 18 '99			

DEMCO 38-296

VITAL SIGNS

Vital Signs

ESSAYS ON AMERICAN LITERATURE AND CRITICISM

James W. Tuttleton

CHICAGO   IVAN R. DEE   1996

VITAL SIGNS. Copyright © 1996 by James W. Tuttleton. All rights reserved, including the right to reproduce this book or portions thereof in any form. For information, address: Ivan R. Dee, Inc., 1332 North Halsted Street, Chicago 60622. Manufactured in the United States of America and printed on acid-free paper.

Library of Congress Cataloging-in-Publication Data:
Tuttleton, James W.
  Vital Signs : essays on American literature and criticism / James W. Tuttleton
    p. cm.
  Includes bibliographical references and index.
  ISBN 1-56663-100-9 (alk. paper)
    1. American literature—History and criticism—Theory, etc.
  2. American literature—History and criticism. 3. Criticism—United States. I. Title
  PS121.T88 1996
  810.9—dc20   95–35948

For Patricia

cara sposa

La dolce donna dietro a lor mi pinse
con un sol cenno su per quella scala,
sì sua virtù la mia natura vinse;

né mai qua giù dove si monta e cala
naturalmete, fu sì ratto moto
ch'agguagliar si potessse a la mia ala . . .

Preface

Vital Signs brings together a great many observations about American literature and criticism that turn out to be somewhat more polemical than I first intended. If they echo with the overtone of argument and debate, they do so despite some reluctance and against the will. Criticism, I think, ought to be—and in this book *is*—an explication and celebration of imaginative genius. I see, however, that my vexation has risen in reaction to recent tendencies in linguistic and literary criticism, tendencies that have tried to drain literature not only of its traditional capacity to illuminate human experience but also of its ability to give aesthetic pleasure. I have in mind the effect of such "schools of criticism" as neo-Marxism, Queer Theory, the new historicism, feminism, multiculturalism, reader-response theory, deconstructionism, and the so-called "creative criticism" by would-be (but failed) professor-poets.

In recent years these disfigurations in criticism, as I regard them, have had dismaying effects on readers of literature. In declaring that language is disjunct from reality and cannot therefore represent it, the deconstructionist, for instance, has convinced a great many people that there is no point in reading plays or novels to discover what society was like in the eighteenth century or what notions of virtue may have governed conduct in the Renaissance. Literature, we are told, can no longer be thought of, in Kenneth Burke's phrase, as equipment for living. In fact, by the deconstructionist's account, there is no literature as such —no verbal art, no elevated, distinguished body of superior imaginative writing—but only discourse, endless discourse, all of which can be deconstructed, demystified, and shown to be mere verbal production. This view, recently enunciated by a president of the Modern Language Association, has entered into the thinking of many students, teachers, and general readers and has transmogrified literature into a mere interplay of linguistic elements, the equivalent of a *Times* cross-word puzzle for people who want to play with notions like *aporia*, *différance*, or *diachresis*, and who think that, since *discours* is just *discours*, *The Honeymooners* is the equivalent, for criticism, of *King Lear*.

As dismaying as deconstructionism may be in trivializing literature as a mere freeplay of linguistic undecidabilities, other viewpoints are for me equally noxious. These are the recent modes of applied criticism that manipulate literary texts so as to endorse the critic's political viewpoint or to serve as a cautionary instance of some retrograde position that is now felt to be politically incorrect. Feminism, black and Latino studies, lesbian and gay criticism, multicultural studies, neo-Marxism—all are very prominent in the American classroom today. And the journals of criticism and programs of the learned societies are raucous with their strenuous rhetoric. Each of these approaches has a social or sexual agenda (or both), an agenda felt to be more important than the litera-ture that is invoked to present it. Citizens may wish to act upon such social or political agendas in the public arena. But whatever we may think of them, the reduction of the literary work to an instrument of social change (of whatever kind it may be) has manifestly deformed our subject, corrupted judgment, and falsified the critical enterprise itself.

In the essays that follow I cite evidence of those tendencies that I regard as inimical to literature as the precious vision of the American creative imagination, or that I see as subversive of American history as a complex and difficult but nonetheless intelligible record of the past. The essays on Parkman and Irving, for instance, reject emphatically the "creative historiography" of the kind appallingly advocated by Hayden White and recently concocted by Simon Schama. The essays on Fuller, London, and the modern Sophists are meant to remind the reader of how insidious has been the utopian appeal of socialism; with the best of intentions, it has seduced and betrayed many well-meaning American writers and critics. Even though socialism has clearly subverted every society where it has been implemented; even though, as a political and economic ideology, it has collapsed in Eastern Europe and the former Soviet Union; and even though socialism can be imposed on people, as in China and Cuba, only at the point of a gun, it remains the mindless sentimental hankering of many American university faculties. In this respect I concur with those, like Roger Kimball and Dinesh D'Sousa, who have shown the universities to be permeated with sixties radicals who have attained tenure and who now use the college classroom to restate the failed policies of the SDS and like radical organizations.

Of course it cannot be said of me, as Gerald Graff has complained of Kimball and D'Sousa, that I am not an academic and therefore really do not know what goes on in the academy. I have been a teacher for a great many years, and for quite some time I have observed closely faculty meetings, conferences, and scholarly publications. And, as a sometime chairman and associate graduate dean, I have seen critical enthusiasms come and go. But the kind of ideological assault on literature that has emerged in the past decade or two is unparalleled in my experience.

One form of the assault can be seen in women's studies. The essays herein on Emerson and Hawthorne, Fuller, Chopin, Fitzgerald, Green, and Hemingway look at the effects on some American literary criticism of what I regard as desperate and misguided thinking. This criticism takes one of three forms. First, since there are few serious women writers who agree with the purposes of radical feminism, one type of feminism exaggerates the importance of politically correct but distinctly second-order women writers on the radical fringes of mainstream literature. Margaret Fuller, for example, is routinely overpraised for literary virtues that an examination of her work will not sustain.

Second, if the writer really *is* distinguished, like Edith Wharton or Kate Chopin, feminist arguments are sometimes made in her name that letters, journals, and other documents cannot support. It makes academic women very uncomfortable to turn from *The House of Mirth*, with its poignant sacrificed heroine Lily Bart, to *French Ways and Their Meaning* or to Mrs. Wharton's journals and letters with their sharply expressed critiques of the deficiencies of American women. A few years ago Susan Goodman began a book on Edith Wharton with confidence that Mrs. Wharton would have approved of her project—only to discover a Wharton letter stating that "women scholars would be better off staying home and having babies." [1] Whether they should or not is a debatable question, but Mrs. Wharton's viewpoint cannot be aligned with that of the feminist ideologues in the universities or in NOW. Nor can that of Kate Chopin.

I confess to a certain discomfort in raising the flaws of feminist criticism, partly because I am a Southerner and it seems discourteous ever to contradict a lady, partly because I am in sympathy with a great many goals of feminism. On the other hand, genuine liberation is not likely to result from gross distortions of literary fact, and candor compels strict attention to the biographical and textual evidence. If this seems antifeminist, I trust that the reader will note my acclamation of the literary genius of Mrs. Wharton, Ellen Glasgow, and Kate Chopin, and observe that my praise of them has a great deal to do with their refusal to

---

1 Susan Goodman, *Edith Wharton's Inner Circle* (Austin: University of Texas Press, 1994), p. xi.

degrade the art of fiction into mere propaganda, however noble the cause.

The third form of misguided feminism is that which attacks the literature liked by men (tales by Hemingway and Faulkner, for instance), or that attacks men for being men, for liking the things that men customarily like—hunting, fishing, cussing, card-playing, endless palaver about sports, and the pursuit of women. We are apparently still fated to hear, on every other hand, that men are patriarchal tyrants, brutal oppressors, or fiendish exploiters and therefore ought to be continually trashed until they become more like women. This sounds odd, especially when it comes from the lesbian wing of the critical establishment, but we live in an odd age when even human sexuality is a "social construction" and the aberration is called the norm. If men are indeed unjust, and too many are, perhaps they ought to behave more like men, rather than women, men who have been brought up by their fathers to respect their mothers and sisters and other women. In any case, living as I do in the heart of Greenwich Village, seeing as I see, on a daily basis, men who think they are women and women who think they are men, I am not impressed by the usual run of arguments against essentialism in gender matters. Psychosexual abnormality, whether decked out in tweeds or combat boots and power shoulder pads, does not add up to psychological or emotional good health. If we live in a decadent era, one sign of it is the hostility to writers who were manifestly men and who wrote well about experiences that men have always enjoyed.

The essays in *Vital Signs* have arisen out of many different contexts and claims upon my attention. In some cases a particular book or critical issue provoked an exploration; in others I was commissioned to write on a particular topic; in a few others I was asked to give a talk that evolved into an essay. Doubtless the individual pieces will reflect the point of origin, however much I may have revised them. Here I will specify only the last two essays: "Jacques et moi" and "Some Modern Sophists." These arose out of an NYU faculty colloquium on modernism and postmodernism and reflect the thought of a number of professors, graduate students, and several editors at *The New Criterion,* including Hilton Kramer, Roger Kimball, Robert Richman, and Christopher Carduff. To all of the seminar members I wish to express my thanks for their incisive criticism. Both of these essays deal with what I regard as the deficiencies of deconstructionism and its critical affiliations and derivatives. (By way of contrast, the attentive reader will have found in my remarks on Parkman, James, Howells, and Wharton an appreciation of their scrupulous critical conduct in the presence of the texts of history and literature.)

But *Vital Signs* is not, I hope, handcuffed to the expiring corpse of an abstract academic argument about "isms." A more vivid and personal element, touching these authors, is apparent in the genesis and affect of these essays. I do not mean—like Geoffrey Hartman and Harold Bloom —that the critic is a poet and that his work is "as creative as that of the imaginative writer." For me, the critic must be the servant of the creative work and not its jealous rival. In my view, genuine literary art is a priceless gift, and the author of it—far from being defunct, as modern sophistry has it—is a richly important element in understanding its genesis and its evolving aesthetic form. Consequently, the "death-of-the-author" nonsense, as it descends from Heidegger, Barthes, and Foucault, I reject with absolute finality. The literary works discussed here are too various to have been composed by "language itself" and are in fact products of richly differentiated personalities whose identities are worth keeping present to consciousness and indeed worth celebrating. I have therefore not hesitated to open up questions of biography in an effort to make the meaning of texts clearer.

No work of literature, of course, comes down to a restatement of the author's intention, supposing that the critic could ever fully reconstruct it. Literary purpose is complex, obscure in its origins, and masked by "obvious" biographical details. Authors, moreover, do not always consciously know what their own aesthetic intention is and are often guided by a subterranean wisdom that defies immediate comprehension. One of the most engaging avenues of criticism is thus to trace the ways in which a work of art seems to break away from a writer's avowed intention and assert its own independence. It never really does so, of course. The poem, to the extent that it has been completed by the poet, is adequate unto itself. As Wallace Stevens put it in "So-and-So Reclining on Her Couch," "The arrangement contains the desire of / The artist."[2] It is this arrangement, rightly evident in the completed work, in the artifact present to criticism, that most concerns me here.[3] Indeed, I find that the essays below that gave me greatest pleasure were those in which I surrendered fully to the mystery of a novel or story and tried to work out, for myself, the hidden significance of its engaging questions. In the process of doing this I have found it necessary, from time to time, to address gross misreadings, in the criticism, of the works I love. But

---

2 *The Collected Poems of Wallace Stevens* (New York: Alfred A. Knopf, 1964), p. 296.

3 I am of course in full agreement with Hershel Parker's observation that some literary works are not complete, are complete in some defective form, or coexist in such variant forms that locating the object of criticism is difficult. Such problems, however, are not usually fatal to the production of judicious criticism. Otherwise we should all be mute. See Parker's *Flawed Texts and Verbal Icons: Literary Authority in American Fiction* (Evanston, Ill.: Northwestern University Press, 1984).

whether I attend to other critics or not, if my analysis of what our writers seem to have meant is helpful in any degree to the reader, I shall be content.

My title, *Vital Signs*, is meant to point to the status, in poetry and reflective thought (if I may so claim the term), of the literary works I discuss below. These works of art appeared at the particular historical moment of their birth or creation. I do not know how long they will go on living. But they span up to a century and a half of our literary history and have survived the changing historical contexts in which the American imagination has excelled. Despite the passage of time, then, there is every reason to regard them as having a vital existence. In contemplating the nature of this vitality, I have returned again and again to Emily Dickinson's stunning verse 883:

> The Poets light but Lamps—
> Themselves—go out—
> The Wicks they stimulate
> If vital Light
>
> Inhere as do the Suns—
> Each Age a Lens
> Disseminating their
> Circumference—.[4]

The poem is brilliant in its assertion of the felt infinitude of the living poem. This kind of poem casts its light out of the intensity of its inherent, perhaps even inexhaustible energy. The poem concedes the finitude of the poet, or the death of the author, though not in the sense in which Heidegger and others have claimed it. The image of the poem as a light that enlarges its circumference of passion, insight, and understanding from age to age, indicates that the poem as such has a life of its own. It is really independent of the manuscripts, the holographic scribble, the typescripts and carbons, the stereotyped print runs, the hot metal text or computer printouts, the webbed versions in cyberspace, or the platform and classroom declamations. What is this vitality? I do not mean to suggest that these works of art are alive like a human being. But they do have a "life" of a special kind, a life independent of their material incarnations, an ontology that is denied in much of the tendentious criticism of the day.[5]

---

4 *The Complete Poems of Emily Dickinson*, ed. Thomas H. Johnson (Boston: Little, Brown, 1960), p. 419.

5 Readers with an interest in the ontological *situs* of the poem may find helpful "The Mode of Existence of a Literary Work of Art," by René Wellek and Austin Warren, in *Theory of Literature* (New York: Harcourt, Brace, 1956), pp. 129–145.

Once created or "brought into being" by the artist, the ontological character of the artwork does not inhere in any particular graphological or phonological manifestation of it; and it certainly does not inhere in my response to it as a reader—or in yours. We must of course read or hear it. Without that, we cannot know the form in which it exists or "lives." Knowledge of the life of the literary work is then, for us, inevitably experiential. And in the experience of our reading it or hearing it, the mysterious remarkable ideal "life" of the artwork is heard and felt in its expression and utterance. It is acquired by us and becomes an object of knowledge available to reflective thought and susceptible to literary criticism.

As my remarks on Jacques Derrida suggest, deconstructionism undertakes to kill this, the being of the text. It announces that all texts are already dead, and its operations take the form of an autopsy on what is now alleged no longer to have any life or "presence." But its error is in mistaking the absent "presence" as that of the vanished author, who supposedly left merely inert graphemes, phonemes, and morphemes in his stead. But the real presence, which survives the mortal poet, is that which inheres in and vitalizes the living work of art. In this sense, and to the extent that it is a genuine manifestation of literary genius, the work of art is a system of "vital signs" which testify to its "existence," to an expression of genius that "lives" from generation to generation. There are many kinds of literature. But in its simplest and most important manifestation, the "existence" created in a poem or a novel or a play is generally a representation of a world alternative to our own. It is this alternate world, this imaginative variation on the real, to use Paul Ricoeur's phrase, that opens up modes of being that might be our own. As I suggest below, we turn to literature precisely to discover other worlds, to encounter those modes of being that once were, are now, and that might in the future become our own. Because a great imaginative work disseminates its life as Dickinson (rather than Derrida) suggests, it enlarges the mind and opens the heart, and is a precious gift of culture, both a doorway to understanding and the occasion of instructive aesthetic pleasure. In the present critical climate, I believe that we need to be reminded of that.

J. W. T.

New York University
March 1996

Contents

VITAL SIGNS

Parkman and the Emptiness of Postmodern History

And Kung said "Wang ruled with moderation,
In his day the State was well kept,
And even I can remember
A day when the historians left blanks in their writings,
I mean for things they didn't know,
But that time seems to be passing."
  —Ezra Pound, *The Cantos*

One of the more interesting recent sensations in the field of American history has undoubtedly been the appearance of Simon Schama's *Dead Certainties: (Unwarranted Speculations)*. Readers had come to expect, from this Mellon Professor in the Social Sciences at Harvard, the writing of rather conventional, even massively detailed and documented histories like his *Patriots and Liberators: Revolution in the Netherlands, 1780–1813* (1977), *Two Rothschilds and the Land of Israel* (1978), or *The Embarrassment of Riches: An Interpretation of Dutch Culture in the Golden Age* (1987). But in *Dead Certainties* Schama gave us a radically different kind of book—and set the discipline of history buzzing. *Dead Certainties* brought together several historical episodes, having an unclear logical or chronological connection, in order to illustrate some generalizations about historiography. There are several accounts of the death in battle of General James Wolfe, who led the victorious British forces against Quebec in 1759 and so forced the French out of North America. (The story of his death—as well as that of his antagonist Montcalm, who also died in the battle—is responsibly told in Francis Parkman's superb history *Montcalm and Wolfe* [1884].) Schama also provided an account of Benjamin West's painting *The Death of General Wolfe* (1770), which idealized the heroic British commander, took London by storm, and assured West's artistic fame. We are also presented a wholly invented diary entry of a British common soldier, who is imagined to have been present at the battle where Wolfe fell. And finally, among other things, Schama gave us a narrative of the murder in 1849 of George Parkman, the historian's uncle, by a disgruntled Harvard professor who owed him money.

Each of these separate subjects might have been the centerpiece of its own historical study. But Schama violently yoked them together—as he explains it in his afterword—so as to dislocate "the conventions by which histories establish coherence and persuasiveness." Coherence and persuasion are out. This is his way of urging upon us "the teasing gap separating a lived event and its subsequent narration."[1] In his insistence on this gap between the event and the narrated representation of it, Schama has apparently gone to school to the skeptics now permeating the profession of history, of whom Hayden White is exemplary. In *Tropics of Discourse* (1978), White tells the profession that

> the historian serves no one well by constructing a specious continuity between the present world and that which preceded it. On the contrary, we require a history that will educate us to discontinuity more than ever before; for discontinuity, disruption, and chaos is our lot.

It is certainly our lot if we choose to make it so, but many will feel that "discontinuity, disruption, and chaos" are the usual Nietzschean buzzwords expressing the trendy nihilism of the moment. No one wants from the historian a "specious continuity." Isn't that why we invariably test narrative sequences according to historical evidence, a plausible chronology, our grasp of human psychology and motivation, and what we know of the logic of cause and effect?

But a more decisive question is this: are *all* efforts at representing the continuity between the past and present specious? White appears to think so. Hence, he deplores the reluctance of historians

---

1 Simon Schama, *Dead Certainties: (Unwarranted Speculations)* (New York: Alfred A. Knopf, 1991), pp. 321, 320. Citations from this work will hereafter be given as *DC*, in parentheses, in the text.

to consider historical narratives as what they most manifestly are: verbal fictions, the contents of which are as much *invented* as *found* and the forms of which have more in common with their counterparts in literature than they have with those in the sciences.[2]

White need worry no more about historians' reluctance to equate history and the novel: he appears to have found in Schama a disciple willing to profess historical narration as always a constructive invention. (In fact, in *Dead Certainties*, invention takes in part the form of a collage of merely juxtaposed elements). For Schama, "even in the most austere scholarly report from the archives, the inventive faculty—selecting, pruning, editing, commenting, interpreting, delivering judgments—is in full play" (*DC*, 322). Are these indeed modes of *invention*? Anyone less given to the view that history writing is an inventive freeplay might describe these activities as signs of the rational intelligence at work, in sifting evidence in search of the essence of meaning about men and events in their interaction. At least this is the view held by Francis Parkman, in opposition to whom, in *Dead Certainties*, Schama unwisely aligns himself.

To give Schama due credit, historians *are* "painfully aware of their inability ever to reconstruct a dead world in its completeness, however thorough or revealing their documentation" (*DC*, 320). But the lack of completeness of information or objects—and, on the philosophical plane, even the absence of selfsameness between the historical event and its narrated form—hardly warrants the historian's abandoning his usual empirical method, however incomplete the data or imperfect the execution, for the imaginative liberties claimed by the novelist.[3] Completeness is in any case impossible, for documents, objects, and other testimony of the past are inevitably lost or destroyed over time. More useful to everyone is an historiographical method based on what *is* available, a

---

2 Hayden White, *Tropics of Discourse: Essays in Cultural Criticism* (Baltimore: Johns Hopkins University Press, 1978), pp. 50, 82.

3 A recent instance of the pernicious effect of Schama's historiography is Joe McGinniss's *The Last Brother* (1993). It purports to be a biography of Senator Edward Kennedy. But, lacking demonstrable evidence about a number of areas in Kennedy's life, McGinniss nevertheless reads Kennedy's mind and invents with wild abandon some material about Chappaquiddick, the alleged Mafia connection, the brothers' "affairs" with Marilyn Monroe, and so forth. All of this is given—as Francis X. Clines put it—for "the sheer E. L. Doctorow fun of it." (The historical novelist's wilful distortion of the lives of real people is another abuse deserving of contempt, but that is matter for another paper.) When a furor erupted at McGinniss's invention of "facts" and at the resultant injustice to Kennedy, McGinniss justified himself by invoking the example of Schama. See Clines's "'See What You've Done Now, Camelot Dweeb?'" *New York Times Book Review*, August 22, 1993, p. 6. Schama is said to be dismayed that McGinniss has connected this travesty to *Dead Certainties*. But the link speaks for itself.

method sufficiently comprehensive to allow the historian to capture the substance of the historical subject, a subject like Wolfe's defeat of Montcalm on the Plains of Abraham in 1759 and the consequent fall of the empire of New France. But to accomplish this end it is of course essential to be an essentialist. I propose, then, to contrast Parkman and Schama as modern and postmodern historians. The result tells us much about the writing of history in our universities today.

I

Like every great historian, Francis Parkman thought that a serious historical method required him to read every scrap of paper and examine every extant material object pertinent to his subject, even if it took him off to public and private collections in Montreal, Washington, Paris, or elsewhere. He had exact copies made of everything germane to his subject—the command rosters, diaries, lists of orders, ordnance requisitions, army field correspondence, battle memoirs, governors' reports, missionary accounts, and the like. These he collated with all other documents about the same subject so as to determine whether witnesses were indeed at the scene and were reliable observers. Surviving physical objects, maps, and locations of historical importance were studied intently. It was Parkman's usual custom to visit the site where an event of historical importance had occurred, like the Plains of Abraham, to walk over the terrain, to visualize the layout of the contending armies, so as to recreate the event as it must have occurred. He was striving, he said in *The Jesuits in North America,* "to secure the greatest possible accuracy of statement, and to reproduce an image of the past with photographic clearness and truth."[4] After minute inspection of all the documents pertinent to the history of *La Salle,* Parkman went to the Midwest, and so precise was his geographical understanding that, in tracing La Salle's movements down the Mississippi, he actually found the archeological remains of an important Indian village lost in oblivion, its exact whereabouts disputed for more than two hundred years.

---

4 All of my citations from the works of Parkman, unless otherwise indicated, may be found in the Library of America editions: *Francis Parkman: France and England in North America,* 2 vols., ed. David Levin (New York: Library of America, 1983). Volume I includes *Pioneers of France in the New World,* hereafter abbreviated as *PF; The Jesuits in North America in the Seventeenth Century* (abbreviated as *J*); La Salle and the Discovery of the Great West (*LaS*); and *The Old Régime in Canada* (*OR*). Volume II includes *Count Frontenac and New France Under Louis XIV* (*CF*); *A Half-Century of Conflict* (*H-C*); and *Montcalm and Wolfe* (*M&W*). Quotations from *The Oregon Trail* (*OT*) and *The Conspiracy of Pontiac* (*CP*) are drawn from *Francis Parkman,* ed. William R. Taylor (New York: Library of America, 1991). The quotation just cited appears in *J,* I, 344. Hereafter, all my page references using these abbreviations will be given in the text.

Parkman's historical method was purchased at considerable pain to himself. Sorely afflicted by poor eyesight, migraine headaches, an inability to concentrate, and persistent insomnia, he often found it impossible to work. Whenever "The Enemy," as he called his ailment, overcame him, he had his assistants read to him and take his dictation. He even constructed a wooden frame the size of a sheet of paper, with wires to guide his fingers along the lines. He put the paper between the pasteboard and wires and, using a black lead crayon, he could write with closed eyes. In the introduction to *Pioneers*, he observes:

> During the past eighteen years, the state of his health has exacted throughout an extreme caution in regard to mental application, reducing it at best within narrow and precarious limits, and often precluding it. Indeed, for two periods, each of several years, any attempt at bookish occupation would have been merely suicidal. A condition of sight arising from kindred sources has also retarded the work, since it has never permitted reading or writing continuously for much more than five minutes, and often has not permitted them at all (*PF*, I, 17).

Physicians had no idea of how to cure him and tried various remedies to no avail. One even predicted an early death. Yet Parkman's stoic determination to finish *France and England in North America* drove him, over a period of decades, to the completion of it.

Schama believes that Parkman heroized Wolfe as he prepared the narrative of the Battle of Quebec, because he could identify with a general who also suffered debilitating physical ailments during his campaign against the crafty Montcalm:

> Past and present dissolved at this moment. [Parkman] became Wolfe and Wolfe lived again through him; the man's perseverance and fortitude; the punishments of his body; the irritability of his mind; the crazy, agitated propulsion of his energies all flowed between subject and historian; overtook and consumed him, robbed him of sleep and colonized his days so that the writing of it all, the remembering, the recitation drove him on, relentlessly, became akin to and part of the hard, forced climb [of the British soldiers] upwards to the heights; the drum-measured advance across the field [of the Plains of Abraham], unstoppable till the very finish (*DC*, 65).

But in fact a perusal of Parkman's histories will disclose that Wolfe was only *one* of his favorites. He was drawn to any historical figure whose vision, energy, will, and stoic determination sufficiently distinguished him from the bit players of history. The redoubtable Champlain was "the Aeneas of a destined people" (*PF*, I, 241); the wily old courtier

Count Frontenac, who took up the hatchet and danced the war dance before his Indians, was "the most remarkable man who ever represented the crown of France in the New World" (*CF,* II, 9); Father Brébeuf was the type of a pure saint and martyr; and La Salle

> was the hero, not of a principle nor of a faith, but simply of a fixed idea and a determined purpose. As often happens with concentred and energetic natures, his purpose was to him a passion and an inspiration; and he clung to it with a certain fanaticism of devotion. It was the off-spring of an ambition vast and comprehensive, yet acting in the interest both of France and civilization (*LaS,* I, 1012).

Parkman tried, like La Salle, to be "a tower of adamant, against whose impregnable front hardship and danger, the rage of man and of the elements, the southern sun, the northern blast, fatigue, famine, and disease, delay, disappointment, and deferred hope emptied their quivers in vain" (*LaS,* I, 1012). And, to a substantial degree, Parkman succeeded. Even so, psychobiography has its limits. Although Parkman was a romantic historian who appears to have held the Emersonian view that history is the "lengthened shadow" of the Great Man, he actually seized upon these figures for their symbolic value. As he remarks in the preface to *Montcalm and Wolfe,* "the names on the title page stand as representative of the two nations whose final contest for the control of North America is the subject of the book" (*M&W,* II, 841).

Parkman's extensive research, voluminous reading, and personal travel, despite his ill health, was, he said,

> essential to a plan whose aim it was, while scrupulously and rigorously adhering to the truth of facts, to animate them with the life of the past, and, so far as might be done, clothe the skeleton with flesh. If, at times it may seem that range has been allowed to fancy, it is so in appearance only; since the minutest details of narrative or description rest on authentic documents or on personal observation.

But fidelity to the past involved far more, for Parkman, than patient and scrupulous research into the facts. He thought that the historian had to "imbue himself with the life and spirit of the time. He must study events in their bearings near and remote; in the character, habits, and manners of those who took part in them. He must himself be, as it were, a sharer or a spectator of the action he describes" (*PF,* I, 16). This is why he enters so fully into the story of his heroes and appears, in fact, to identify with them.

If new information developed after he had completed a book, Parkman revised it immediately so as to bring his account into conformity with all the known facts. For years he tried to gain access to the La Salle documents controlled by the French colonial archivist Pierre Margry, who refused to let them be seen until he could publish them. Parkman finished *La Salle* anyway, confident that his narrative was right in the main. But since no one in Paris would publish Margry's sequestered documents, Parkman persuaded the United States Congress to fund the publication of the French collection. Parkman's only compensation was that he was then able to correct and enlarge *La Salle*. Finally, footnotes (which seem to have gone out of favor with many contemporary historians) Parkman amply provided; and in case anybody wished to check his conclusions against the evidence, he always left all copies of his research materials, clearly indexed, for later historical investigators.[5]

II

What, however, is Schama's method in *Dead Certainties,* a book without footnotes? *Without forewarning us,* Schama gives us in his volume concocted scenes, interior monologues, and fabricated diary entries. His narration of Wolfe and Montcalm at war consequently blurs the boundary between history and fiction. The effect is of a book not differing in kind from, say, James Fenimore Cooper's *The Last of the Mohicans.* Schama's approach thus aligns him with the intelligentsia who nowadays tell us that there is no such thing as an essence of an event, that there are really no genres like "history" or "fiction," and that there is no line between expository and narrative prose: there is only discourse, verbal production, *écriture.* It seems probable that our grandchildren will one day regard as juvenile this postmodern penchant for intellectual indiscrimination.

Schama insists in *Dead Certainties* that he does not really scorn "the boundary between fact and fiction"; but an interviewer for the *Guardian* reported him to be pleased with his role in the profession—"the bad boy of the class enjoying the trouble he didn't quite mean to cause."[6] But for all of this asserted respect for the differences between the two genres, I am inclined to say that Schama *meant* to stir up the ruckus: his treat-

---

5 Like Gertrude Himmelfarb, I find dismaying the decline of scholarly citation in works purporting to be learned. In addition to their value for readers (as she remarks in "Where Have All the Footnotes Gone?"), footnotes "make it a little harder for authors . . . to distort the source or deviate too far from it. If footnotes do not quite put the fear of God into scholars, they do make them more fearful than they might otherwise be of colleagues so inconsiderate and untrusting as to check their citations and actually read their sources." See Gertrude Himmelfarb, *On Looking into the Abyss: Untimely Thoughts on Culture and Society* (New York: Alfred A. Knopf, 1994), p. 128.
6 See Gordon S. Wood, "Novel History," *New York Review of Books,* June 27, 1991, p. 12.

ment of this boundary was not merely playful but perverse. Thus, after giving us what pretended to be solid history, Schama himself admitted that *Dead Certainties* was less a work of historical scholarship than a collection of "historical novellas." One appreciates the candor, but, coming as it does in an afterword, it can only irritate the reader that a deception has been practiced upon him and then—surprise!—the deceit is revealed. The confession of his "committing a fiction" does not, then, redeem the book: it fails as history. As fiction it is likewise a flop: Schama is no novelist.

For Schama, disrupting the conventions aiming at coherence and persuasion justifies itself because, he believes, "historical knowledge must always be fatally circumscribed by the character and prejudices of its narrator" (*DC*, 322). Don't we all concede that an historian's character and prejudices may at times distort his understanding? But are we not capable, as readers, of detecting, at least in some degree, most distortions that arise from prejudice, even as in real life we can detect biases in the attitude of friends and acquaintances? When we do recognize a bias, we engage in the rational act that weighs it and that discounts the distortion in its apparent degree; that is, we try to see through and beyond it to the form of truth that is warped by the writer's bias. Of course, it may be harder to see through a lie, unless it is voluntarily confessed—as Schama does, belatedly.

But one notes Schama's term *"fatally* circumscribed." That implies the epistemological skepticism about the truth, or truth-telling in narrative form, that has now permeated the profession of history. That a distinguished historian, at the top of his profession at Harvard, should dismiss as fatally false every historical account—because of the personal perspective of the author—is a scandal that the wise will ponder in dismay.[7] It suggests that no historian can be self-conscious enough or objective enough to rise above his own horizon in contemplating the horizon of the past; and it implies that no reader is competent to judge whether or not the historian has sufficiently done so.

Although the writing of history is not a branch of fiction, narrative does offer a mode of myth-making and is thus adjunctive to the feigning typical of fiction. But storytelling is also a significant mode of thought, a linear, temporal mode of discourse central to the mind's grasp of truth

---

7 Since writing this sentence I see that Professor Schama has left Harvard for Columbia, where his faculty appointment was apparently imposed on the Department of History by an administration that really wanted his scientist wife. When the acting chairman was asked whether there was opposition to the appointment and whether the Columbia history faculty approved the hiring of Schama, he remarked, "Those are internal matters which I do not wish to discuss." See Peter Stevenson's essay "Lights, Camera . . . Schama!" *New York Observer,* September 27, 1993, p. 15.

in the unfolding of events sequentially through time. Perhaps it is more central than logic, inference, deduction, and analogical reason. Surely it is much more *common,* and it is essential to the mental operations by which the truth about that which happened in the past is communicated to our contemporaries and, down the line, to future generations. Of course, any utterance about the past (or the present, for that matter) may express the truth, tell a lie, or misrepresent the truth through epistemological error. But telling the truth, as Heidegger reminds us in *Being and Time,* is not a matter of mere assertion about what happened but of uncovering and disclosing the past in its essential character. Whatever is asserted to be true, and is true, discloses the primordial character of Truth itself. The very existence of what we may—without irony—call Truth is "the ontological condition for the possibility that assertions can be either true or false—that they may uncover or cover things up."[8] Without confidence that a thing or a man or an event has an essence; without credence in an objective anterior primordial Truth; and without confidence in the capacity of the *logos* or discourse sufficiently to disclose it, everything quite naturally dissolves into an epistemological skepticism, radical subjectivity, willed assertion, and methodological anarchy—which pretty much describes the sad state of the profession of history at the moment. Essentialism, like coherence and persuasion, is also, with trendy intellectuals, out.

III

It is a great pleasure, then, to turn away from contemporary skeptical play, as represented by Schama's unwarranted speculations, to the work of Francis Parkman (1823–1893). This superb writer, the greatest historian America has ever produced, has recently been republished in three splendid volumes in the Library of America series. The first two of these volumes, ably edited by David Levin, present Parkman's lifetime project, a series of seven full-length, independently written yet interconnected and sequential historical studies gathered under the title of *France and England in North America.* Levin's edition includes *Pioneers of France in the New World* (1865), *The Jesuits in North America in the Seventeenth Century* (1867), *The Old Régime in Canada* (1874), *Count Frontenac and New France Under Louis XIV* (1877), *La Salle and the Discovery of the Great West* (1879), *Montcalm and Wolfe* (1884), and *A Half-Century of Conflict* (1892). The third volume, edited by William R.

---

8 Martin Heidegger, *Being and Time,* trans. John Macquarrie and Edward Robinson (New York: Harper and Row, 1962), p. 269.

Taylor, includes *The Oregon Trail* (1849) and *The Conspiracy of Pontiac* (1851). These last two titles, incidentally, although technically not a part of the *magnum opus*, are yet so germane to the issues raised in the larger work that they have a most pertinent bearing on Parkman's magisterial accomplishment. That accomplishment was to give us an American epic history: the most detailed, comprehensive, and definitive account of the transformation of the North American continent from forest savagery to civilization and of the transition from an Anglo-French to a Canadian and an American culture.

The subject of *France and England in North America* is the epic of these two countries in the American wilderness from 1488 onward. *Pioneers* recounts the initial explorations and settlements in Florida up to the sixteenth century (all destroyed) as well as the rise of Samuel de Champlain as an early explorer and heroic founder of modern Canada. *Jesuits* narrates the history of the Indian missions, which came to ruin in the Iroquois slaughter of the Christianized tribes. *The Old Régime* has a medley of themes: French conflicts with the Spanish, Dutch, and English (who were simultaneously founding New World settlements); the gradual rise of the military outposts and settlements in Canada and Acadia; the stumbling development of a French colonial policy; and French failures with the Indian tribes. As these books somewhat overlap in chronology, *Count Frontenac* deals with the royal governor who supported La Salle's explorations and rising conflict between the civil and ecclesiastical authority in France and Canada. *La Salle* relates the tale of the great explorations of the Mississippi Valley region, culminating in La Salle's objective of founding a colony on the Gulf of Mexico, the public and private jealousies he provoked, and his assassination in 1687 by his own mutinous crew. *A Half-Century of Conflict*, written out of sequence, covers the seventeenth-century French and Indian border wars against English settlers, and their mobilization, supported by the mother country, for self-defense. The final death-struggle between England and France for the control of North America is narrated in *Montcalm and Wolfe*, Parkman's masterpiece. It recounts General Wolfe's impossible assault on Quebec, in which the British troops, in a lunatic feat, scaled the perpendicular cliffs at the base of the city, surprised the French on the Plains of Abraham—a meadow at the top—and routed them, killing Montcalm. This victory in 1759 led to the expulsion of the French from North America and the loss of the empire of New France. *The Conspiracy of Pontiac* may be said to conclude Parkman's vast historical overview by recounting the aftermath: the Indian uprising, under Pontiac, against the British in the 1760s and the defeat that doomed the Indians to near extinction.

Although *Pioneers* traces the early southern explorations, when the whole continent was an unknown world, Parkman's real story begins with Verrazzano's northern voyages, in the 1520s, in search of an alternative route to Cathay. His expeditions opened the northern wilderness to exploration, and Jacques Cartier followed in 1535, coasting the Bay of St. Lawrence, the site of what is now Quebec City, and a place he called Mont Royal, now Montreal. Isolated settlements were founded by these redoubtable explorers in Cartier's time, but, a half-century later, when the French returned, they had all disappeared—along with all the tribes of the area.

For Parkman, it is with Samuel de Champlain (1567–1635) that we see "the true beginning" of Canada's extraordinary history. "The Father of New France," Champlain traversed the virgin wilderness of eastern Canada, discovered some of the Great Lakes, and mapped the territory afterward made accessible to settlement. The easy availability of beaver skins, codfish, train oil, and marine ivory thus awoke in the French the spirit of commercial enterprise. Between about 1604 and 1635, the French set up principal outposts at Montreal, Three Rivers, and Quebec and opened avenues of trade with the Indians. Along with them, on an errand of Indian salvation, came of course the Jesuits.

What was Parkman's view of these Europeans in Canada? Was it like that of several postmodern American historians in the year 1992? The quincentenary of the discovery of America—it should be remembered to our shame—was defiled by a great many revisionist historians who trashed Columbus as another Hitler who invaded, brutalized, enslaved, and exterminated the red man. A Minneapolis group calling itself the Alliance for Cultural Democracy denounced Columbus as the father of colonial imperialism and advised us to skip the celebration. Academic anthropologists maligned whites for having decimated the Indian tribes, and environmentalists vilified those responsible for the "ecocide" said to have occurred with the advancing westward civilization. The National Council of Churches—preserving its record for getting nearly everything wrong—even characterized the arrival of the *Niña*, the *Pinta*, and the *Santa Maria* as "an invasion and colonization with legalized occupation, genocide, economic exploitation and a deep level of institutional racism and moral decadence."[9] The implication was that the white men who followed in Columbus's wake inaugurated in North America a reign of racist violence over peaceful Indian tribes and all but wiped them out.

---

9 See "Columbus and the Quincentenary," *Social Studies Review,* 8 (Spring 1991), 12–13; "The Invasion of the Niña, the Pinta and the Santa Maria," *New York Times,* June 2, 1991, p. E-4.

As one descended in part, on my mother's side, from the Cherokee Nation in the Carolinas, I find fascinating this new attention to the Indian tribes. Certainly in my childhood my parents instilled in us great pride in our Cherokee ancestors, whose lives seemed much more adventurous, tragic, and romantic to us, as children, than that of our other forebears—the English, Scotch-Irish, and German ancestors who filled out our "typically American" inheritance. (My father, in a tobacco metaphor, used to speak of the *true* American as a "Duke's Mixture" of blended ethnic and national origins.) Off and on I count myself a full Cherokee, although I do not have the copper complexion, black hair, and high cheekbones of my uncles, and even today I have the illusion that I am a crack shot and have an unerring instinct in the woods. However that may be, I must remark that I find the current eruption of white guilt over the fate of the primitive Native American tribes to be as dubious as it is ignorant of the historical reality of aboriginal existence. What, in fact, did Champlain and his followers discover about the character of Indian life in 1600?

I shall pass over the ethnographic charm of life in the long house, where up to ten families might live in filth, smoke, and vermin-infested proximity. Nor is there any point in discussing the malnutrition arising from a diet of whatever animals could be killed and of maize (if the tribes bothered to plant and remained to harvest). Periodic starvation was a given and dislocation in search of game a constant. Parkman's account of various Indians and French explorers reduced to starvation is graphic. Here is one account, in *Pioneers*, from Florida in 1564:

> "Our miserie," says [René de] Laudonnière, "was so great that one was found that gathered up all the fish bones that he could find, which he dried and beate into powder to make bread thereof. The effects of this hideous famine appeared incontinently among us, for our bones eftsoons beganne to cleave so neere unto the skinne, that the most part of the souldiers had their skinnes pierced thorow with them in many partes of their bodies" (*PF,* I, 73).

Subsistence was more difficult in the north, where the French, battling the wintry cold, were all too often reduced to a diet of "moss, the bark of trees, or moccasins and old moose-skins cut into strips and boiled." If suffering was the native way of life, the starving French explorers turned hardship into culinary advantage—in preparing what they called "*tripe de roche,* a species of lichen, which, being boiled, resolved itself into a black glue, nauseous, but not void of nourishment" (*LaS,* I, 750). Life for Indian women was particularly brutal. While the braves lusted for war, conquest, and scalps, their squaws had to gather the firewood, sow, till, harvest, cook, smoke fish, dress skins, and make their rude garments. In the words of Champlain, "their women were their mules." No wonder this life broke them down. Parkman concludes of this female brutalization: "In every Huron town were shrivelled hags, hideous and despised, who, in vindictiveness, ferocity, and cruelty, far exceeded the men" (*J*, I, 358).

Champlain found, and generations of later observers have confirmed, that North American Indian life was one of constant savage tribal warfare. (Columbus found the same thing among the Caribs, Arawaks, and other tribes of the Southern Sea.) Any Indian with sufficient personal credit, Parkman reminds us, could dance a wardance, sing a warsong, bury his hatchet in the warpost, and inflame his tribesmen to follow him on the warpath against some nearby (or even distant) tribe. A war party, seized with homicidal fury against another tribe, might paddle fifty or five hundred miles to butcher a rival.

In 1600, to the east, in what is now New York and southern Canada, the Five Nations of the Iroquois (the Mohawks, Oneidas, Onondagas, Cayugas, and Senecas—and later the Tuscaroras) were brutally ravaging the Algonquin tribes along the Great Lakes. War parties of one tribe or another were continually assaulting enemy villages, braining the inhabitants in their sleep, butchering those who could not escape, and taking the rest prisoner. Even an enemy tribe's burial grounds were not sacrosanct. After a raid, victorious Indians often dug up the enemy dead, took scalps as trophies, stole the clothes, burnt the bodies, and danced in victory.[10]

The modern anthropological view—that theirs was "a warrior culture," with which they were of course in "natural harmony"—will not do. Women and children, and the old and the infirm, were choice victims—especially when the braves of an enemy village were away in the maize fields or, often enough, on raiding parties of their own. In his *Relation* for 1642, Father Vimont reports on the fate of several captured Algonquins:

> Among these were three women, of whom the narrator was one, who had each a child of a few weeks or months old. At the first halt, their [Iroquois] captors took the infants from them, tied them to wooden spits, placed them to die slowly before a fire, and feasted on them before the eyes of the agonized mothers, whose shrieks, supplications, and frantic efforts to break the cords that bound them were met with mockery and laughter (*J*, I, 573).

---

10 The buried clothes were of course often infected with the smallpox germ, which did more to decimate the tribes than the French and English combined.

What seems inescapably evident, from an overwhelming mountain of evidence, is that only butchery and torture could slake an Indian blood-lust that afflicted every tribe, in one degree or another, from the Canadian wilderness to Florida, and from the Eastern seaboard to the Pacific forests.

Indian torture was especially diabolical. If prisoners were taken, they were tied up and marched around, from village to village, and mounted on scaffolds as a public spectacle. Hair and beards were torn out, their fingernails were gnawed, or fingers burnt off. A favorite device was the sharpened splinter rammed up the penis. A fiendish effort was made to preserve the life and prolong the conscious agony of the victim. Any sign of pain produced paroxysms of public glee and was ridiculed as cowardice. "In the torture of prisoners," Parkman remarks, "great deference was paid to the judgment of the women, who, says Champlain, were thought more skillful and subtle than the men" (*OR*, I, 1126n). Even the Indian children, spurred by the savagery of their parents, "amused themselves by placing live coals and red-hot ashes on the naked bodies of the prisoners, who, bound fast, and covered with wounds and bruises which made every movement a torture, were sometimes unable to shake them off" (*J*, I, 555). Prisoners were often burnt alive. Equally as often the victim was slit open and his blood drunk by the savages. Thereupon the body was cut into quarters like butcher's meat, cooked in kettles, and eaten with voracious satisfaction. As Parkman dryly remarks in *A Half-Century*, "the benevolent and philanthropic view of the American savage is for those who are beyond his reach. It has never yet been held by any whose wives and children have lived in danger of his scalping-knife" (*H-C*, II, 484).

Parkman gives full play to the frenzy of these Indian atrocities, which were stupefying to the French, but they are frankly so com-monplace in the history of these tribes that some of the accounts he passes over as too repetitive or "too revolting to be dwelt upon" (*J*, I, 457n). Parkman rightly remarks that there is reason to believe that the "process of extermination, absorption, or expatriation" had "for many generations formed the gloomy and meaningless history of the greater part of this continent" (*J*, I, 572). Of this record of Indian-versus-Indian carnage, which "had existed time out of mind," he concludes:

> There is a disposition to assume that [such] events . . . were a conse-quence of the contact of white men with red; but the primitive Indian was quite able to enact such tragedies without the help of Europeans. Before French or English influence had been felt in the interior of the continent, a great part of North America was the frequent witness of

scenes still more lurid in coloring, and on a larger scale of horror. In the first half of the seventeenth century, the whole country, from Lake Superior to the Tennessee, and from the Alleghenies to the Mississippi, was ravaged by wars of extermination, in which tribes, large and powerful, by Indian standards, perished, dwindled into feeble remnants, or were absorbed by other tribes and vanished from sight. French pioneers were sometimes involved in the carnage, but neither they nor other Europeans were answerable for it (*H-C,* II, 532–533).

Parkman's analysis of the tribes' relations with one another, over two centuries, based on the records, ought to dispel forever the current myth of the natives' congenial existence wiped out by the warmongering of genocidal whites. At most one can say that, in later giving the Indians guns, Europeans merely accelerated the pace of the slaughter and became complicit in it by siding with now one tribe or the other, for commercial ends.

It is no wonder, in any case, that the Ottawas, Mohicans, Wampanoags, Hurons, and other Algonquins—in awe of French cannon and musketry—petitioned Champlain to defend them from the savage fury of the Mohawks, the Senecas, and others of the Five Nations. Likewise, the Iroquois sought Dutch and English weapons and intelligence to prosecute their killing. Out of these early Indian appeals to Champlain for protection developed the French policy in dealing with the Indians:

> It was the aim of Champlain, as of his successors, to persuade the threatened and endangered hordes to live at peace with each other, and to form against the common foe [the Iroquois and the English] a virtual league, of which the French colony would be the heart and the head, and which would continually widen with the widening area of discovery. With French soldiers to fight their battles, French priests to baptize them, and French traders to supply their increasing wants, their dependence would be complete. They would become assured tributaries to the growth of New France (*PF,* I, 286).

This policy, of course, brought down on Champlain the wrath of the Iroquois, who slaughtered or enslaved many of his soldiers and with great regularity destroyed the continually rebuilt French settlements. (The slaughter would likely have occurred whatever policy had been in effect.) In any case, the trading company in Paris, which had a royal monopoly on Canadian imports, virtually went bankrupt, and for a good many decades after the first French settlements "the wilderness of woods and savages had been ruinous to nearly all connected with it" (*PF,* I, 325).

IV

The failure of the earliest outposts to gain a solid foothold in Canada between 1600 and 1650 had much to do with France's failure to grasp the character of the native inhabitants. *The Jesuits in North America in the Seventeenth Century,* which tells the story of the missionaries who accompanied Champlain into the wilderness, throws a clearer light on how the early French and Indians dealt with each other. This book is substantially based on the massive collection of documents called the *Jesuit Relations,* a series of annual missionary reports, composed over nearly two centuries, sent back to the provincial of the order in Paris. Parkman, although rationalist and anticlerical, rightly trusts the essential accuracy of these reports, but he cannot conceal—and indeed makes no effort to conceal—his hostility to the Catholic church and to the Society of Jesus.

For Parkman, the Jesuit was a "moral Proteus" in the service of a monolithic church bent on attaining, at any price, temporal power. Subservient to Loyola's *Spiritual Exercises,* the priests were contemptuous of the body and thus ready to die "in unquestioning subjection to the authority of the Superiors, in whom they recognized the agents of Divine authority itself." Their training, for Parkman, did "horrible violence to the noblest qualities of manhood"; it joined them "to that equivocal system of morality which eminent casuists of the Order have inculcated" and thus produced "deplorable effects upon the characters of those under its influence" (*J,* I, 407, 410). Nothing was more sinister to Parkman's Protestant imagination than the Jesuits' agenda. They were

> everywhere,—in the school-room, in the library, in the cabinets of princes and ministers, in the huts of savages, in the tropics, in the frozen North, in India, in China, in Japan, in Africa, in America; now as a Christian priest, now as a soldier, a mathematician, an astrologer, a Brahmin, a mandarin, under countless disguises, by a thousand arts, luring, persuading, or compelling souls into the fold of Rome (*J,* I, 411).

Although not a Roman Catholic myself, I have no trouble in identifying Parkman's bias and so weighing and discounting it, in the appropriate degree, as I proceed through the narration of these historical events. This is made all the easier because Parkman recognizes the bias in himself and warns us of it. He will occasionally announce something like "This is the view of a heretic" (*J,* I, 510). Thus he himself tries to right the balance. In discussing François Xavier de Laval-Montmorency, the first bishop of Quebec, for example, Parkman realizes that he would offend many pious Canadian Catholics for whom Laval was "an object of veneration." But he nevertheless announces his intention to "regard him from the standpoint of secular history" and so recounts his political machinations as if he were any Machiavellian lay politician. Elsewhere he remarks that "those who wish to see the subject" of *The Old Régime in Canada* "from a point of view opposite to mine cannot do better than consult the work of the Jesuit Charlevoix, with the excellent annotation of Mr. Shea" (*OR*, I, 1068n). In this remark we can observe Parkman's recognition of the way in which his own values might be seen as prejudicial to his evidence. He therefore recommends as a possible corrective the most forceful account from a Catholic perspective. This method is admirable, and the serious reader can do no less than to take up the suggestion to read Charlevoix's *History and General Description of New France*. Whatever Schama may think, I find here—in this candor and in the invitation to consider alternative viewpoints—decisive evidence that not every historian's work must be seen as fatally compromised by a personal perspective.

The salvation of pagan souls, for Parkman, was the Jesuits' sole original motive. (Later on they became involved in the search for copper and other goods.) To this end, *ad majorem Dei gloriam*, they sought out the Indians, settled in their encampments, learned their languages, adopted many of their customs, "studied the nature of the savage, and conformed themselves to it with admirable tact." Instead of treating the Indian as "an alien and barbarian," Parkman observes, "they would fain have adopted him as a countryman." These Jesuits taught the gospel, baptized converts, and inculcated a morality that condemned polygamy, frivolous divorce, licentiousness, murder, cannibalism, feasts, dances, and violent games. "Gentleness, kindness, and patience," Parkman notes, were "the rule of their intercourse" (*J*, I, 494). The Indians were skeptical, yet credulous, and compliant but wildly unpredictable. In any case, they thought that the black-robed strangers had a powerful medicine. Often enough, however, they suspected the Jesuits of causing all the ills that befell them. In the smallpox epidemic of 1636 the priests, desperate to save souls, forced their way into Indian huts to baptize the dying children. The savages of course thought the young died *because of* the baptism and so murdered many of the priests.

Often enough the missionaries were murdered simply because they were Frenchmen—the hated Other in their tribal schema. As Parkman observes, "not the most hideous nightmare of a fevered brain could transcend in horror the real and waking perils with which they beset the path of these intrepid priests" (*J*, I, 576). In 1649 the Iroquois wiped out a whole band of Christian Hurons at St. Ignace. Father Jean de Brébeuf, "the founder of the Huron mission, its truest hero, and its greatest martyr," was put to the stake. Another Jesuit, Father Lalemant, was put to the torch before his eyes. They hung around Brébeuf's neck "a collar made of hatchets heated red-hot." They poured boiling water on his head in a mock baptism. They "cut strips of flesh from his limbs, and devoured them before his eyes."

> After a succession of other revolting tortures they scalped him; when, seeing him nearly dead, they laid open his breast, and came in a crowd to drink the blood of so valiant an enemy, thinking to imbibe with it some portion of his courage. A chief then tore out his heart and devoured it (*J*, I, 671).

Work in the Jesuit missions in the seventeenth century was thus a "living martyrdom." But although these earnest Jesuits "burned to do, to suffer, and to die" (*J*, I, 502–503), their efforts to Christianize the Indians were doomed. The incessant Iroquois slaughter of the lake tribes, and the latter's flight to the west—together with contagious disease and a French policy unequal to dealing with (and even contributing to) Indian violence—wiped out many of the Algonquins, and, by the end of the seventeenth century, most of the missions had failed. Despite his anticlericalism, Parkman had the decency to concede that it was the church's

> nobler and purer part that gave life to the early missions of New France. That gloomy wilderness, those hordes of savages, had nothing to tempt the ambitious, the proud, the grasping, or the indolent. Obscure toil, solitude, privation, hardship, and death were to be the missionary's portion.

Parkman found, in the lives of Fathers Lejuene, Garnier, Jogues, and many others, "a solid nucleus of saint and hero," even though their virtues, for him, shone "amidst the rubbish of error, like diamonds and gold in the gravel of the torrent." He concludes that "the missionaries built laboriously, and well," but they were doomed: "the cause of the failure of the Jesuits is obvious. The guns and tomahawks of the Iroquois were the ruin of their hopes" (*J*, I, 459, 674n, 711–712).

Parkman's friend, the Abbé Henri-Raymond Casgrain, working in the same field of history at Laval University, carried on a lengthy correspondence with Parkman about this anti-Catholic prejudice. Speaking of the Jesuit missionaries, Casgrain wondered how Parkman could draw the line between their heroism and their faith:

> Like me [Casgrain writes], you cannot withhold your admiration of

these men who sacrificed themselves with so much constancy and heroism for the love of mankind. . . . What colossuses, you say, and justly. But are you indeed sure that they would have been such great men without their blind obedience, without their enthusiastic faith?

Parkman could only insist that he was a rationalist, not a super-naturalist. Some pious Canadian Catholics also attacked Parkman when Laval University proposed to grant him an honorary degree. But many others judged him responsible to the evidence and thorough in his narrative account of the Jesuit missions. As Abbé Casgrain put it, "Your book is the work of a thinker and of a great painter; and Canada owes you an eternal debt for having made its history so much admired."[11]

V

In understanding Parkman's view of the Indian, whose soul was the principal concern of these missionaries and whose decline forms the romance of poetry, myth, and legend, there is perhaps no better starting place than the long expository chapter that introduces *The Conspiracy of Pontiac*—"Indian Tribes East of the Mississippi." This ethnographic essay is much too long to summarize, but it knowledgeably recounts the tribal divisions, totem clans, modes of government, myths, arts, agriculture, and the customs and character of the Indian. It also strives for the kind of balance evident in his treatment of the Jesuits. But it must also be said at the outset that Parkman is a cultural anthropologist's worst nightmare. That is, he believed that the Indians were indeed savages, that their "culture" was hardly worth the name, and that the advance of civilization at their expense was not only in-evitable but a manifestation of their own social and psychological deficiencies.

Although Parkman's grasp of Canadian affairs was based on voluminous reading, he was not without a firsthand understanding of Indian character and life. In fact, the 1846 journey recorded in his first book, *The Oregon Trail*, was specifically undertaken "with a view of studying the manners and characters of Indians in their primitive state."

Having from childhood felt a curiosity on this subject, and having failed completely to gratify it by reading, I resolved to have recourse to obser-vation. I wished to satisfy myself with regard to the position of the In-dians among the races of men; the vices and virtues that have sprung

---

11 Mason Wade, *Francis Parkman: Heroic Historian* (Hamden, Conn.: Archon Books, 1972), pp. 387–388.

from their innate character and from their modes of life, their government, their superstitions, and their domestic situation. To accomplish
my purpose it was necessary to live in the midst of them, and become,
as it were, one of them. I proposed to join a village, and make myself an
inmate of one of their lodges ... (*OT,* 111).

In the 1840s, in the far West, the Sioux, Pawnees, Snakes, Arapahoes,
Oglala, and other tribes that he visited had had virtually no contact with
whites, and "their religion, their superstitions, and their prejudices were
the same that had been handed down to them from immemorial time.
They fought with the same weapons that their fathers fought with, and
wore the same rude garments of skins" (*OT,* 176).

In launching out from St. Louis into the unknown world of these
aborigines, in order to observe and record what could be known of
"their vanishing existence," this Boston Brahmin experienced a distinct
"culture shock" for which his education had not prepared him. Despite
a disabling illness that often made it impossible for him to walk or ride,
he nevertheless explored the Fort Laramie and Platte River areas, the
Black Hills, and the interior regions of the Arkansas River country. For
several months he lived with the Sioux. While the time he spent among
them was too brief, and while his lack of the requisite native languages
limited his grasp of what he saw, his report has an authenticity lacking
in, for example, Cooper's account of the Pawnees in *The Prairie* or Irving's treatment of the West in *A Tour on the Prairies*. The adventure of
the uncharted prairies and mountains, the buffalo hunts, the motley
crew of hunters, trappers, migrants, half-breeds, soldiers, Mexicans, and
Mormons is wonderfully detailed. His encounters with the Indians
brought him close to death several times, and he came to value the tools
of survival and self-defense—a good horse, a rifle, and a knife.

Parkman could not help comparing the Indians' condition with his
own in Boston. On the differences, the young Parkman observes:

> For the most part, a civilized white man can discover but very few
> points of sympathy between his own nature and that of an Indian. With
> every disposition to do justice to their good qualities, he must be con-
> scious that an impassable gulf lies between him and his red brethren of
> the prairie. Nay, so alien to himself do they appear, that having breathed
> for a few months or a few weeks the air of this region, he begins to look
> upon them as a troublesome and dangerous species of wild beast, and if
> expedient, he could shoot them with as little compunction as they
> themselves would experience after performing the same office upon him
> (*OT,* 242).

If this remark seems callous, it is. On one reading it reflects the common sense of white men who could not grasp the aims and intentions of dangerous red men who prided themselves on the virtues of their warrior code. But just as easily it may reflect the pull toward savagery, the regression to barbarism in Europeans, oft noted in the literature of the wilderness. (The French were under orders to arrest and rehabilitate their countrymen who had abandoned the outposts and gone native, the *coureurs de bois,* or "white Indians," who had regressed into savagery. La Salle had suffered from such a regression when his mutinous men stole his supplies, wrecked the ship he was building, and took off into the forest. One of them left a message, scrawled on the shattered bows of the hulk, that says volumes about the fragility of the Europeans' claim to civilization: *"Nous sommes tous sauvages"* [*LaS,* I, 867].) Even so, young Parkman made friends with many of the Sioux braves, admired their courage and physical skills, undertook to learn the Dakota language, observed them on the warpath, shared in some of their tribal diversions, and found "at least some points of sympathy" between their savage and his own civilized condition (*OT,* 242).

Nevertheless, the whole experience of living for a time beyond the pale of civilization, beyond the reach of law, in a state of pure anarchic violence, taught him that the "soft-hearted philanthropy" of the Rousseauist was a dangerous illusion. Given the readiness of Indians to go on the warpath, against each other or against whites, he formed, in advance of Darwin, what one might call his philosophy of history: "From minnows up to men, life is an incessant battle" (*OT,* 246). This philosophy, amply illustrated in the voluminous colonial records he assembled, informs his story of the Indian tribes in the contest between France and England for the control of North America. As he remarks in *Pioneers,* "The story of New France is from the first a story of war" (*PF,* I, 14). It was war between France and Spain, France and England, France and the Indians, the Indians and the English, and the Indians against each other. At any time in the first two centuries of European immigration, the Indians—had they united, had they not been driven by their own homicidal fury against each other—could have combined to drive out the whites. Yet, "in this crisis of their destiny, these doomed tribes were tearing each others' throats in a wolfish fury, joined to an intelligence that served little purpose but mutual destruction" (*J,* I, 634). Their incessant intertribal warfare, poor planning for winter subsistence, unsanitary living conditions, susceptibility to disease, and their own fickle passions made them, for Parkman, unequal to the changing circumstances produced by European immigration. "The Indians melted away," Parkman concluded, not because civilization destroyed them, but because their own ferocity and intractable indolence made it impossible that they should exist in its presence. Either the plastic energies of a higher race or the servile pliancy of a lower one would, each in its way, have preserved them; as it was, their extinction was a foregone conclusion (*J*, I, 623).

As for the French, their royalist authoritarianism and religious absolutism unfitted them, in Parkman's view, to succeed in the New World, especially as the English colonies were extending past the Alleghenies the idea of decentralized liberty and religious pluralism. France's "records shine with glorious deeds, the self-devotion of heroes and of martyrs," but for Parkman "the result of all is disorder, imbecility, ruin" (*PF*, I, 312). At the time he wrote his history, he felt confident that the Canadian union represented the triumph of Anglo-American republican principles and that "the French dominion is a memory of the past" (*PF*, I, 15). But many of French descent in Quebec now wish to secede from Canada, to revive in Quebec (as it were) New France; and Indian tribes are newly asserting, in court, "aboriginal rights" to immense tracts of land already long settled with Canadian towns, villages, and farms. One Mohawk tribe, denouncing both the Canadian and American governments for having betrayed and killed Indians "for centuries," has—after a shoot-out with the police—implemented its "aboriginal right" to run a gambling casino in St. Regis, on the Canadian–New York border. Apparently to support this militancy, Col. Muammar el-Qaddafi of Libya has—they say—given the Mohawks a quarter million dollars to carry on the struggle. Meanwhile, the Pequots in New England have grown immensely rich with their own casino. It is not a matter of "spurious continuity," I believe, to observe that these recent events have a connection to the reverberating decisions of Louis XIV and XV, Champlain, Frontenac, La Salle, and Montcalm so many years ago, and a connection to those council decisions made by Indian tribal leaders who worked with and against the British, the Dutch, and the French.

If Parkman composed his history so as to condemn "Feudalism, Monarchy, and Rome," and if he organized his narrative as an illustration of the antagonism between "Liberty and Absolutism," we have at least the verdict of history—what actually happened in New England and New France—against which to test his conclusions. He underestimated the enduring power of the Catholic faith in Canada, but he was right about the end of feudalism and royalism. The verdict about Quebec's remaining within the Anglo-Canadian fold is not yet in. His other faults must also be weighed in the balance—his overemphasis on his thesis, the continual Jesuit-baiting, a rhetorical straining for the purple passage, the exaltation of the great man, "insensitivity" to "politically correct" ethnic attitudes, a suspicion of the democratic mob, and so on. But his scope is vast, his subject compelling, his research as exhaustive as he could make it, and his writing moves: he handles masses of material with vivid power and intensity, maintains suspense with dramatic skill, and is a superb storyteller. And what a story he had to tell—nothing less than the epic struggle of France and England for the control of North America. But of course that story—as superb and comprehensive as it is, in Parkman's version of it—was merely the prologue of another story with, for Americans, even greater import.

Before the middle of the seventeenth century, the English, as Parkman observes, actually "had an interest in keeping France alive on the American continent": the French and Indian threat kept the American colonies loyal to the English crown. But after the defeat of Montcalm, a Boston minister, John Mayhew, observed that, given the French expulsion from North America, "with the continued blessing of Heaven [the American colonies] will become, in another century or two, a mighty empire." Then Mayhew added a "cautious parenthesis": "*I do not mean an independent one.*" As Parkman observes, Mayhew "had read Wolfe's victory aright, and divined its far-reaching consequences" (*M&W,* II, 1419). It would take another twenty years for the restive American colonists to break away from the mother country, but there can be no doubt that, in destroying New France, England inadvertently made possible the new nation of America, founded by her own colonial subjects.

Compared to other nineteenth-century historians like Prescott, Sparks, Bancroft, and Motley, Parkman stands out as the best (as Henry Adams himself conceded). And certainly there has been no one yet in the twentieth century to rival him. As for the future, if current historians follow the postmodern approach of Schama (inventing fanciful scenarios for the sake of imagining "alternative narrations") Parkman will be our most distinguished historian for some time to come.

American
Manhood and the
Literature of
Adventure

It isn't often that one is asked, in a volume of literary criticism, a question on the order of *What is the most important event in modern history?* But this is precisely what Martin Green asks toward the end of *The Great American Adventure,* a book about American fiction. I shall return to his question in due course, but first let me say that Green's study, which is described as dealing with "action stories from Cooper to Mailer and what they reveal about American manhood," is not a work of historical analysis. It is instead a study of a dozen American adventure books seen as a reflection of America's "caste system" and her "imperialism," as these have shaped American "manliness." In fact, *The Great American Adventure* is merely the first of a trilogy of attacks on Western civilization and on its masculine underpinnings. The other two books in the trilogy are (à la William Empson) *Seven Types of Adventure Tale* and *The Adventurous Male: Chapters in the History of the White Male Mind.*

In subjecting these cultural phenomena to a political critique, Green offers a pretense of historical coverage by organizing his books into a triadic scheme. THREE FROM PHILADELPHIA: Cooper's *The Pioneers* (1823), Irving's *A Tour on the Prairies* (1832), and Robert Bird's *Nick of the Woods* (1837); THREE FROM BOSTON: Richard Henry Dana's *Two Years Before the Mast* (1840), Melville's *Typee* (1846), and Parkman's *The Oregon Trail* (1849); THREE ANOMALIES: Kit Carson's *Autobiography* (1856), Mark Twain's *Roughing It* (1872), and Theodore Roosevelt's *Au-*

26

tobiography (1913); and what Green calls THREE AESTHETES: Hemingway's *The Green Hills of Africa* (1935), Faulkner's "The Bear" (1942), and Mailer's *Why Are We in Vietnam?* (1967).

Even a cursory glance will reveal that these triads are not subdivisions of a single whole and form no coherent logical entity. The first two suggest a regional connection; but the third denies any connection altogether; and the fourth—dealing with three of the greatest moralists in American fiction—misdefines them as, of all things, aesthetes. Since logic and intellectual coherence are not Professor Green's long suit, why even bother with Green's lucubrations about the adventure tale? That is a fair question; and it may seem churlish to single out Green when there are so many contemporary literature professors for whom intellectual coherence is a problem. But Green's criticism is worth attending to as an instance of the modern intellectual's loathing of Western civilization, even while he exploits the prestige and creature comforts it affords to the intellectual elite. To fathom this detestation of Western civilization and to trace the weird distortions it produces in our literary criticism is at once to understand what is happening today in the academy and to grasp a salient fact about the modern intelligentsia. What do these adventure tales reveal to Martin Green?

According to Green, these stories disclose a common type of protagonist engaged in a series of exciting or violent events—often far from home or civilization—that call for "such virtues as courage, fortitude, cunning, strength, leadership and persistence." Now, most of us would probably be disposed to admire these qualities as indeed worth cultivating. But to Green these are not virtues at all but rather qualities of an "aristo-military caste" derived from the European class system and therefore implicitly supportive of it. The values of this caste are said by Green to be celebrated by our culture and acclaimed by the specific writers he has adduced here. Reading these books, he says, is recommended by the "establishment" as a means of preparing boys to become leaders, rulers, and accomplished experts in the use of force. For Green, even the Boy Scouts of America is a doubtful organization, no doubt because of its aversion to gays but certainly because it advocates roughing it with tent and backpack. Green sees such groups and these authors as, in effect, servants and sponsors of American imperialist or nationalist objectives, which he describes as capitalist, anti-Christian, and antidemocratic. In consequence, he indicts them as complicit in an immoral and violent American expansionism.[1]

---

1 Martin Green, *The Great American Adventure* (Boston: Beacon Press, 1984), pp. 1, 11. Citations from this work will hereafter be given as *GAA*, in parentheses, in the text.

Two personal observations in the foreword of this book may help us to understand the astonishing premise of this study. First, Green, an Englishman by birth but a longtime professor at Tufts University, remarks that as boy and man he has always preferred domestic fiction to adventure tales. By domestic fiction he means the stories of O. Douglas, Charlotte Brönte, Mrs. Gaskell, George Eliot, Jane Austen, and others who have written what he calls the "serious novel": "stories about marriage and domesticity written in a form of moral realism and woman-centered whereas adventure was man-centered." This preference made Green feel out of step with other boys: "I was not a manly boy." Second, Green is a practitioner of "an English school of criticism, whose major present exponent is Raymond Williams; it looks at literature with strong political and social concerns of a left-wing kind." (He means of a Marxist kind, but no matter.) To Green's left-wing political orientation is added something else. He has been deeply affected by the radical moralism of Gandhi and the later Tolstoy, and he makes admiring references to "radical Christianity" (of a dissenting kind), to Quaker pacifism, and to Eastern nonviolence. What Tolstoy and Gandhi "would ask of a teacher of literature" also informs this critique of American adventure tales (*GAA*, 18, vii, ix). In view of the argument I shall develop, the extraordinary intellectual gyrations by which Martin Green got to this position deserve some brief description.

I

After writing comparatively optimistic, if idiosyncratic, literary analysis in *A Mirror for Anglo-Saxons* (1960), *Reappraisals* (1965), and *The Problem of Boston* (1966), Green was apparently unhinged by the general convulsions of the Vietnam era. *Cities of Light and Sons of the Morning* (1972) showed a man embracing, as the subtitle suggests, "A Cultural Psychology for an Age of Revolution," while abandoning his Catholicism, optimism, and ambivalent love for his adopted country. Following *The Von Richtofen Sisters* (1974), and *Children of the Sun* (1976), Green launched himself into a trilogy of books under the general title *The Lust for Power*. Each, he promised us, would deal with the immorality of adventure and the exploitations of imperialism in the West. In the first of these, *The Challenge of the Mahatmas* (1978), he weighed Western civilization against the pacifist teachings of Gandhi and the later Tolstoy, the two "mahatmas," and found it wanting. In the second, *Dreams of Adventure, Deeds of Empire* (1979), he found English literature before 1918 to be the aesthetic support of an empire-building that created the moral and spiritual crisis of our times. In the third, *Tolstoy and Gandhi,*

Men of Peace: A Biography (1983), he returned to his spiritual heroes for a "joint biography" of two models offering a single solution to the destructive pursuit of power in the West. That trilogy, however, did not exhaust the moral fervor of Green's literary analysis. He followed with *The Origins of Non-Violence: Tolstoy and Gandhi in Their Historical Setting* (1986) and *Gandhi in India: In His Own Words* (1987). *The Great American Adventure*—the study of American fiction with which I am most concerned here—puts American writing on the axis where Marx and the mahatmas meet in Green's mind. Can the Marxist call to violent revolution and pacifist nonviolence be reconciled? On theoretical grounds alone, the task would seem to be formidable.

Given his contradictory premises, it is not surprising that Professor Green has no great admiration for the politics and morality of the adventure books in question, although—like Raymond Williams, Terry Eagleton, and the other left-wing Brits—he thinks them worth a "dialectical" unmasking. What we get, though, is principally the critical distortion produced by looking at them through pink spectacles. The distortions of our literature span a range from minor to major and would not be worth talking about if the literature he invokes did not have a permanent claim on our attention.

A minor distortion is Green's preposterous claim that Washington Irving and James Fenimore Cooper belong to "that Philadelphia school of writers that gave birth to American literature in the generation before Boston established its dominance as a writing and publishing center. . ." (*GAA*, 24). As scholarship, this is nonsense. First, American literature originated in Boston and—from the days of the *Bay Psalm Book* to the 1880s—Boston was the intellectual center of American literature. Second, both Irving and Cooper were deep-dyed New Yorkers, not Philadelphians. That printers in Philadelphia produced some of their books does not make them members of some "Philadelphia school." There was no such school. To suggest this is on a par with describing Louis Auchincloss's Park Avenue and Wall Street fiction as Boston novels of manners because Houghton Mifflin is his publisher. Cooper and Irving selected publishers who promised satisfactory royalties and other benefits. Third, to press this point further, Melville is not a Boston author, though some of his in-laws came from Massachusetts. Melville's essential links were always with New York. Green knows this, I have reason to believe, for in his study of the literature of The Hub in Melville's time, *The Problem of Boston*, Green scarcely ever mentions Melville. These misrepresentations of the regional affiliations of his authors are stupefying in a cultural historian of Green's wide reading and suggest the perils of too procrustean and schematizing a mind-set. Forcing books and writers into doubtful categories, however, is only part of the problem of Green's ongoing literary project.

II

Green's treatment of Cooper's *The Pioneers* offers an instance of how not merely the facts but also the meaning of facts in a narrative can be distorted. According to Green, Cooper's "sense of values is based on adventure, manliness, and patriotism, and he gives Americans a picture of society that assigns a leading part to the aristo-military caste that embodies these values." These caste values are said to be embodied in Judge Temple, Oliver Edwards, and Natty Bumppo (Leatherstocking). To them is contrasted Elizabeth Temple, the Judge's winsome daughter, whom Green astonishingly calls "the social and moral tuning fork" of the novel (*GGA*, 29, 35). I shall return to her in a moment, for she is one of the most interesting characters in the novel. But first we must attend to the central event of the book, the event that provokes Green's accusation about the American penchant for violence.

The central issue in *The Pioneers* is the arrest of Natty Bumppo for shooting a deer in the teeming season. Cooper's point is the tension between the natural liberty that exists for the nomadic hunter in the wilderness, on the one hand, and civilization's constraint upon it when the rise of settlements requires the institution of the law, on the other. At what point can other people in the wilderness, who have now organized for themselves a set of laws, impose their legalities on a hitherto unconstrained hunter who is said by the critic to be a representative of the "aristo-military" caste? This is an important question for criticism, for sociology, and for the law. Let's take a look at this hunter. Natty Bumppo is far from a glamorous aristo-military type. A balding old man of seventy, sporting a single tusk of yellow bone, clad in ratty deerskin leggings, the sartorial wonder "Natty" is a near comic travesty of the vanishing woodsman. About the riskiest adventure in the novel is the hackneyed rescue of Elizabeth from a wild varmint in the woods. Elizabeth tells her father that Natty, her rescuer, saved her life and ought therefore to be pardoned of the charge that he killed a deer out of season. The Judge's reply, in view of Green's spurious claim for Elizabeth's centrality to the moral design of the novel, deserves the greatest attention.

Elizabeth Temple argues that "those laws that condemn a man like Leatherstocking to so severe a punishment [one hour in the stocks, a $100 fine, and a month in jail], for an offence that even I must think venial, cannot be perfect in themselves." For the Judge, however, "the

. sanctity of the laws must be respected." "Society," he tells her, "cannot exist without wholesome restraints," and "it would sound ill indeed, to report that a judge had extended favour to a convicted criminal because he had saved the life of his child." Speaking *in propria persona*, Cooper says that Miss Temple spoke with "a logic that contained more feeling than reason." And into the Judge's mouth Cooper puts the concluding, decisive argument. After giving Elizabeth money to pay Natty's fine, the Judge remarks: "Thou hast reason, Bess, and much of it too, but thy heart lies too near thy head. . . ." He asks her to "try to remember, Elizabeth, that the laws alone remove us from the conditions of the savages; that he has been criminal, and that his judge was thy father."[2] The general construction of plot and character confirm this viewpoint. At the end of the novel, Leatherstocking strikes deeper into the wilderness, leaving civilization and its laws behind, unable to conform to these newfangled legalities meant to socialize us.

Of course it could be argued, I suppose, that in structuring the plot in this way, Cooper is embodying in the Judge this "aristo-military" threat to humane values. But this approach would in my view need to assume the paranoid proposition that laws are per se unfair, that the socialization of individuals through legislation is inherently oppressive, and that the judicature must always be subverted in favor of an anarchical libertarianism. Is the Judge a front for The System? Is he simply a tool for the moneyed interests and the class-oriented power structure? Only in the sense that he is an educated, thoughtful, and articulate spokesman for civilized values. In making his claim for these values he of course defends the institution of the law and the rights of property. Such constitutional principles were for Cooper inseparable from a true American democracy. As *The American Democrat* (1838) makes plain, men of the Judge's type, members of the American gentry, are democratic gentlemen, from whom, as a class, we have less to fear than from any other class in society.[3] Green doesn't like gentlemen, however, for they imply the English class structure, and they defend property rights with the support of the military. But if the Judge's reasoning is an instance of the "aristo-military" mind, I can only commend it. The idea of natural liberty is an interesting proposition in one's cozy study, but in the state of lawless nature, life is nasty, brutish, and short: it is the liberty of every man for himself. We see this in Cooper's *The Prairie*, where certain frontiersmen, having pushed too far ahead of civilization, regress to barbarism and savagery. Every witness to deep penetration

---

2 Cooper, *The Pioneers,* ed. Leon Howard (New York: Rinehart, 1959), pp. 394–95

3 Cooper, *The American Democrat,* ed. Robert Spiller (New York: Vintage, 1956), p. 89.

into the Western wilderness—see particularly the Western works of Parkman and Irving—has testified to the kind of barbaric regression that often produced "white Indians."[4] But Green thinks the century's natural fear of atavistic regression a mere capitalist's trick.

III

Many of the tales dealt with by Green pose just this kind of tension between anarchy and order, between lawlessness in the wilderness (or on the remote prairie, the high seas, or on a Polynesian isle) and the necessary legal codes of conduct that must be introduced when a society begins to form in that lawless space. In the conflicts that result (whether with savage Indians, cannibals, mutinous sailors, or wild animals) most authors have preferred order to anarchy and have approved the imposition of humane law and even the judicious use of force, if necessary, to guarantee the conditions under which civilized existence can be nurtured. Green finds the resultant society not worth the immoral price. He sees in the expansion of Western civilization (through the Americas, Polynesia, and the Orient) a bloody record incompatible with Christian pacifism, Gandhian nonviolence, and universal brotherhood; and he has recoiled in disgust.

In any clime, coexisting with cannibals and Apaches, panthers and bears, has been harder in practice than the moral absolutist will allow. Green falls back on the old accusation that "white culture is built on guns and explosives." (Cooper thought it was built on liberty, law, and the rights of property.) For Green, "Officer or pioneer, the hero is a man of blood" (*GAA*, 37). This tiresome canard reminds us of another Englishman, D. H. Lawrence, who also reduced the typical American of our classic literature to the blue-eyed killer: "The essential American soul is hard, isolate, stoic, and a killer."[5] Green finds the image of his disgust everywhere—in kindly Irving, in Dana, Faulkner, Mailer, and the rest. They are all complicit in glorifying bloodlust, the social caste system, and the capitalist extermination of aborigines.[6]

---

4 For an impressive treatment of Irving and the topic of adventure, see Peter Antelyes, *Tales of Adventurous Enterprise: Washington Irving and the Poetics of Western Expansion* (New York: Columbia University Press, 1990). On Parkman, see the previous essay and *La Salle and the Discovery of the Great West*.

5 D. H. Lawrence, *Studies in Classic American Literature* (Harmondsworth, England: Penguin, 1977), p. 68.

6 A cogent answer to the disgust with civilization found in certain contemporary leftist literary critics, of whom Green is merely typical, will be found in Peter Shaw's splendid critical study *War Against the Intellect: Episodes in the Decline of Discourse* (Iowa City: University of Iowa Press, 1989), especially "Literary Scholarship and Disparaging American Culture" and "Civilization's Malcontents: Responses to *Typee*" (pp. 91–120).

So sweeping an indictment of our action stories of course prevents Green from making any moral discriminations whatsoever. But for us the task of the ethical sensibility is precisely to make moral discriminations, and, in respect to most of these writers, Green's indictment can have little value. Virtually every one of these writers abhorred anarchic violence and affirmed the sanctity of the law. With Mailer, however, Green is absolutely right. He has got his target right in the center of the cross hairs. *Why Are We in Vietnam?* does legitimate, without remorse, the acting out of murderous impulse, in Mailer's case as a means of discovering one's so-called "existential being." Even so, Green's reading of Mailer is off to the left in its emphasis on his supposed aestheticism. Mailer's thinking is eccentric and morally incoherent. But his concerns in the novels of the 1960s were moral concerns and involved a theology of Manichean struggle in the cosmos between God and the Devil. He cannot be written off as intending merely to "aestheticize violence." Nor is it appropriate to claim such an intention for Hemingway and Faulkner.

It is a hard saying but a true one that we live in a complex world of predation and death-dealing. Nature red in tooth and claw can horrify; and it will not change matters much if we euphemize this nature-system as an ecological food chain, rather than calling it the bloody arena of Darwin's "struggle for survival." (All the more reason to affirm the law: to restrain human predation.) But if Hemingway and Faulkner ritualize the ubiquity of death-dealing, in their hunting stories, they do so for a religious rather than for an aesthetic purpose. Sam Fathers in "The Bear," and Ike McCaslin, his young protégé initiated into the hunter's code, both articulate a reverence for life—for all being—that is communicated in their sympathetic identification with the magnificent buck, the towering bear, and other such creatures, and in the guilt they feel upon killing animals.

Something of the same religious identification with the order of being itself is expressed in Hemingway's elaborate rituals of hunting and fishing, not to speak of bullfighting. I cannot defend bullfighting here, but anyone opposed to this "sport" must engage with the evident fact that the rites and rules of the *corrida*, which have compelled the Mediterranean imagination for at least four thousand years, formalize the inevitability of death-dealing in an obscurely moral and primordially religious way. Like Faulkner, Hemingway expresses the immense pity of the human plight in knowing, consciously, its place in this scheme of predation. This pity is movingly expressed in *The Old Man and the Sea*, a work that Green avoids because it obviously cannot serve as ammunition for his left-wing attack. Old Santiago loves and respects the fish he kills, calls it his brother, and begs its pardon as he reels it in. "Perhaps it was a sin to kill the fish," he thinks to himself, "even though I did it to keep me alive and feed many people." Later he thinks, "You did not kill the fish only to keep alive and to sell for food. . . . You killed him for pride and because you are a fisherman. You loved him when he was alive and you loved him after." He wonders, "If you love him, it is not a sin to kill him. Or is it more?"[7] The meaning of such moral reflection—which points to the ineluctable fatality of the human condition in a world where life feeds on life—is beyond Green's understanding. He is impatient and dismissive of all such anguished moral struggle as so much macho rationalization.[8]

Of course "The Bear" and *The Old Man and the Sea* may be accused of a false primitivism, of presenting an extinct animism, a regression to some pantheistic morality now obsolete for urban critics like Green, who have left errant humanity behind for the higher planes of sainthood, where Mahatma Gandhi, Tolstoy, and Albert Schweitzer abide. But in terms of practical morality, what do we do when the tsetse fly is about to bite, when the bear is about to kill the livestock, when game presents itself to one whose family must be fed? For most of us there is no escaping this human dilemma, however much it may be disguised in city life. It will not serve to reduce this universal problem to the excesses of individualism, capitalism, and imperialism. Most American pioneers tried to be good Christians, but the doctrine of turning the other cheek presented too many problems to (let us say) the peaceful immigrant farmer from Yorkshire whom the Iroquois warrior had got by the throat.

Green's anti-imperialism is that of an Englishman who feels guilt at the moral cost of his country's worldwide imperial adventures. But Americans never had a world empire and, in my view, never wanted one. Even the forays into Mexico in the 1840s and the Cuban and Philippine hullabaloos at the *fin de siècle* were short-lived anomalies. Green treats the slow and spreading settlement of the American West as if it were identical with a planned, armed British military takeover in India or Africa, when in fact the American militias were called out essentially to protect from Indian savagery peaceable settlers on the frontier.[9]

---

7 Ernest Hemingway, *The Old Man and the Sea* (New York: Scribner's, 1952), pp. 50, 54, 105.

8 On the matter of the food, Green opines that meat-eating *produced* the warrior class. But vegetarianism also involves the killing of life forms for our alimentary sustenance. So vegetarians cannot claim, in my view, any moral superiority to meat-eaters, nor does vegetarianism deliver us from the offense of killing.

9 European colonial masters in the Third World could be a brutal lot; but anyone reflecting on the history of postcolonial life in India and Africa must be horrified at what has hap-

IV

If American adventure stories condone or aestheticize violence, what kind of fiction does Green admire? Green most values the social novel which deals with money, property, class, marriage, and the domestic scene. One may sympathize with this preference. James, Wharton, Austen, and George Eliot—practitioners of this kind of fiction—*are* artists of a major order. But even here rigid generic distinctions are perhaps unwise. Cooper wrote some of our best early novels of manners—for example, *Satanstoe* and *Home As Found*; and James's "The Beast in the Jungle" is an adventure tale transcendently superior to most of Green's examples. Indeed, as James asks in "The Art of Fiction," "What is adventure, when it comes to that, and by what sign is the listening pupil to recognize it?" [10] Green can recognize adventure only by tracking down the aristo-military type. But for James, the drama of a rejected marriage proposal was adventure incarnate. And as he remarked of Isabel Archer's midnight vigil, when she reflects on the failure of her marriage in *The Portrait of a Lady*, the "representation simply of her motionlessly *seeing*," "the mere still lucidity of her act," was "as 'interesting' as the surprise of a caravan or the identification of a pirate." [11]

It is true that the attempts by Howells, James, Wharton, and other novelists of manners to register the adventure of the mind, to catch the finer vibrations of the moral sense, may seem rarefied to readers demanding the kind of violent adventure reflected in the books of Mailer, Faulkner, Hemingway, and others. Our appetite for them leads Green to characterize books of this kind—in the language of his mentor, F. R. Leavis—as "the great tradition, the central tradition, in American literature." [12] But this formulation makes too much of the romance as *the* tradition, a mistake that Richard Chase inaugurated in *The American Novel and Its Tradition*. I for one think that the great tradition in America, as in England, is in the social novel and have so argued at some length. [13] But there is no denying that our frontier experience has

---

pened since the European oppressors left: the pervasive increase in poverty; the decline of the standard of living; the breakdown of law and order; the lack (indeed loss) of political liberties that originated with the colonial administrations; the rise of savage strongmen; and the constant tribal, ethnic, and religious warfare that has produced horrific widespread starvation and, in fact, wholesale regressions to barbarism. But of course there will always be those who see in American foreign policy, like the rescue of starving Somalis, some kind of covert imperialism.

10 Henry James, *Literary Criticism: Essays on Literature, American Writers, English Writers* (New York: Library of America, 1984), p. 61.

11 Henry James, *The Art of the Novel: Critical Prefaces*, ed. R. P. Blackmur (New York: Scribner's, 1934), p. 57.

12 F. R. Leavis, *The Great Tradition* (New York: George W. Stewart, [1948]).

13 James W. Tuttleton, *The Novel of Manners in America* (New York: W. W. Norton, 1974.)

produced compelling fictive representations and that the romance genre is marked by some splendid instances of the form.

I find interesting Green's direct appeal to English teachers, especially academic feminists, to turn away from these adventure stories "toward others—those about 'strong women'—who can do more to build up the communal pride and energy of readers who want to resist imperialism and to change the meaning of 'America'" (*GAA*, 219). Except for "The Bear," I suspect that the works of Green's "great tradition" of violent adventure are not widely taught, except perhaps in the odd doctoral seminar at Tufts.

In any case, if English teachers do transform the canon as Green proposes, they will finally feminize American literary culture. [14] This would appear to be Green's objective, for he has elsewhere quoted Gandhi's call for more feminized men:

> I have repeated times without number that nonviolence is the inherent quality of women. For ages men have had training in violence. In order to become nonviolent they have to cultivate the qualities of women. Ever since I have taken to nonviolence, I have become more and more of a woman. [15]

No one can object to the growth of women's wise influence on American culture. Certainly we need all the wisdom we can get, especially if the effect is a decline in violence. But I am not convinced that those in our society who wish to emasculate males—especially white males, of which I am one—or who wish to effect an androgynous merger of genders so that men and women become less distinguishable, are really speaking in the best interests of either sex or of their relationship to each other or of the future of the race. All too often what is at work is a sexism directed at men, not only by feminist ideologues but even by "liberated" men. A typical instance is this remark of W. P. Day, whom Green cites with approval: "Violence is, of course, the natural expression of the masculine in its purest form, the application of force to the world to assert its power and identity." [16] But is violence *the* natural expression of masculinity? Is it identical with "force," and, if so, what is force? Does it mean energy? If so, I see no moral flaw inherent in the application of *energy* to the world, so as to assert power, effect change,

---

14 See Ann Douglas's treatment of the nineteenth-century forces working to effeminize our society in *The Feminization of American Culture* (New York: Alfred A. Knopf, 1977).

15 Quoted in Martin Green, *The Challenge of the Mahatmas* (New York: Basic Books, 1978), p. 42. In calling women inherently nonviolent, the mahatma had clearly never visited a public junior high school in New York City.

16 Quoted in Martin Green, *The Adventurous Male: Chapters in the History of the White Male Mind* (University Park: Pennsylvania State University Press, 1993), pp. 18–19.

and actualize identity. That is what produced the Chartres cathedral, Mozart's sonatas, the vaccine of Jonas Salk, the four-minute mile, the moon landing, and *The Old Man and the Sea*. Of course, many intellectuals have a problem with the exertion of physical energy, which they must be at pains to discredit as they are not good at it. And of course, in some strains of oriental thought, all exertion of energy is vain. But most boys and men are not Eastern passivists or armchair intellectuals. And the attempt to neuter them through discrediting the active life is, as Camille Paglia has shown, a form of sexual decadence. [17] But sexual decadence offers a critical thrill for English teachers nowadays. The freakish is now "in." Thus academic intellectuals are usually the least trustworthy guides as to what forms of conduct and being constitute man- and womanhood. Yet the manly women, the feminized men, and the whole carnival of lesbians and homosexuals now proclaiming what is pretentiously and risibly called "Queer Theory" do not scruple to tell us what, genderwise, we ought to be.

What will be the case if, as I suspect it to be, women readers and teachers admire adventure stories too, even as men admire good novels of manners? As James remarked in "The Art of Fiction": "There are some subjects which speak to us and others which do not, but he would be a clever man who should undertake to give us a rule—an index expurgatorius—by which the story and the no-story should be known apart." [18] Yet Green and like-minded ideologues want to declare as forbidden and undesirable our classic tales of adventure.

It is perhaps a sign of the times that Green must be so apologetic about his preference for the novel of manners. The prisoner-of-sex syndrome seems to have affected a good many male critics as well. In an essay called "The Ways of a Wimp," the novelist Thomas Flanagan has expressed uneasiness over his liking for Austen, Proust, and James because he thinks that Americans automatically identify such a preference with something less than full masculine intelligence and aesthetic understanding. Of course Flanagan does not consent to this charge of wimpiness, but the uneasiness is still there. Something of the same discomfort arises in Alfred Habegger's *Gender, Fantasy, and Realism in American Literature* (1982), which contains a chapter called "Henry James and W. D. Howells as Sissies." Doubtless some adventure-writing he-men, like Frank Norris and Jack London, disliked the domestic realism of Howells and James, with its "drama of a broken teacup, the tragedy of a walk down the block, the excitement of an afternoon call,

---

17 Camille Paglia, *Sexual Personae: Art and Decadence from Nefertiti to Emily Dickinson* (New Haven: Yale University Press, 1990), *passim*.
18 Henry James, "The Art of Fiction," p. 60.

the adventure of an invitation to dinner," as Norris described it.[19] But
Norris, London, and the others were merely trying to make a critical
space for their own brand of fiction, a sensational naturalism intended
to shock genteel Victorian America, or what was left of it. No wonder
Alexander Harvey in *William Dean Howells* (1917) put Howells "at the
head of the sissy school of American literature." But need anybody be
troubled in his manhood by the macho posturing of the naturalists?

As it turns out, both Harvey and Habegger, as well as Martin Green,
really like the domestic realism of Howells and James. So do I. There is a
great deal of sheer aesthetic pleasure to be derived from Howells's modest comedies of manners like *A Chance Acquaintance* or *The Lady of the
Aroostook*. There is also stunning depth of human understanding disclosed in novels like *The Wings of the Dove* and *The Golden Bowl*. And I
would not give up Cooper's *Satanstoe* as a portrait of colonial domestic
manners. But one is frankly appalled at the morbid self-consciousness,
the sexual anxiety, and the embrace of hysterical thinking about manliness and womanliness evident in these critics and projected by them
onto the whole of American culture. I can see no necessary contradiction between the pleasures of a good narrative about a wilderness hunt
and the pleasures of a domestic narrative about pride and prejudice.
James had it right in saying that there is simply good fiction and bad
fiction.

V

A central issue here is the pleasure of the text. Green can get no pleasure
from a novel in which an Osage Indian or a blue-coated cavalryman
bites the dust, or in which the hunt for game in the wilderness turns
sanguinary. He cannot have us read these narratives "with total assent or
complicit enjoyment" (*GAA*, ix). Pleasure is capitalist corruption, and
literary pleasure corrupts absolutely. But this fear of pleasure neither allows the author his *donnée* nor permits the reader any willing suspen-
sion of disbelief, even for the moment. The *reductio* of Green's dour
moralism is Tolstoy's "What Is Art?"—which insists that the only justification of art is its promotion of brotherhood and human happiness.[20]
But in fact Tolstoy wasn't even content with *that* formulation and eventually renounced the vanity of all literature, including his own; and
Gandhi had no use whatsoever for the fruits of aesthetic invention.

19 Frank Norris, "A Plea for Romantic Fiction," *The Responsibilities of a Novelist* (New York:
    Doubleday, Page, & Co., 1903), p. 215.
20 Leo Tolstoy, "What Is Art?" in *Critical Theory Since Plato*, ed. Hazard Adams (New York:
    Harcourt, Brace, Jovanovich, 1971), p. 716.

Green is sincere enough to know that his continued preoccupation with art constitutes a rejection of the lesson of the mahatmas, but he rationalizes his lecturing and writing about art as a mode of "contemplation" in which his unmasking of the literature of empire somehow saves his honor and redeems his refusal of their oriental asceticism. But this activity is not contemplation, in the Eastern meaning. The renunciation commanded by Gandhi is quite plain: "All attachment to the senses is death."[21] If Green cannot yet submit himself to it, which of us could, even if we wanted to? Meanwhile, both the Tolstoyan and Marxist instrumental views of literature are hopelessly reductive of art's rich complexity of being. And the danger of adopting this functionalist view of art is that it impels us headlong toward the *index expurgatorius* with the clever left-wing authoritarian telling us what we can and cannot read.

Green's moralism runs counter to the whole affective psychology of "violence in art." I have in mind here Aristotle's observation, in the *Poetics,* that such is the pleasure of poetic *mimesis,* or imitation, that, although "there are some things that distress us when we see them in reality," "the most accurate representations of these same things we view with pleasure—as, for example, for forms of the most despised animals and of corpses."[22] Likewise, Sir Philip Sidney in "An Apology for Poetry" speaks of "the sweet violence of a tragedy."[23] And Dr. Johnson remarks that "the delight of tragedy proceeds from our consciousness of fiction; if we thought murders and treasons real they would please no more."[24] Wallace Stevens has even suggested, in *The Necessary Angel,* that the literature of violence, when it achieves true aesthetic nobility, may have a genuine existential value: "It is a violence from within that protects us from a violence without. It is the imagination pressing back against the pressure of reality. It seems, in the last analysis, to have something to do with our self-preservation; and that, no doubt, is why the expression of it, the sound of its words, helps us to live our lives."[25]

But Green won't draw a line between fiction and reality. He would make us feel guilty for the pleasure we take in literature's capacity to represent life, including life's violence. That capacity, for him, amounts to aesthetic hedonism, literature as "a pleasure garden for the socially privileged" (*GAA,* viii). Like Plato, or like the commissars whose politics Green espouses, he would deny such pleasurable adventure stories and

---

21 Quoted in Green, *The Challenge of the Mahatmas,* p. 230.

22 Aristotle, *Poetics,* trans. Leon Golden (Englewood Cliffs, N.J.: Prentice-Hall, 1968), p. 7.

23 Sidney, "An Apology for Poetry," in *Critical Theory Since Plato,* p. 106.

24 Samuel Johnson, "Preface to Shakespeare" (1756), in *Criticism: Major Statements,* eds. Charles Kaplan and William Anderson (3rd ed., New York: St. Martin's Press, 1991), p. 233.

25 Wallace Stevens, "The Noble Rider and the Sound of Words," in *The Necessary Angel: Essays on Reality and the Imagination* (New York: Vintage, 1951), p. 36.

admit to his utopia only tales that emphasize the pastimes of the domestic circle, the joys of economic production, the drama of social justice triumphant, the elimination of class conflict. These, for Green, express *the most important event in modern history,* which he identifies, following "Sartre and most Marxists (and most modern intellectuals)," as "Europe's industrialization of its economy" (*GAA,* 228).

I confess here to a sense of deflation at the answer to this great question about the most important event in European history. Sartre is hardly an economic historian, and no rational argument for this astonishing proposition is offered. The industrialization of Europe's economy was a fine thing—achieved without Marx's help, thanks to aggressive entrepreneurs building a better mousetrap. But the application of industrial techniques to production, distribution, and consumption, as an answer to a question about the most important event in human experience, grotesquely materializes history and robs it of the transcendental meaning it had for Gandhi and Tolstoy. In reality, *The Great Adventure* has unwittingly led us to believe that *the westward expansion of civilization* was the major event in modern history. But Green will have none of this because to assent to the literature of expansion is to recognize the rise of civilization in wilderness and prairie, the extension of law, the creation of wholesome socialized existence where once there was anarchy and savagery. This grand movement, afoot since 1492, is advancing Western civilization, and Green detests it for its ideology of personal liberty, its individualistic energy and success, its foundation on private property and the protection of the law, and its resignation to the inescapable fact, on the individual level, of human inequality. Behind Green's detestation of Western civilization is a racist self-loathing, reflected in his approval, in *The Challenge of the Mahatmas,* of Susan Sontag's calumny that "the white race is the cancer of human history."[26] Behind Green's work lies an undeclared romance with the utopian antithesis of the West, never quite defined, that inheres in the "countercultures" that he praises—the world of Tolstoy's peasants, the Quakers' Holy Experiment in Pennsylvania (1682–1775), Ascona, or in the ashrams of Gandhians in India.[27]

Can Green's Gandhism be reconciled with his left-wing politics, with what he calls "Marx and his revenge, his call to action, to praxis, to political rising"? This book certainly fails to harmonize them. Indeed, it cannot be done. Even Green has to confess in *The Challenge of the Mahatmas:* "Marxism-modernism is no option for a man opposed to

26 Green, *The Challenge of the Mahatmas,* p. 179.
27 See Green's *Mountain of Truth: The Counterculture Begins, Ascona, 1900–1920* (Hanover, N.H.: University Press of New England, 1986.)

violence; and Gandhism is antiintellectual and antiaesthetic."²⁸ My complaint here is not with the dedicated Marxist. He knows what he wants—a violent revolutionary overthrow of the capitalist system. Nor do I fault the Christian pacifist and nonviolent Gandhian. Both are sincere in believing that the martyr to faith will shame into conversion his violent oppressor. Such men of faith and private conviction can at times effect useful moral change. But what one faults here is the intellectual muddlement of a critic who tries to have it both ways: a nonviolent overthrow of the capitalist system in which those who have accumulated property through hard work or inheritance will somehow peacefully allow themselves to be stripped of it by intellectual leftists like Green. He has painted himself into a corner from which he cannot escape, and his work reflects this paralysis. The sensible option would be to abandon Marxism, but Green has not to my knowledge renounced it despite its call to violence.

When Marx *has* had his revenge, when left-wing revolutions have erupted, men of moral conscience, of pacifist belief, and of Christian conviction have been among the first to be liquidated as reactionary vestiges of obsolete bourgeois morality. One of the greatest moral abominations of modern history was the wholesale slaughter of millions of Tolstoy's peasants, civil servants, doctors, merchants, artists, liberal humanists, and even dedicated Marxist functionaries (and their wives and children) in the name of that leftist ideology that that now permeates the American university; our intellectual life is rotten with its false pieties and bogus sentimentality. In *The Challenge of the Mahatmas,* Green confesses: "I could not describe even theoretically the kind of political radicalism that I could subscribe to authentically."²⁹ When we think about the totalitarianism of Cuba and China and about how democracies perish, such confusion in our university intellectuals is instructive. Given the social wreckage produced by Marxist revolutions in this century, no one pretending to call himself a humanist can ignore the ways in which political radicalism has created an intolerant and repressive Marxist praxis. By every rational, religious, and humanly civilized criterion, that ideology has proven itself totally and horridly bankrupt. We need a better dream of the future; the Marxist polity, in all its bloody actuality, has been and is still a nightmare.

---

28 Green, *The Challenge of the Mahatmas,* pp. 229, 87.
29 Green, *The Challenge of the Mahatmas,* p. 150.

Irving's Spaniards: The Romance of History

The relationship of historical fact to the American imagination is one of the most engaging aspects of the study of genres during the American Renaissance. We are accustomed to think of it in connection with historical romances such as *The Last of the Mohicans, The Yemassee,* and *The Scarlet Letter.* But it is worth remembering that the historians Bancroft, Prescott, Motley, and Parkman thought of themselves as, broadly, men of letters sharing in the national literary enterprise along with the romancers Cooper, Simms, Hawthorne, and Irving. Though best known for *The Rise of the Dutch Republic,* Motley was also the author of two historical novels, *Morton's Hope* (1839) and *Merry-Mount: A Romance of the Massachusetts Colony* (1849). And Parkman's magisterial *France and England in North America* should not obscure for us his fictional ambition in *Vassal Morton* (1856). Washington Irving shared with these writers a profound interest in the relationship between men, events, historical records, and the creative faculty which brings them together in the imagined form of history and romance. His career reflects his wavering between the two genres and, occasionally (as in *Granada*), his attempt to fuse them in a special way.[1]

Irving's interest in history was appropriated from his literary culture—the long Puritan tradition of history as the wonder-working of God's providences; from his formal reading of the Greek and Roman historians, as well as Enlightenment historians like Gibbon; and from

---

1 For Irving's remarks about the fusion of history and romance, see Stanley T. Williams, *The Life of Washington Irving* (New York: Oxford University Press, 1935), I, 344–345.

that American nationalism in the early federal period which made works like William Robertson's *History of America* (1777) central documents in the American literary consciousness. Before his first Spanish period (1826–1831), he was chiefly known for the whimsies of *Salmagundi, The Sketch Book, Tales of a Traveller,* and Diedrich Knickerbocker's comic *A History of New York.* The latter delightful book still has a rich value for the appreciative reader. One of the pleasures of the work arises from Irving's wish, as a "sentimental historian," to save colonial New York from "entering into the wide-spread, insatiable maw of oblivion." Irving's readings in the history of the Dutch exploration and settlement in New Amsterdam were quite extensive; and he thoroughly prepared himself, in the library, to tell the stories of Hendrik Hudson, Wouter Van Twiller, Peter Stuyvesant, and William the Testy—however comically. But, as a "modern historian," Irving complains (through Diedrich) that he is "doomed irrevocably to . . . dull matter of fact" when he would prefer, like a poet, to "wander amid . . . mouldering arches and broken columns, and indulge visionary flights of his fancy."[2] Since colonial New York—at least during the Dutch administrations—did not offer an adequate appeal to his poetic sensibility, it could be treated only comically.

Irving's irritation, expressed in the remark above, shares much with Cooper's condemnation, in *Notions of the Americans, Picked Up by a Travelling Bachelor* (1828), of the American scene as inadequate for any kind of serious literary enterprise. (Henry James's notorious list, in *Nathaniel Hawthorne* [1879], of the elements of true civilization that were still missing in America has a long history of predecessors.) Irving's rhetorical problem was also quite similar to the struggle of William Hickling Prescott to define the literary form of his Mexican historical materials. Prescott solved his dilemma by thinking big, by aiming high, by inflating his subject with epic largeness. In his notebooks on the conquest of Mexico, Prescott reminded himself that

> the true way of conceiving the subject is, not as a philosophical theme, but as an epic in prose, a romance of chivalry; as romantic and chivalrous as any which Boiardo or Ariosto ever fabled . . . ; and which, while it combines all the picturesque features of the romantic school, is borne onward on a tide of destiny, like that which broods over the fiction of the Grecian poets; for surely there is nothing in the compass of Grecian

---

2 Washington Irving, *A History of New York,* in *Washington Irving: History, Tales and Sketches,* ed. James W. Tuttleton (New York: Library of America, 1983), p. 380. For a comprehensive assessment of Irving's early historical prose, see William L. Hedges, *Washington Irving: An American Study, 1802–1832* (Baltimore: Johns Hopkins University Press, 1965), especially pp. 236–267.

epic or tragic fable, in which the resistless march of *destiny* is more discernible, than in the sad fortunes of the dynasty of Montezuma. It is, without doubt, the most poetic subject ever offered to the pen of the historian.[3]

I

A poetic subject—conceived of as "an epic in prose, a romance of chivalry" full of picturesque romantic episodes, tending toward pathos and tragedy—was exactly what Irving needed to write the kind of history to which he was drawn. He was offered such a subject in 1826 when Alexander Hill Everett, of the American legation in Madrid, invited him to come to Spain in order to translate Martin Fernández de Navarrete's recently published collection of materials relative to the voyages of Columbus and his companions. Reading the two-volume *Colección de los viages y descubrimientos, qui hicieron por mar los españoles desde fines del siglo XV*[4] awakened Irving to the possibilities of this subject for "the visionary flights of his fancy." Nothing less than a biography of Colum-

---

3 Quoted in David Levin, *History as Romantic Art: Bancroft, Prescott, Motley, and Parkman* (New York: Harcourt, Brace and World, 1959), p. 3. Though Levin does not discuss Irving at any length, many of his conclusions about romantic history are, as I have tried to show here, applicable to *Columbus* and *Companions.*

4 The full title of Navarrete's compilation may be translated as "Collection of sea voyages and discoveries made by the Spaniards, from towards the close of the 15th century—with various documents, hitherto unpublished, relating to the history of the Spanish marine, and the establishments of Spain in the Indies, arranged and illustrated by Don Martin Fernández de Navarrete." For a discussion of Irving's judicious use of Navarrete's *Colección,* and for a refutation of Stanley T. Williams's unwarranted claim, in the *Life,* that Irving was guilty of a "near-plagiarism" of the Spanish historian's compilation, see John Harmon McElroy's "The Integrity of Irving's *Columbus,*" in *Washington Irving: The Critical Reaction,* ed. James W. Tuttleton (New York: AMS Press, 1993), pp. 126–136. And further evidence that Irving made right and appropriate use of the *Colección* in writing *Companions of Columbus* is this remark in a letter Navarrete sent to Irving on April 1, 1831:

> I congratulate myself that the documents and notices published in my collection about the first events in the history of America have fallen into hands so able to appreciate their authenticity, to examine them critically, to propagate them, and establish fundamental truths which have been adulterated by partial and prejudiced writers.

These are not the remarks of a man whose works, as Williams claimed, had been virtually plagiarized. Moreover, it is inconceivable that Irving would have been elected to the Royal Society of History in Madrid had Navarrete, or any of his fellow Spanish historians believed that Irving had plagiarized Navarrete's work or failed to give it—and the other Spanish historians he cites—due and appropriate acknowledgment and full citation. For the complete texts in Spanish and English of Navarrete's highly complimentary letters to Irving, expressing his admiration for the gift of *Columbus* and *Companions,* see Volume XII of *The Complete Works of Washington Irving,* specifically Tuttleton's introduction to *Voyages and Discoveries of the Companions of Columbus* (Boston: Twayne Publishers, 1986), pp. xxx–xxxi.

bus and his companions would do. And during the next five years, he exploited these and other Spanish manuscripts and documents in composing *A History of the Life and Voyages of Christopher Columbus* (1828) and *Voyages and Discoveries of the Companions of Columbus* (1831).

The earnest historical character of these books represented a new literary departure for Irving, who aspired to "weightier" productions which would characterize him as a more "serious" man of letters. He suffered considerable anxiety about this new enterprise. As he told Henry Brevoort, "How it will please the public I cannot anticipate. I have lost confidence in the favourable disposition of my countrymen and look forward to cold scrutiny and stern criticism, as this is a line of writing in which I have not hitherto ascertained my own powers." He worried that many people would "suppose, from my having dealt so much in fiction, it must be impossible for me to tell truth with plausibility." [5] Nevertheless, during this period in Spain, Irving persevered with the patient work of translating, collating historical narratives, and composing *Columbus* and *Companions*. As he told Thomas T. Storrow in February 1828, if this work "takes with the public its success will have a most favourable effect upon any thing I may afterwards produce." [6]

In the course of more than three years, while Irving plumbed the old Spanish documents relative to Columbus, he assembled an enormous quantity of material dealing with *other* exploratory voyages to the New World. Though much of it had an intrinsic interest of its own, the documents touching the voyages of the companions of Columbus, navigators such as Alonzo de Ojeda, Diego de Nicuesa, Vasco Nuñez de Balboa, and Juan Ponce de Leon, had no direct pertinence to the Columbus project; in any event, their expeditions extended well beyond the fate of the admiral, who had died in 1506. Ever anxious to explore whatever might be turned to profit and literary applause, Irving wisely decided to make a separate book narrating the adventures of these companions of Columbus. Apparently the suggestion to exploit them in a separate book came from his brother, who was with him in Spain, for Pierre M. Irving calls *Companions* "a work to which he had been prompted by Peter." [7] Apparently Peter Irving was first to realize that the story of these companions might form some of "the most beautiful and

---

5 *The Letters of Washington Irving to Henry Brevoort,* ed. George S. Hellman (New York: G. P. Putnam, 1915), II, 204.

6 *Washington Irving and the Storrows: Letters from England and the Continent, 1821–1828,* ed. Stanley T. Williams (Cambridge: Harvard University Press, 1933), p. 127.

7 Pierre M. Irving, *The Life and Letters of Washington Irving* (New York: G. P. Putnam, 1865), II, 447.

striking incidents in the history of the New World," and that their fates might "furnish a theme of wonderful interest for a poem or drama."[8]

II

Columbus is of course the better known of the two books. It is a life so monumental that the brief lives in *Companions* are sometimes over- looked—as when Elsie Lee West casually remarked that, after *Columbus,* Irving undertook no biographical writing for the next fifteen years.[9] Most of Irving's biographical writing is monumental: the life of George Washington, for example, ran to five volumes in its original publication. So it is easy to forget about his briefer productions. But since both *Columbus* and *Companions* contain events that "rival the exploits recorded in chivalric romance" and "have the additional interest of verity" (*CC,* 5), I propose to look at the neglected *Companions* as an in- stance of romantic history that required Irving to think deeply about the poetic and dramatic aspects of its organization, its characterization, and about the ideological significance of the events. As he wrote the work, it was intended to be not a loose account of exploratory voyages but a moral drama illustrating in all its parts the providential design of civilization extending itself into the wilderness, a tale of reason tri- umphing over superstition, of common men rising to distinction in adumbration of New World democracy. How to celebrate these values constituted a serious ideological problem, for the Spanish church and crown embodied forces of reaction which Irving deplored. Moreover, the enterprise of exploration had as a principal aim the commercial plunder of New World riches (gold, silver, pearls, and slaves) for the royal treasury, an objective appalling to the writer.

Irving anticipated the rationale of later historians like Parkman by focusing on biography as the key to the presentation of this Spanish colonial enterprise. "All history becomes subjective," Emerson was later to say: "in other words, there is properly no history, only biography."[10] Irving would offer historical events in abundance, wild stirring events crowded together in succession, as in a romance. But *character* would be the focus, the adventure of the central man. This subjective focus is

---

8 Irving, *Voyages and Discoveries of the Companions of Columbus,* p. 5. Although this text was originally published (by John Murray in London in 1831) under the title here given, it is familiarly referred to as *Companions of Columbus.* Quotations from it will therefore hereafter be cited as *CC,* in parentheses, in the text.

9 See Elsie Lee West's "Washington Irving, Biographer," in *Washington Irving: The Critical Reaction,* p. 201.

10 Ralph Waldo Emerson, "History," in *Ralph Waldo Emerson,* ed. Joel Porte (New York: Library of America, 1983), p. 240.

especially suggested in Irving's narrative of the life of Ojeda, whose "whole career," remarked one reviewer, "is beyond a romance."[11]

A biographical focus in a work of history has, of course, its limitations, and they are manifest in the structure of *Companions of Columbus*. In digressing briefly to discuss the enterprises of Morales and Pizarro, for example—while he was narrating the life of Balboa—Irving notes that "we have been tempted into what may almost be deemed an episode, though it serves to place in a proper light the lurking difficulties and dangers which beset the expeditions of Vasco Nuñez to the same regions, and his superior prudence and management in avoiding them." Irving defends his digression on the ground that "it is not the object of this narrative . . . to record the general events of the colony under the administration of Don Pedrarias Davila. We refrain, therefore, from detailing various expeditions set on foot by him to explore and subjugate the surrounding country. . ." (*CC*, 149).

This kind of justification did not, however, satisfy all of his readers. *The Athenaeum*, in particular, raised "objections to the plan of his work: it is neither biographical nor historical. . . ." This reviewer complained that "Mr. Irving's narratives want connexion" and that, in consequence, Irving was frequently "obliged to repeat what he has said before. . . ." Although the objection was directed against the biographical focus of the work and grew out of the reviewer's belief that Irving ought to have written a conventional history of the Spanish exploration, its critical pertinence—for the writing of historical fiction as well as for conventional history—is unarguable. Thus the reviewer concluded that, although *Companions* would "be read with great satisfaction" by some, "by others, and there are many, these unconnected narratives will be *more like novels*, and the historical knowledge gained will be but trifling."[12]

Structurally for better or for worse, then, Irving chose Balboa, Nicuesa, Ponce de Leon, Ojeda, and the others to be each the center of a separate narrative. The tales are remarkably individualized brief lives, but character typology governs his conception of each navigator. Each is made to be a representative of some aspect of the "bold and heroic qualities inherent in the Spanish character, which led that nation to so high a pitch of power and glory; and which are still discernible in the great mass of that gallant people, by those who have an opportunity of judging of them rightly" (*CC*, 5). Each is an instance of courage or reason (balanced or overmastered by passion), of endurance or con-

---

11 Review of *Voyages and Discoveries of the Companions of Columbus*, in the *Literary Gazette* (London), 729 (January 8, 1831), 22.
12 *The Athenaeum*, 169 (January 22, 1831), 51–52. Emphasis added.

stancy, of loftiness, isolation, acute sensibility, or suffering. Irving cast himself in the role of the painter, sketching lifelike portraits of "real" men (however "typical" of Spanish character) arising in three-dimensional form from the dust of moldering parchment. He also undertook to be the landscape painter of the Atlantic high seas and the virgin forests of the New World in the Caribees.

Companions, then, manifests a virtually postmodern fusion of multiple genres—the romance, the epic, the tragic, biography, and history. In addition, Irving claimed the role of dramatist, shaping his historical materials into scene and dialogue—sometimes invented, sometimes reported, often based on the authorities on which he relied—Bishop Las Casas, Herrera, Oviedo, and others. Of *Columbus,* W. L. Hedges has observed that Irving had an inclination, on occasion, to

> compensate for the impossibility of doing exhaustive research, to "let his imagination go completely," reconstructing colorful scenes not only from what existing records clearly indicated had happened, but from what a knowledge of the era of discovery led him to believe *might* have happened. And he heightened diction, tone, and characterization to the point of inviting criticism.[13]

Is criticism over Irving's "inventions" justified? I believe so. Although Irving's *Companions* is no different in kind from the historian Simon Schama's recent *Dead Certainties: (Unwarranted Speculations)* (1991), which invented scenes and even documents in narrating the history of General Wolfe's defeat of Montcalm on the Plains of Abraham, the deliberate blurring of the genres of history and biography, on the one hand, with fiction and drama on the other, violates an implied pact with the reader—that what is being presented is, or is not, factual, expositional, documentable, and faithful to what really happened. Nevertheless, when the historical archives did not supply the requisite information to the romantic historian, Irving, in *Companions,* imagined it. The accounts of Balboa's discovery of the Pacific, for example, left out the subjective feelings of Vasco Nuñez and his men, so Irving invented them. Noting that the discovery of the Pacific was "indeed one of the most sublime discoveries that had yet been made in the New World," Irving observes that it

> must have opened a boundless field of conjecture to the wondering Spaniards. The imagination delights to picture forth the splendid confusion of their thoughts. Was this the great Indian Ocean, studded with

---

13 William L. Hedges, "Irving's *Columbus:* The Problem of Romantic Biography," *The Americas,* 8 (1956), 127.

precious islands, abounding in gold, in gems, and spices, and bordered by the gorgeous cities and wealthy marts of the East? or was it some lonely sea, locked up in the embraces of savage uncultivated continents, and never traversed by a bark, excepting the light pirogue of the savage? The latter could hardly be the case, for the natives had told the Spaniards of golden realms, and populous and powerful and luxurious nations upon its shores. Perhaps it might be bordered by various people, civilized in fact, though differing from Europe in their civilization; who might have peculiar laws and customs and arts and sciences; who might form, as it were, a world of their own, intercommuning by this mighty sea, and carrying on commerce between their own islands and continents; but who might exist in total ignorance and independence of the other hemisphere.

Such speculations, Irving concludes, "may naturally have been the ideas suggested by the sight of this unknown ocean" (*CC*, 111–112).

Irving takes considerable liberty here in "picturing forth" the splendid profusion of their thoughts. But in fact it is his imagination at work, acting, it should be noted, on considerable subsequent historical knowledge—knowledge of, for example, the subsequent discovery of Peru. We may forgive this liberty, as we cannot in the case of Schama, because Irving forewarns us that what is about to follow is what "the imagination delights to picture forth." (Schama tells us only afterward that some of his "historical material" was invented.) But Irving thought the liberty was warranted by the dramatic necessities of the form he had elected. The paucity of fact required the superimposition of "color." Consequently he began his fictionalization. The drama of history would have its hero (here the man of wonderment) as the biographical focus, with his emotions imagined, if historical records failed to supply them. But the story would also have its villains, like Pedrarias; its stock characters, like the faithful Juan de la Cosa; and its romantic interracial love story (à la Pocahontas) in the relationship of Vasco Nuñez and Fulvia, the ravishing Indian princess.

III

The object of the narrative of the past, for Irving, the function of this multigeneric historical writing in *Companions*, was threefold. First, it would impart the facts of the New World discovery as an illustration of national and racial characteristics, as these were shaped by the pressures of fifteenth- and sixteenth-century cultural institutions. Yet, second, it would search beneath the merely historic in order to exemplify some general truths about human nature, the same from age to age. Finally, it would find in the New World navigations and settlements the unfolding of the divine plan. Let us take the elements of Irving's intention seriatim.

Irving's introduction to *Companions* takes great pains to establish the principle of historical continuity as explaining the impulse behind the New World explorations. Various motives lured individual navigators to the New World—the example of Columbus, the love of discovery, the hope of finding the Indies, fame, and the expectation of wealth and profit. But the avidity of Spanish behavior, in the presence of the opportunity posed by Columbus and the others, was to be accounted for by "the spirit of chivalry" implicit in "the domestic history of the Spanish during the middle ages." Irving observes that "eight centuries of incessant warfare with the Moorish usurpers of the Peninsula" had produced a culture of born soldiers. The character of the Spaniard was that of a "chivalrous marauder," delighting in "roving incursions and extravagant exploits," "the cavalagada of spoils and captives driven home in triumph from a plundered province" (*CC*, 3–4). The conquest of Granada put an end to the Moorish wars, Irving reasoned, thereby depriving the chivalric Spaniards of a proper arena in which to perform their military exploits.

The plans of Columbus and his fellow navigators to sail westward to the Indies thus fired the imagination of young men, who "panted for some new field of romantic enterprise." In Irving's account of the secularization of the spirit of the Crusades, "Chivalry had left the land and launched upon the deep." The Spanish cavalier "embarked in the caravel of the discoverer." Irving's biographies of Ojeda, Nicuesa, Balboa, Valdivia, and the others dutifully listed the national characteristics of the Spanish cavalier shaped by the peninsular wars: "contempt of danger and fortitude under suffering"; a "restless, roaming spirit"; a "fervent, and often bigoted zeal for the propagation of his faith, that had distinguished him during his warfare with the Moors" (*CC*, 5). The bigotry of inquisitional Catholicism, for example, was made incarnate in Ojeda, who converted Indians by force, enslaving and even exterminating them. The loftiness, anguish, and suffering of the romantic were embodied in *el desdichado Nicuesa,* "the unfortunate Nicuesa," repudiated by his subjects and put to sea in a ship which went down off the coast of Hispaniola. The vanity of human wishes was reflected in Ponce de Leon's search for the fountain of youth. And Balboa was projected as a type of the common man rising to distinction, together with the melancholy that attends the ruin of a great man, betrayed by his lesser enemies at court.

Romantic history, at least as Irving conceived it, was preoccupied with the interpretation of such events in light of the determinant of race as well as nationality. In the "American Renaissance," the racial character of the Indians, Negroes, South Sea islanders, and other "primitives" was as important an index to the meaning of history as the attributes of the Anglo-Saxon, Celtic, Mediterranean, or other European "races." The Enlightenment ideology of history presupposed "progress" founded on irresistible natural or moral laws. One of the concomitants of progress was the extension of civilization into the New World wilderness at the expense of the indigenous savage population. Irving's *ex post facto* presumption in *Companions* is likewise that the destiny of the Indians was to give way to the advancing white civilization. Their decline was warranted for us by Irving's presentation of the Indian as cruel, treacherous, wily, deceitful, subtle, devious, superstitious, cannibalistic, and diabolical. Resistant to right reason, in the form of submission to the crown of Ferdinand and Isabella and to the authority of the pope, the infidels thus guaranteed—to the Spanish, if not to the reader—their own fate: capture, enslavement, death—in fact, near genocide.

While Irving is subtle and indirect in making these points, the reviewer of *Columbus* and *Companions* for *The Gentleman's Magazine and Historical Chronicle* makes them explicit. Commenting on the abridgment of *Columbus*, the reviewer finds in the subjugation of the natives

> new illustrations of the history of man—especially on this point, that the gregarious principle cannot be acted upon so far as regards progressive improvement and solid happiness, except in a state of civilization. The history of America, in all other respects, lies in a nutshell. It is merely that of savages, from whom nothing could be learned, and of civilized Europeans labouring to overcome physical difficulties.

Providence, he concluded, "does not permit population to increase in a state where land is not reduced to private property, and cultivated. In short, all the progressive conditions of man are exhibited in the history of America, as if it had been intended for a series of philosophical and political illustrations."

Later, in reviewing *Companions*, doubtless the same writer argued the impossibility of "a civilized people" making "a beneficial settlement in a barbarous country." For this reviewer,

> the liberty of civilized countries can no more be allowed to a savage, than fire-arms to an idiot. It is not that the mode of subjugation may be correct, but subordination there must be; or no good can be done to the

people themselves. Could South America, or North America, ever have been what they are now, if the Indians of either country had been suffered to be triumphant? We speak only *en philosophe* in vindication of Providence, which extracts only good out of evil; and openly manifests, that power cannot be entrusted to barbarians, without injury to the species.[14]

It is against this point of view that, during the quincentary in 1992, some contemporary historians, anthropologists, and Native Americans were protesting the arrival of the Columbus and his companions as an invasion, followed by enslavement, brutalization, and even genocide. And, despite the sheer human grandeur of the great discovery, we were urged to boycott the Columbian celebration. Irving would not have agreed with this kind of neo-Rousseauvian aversion to the advancement of civilization.

At the same time, however, Irving shares a romantic double view of the native. He is in some respects a *noble* figure, whatever his savage limits. *Companions* abounds with scenes in which Indian nobility, dignity, marvelous physique, bravery, and depth of humanity exceed that of the Spaniards. When Ojeda and his men barely escape starvation and death in the swamps of Cuba, they are rescued by natives who "exhibited a humanity that would have done honor to the most professing Christians. They bore them to their dwellings, set meat and drink before them, and vied with each other in discharging the offices of the kindest humanity" (*CC*, 59). Such kindness, Irving writes, "seems almost invariably the case with the natives of the islands, before they had held much intercourse with Europeans" (*CC*, 61). Given the intertribal warfare among the Indians, remarked by nearly all disinterested European observers, Irving's sentimental reduction here may be confidently doubted.

Some justification of Irving's double view of the Indian is found in the fact that there were broadly two families of Indian tribes in the islands of the New World—the more pacific Arawaks and the cruel, cannibalistic Caribs. The Spaniards, of course, made no distinction, slaughtering the Caribs (often at the weaker Arawaks' instigation) and enslaving both tribes in *repartimientos* and *encomiendas*. The total effect was the same: a brutality so devastating that, under the prompting of Bishop Las Casas, the Spanish crown formed a commission in 1516

---

14 Review of the abridgment of *Columbus* in *The Gentleman's Magazine and Historical Chronicle*, 100 (April 1830), 338–339. Review of *Voyages and Discoveries of the Companions of Columbus* in *The Gentleman's Magazine and Historical Chronicle*, 101 (February 1831), 143–144.

"clothed with full powers to inquire into and remedy all abuses, and to take all proper measures for the good government, religious instruction, and effectual protection of the natives" (*CC*, 156n). One of the executive acts of the Spanish crown was to order the importation of Negro slaves into the colonies on the ground that blacks withstood the rigors of slave labor much better than the weaker and useless Indians.

By way of concluding this discussion of *Companions* as an illustration of national and racial character, we ought to note Irving's observation of the

> singular difference in character and conduct of these Spanish adventurers when dealing with each other, or with the unhappy natives. Nothing could be more chivalrous, urbane, and charitable; nothing more pregnant with noble sacrifices of passion and interest, with magnanimous instances of forgiveness of injuries and noble contests of generosity, than the transactions of the discoverers with each other; but the moment they turned to treat with the Indians, even with brave and high-minded caciques, they were vindictive, blood-thirsty, and implacable . . . [inflicting] atrocious cruelties upon its inhabitants (*CC*, 61–62).

Some Spaniards were of course chivalric in their dealings with each other. But this observation is largely nonsense, as Irving's own text provides abundant illustration of intra-Spanish duplicity, intrigue, violence, and murder. But Irving's attitude toward the natives is, finally, very much like that of Bancroft, who observed in his *History*:

> The picture of the unequal contest inspires a compassion which is honorable to humanity. The weak demand sympathy. If a melancholy interest attaches to the fall of a hero, who is overpowered by superior force, shall we not drop a tear at the fate of nations, whose defeat foreboded exile, if it did not indeed shadow forth the decline and ultimate extinction of a race?[15]

If *Companions* is a romance illuminating history as a conflict between the distinctive characteristics of the Indian and the Spaniard, it is also a tract of sorts on the attributes of human nature, brought under the moral scrutiny of the author. Irving clearly admired the courage, endurance, vision, and enterprise of the Spanish, even though one of his Southern reviewers, with a different definition in mind, expressed surprise that Irving "should insist so strenuously upon the influence which chivalry exerted over these Western discoveries. We cannot for the

---

15 Quoted in Levin, *History as Romantic Art*, p. 126.

life of us, see any chivalry in the matter."[16] But Irving did not skirt the issue of moral judgment.[17] He found in the history of Ojeda, Nicuesa, Balboa, and the others irrefutable evidence of the cupidity and greed of wild, mercantile adventurers whose evangelical Catholicism insufficiently restrained them from the plunder of the Americas. As he sardonically observed, gold covered all sins in the New World. If the navigators' enterprises were heroic in scope and attended with gallantry, they were also marked by vanity, pride, the lust for power and glory, and endless jealousies. These are timeless vices that transformed the settlers into ungovernable mobs, fickle in their support of the duly appointed and elected leaders, who themselves intrigued and conspired at court to destroy one another. In presenting this panorama of continuing disorder, Irving was, as the reviewer Henry D. Gilpin pointed out, "the same undeviating, but beautiful moralist, gathering from all lessons to the present, in striking language, to reason and the heart."[18]

The effect of Irving's biographical method, his organizational plan, was to give his narrative a general literary unity and an historical overview of significant philosophical meaning. These merits, I believe, rescue the book from the charge of incoherent anecdotalism. At the same time, this plan showed the ironies of Providence in bringing to despair some of the most heinous criminals against humanity who ever lived—although always, as the man of sensibility and feeling, Irving absolves the navigators in death: "who does not forget [Ojeda's] faults and errors at the threshold of his humble and untimely grave!" (*CC*, 64). "How vain are our most confident hopes, our brightest triumphs!" he remarks of the fall and execution of Balboa, who first discovered the Pacific.

> Behold him . . . betrayed into the hands of his most invidious foe, the very enterprise that was to have crowned him with glory wrested into a crime, and himself hurried to a bloody and ignominious grave at the foot, as it were, of the mountain whence he had made his discovery! His fate, like that of his renowned predecessor, Columbus, proves that it is sometimes dangerous even to deserve too greatly (*CC*, 162–163).

This tone of tragedy, or at least of pathos, marks all these narrative biographies. As another reviewer remarked, no mean sentimentalist

---

16 "Irving's *Voyages and Discoveries of the Companions of Columbus*," *Southern Review*, 13 (May 1831), 217–218.

17 Irving tried to avoid extremes of judgment, preferring to balance his subjects' virtues against their vices, and often attained a balance by citing positive and negative attitudes of previous annalists who had witnessed the events.

18 Henry D. Gilpin, "Irving's Spanish Voyages of Discovery," *American Quarterly Review*, 9 (March 1831), 184–185.

himself, "the careers of all end sadly and disastrously—in the great cause of discovery they suffered imprisonment, persecution, exile and death. The history of genius is the saddest of all histories."[19]

"The trouble with *Columbus* today," W. L. Hedges has observed of Irving's *magnum opus*, "is that there is not enough factual weight to hold it down. Even as 'literary' history it is not sufficiently informative. Students of Irving look upon it as simply romantic, like romance, or like fiction. Stanley T. Williams goes so far as to say it really is a romance."[20] But is *Columbus*, or *Companions*, for that matter, a romance? Is it really fiction? This was a commonplace viewpoint one used frequently to encounter in Irving criticism. But a great many judgments like this, founded on the authority of Irving's first notable academic biographer, Stanley Williams, have recently been called into question. And in light of the recent research of John H. McElroy, whose superb investigation into the sources of *Columbus* is definitive, Williams's description of the book must now be rejected as partial, defective, and biased.

Nevertheless, the viewpoint persists that Irving was good for only comic treatments of the past—as in Knickerbocker's rollicking *A History of New York*. If not that, Irving is usually seen as the dabbling, drifting dilettante that he himself invented in Geoffrey Crayon—an idle, whimsical, mindless dreamer incapable of sustained intellectual labor of any kind and only to be counted on for shallow verbal whimsies and superficial literary whim-whams. I am surprised that no one has confused Irving with Fray Antonio Agapida, Jonathan Oldstyle, or any of his other invented narrators. The biography of Stanley T. Williams, published in 1935, is substantially responsible for the indifferent opinion—on the part of Hedges and a number of others—of Irving's attainments as a historian and biographer of Columbus, of his fellow Spanish navigators, and of George Washington. For it was Williams who, in presenting his massive two-volume biography of Irving, dismissed him in the following words:

> Indeed, as I continued my study of the age in which Irving lived, the question became not at all the measuring of his literary work by the immemorial touchstones of the past, tested by which he is often trivial, or by the standards of to-day, by which he has been outmoded, but a study of his career and writings in fusion with the literary criteria of his own time. For through such an approach he becomes a clarifying mirror of some aspects of culture in America during the first half of the

---

19 Review of *Voyages and Discoveries of the Companions of Columbus, The Athenaeum*, 166 (January 1, 1831), 9.
20 Hedges, "Irving's *Columbus*," p. 128.

nineteenth century. To understand Irving's hold upon his generation is to understand a dominating tendency of American literature prior to the Civil War, which, beginning only two years after Irving's death, helped to destroy the cult of elegance and made comprehensible the voices of a Whitman or a Clemens.[21]

A member of the cult of elegance? Trivial? Outmoded? This writer who was called the "Father of American Literature" and whose works were universally beloved? These are the words of a left-leaning depression-era critic whose judgment was clouded by the socialist indictment of the middle class and by the romantic glorification of the American counterculture. There is nothing wrong with having a literary counterculture, insofar as it may produce a Whitman or a Twain. But the prejudice against educated, well-born, or well-to-do American writers such as Irving, on the part of critics on the left, has frequently led them to faulty aesthetic judgments.

This is the case with Williams's view of *Companions of Columbus:* "upon Irving's reputation this *addendum* [to *Columbus*] had no effect."[22] I have no wish to inflate the reputation of *Companions* today. But such was not the view of Irving's contemporaries, who felt that *Voyages and Discoveries of the Companions of Columbus* had added "to the already well-deserved reputation of Mr. Irving." It had the merit, Gilpin wrote in the *American Quarterly Review,* "of which so few American books can boast, of going to the bottom of its subject." For Gilpin and his contemporaries, *Companions* entitled Irving to "take his stand among those writers who have done more than amuse the fancy, or even gratify the heart. He is to be classed with the historians of great events. . . ."[23] *Companions* is distinctly a lesser book than *Columbus*. It is, without question, an offshoot of the research that produced a greater book. But it is an eminently readable, stirring, suspenseful set of brief lives. One is therefore inclined to assent to the view of Van Wyck Brooks, who praised its "glowing chapters," chapters that "can hardly be excelled in human feeling and romantic enthusiasm." For Brooks, as perhaps for those who will take the trouble to read *Companions,* "these chapters are chips from the workshop that produced the great *History,* but they are chips of the rarest material."[24]

---

21 Stanley T. Williams, *The Life of Washington Irving* (2 vols., New York: Oxford University Press, 1935), I, xiii–xiv.
22 Williams, *Life of Washington Irving,* II, 24.
23 Gilpin, "Irving's Spanish Voyages," pp. 163–165.
24 Van Wyck Brooks, "Foreword," in *Voyages and Discoveries of the Companions of Columbus,* by Washington Irving (New York: Rimington and Hooper, 1929), pp. xii, viii.

Consecrating Evil: Emerson and Hawthorne

To speak of Emerson and Hawthorne together is to recollect one of the most lively and creative periods in American literary history and to remember a specific place (the Boston-Cambridge-Concord axis) where they and their friends lived. The friends and acquaintances of Emerson and Hawthorne are not without their own independent interest—people such as Henry Wadsworth Longfellow, John Greenleaf Whittier, James Russell Lowell, Oliver Wendell Holmes, Margaret Fuller, Theodore Parker, Bronson and Louisa May Alcott, the Peabody sisters, and Henry David Thoreau, among others. This period is often called the American Renaissance because it produced such a brilliant flourishing of the literary imagination in New England between the 1830s and 1860s. There seems general critical agreement that few periods before—or since—have produced so many writers and so many works of such great imaginative distinction.

One of the reasons why the epithet "renaissance" is given to the period is that Emerson and his followers inaugurated a spiritual movement that permeated New England culture and, as New England was the cultural capital of the United States, the rest of American culture as well. This upsurge of spiritual intensity was inchoate in its origins, and people did not know what to call it, so they called it at first "The Newness."[1] Theodore Parker's sermons and the lectures and essays of Emer-

---

1 Irving Howe recently revived the term in *The American Newness: Culture and Politics in the Age of Emerson* (Cambridge: Harvard University Press, 1986). But as Howe accorded no importance to the Newness as a manifestation of a distinctively religious spirit, the book was of scant value in understanding Emerson and his circle. The intent of the book was in

son, particularly *Nature* (1836), "The American Scholar" (1837), "The Divinity School Address" (1838), and "Self-Reliance" (1841), expressed the basic faith of the movement. We now call it transcendentalism rather than the Newness.

Emersonian transcendentalism was a faith in spiritual intuition as the guide to truth, and in reliance on subjective feeling as the validation of reality. The transcendentalists subordinated the rational faculty to intuition and subordinated history and tradition to the urgencies of the immediate present. Transcendentalism elevated nature into a symbol of the benignant spiritual center of the universe and urged men to get in touch with that Divine Oversoul by listening to the inner voice. The discovery of Emerson, Thomas Wentworth Higginson was later to say, would be for any young man "a great event in life, but in the comparative conventionalism of the literature of that period it had the effect of a revelation."[2] The key to the period—as Emerson observed in "Historic Notes on Life and Letters in New England"—"appeared to be that mind had become aware of itself. Men grew reflective and intellectual. There was a new consciousness."[3]

I

It is the content of this new consciousness that I want to consider, and the reaction it provoked in one of Emerson's most profound and talented contemporaries, Nathaniel Hawthorne. But let me proceed for a moment further with what transcendentalism stood for. "The summer of 1839," William Ellery Channing later remarked, "saw the full dawn of the Transcendental movement in New England." Channing defined it as "an assertion of the inalienable integrity of man, of the immanence of Divinity in instinct. In part, it was a reaction against Puritan Orthodoxy; in part, an effect of renewed study of the ancients, of Oriental Pantheists, of Plato and the Alexandrians, of Plutarch's *Morals,* Seneca and Epictetus; in part, the natural product of the culture of the place and time."

Partly what happened was that the German idealism of Kant, Jacobi, Fichte, and Novalis, reinforced by the teachings of Schelling, Hegel, Carlyle, and Schliermacher, was engrafted onto the "stunted stock of

---

fact to try to resuscitate the "progressive spirit," by claiming Emerson as its father, since worldwide socialism and communism had begun to collapse. Emerson, who is the father of radical individualism, spurned the appeal of the Brook Farm socialists and would have been stupefied at the way his doctrines have been coopted by the radical left.

2 Thomas Wentworth Higginson, *Contemporaries* (Boston: Houghton Mifflin, 1899), p. 10.

3 "Historic Notes on Life and Letters in New England," in *The American Transcendentalists,* ed. Perry Miller (Garden City, N.Y.: Doubleday, 1957), p. 5.

Unitarianism." And the result, as Channing called it, was "a vague yet exalting conception of the godlike nature of the human spirit." For these disciples of "The Newness," transcendentalism was "a pilgrimage from the idolatrous world of creeds and rituals to the temple of the Living God in the soul. It was," he said, "a putting to silence of tradition and formulas, that the Sacred Oracle might be heard through intuitions of the single-eyed and pure-hearted." Essentially a romantic epistemology, transcendentalism took as many forms and shapes as its individualistic adherents could devise, but they shared a common belief in what Channing called "perpetual inspiration, the miraculous power of the will, and a birthright to universal good." [4] The New England sense of sin and damnation, endemic in the vestigial Puritan culture, even in Unitarianism, was abandoned in favor of a belief in the essential goodness of humanity and the possibility, by will and action, of fulfilling the imperatives of the self. Anti-institutionalists and "come-outers," the transcendentalists passed severe judgment on what they called the fossilized institutions of New England society—the church, the college, political parties, and the government. Still, they sometimes banded together to effect social reforms and to publish their views—principally in *The Dial*, the *Harbinger*, and the *Boston Quarterly Review*. A fellowship of the "like-minded," who on specific issues disagreed more often than not, transcendentalism was a brotherhood of free and independent thought and of a liberal and hopeful spirit.[5]

II

Some sense of the radical stance of Emerson and his circle is suggested by his essential position on human nature and good and evil in the universe. For Emerson, the Christian idea of God was to be replaced by a conception of the deity as a Divine Oversoul, a quasi-pantheistic Vital Energy, fundamentally benignant in its nature, irradiating all mind and matter. A man could know this divine presence within his own soul, for it circulated through man as well as through all of creation. Through the faculty of intuition (what Kant had called *Vernunft*) a man could know his divine mission in the world—not through consulting decalogues, articles of faith, sacred scriptures, or church doctrine, but simply

---

4 William Ellery Channing, "A Participant's Definition," in *The American Transcendentalists*, pp. 36–38.
5 Among critical works valuable for an understanding of transcendentalism, readers may consult William R. Hutchinson's *The Transcendentalist Ministers*, Lawrence Buell's *Literary Transcendentalism*, and F. O. Matthiessen's *American Renaissance*. Joel Myerson's *The Transcendentalists* gives a comprehensive, indispensable review of research and criticism relevant to this movement.

through passively awaiting the monitions of the Oversoul as it manifested itself with him. Since all creation is divine and moral, all communiqués or calls to action from the Oversoul have a divine origin and sanction. No inspired act can be immoral since God, or the Oversoul, or the divine current of being within us, is always benign. Evil, as such, does not exist, Emerson tells us in "The Divinity School Address": it is merely the "privation of good," that is, the absence of good. If we fill up our lives with virtuous action, evil has no space, as it were, to exist.[6]

The notion that there is no active principle of evil, no agency that has as its central intention the corruption of human virtue, such as men have called Satan or the Devil, freed Emerson and his followers to think that each one alone could perpetually recreate the world in the image of the divine, that is, in the image of personal desire. Emerson granted that most men live a mundane, this-worldly existence, misled by their senses and their merely rational faculties (Kant's *Verstandt*) into living on a material plane of existence. "Man is a god in ruins," he complains in *Nature*. "Man is the dwarf of himself," (*E*, 45–46) because he heeds not the voice of the God within. There is something sublimely hortatory in Emerson's calling us to the full measure of our divinity and in his urging us each to build our own worlds, as the God within bids us. If we do so, he promises, we will discover that evil has evaporated into so much nonentity (*E*, 48–49).

In the struggle to live the virtuous life, Emerson turned away from the prescriptions of sacred scripture, from prohibitive decalogues with their "shalt nots," from religious commandment of every kind. The ground of ethical behavior, for Emerson, was to be discovered by consulting the self. Ethics could not consist in following the commandments of an outward authority, however august. In this rejection of the ethical mandates of institutional religion we have not only a rejection of the idea of divine revelation on which these mandates are claimed to have been founded but also a rejection of the past—the past of historical tradition, the past of received theological pronouncements, of binding doctrine and dogma. But even if, say, Christian revelation were true, Emerson would reject any received moral law and doctrine simply because it is received: "Why," he asks in *Nature*, "should not we also enjoy an original relation to the Universe?" (*E*, 7). Thus the accumulated wisdom of the race, the amassed and analyzed experience of mankind, over generations, over centuries, counts for naught, for Emerson, in comparison with the self's intuitive flash of understanding as to what at the

---

6 "The Divinity School Address," in *Ralph Waldo Emerson: Essays and Lectures*, ed. Joel Porte (New York: Library of America, 1983), p. 77. Unless otherwise indicated, citations from Emerson will hereafter be given as *E*, in parentheses, in the text.

moment is to be done, the quasi-mystical impulse, validated by feeling, of what the individual's course is to be. "What have I to do with the sacredness of traditions, if I live wholly from within?" (*E*, 262) he asks.

When Emerson was asked how he could know that his actions might not be evil, his reply in "Self-Reliance" will seem astonishing: ". . . they do not seem to be such; but if I am the devil's child, I will live then from the devil." "No law," he remarks, "can be sacred to me but that of my nature. Good and bad are but names very readily transferable to that or this; the only right is what is after my constitution, the only wrong what is against it." In sacralizing all of nature as an expression of divinity, in sacralizing human nature as divine, Emerson readily dispenses with confession, penance, and absolution: "Absolve you to yourself and you shall have the suffrage of the world" (*E*, 261–262).[7]

III

Absolution is a frequent theme in Hawthorne as well as in Emerson, but it would be hard to image two neighbors so close who had so different a view of human nature, history and tradition, and the workings of good and evil in human experience. Emerson, for Hawthorne, was "that everlasting rejecter of all that is, and seeker for he knows not what," a thinker for whom the facts of the moral life "melt away and become insubstantial in his grasp."[8] Hawthorne was disturbed at the discrepancy, as he saw it, between the Emersonian theory of human perfectibility and the reality of human thought and behavior in ordinary quotidian experience. Descended from the Puritans, as he tells us in "The Custom House" prologue to *The Scarlet Letter*, he remarks that "strong traits of their nature have intertwined themselves with mine."[9]

One aspect of the Puritan influence over him, two centuries afterward, was his recognition of the fallen nature of mankind, the tendency in men and women to moral error. In story after story Hawthorne sought to answer Emerson's unrealistic optimism about human nature.

---

7 Self-absolution for acts that others regard as evil appears also in Melville. Captain Ahab justifies his destructive monomaniacal quest for Moby Dick, which leads to the death of all his crew (save Ishmael) by a like Emersonian maneuver. When the *Pequod* encounters the *Rachel*, crazy Ahab will not pause in his mad pursuit of Moby Dick to search for Captain Gardiner's son, who is lost at sea: "Captain Gardiner, I will not do it. Even now I lose time. Good bye, good bye. God bless ye, man, and *may I forgive myself*, but I must go." See *Moby-Dick*, ed. Charles Feidelson (Indianapolis: Bobbs-Merrill, 1964), p. 671. My italics.

8 *Centenary Edition of the Works of Nathaniel Hawthorne*, ed. William Charvat (Columbus: Ohio State University Press, 1962–), VIII, 357, 336.

9 Nathaniel Hawthorne, *The Scarlet Letter and Other Tales of the Puritans*, ed. Harry Levin (Boston: Houghton Mifflin, 1961), p. 12. Hereafter, quotations from the novel will be cited as *SL*, and page numbers will be given in parentheses in the text.

In "Young Goodman Brown" his theme is the youth's discovery of the ubiquity of evil in the human heart. Not even his wife, Faith, glimpsed through the trees at the Black Mass initiating the innocents into the service of the Devil, is apparently as innocent as she seems. In this scene the Devil speaks to the new communicants:

> "Depending upon one another's hearts, ye had still hoped that virtue were not all a dream. Now ye are undeceived! Evil is the nature of mankind. Evil must be your only happiness. Welcome, again, my children, to the communion of your race!"[10]

Hawthorne himself did not of course believe that virtue was a dream; and we should note that it is the Devil, the Father of Lies—not Hawthorne—who defines evil as man's nature. The whole matter, moreover, might well have been Brown's nightmare. But Hawthorne is clear enough in this tale and in many other places that a rosy transcendentalist view of the perfectibility of mankind, its claim for man's ability to banish evil impulse, was a delusion. Hawthorne was hardly an orthodox Christian, but he found in Christianity's view of fallen human nature a more nearly accurate description, if only on the psychological level, of what people are really and fundamentally like: "There is evil in every human heart," he observes in his notebook, "which may remain latent, perhaps, through the whole of life; but circumstances may round it to activity."[11] In his short story "Earth's Holocaust," he satirizes both transcendental reformers and exotic Christian cults awaiting the Second Coming. These religious reformers have a desire for moral perfection so intense that it becomes a lust for destruction and utopian purification from tainted this-worldliness. It leads them to ignite a bonfire upon which they cast all the monuments of civilization and learning that have lifted man out of barbarism. The Devil appears at the end of the tale, his eyes glowing "with a redder light than that of the bonfire," to mock these idealistic reformers because they have forgotten to incinerate the human heart: "And, unless they hit upon some method of purifying that foul cavern, forth from it will re-issue all the shapes of wrong and misery—the same old shapes, or worse ones—which they have taken such a vast deal of trouble to consume to ashes" (*NHT,* 158–159).

Hawthorne's Puritan ancestors did of course embrace a belief in the absolute depravity of man, who in his fallen condition was a foul cavern

---

10 Nathaniel Hawthorne, "Young Goodman Brown," in *Nathaniel Hawthorne's Tales,* ed. James McIntosh (New York: W. W. Norton, 1987), p. 74. Hereafter quotations from the short stories will be cited as *NHT,* and page numbers will be given in the text.

11 *The Centenary Edition of the Works of Nathaniel Hawthorne,* VIII, 29. See also IX, 220 and 226, for other reflections on evil in the human heart.

full of lust, envy, anger, gluttony, pride, and the rest of the Seven Deadly Sins. The fate of the natural man, unredeemed by God's grace and conversion, was to the Puritans inevitably perdition. Hawthorne lived two hundred years later than the Puritans, lived in a more charitable and latitudinarian age. His works do not evince a belief in the absoluteness of human depravity, but they are so full of the sense of sin and guilt, of transgression and error, and of the need of confession and absolution, as psychological realities, as truths of the moral life, that there can be no doubt that his work is a dramatic protest against the Emersonian faith in man's fundamental perfectibility. In "Ethan Brand" the title character goes throughout the world in search of the Unforgivable Sin, only to find it lodged in his own heart, which is transformed into stone at the end of the story.

"Ethan Brand" is worth attending to for a moment longer, in connection with Emerson. Emerson had announced in "Self-Reliance" that every individual who would be an individual must go it alone, must live by his own lights, rejecting tradition, history, and the accumulated wisdom of the past. Society, in that essay, is viewed as inimical to the full actualization of the individual. "Whoso would be a man must be a nonconformist" who resists the blandishments of society, its threats, its coercive pressures, in order to be himself. In "Self-Reliance" he observes: "Society everywhere is in conspiracy against the manhood of every one of its members. Society is a joint-stock company in which the members agree for the better securing of his bread to each shareholder, to surrender the liberty and culture of the eater. The virtue in most request is conformity. Self-reliance is its aversion" (*E*, 261).

Now, this view of society, which emphasizes only our craven security at the price of individual liberty, leads Emerson to affirm the necessity, as it may be, of rejecting community, friends, and even family: "I shun father and mother and wife and brother, when my genius calls me. I would write on the lintels of the doorpost *Whim*. I hope it is somewhat better than whim at last, but we cannot spend the day in explanation. Expect me not to show cause why I seek or why I exclude company" (*E*, 262). And again: "Check this lying hospitality and lying affection. Live no longer to the expectation of these deceived and deceiving people with whom we converse. Say to them, O father, O mother, O wife, O brother, O friend, I have lived with you after appearances hitherto. Henceforth I am the truth's" (*E*, 273). Emerson has as his model here Christ himself, who spurns Mary in favor of doing his Heavenly Father's will. Most of Emerson's audience would have accepted the necessity of Christ's resistance to his mother. But Emerson believes that we are all potential Christs who need only consult ourselves—that is, our Divinity Incarnate—to relegate to their subordinate rank relatives, friends, and community.

Such a radical individualism as is expressed in these remarks from "Self-Reliance" is very far distant from the sentiment in favor of the individual's full integration into the fabric of society that we find expressed repeatedly in Hawthorne's fiction. Hawthorne's claim for the value of integratedness into the community is repeated so frequently in his stories that it emerges as an element in the grand design of his fiction, as a basic attribute of the value system inherent in his art. In "Ethan Brand" the Unforgivable Sin turns out to be Brand's repudiation of our common fallen humanity. He rejects society and his role in it in favor of a Faustian ambition for godlike individual superiority. This sublime egotism leads him to spurn the human claims of others; because they are weak, he comes to be a fiendish manipulator of other people. At the end of the story, as Ethan Brand reviews his life just before he throws himself into the burning lime kiln, Hawthorne writes that Brand

> remembered with what tenderness, with what love and sympathy for mankind, and what pity for human guilt and woe, he had first begun to contemplate those ideas which afterwards became the inspiration for his life [that is, discovering what and where is the Unforgivable Sin]; with what reverence he had then looked into the heart of man, viewing it as a temple originally divine, and, however desecrated, still to be held sacred by a brother; with what awful fear he had deprecated the success of his pursuit, and prayed that the Unpardonable Sin might never be revealed to him. Then ensued that vast intellectual development, which, in its progress, disturbed the counterpoise between his mind and heart. . . . [His heart] had withered—had contracted—had hardened—had perished! It had ceased to partake of the universal throb. He had lost his hold of the magnetic chain of humanity (*NHT,* 241).

Throughout Hawthorne's work, in "Lady Eleanor's Mantle," "Ethan Brand," "My Kinsman, Major Molineux," and *The Scarlet Letter,* whatever may be the deficiencies of society we cannot exist without it; we fare better when we are in vital connection with it; and the individual who dissents from society and estranges himself from his fellows suffers an alienation that inwardly, and perhaps outwardly, destroys him. This I take to be the fate that overcomes the principals of *The Scarlet Letter,* Coverdale in *The Blithedale Romance,* the pastor in "The Minister's Black Veil," and many others. The Emersonian claim for liberty as the prior condition of all values, all politics, all religion, and all social organization is hortatory and inspiring. But its consequences, as dramatized by Hawthorne, are not beneficent. In his fiction, disaster follows when the individual sets himself apart from his fellows in some assertion of spiritual superiority or godlike divinity.

These issues involving good and evil and the self and society, asserted in Emerson's essays and challenged in Hawthorne's stories, bear upon the question of how one can know that the assertion of one's liberty will result in virtuous conduct. What is the ground of one's belief that what he does is beneficent and not immoral? What validates an action as indeed virtuous and not the act of a child of the Devil? Emerson is quite clear in "Self-Reliance": trust your intuition; trust your emotion; trust your feeling—this validates the conduct out of which impulse springs. Of course, Emerson believes that the voice of the God or the Oversoul speaking to man's feeling self, to his intuitive faculty, cannot delude or deceive him, that the monitions of the divine that flood the soul cannot but be positive. Ah, but how many crimes of the heart have been committed in the name of a belief that God personally directed one to act as he did? Quite a few more, I should think, than "the Devil made me do it."

The status of the feelings—as a source of truth and as the ground of ethical conduct—is what is here in question. The great religions offer theological commentary on this point, and I think I am not blurring specific distinctions when I observe that in religious thought the feelings and appetites are understood to be inimical to spiritual perfection. The way of the disciple—whether in Christianity, Islam, Buddhism, or Hinduism—is detachment from the appetites, an asceticism in which the aspiring soul frees itself from the seductions of the world, the flesh, and perhaps the Devil. Moreover, in the history of philosophy, most reflective thought on moral conduct tells us that feeling is an unstable basis on which to decide the great ethical questions of our lives. Short of Epicureanism, with its *carpe diem* injunction, philosophers from Plato and Aristotle onward have commended conduct based on rational principle rather than feeling, which is fickle, transient, and easily self-deceived. To these two modes of thinking, the theological and philosophical, we must add the commonsense conclusions men have reached, after centuries of human experience, about how to behave and act in difficult ethical dilemmas that are always recurring, virtually identically, from generation to generation. But "Trust your emotion": that is just what the saintly Emerson, the former Unitarian minister of Boston, would have us do. No wonder Emerson has been such a popular guru since the sixties: just do your own thing. Doing one's own thing is not a bad thing to do, if, like Emerson, one's moral sense is shaped by the mandates of Christian ethical thought. Taught self-discipline by a

Calvinist aunt, educated at a Christian divinity school, constrained by the discipline of a congregational ministry, Emerson's exemplary personal life was lived on the borrowed capital of Christian ethical thought. The lives of his more recent disciples are another matter.

IV

In *The Scarlet Letter* Hawthorne explores what happens when a couple, Hester Prynne and Arthur Dimmesdale, act on the imperative of feeling. The novel opens with Hester Prynne on the scaffold outside the jail, punished for her adultery and for the bastard child in her arms. She is commanded by the community, through the agency of the ministers and magistrates, to wear the scarlet *A* on her breast as a sign of her immorality. She is seen by the community, especially by the goodwives, as subversive of its values, which affirm the rightness of monogamy in marriage and the wrongness of sex with another man's wife.

These days it is customary for us to think the seventeenth-century Puritans harsh in their modes of punition. When Dimmesdale is too craven to confess his fatherhood of Pearl, we therefore sympathize with Hester in her solitary punishment. Dimmesdale ought to have confessed his part in the adultery at once, but he does not do so. And the consequence for both of them, as well as for Pearl and Hester's husband, Roger Chillingworth, is a train of even greater moral disasters that impel the plot toward Dimmesdale's final sermon, confession, and penitent death. These disastrous consequences include Pearl's fatherlessness and the distortions of her personality therefrom; Dimmesdale's increasing remorse, gnawing within him, that produces its own scarlet letter said to ulcerate his chest; Chillingworth's appetite for revenge against the man who cuckolded him (leading to the infernal diabolization of his character); and Hester's more or less complete estrangement from the community's religious, moral, legal, and domestic values.

All these are interesting characters, and their entanglements provide many fascinating plot developments. But I want to focus on Hester Prynne, on the consequences of her self-estrangement from the old Boston social order (it is self-estrangement: if she is ostracized by the town it is because she is impenitent and denies that she has done anything wrong), and on the role of her feelings in the definition of her character.

Hester is one of the most beautiful, passionate, strong, self-reliant, and independent heroines in our literature. The sexually fallen, utterly abandoned single mother is a frequent focus of social and literary compassion. It is clear that Hawthorne, like Dimmesdale (and many readers), was deeply in love with her. Her beauty, her passion, her strength as a woman, her resistance to the perceived unjust authority of the ministers and magistrates, her remarkable powers of stoic endurance in the face of ostracism—all these are so striking that many see her as deserving our full and absolute admiration. This is especially evident in much recent feminist criticism of the novel.[12] But in my view it is a misreading of the novel to admire Hester too much.

Hawthorne makes it quite plain that Hester's resistance to the ministry of the town elders estranges her from the community. In her pride and rebellion, "The links that united her to the rest of human kind . . . had all been broken." During the seven years of her isolation from intimate involvement with the town life, she was "little accustomed, in her long seclusion from society, to measure her ideas of right and wrong by any standard external to herself," (*SL*, 158). She has become, in other words, a perfect Emersonian. Harold Bloom is quite right to see Hester as "a prime instance of Emerson's American religion of self-reliance"; and Nina Baym accurately observes that Hester "represents everything the transcendentalists believe and more besides, for in her Emerson's 'Spirit' is transformed into Eros and thus allied to sex, passion, eroticism, flesh, and the earth."[13] For Bloom and Baym, such asserted freedom from external social constraint is positive; for Hawthorne it is not.

Hawthorne associates Hester with Anne Hutchinson, the Puritan woman preacher whose violation of Massachusetts Bay Colony laws in the seventeenth century led to the charge of antinomianism and exile, doubtless because the Emerson crowd thought her to be "the first Transcendentalist and, by extension, the first feminist in America."[14] He

---

12 See, for example, Nina Baym's "Thwarted Nature: Nathaniel Hawthorne as Feminist," in *American Novelists Revisited: Essays in Feminist Criticism*, ed. Fritz Fleischmann (Boston: G. K. Hall, 1982), pp. 58–77; the risible reading of the novel by Shari Benstock in "*The Scarlet Letter* (a)dorée, or the Female Body Embroidered," in *The Scarlet Letter: Complete, Authoritative Text with Biographical Background and Critical History Plus Essays from Five Contemporary Critical Perspectives. . .* , ed. Ross C. Murfin (Boston: Bedford Books of St. Martin's Press, 1991), pp. 288–303; and Nina Auerbach's preposterous claim that Hester is a "defiant icon" of women's hidden power, a "feminist saint, the vehicle for 'a new truth' of empowered and transfigured womanhood," argued in *Woman and the Demon: The Life of a Victorian Myth* (Cambridge: Harvard University Press, 1982), pp. 165–166. Auerbach is claiming for Hester exactly that which, because of her sexual fall, Hawthorne denies to Hester.

13 See *Nathaniel Hawthorne*, ed. Harold Bloom (New York: Chelsea House, 1986), pp. 5–6; and Nina Baym's *The Shape of Hawthorne's Career* (Ithaca: Cornell University Press, 1976), p. 147, reprinted in "The Major Phase I, 1850: *The Scarlet Letter*," in *Critical Essays on Hawthorne's The Scarlet Letter*, ed. David B. Kesterson (Boston: G. K. Hall, 1988), p. 148.

14 B. Welter, *Dimity Convictions: The American Woman in the Nineteenth Century* (Athens: Ohio University Press, 1976), p. 94.

tells us that Hester was living in "an age in which the human intellect" was "newly emancipated" from ancient ideas. One of these ancient ideas had to do with the role of woman in society. Hester's radical freethinking leads her to the appalling view that

> the whole system of society is to be torn down, and built up anew. Then, the very nature of the opposite sex, or its long hereditary habit, which has become like nature, is to be essentially modified, before woman can be allowed to assume what seems a fair and suitable position. . . . Thus, Hester Prynne, whose heart had lost its regular and healthy throb, wandered without a clew in the dark labyrinth of mind. . . . At times, a fearful doubt strove to possess her soul, whether it were not better to send Pearl at once to heaven, and go herself to such futurity as Eternal Justice should provide.
>
> The scarlet letter had not done its office (*SL,* 163–164).

It is because the scarlet letter has not done its office that Hester here contemplates the murder of Pearl and her own suicide. Hawthorne's remark suggests that the scarlet letter has an office to perform, a role to play in her life; and indeed it is to be the instrument of her redemption. But this is to get ahead of our story, which holds Hester yet awhile in her unregenerateness. Since the scarlet letter has not done its office, Hester suggests to Dimmesdale—when she sees how he is being destroyed by his guilt and by Chillingworth's diabolical torture—that they run away together, into the forest or to Europe. In a scene of passionate sensuality, Hester meets Dimmesdale in the forest (probably where the adultery had taken place before). There Hester expresses again her love for him, removes the scarlet letter from her breast, takes down her hair (an act of unparalleled erotic suggestiveness), and proposes their flight from the scene of their guilt.

We note in that scene, however, that the elfin daughter Pearl—whose preternatural behavior symbolizes that she is not merely a natural child but the issue of a moral crime, adultery—refuses to recognize her mother and demands that the scarlet *A* be resumed. The allegorical significance of the forest should not be minimized. It is Dante's *selva oscura,* Spenser's "Wood of Errour," Bunyan's site of the temptation to sin. Melville called Hawthorne as deep as Dante because, in part, both allegorized the forest as the appropriate scene of the *natural* act; it is not the scene of the *civilized* act. Civilization is the scene where, for the general good, men and women bind themselves under civil law, religious commandment, and socially constraining yet unifying manners and mores. Still, this forest scene is poignant, as the couple forgive each other for the wrongs they have unintentionally inflicted on each other.

But more striking is the position Hester expresses about their adulterous act seven years before. Dimmesdale says:

> "May God forgive us both. We are not, Hester, the worst sinners in the world. There is one worse than even the polluted priest! That old man's revenge [Chillingworth's] has been blacker than my sin. He has violated, in cold blood, the sanctity of the human heart. Thou and I, Hester, never did so!"
>
> "Never, never!" whispered she. "What we did had a consecration of its own. We felt it so! We said so to each other! Hast thou forgotten it?"
>
> "Hush, Hester!" said Arthur Dimmesdale, rising from the ground. "No; I have not forgotten!" (*SL*, 194).

Hester justifies the original adultery in that it had a consecration of its own. It is not their love that she consecrates but "what we did," the act itself, the act of adultery.

Now, that which is consecrated is set apart as holy; it is blessed; it is invested with religious meaning and value. Yet here we are talking about an act of adultery, which throughout the long millennia of human history has been well nigh universally condemned in all societies with any kind of developed ethical consciousness. But what interests me is the ground of her consecration of this adulterous act: "We felt it so." That she validates their conduct on the basis of feeling clearly makes her the Emersonian transcendentalist I have been describing. Such a person finds a warrant for behavior in how she feels. "If it feels right, do it": the message of *Playboy* and television shows like *Studs* and *Murphy Brown*. Emerson, minus his ethical rigor, lives on today.

If I seem to have trivialized Hester's position, it is because her suggestion is not only morally doubtful but made in absolute ignorance of the character of Dimmesdale. To follow her suggestion would be the utter ruination of Dimmesdale, who has already once yielded to the seductive appeal that feeling validates conduct as ethical—and look at the disasters that have happened to them. Moreover, if he succumbed to this idea *this time*, we can be sure that this conscience-stricken minister would be utterly destroyed—morally, psychologically, and spiritually. For he is a believer in the divine commandment against adultery, in the rule of Boston civil law condemning it, in the propriety of the community's social stand against it. What Hester is thus suggesting is the most dangerous moment in the novel, when their immortal souls are hanging in the balance. His admonition to her to hush is his gentle way of declining a course of action that would be even more immoral than the original adultery.

Hawthorne is not content to let the matter rest there. The ethical and psychological risk implicit in Emersonianism made him abandon the scenic presentation of the action and comment, in his own person, on the meaning of Hester's overture to run away so that they can cohabit together in what will be for Dimmesdale a state of sexual lawlessness. Hawthorne remarks in the next chapter that Hester Prynne

> with a mind of native courage and activity, and for so long a period not merely estranged, but outlawed, from society, had habituated herself to such latitude of speculation as was altogether foreign to the clergyman. She had wandered, without rule or guidance, in a moral wilderness; as vast, as intricate and shadowy, as the untamed forest, amid the gloom of which they were now holding a colloquy that was to decide their fate. Her intellect and heart had their home, as it were, in desert places, where she roamed as freely as the wild Indian in his woods. For years past she had looked from this estranged point of view at human institutions, and whatever priests or legislators had established; criticizing all with hardly more reverence than the Indian would feel for the clerical band, the judicial robe, the pillory, the gallows, the fireside, or the church. The tendency of her fate and fortunes had been to set her free. The scarlet letter was her passport into regions where other women dared not tread. Shame, Despair, Solitude! These had been her teachers,—stern and wild ones,—and they had made her strong, but taught her much amiss (*SL*, 198).

I cannot think of another passage in all of Hawthorne's fiction where the narrative voice of the author is so unambiguous and insistent in directing us to a negative judgment on the consequences of radical freethinking, such as we find in Emerson and his school. The manifest evidence of Hawthorne's cultural conservatism here has apparently been too much to bear for some recent critics. His view of marriage, sex, and adultery is simply too retrograde for our enlightened and emancipated academic critics. Yet he is such a great writer! To avoid attacking him, some way around Hawthorne's moral conservatism must therefore be found. Some way of denying what he wrote has become the business of criticism. David Leverenz, for example, disposes of this passage by a deconstructionist maneuver. Despite the excellent demonstration by Wayne C. Booth in *The Rhetoric of Fiction* of the ways in which an author embodies his vision in a narrative voice, Leverenz attacks the narrative voice by saying it is not that of Hawthorne; it is that of "a gentlemanly moralist" who cannot cope with "what starts as a feminist revolt against punitive patriarchal authority" and so "ends in a muddle of sympathetic pity for ambiguous victims."

D. H. Lawrence's directive to trust the tale, not the teller, rightly challenges the narrator's inauthentic moral stance. . . . In learning to see beyond Hawthorne's narrator, readers can see what lies beneath the author's distrust of any coercive authority, especially his own. Though the narrator sometimes seems quite self-consciously fictionalized, he functions less as a character than as a screen for the play of textual energies.[15]

What a distortion of Lawrence's point! Lawrence said that we ought not to trust what a writer may say, in letters, speeches, or diaries, about a story he has written or intends to write. We are to trust the story as written. But Leverenz doesn't care for the story as written, because the story as written is conveyed by the narrative voice that defines Hester's condition as one of sinful behavior, disoriented thought, and moral confusion. If we dismiss Hester's experience as it is interpreted by the narrative voice, the result will be critical chaos. But chaotic judgment, on the part of those who think Hester never does anything wrong, is the usual thing in the radical criticism of Hawthorne. Frederic I. Carpenter, for example, complained that, while the novel has "dramatic perfection," it is flawed by the author's "moralistic, subjective criticism of Hester Prynne." She is a character "embodying the authentic American dream of freedom and independence in the new world," and Carpenter was affronted by Hawthorne's insistence that her claim for perfect freedom was delusional and by his criticizing her "for being romantic and immoral."[16]

Such critical gyrations as we see in Auerbach, Leverenz, and Carpenter are a scandal in Hawthorne criticism. If such critics do not like Hawthorne's moral vision, it is quite enough to say so, in a final summing-up of his work. There is no need to misrepresent what he in fact wrote and thought. This scandal has led Sacvan Bercovitch to complain at the doubtful character of such postmodern criticism. The older critics believed that

> if the narrator said it the author meant it; the new view is that if we do not agree the author must have meant something else. The license this gives to pluralist interpretation—a license (among other things) to create an interpretive gap through which we can attribute our concerns

---

15 David Leverenz, "Mrs. Hawthorne's Headache: Reading *The Scarlet Letter*," *Nineteenth-Century Fiction*, 37 (1983), 553–554. A like attack upon the narrator, for not being a liberal feminist, is to be found in Mary Suzanne Schriber's *Gender and the Writer's Imagination: From Cooper to Wharton* (Lexington: University Press of Kentucky, 1987).

16 Frederic I. Carpenter, "Scarlet A Minus," in *The Scarlet Letter: An Authoritative Text, Essays in Criticism, and Scholarship*, ed. Seymour Gross, *et al.* (3rd ed., New York: W. W. Norton, 1988), pp. 298–300.

and beliefs to the secret "true" author—has certain affinities to Hawthorne's techniques, but it does not therefore bring us closer to *The Scarlet Letter.*

Bercovitch's own interpretation, however, turns out to be little different from what he affects to dislike. He finds himself "aversive" to the moral conservatism of the narrator. The office of the scarlet letter—to signify the crime and to effect the reconciliation of Hester to the old Boston community—must, of course, be accomplished; the novel indeed compels us to accept it "as a grim necessity." But the moral vision of the narrator—which affirms sexual virtue, openness, candor, communal solidarity, and moral truth—is dismissed as a form of "compulsion," "a special form of pleading," "some equivalent in the liberal imagination for the Thou Shalt Not's [sic] delivered from Mount Sinai." The moral conservatism of the narrative "adds a discordant note to Hawthorne's orchestration of pluralist points of view." But does Hawthorne, like Bercovitch, have a "liberal imagination"? If Hawthorne does present rival interpretations in conflict, does that mean he has no moral or social viewpoint of his own? Hardly.

Bercovitch certainly wants us to believe so, and he therefore concocts his own "interpretive gap" that allows him to "attribute" his own "concerns and beliefs" to Hawthorne. Bercovitch constructs a "secret Hawthorne" and a "hidden Hester" who form an "illicit bond" expressing their "marginal consensus-in-dissent."[17] But it gets even worse. This "secret Hawthorne," an imaginary Emersonian who never existed, is invented in order to couple him with an equally imaginary "hidden Hester." The purpose of these shadowy inventions, it would appear, is to facilitate the critic's devising some kind of imaginary adultery between the author and his own character, with whom he must be in love and whom he would never criticize, really, for her defections from a sound moral and a high intellectual standard.

Now, characters—and the novelists who invented them—copulate with abandon in the novels of antirealists such as John Barth, Robert Coover, and William Burroughs. But Hawthorne, for all the complexities of his method, is not a postmodern novelist; nor can he be transmogrified into a crypto-transcendentalist. Yet one or another of these critically bankrupt maneuvers appears to be the only way that liberal critics can live with the morally conservative Hawthorne.[18]

---

17 Sacvan Bercovitch, *The Office of the Scarlet Letter* (Baltimore: Johns Hopkins University Press, 1991), pp. 119n, 156–157.

18 This kind of radical criticism is morally reprehensible and patently unfair to Hawthorne; and these critics, if they want to rewrite *The Scarlet Letter* as a postmodern nihilist text, ought to write another novel. John Updike, for one, has answered Hawthorne in his Scarlet

Hester's antisocial view of the institutions of society is, in any case, like Emerson's: institutions are in conspiracy against the manhood—or here womanhood—of all its members. The institutions which she rejects—the clerical band (organized religion), the church (in its institutional character), the judicial robe (the rule of law), the pillory and the gallows (society's modes of punition for crime), and the fireside (the domestic scene or center of familial values)—these institutions are the very bonds that unite us in our social existence, in the absence of which we would live in a state of absolute anarchy. But, then, anarchy was Hawthorne's sense of the likely consequence of revolutionary Emersonianism if its practitioners got their way. It is no wonder Emerson told E. P. Whipple that *The Scarlet Letter* was "ghastly."[19]

The Scarlet Letter is, in any case, clearly a novel as much about nineteenth-century radical thought in Concord as it is about seventeenth-century Puritanism in Boston. It addresses, only to reject, the radical antinomianism inspired by Emerson; it rejects the arrant individualism of the transcendentalists; it calls into question a feminism that would seek to destroy the existing social order, with all its faults, in favor of theoretical or utopian speculation about how things ought to be. And finally, *The Scarlet Letter* attacks the notion that emotion, rather than principle, should guide us in ethical dilemmas. Hawthorne thus speaks for a conservative vision—a vision of limited human possibility, of a frank recognition of our fallibility, of the need for a social order based on communal values, of a moral system pertinent to actual human experience. "Be true, be true" (*SL*, 258), the novel admonishes. If we err we confess our error, ask forgiveness, seek absolution outside ourselves, and do whatever penance is necessary. But, according to Hawthorne, we must maintain our connection to the "magnetic chain of humanity."

The novel, then, is essentially a tale of Hester's redemption and reconciliation to society. After Dimmesdale's death she goes to Europe with Pearl, drifts about until her daughter's marriage, but then comes back to the scene of the crime and reattaches the scarlet letter to her bosom. At this point in the novel we are meant to understand that Dimmesdale's refusal of her offer to flee, his confession and death, and her subsequent experience in Europe have awakened her to the reality

---

Letter trilogy. But Updike turns out to be as conservative in his exposure of the enormities of Emersonian subjectivism as anything in Hawthorne. See Updike's *A Month of Sundays*, the minister's story; *Roger's Version*, the husband's bill of indictment; and *S*, the tale of the modern feminist as descended from Hester's muddled thought. For an excellent study of Hawthorne's impact on Updike, see also James A. Schiff's *Updike's Version: Rewriting The Scarlet Letter* (Columbia: University of Missouri Press, 1992).

19 E. P. Whipple, *Recollections of Eminent Men* (Boston: Ticknor, 1889), p. 149.

that a great wrong really *was* committed in their adultery and in their resistance to confessing it as a wrong. And we are also meant to understand that her working out of the spiritual consequences of it, the atonement for it, is to be performed in the community where that crime occurred. The *A* on her breast becomes not only the sign of Able now, but Angel too, as she, with a truer knowledge of the realities of good and evil, becomes the friend and counselor of Boston youth, especially the young women.

The self versus society, feeling versus rational thought, freedom versus responsibility, the passions of the individual versus received religious and social values, the role and status of men and women: much of the literary expression of the "American Renaissance" is a manifestation of cultural struggle where contending values are dramatically debated and tested, an arena where principles are implicitly analyzed and their consequences figuratively represented. Freedom was assumed as a given by both Emerson and Hawthorne. But Hawthorne refused to go along with an absolute exaltation of freedom. Freedom for him was not the *source* of values. It was rather the metaphysical condition, the moral arena, within which one acted or did not act out one's principles. If one lives by the wrong principles, one will pay a moral and social price. The exaltation of liberty, so as to posit any subjectively derived ethic as of transcendent origin, was thus for Hawthorne a sign of the moral confusion of his time. And so it is of ours.

Sex and Socialism: Becoming Margaret Fuller

Margaret Fuller (1810–1850) is without question one of the most fascinating and provocative women of nineteenth-century America. She deserves to be better known than she is, for her contribution to American culture was indeed significant—especially in four important areas: transcendental thought, American feminism, American newspaper and magazine journalism, and promoting Italian revolutionary activism. Briefly to survey her life, one may note that Fuller grew up in Massachusetts in the Boston area, taught young ladies in Providence, dazzled her contemporaries with her formidable learning, conducted "Conversations" (or early consciousness-raising sessions) with transcendental women, edited (with Emerson) *The Dial*, and, after moving on to New York, served as literary editor for Horace Greeley's *New-York Daily Tribune*. After 1844 she traveled in Europe, lived in Italy, became involved with the revolutionaries attached to Mazzini, bore a perhaps illegitimate child to a rebel nobleman, the Marquis Giovanni Ossoli, and, after the collapse of the first campaign of the Risorgimento, returned to America. On the return voyage, Margaret, Giovanni Ossoli, and their child, Angelo, were shipwrecked and drowned off Fire Island. She was forty years old.

A distinctive personality clearly emerges from Margaret Fuller's writing and from the memoirs and letters of those who knew her well. This personality is not the Fuller of the "Margaret cult" recently espoused in contemporary feminism. It is rather a complex identity that expressed itself (sometimes with remarkable force) in, among other works, *Eckermann's Conversations with Goethe* (1839), *Günderode*

(1842), *Summer on the Lakes* (1844), *Papers on Literature and Art* (1846), and *Woman in the Nineteenth Century* (1845), of which only the last survives—principally as a sacred unread feminist text.

I

Like Mme. de Staël's *Corinne*, Margaret Fuller was essentially a talker rather than a writer. Henry James, who remembered being with his father as a boy and hearing from Washington Irving that Margaret Fuller had drowned off Fire Island, called her a dazzling "moral improvisatrice" who "left nothing behind her, her written utterance being naught."[1] This is harsh, but not unjustifiably so. Even her close friend Elizabeth Barrett Browning remarked that "If I wished anyone to do her justice, I should say, as I have indeed said, 'Never read what she has written.'"[2] The judgment of Eleanor Roosevelt still seems true of the bulk of her writing: "To us to-day [1930] much of what she said and wrote seems pedantic and the language, which was that of the scholar of her day, smacks somewhat of the Blue Stocking." Emerson called her pen a "non-conductor,"[3] in a phrase open to several possible interpretations. It seems a general consensus that Fuller is not a great stylist who gives us unalloyed pleasure. But what we do find in her work is what Roosevelt called the "enthusiasm for greatness of mind and soul" that marks this most remarkable woman.[4]

The principal interest now attaching to Margaret Fuller is her place in the American literary canon. For some decades nineteenth-century literature courses presented the "American Renaissance" with little of Margaret Fuller, concentrating instead on writers like Emerson, Thoreau, Hawthorne, Melville, Whitman, Poe, Irving, Cooper, Whittier, Lowell, Longfellow, and Oliver Wendell Holmes. In short supply in the curriculum studied in graduate school, years ago, were women writers such as Fuller, Harriet Beecher Stowe, the domestic sentimental novelists Mrs. E. D. E. N. Southworth, Maria Cummins, Eliza Phelps, Fanny Fern, and others now renascently esteemed. Writers such as Margaret Fuller were not then regarded as part of the literary canon because of writerly imperfections and marginal influence on their contemporaries

1 Henry James, *William Wetmore Story and His Friends* (Boston: Houghton Mifflin, 1903), I, 127–128.
2 *Letters of Elizabeth Barrett Browning*, ed. F. D. Kenyon (New York: Macmillan, 1898), II, 59.
3 Ralph Waldo Emerson, William Henry Channing, and James Freeman Clarke, *Memoirs of Margaret Fuller Ossoli* (Boston: Phillips, Sampson, 1852), I, 294. Hereafter, quotations from the *Memoirs* will be cited as *M*, in parentheses, in the text.
4 Eleanor Roosevelt, "Introduction," in Margaret Bell's *Margaret Fuller: A Biography* (New York: Albert and Charles Boni, 1930), p. 13.

or later writers. The feminist movement has undertaken to change all that, demanding attention to writers such as Fuller on the ground that the principle of exclusion reflects male prejudice and a false criterion of aesthetic excellence. This kind of excellence has been hooted down as a mask for male bourgeois conservatism; and the argument is often advanced that, since there are no objective standards of literary quality, no decisive argument against a writer like Fuller can be credited. A corollary argument of the deconstructionists is that since there is no such category as literature—all is *écriture* or discourse—there is no principle of discrimination according to which a writer like Emerson may be included and a writer such as Fuller excluded. There are, of course, literary standards, measured by which Fuller's style is impossibly affected. Yet Margaret Fuller has a cultural importance that deserves continued recognition.

The whole body of Margaret Fuller's prose is intended to throw light on her sense of herself as a woman and on her attempt to define herself against the constraints of what she perceived as a repressive patriarchal society. In her childhood, her father, Timothy Fuller, a lawyer, provided her with a thorough education in languages and literature, philosophy, history, and religion. His regimen was demanding and, since she deeply loved him, she was overly conscientious. Something of her youthful life of studies is suggested by this letter to Susan Prescott in 1825, written when she was fifteen:

> I rise a little before five, walk an a hour, and then practise on the piano, till seven, when we breakfast. Next I read French,—Sismondi's Literature of the South of Europe,—till eight, then two or three lectures in Brown's philosophy. About half-past nine I go to Mr. Perkins's school and study Greek till twelve, when, the school being dismissed, I recite, go home, and practise again till dinner, at two. Sometimes, if the conversation is very agreeable, I lounge for half an hour over the dessert, though rarely so lavish of time. Then, when I can, I read two hours in Italian, but I am often interrupted. At six, I walk, or take a drive. Before going to bed, I play or sing, for half an hour or so, to make all sleepy, and, about eleven, retire to write a little while in my journal, exercises on what I have read, or a series of characteristics which I am filling up according to advice. Thus, you see, I am learning Greek, and making acquaintance with metaphysics and French and Italian literature.

She told Susan Prescott that, since "the power of industry" was growing in her every day, "nothing, no! not perfection, is unattainable. I am determined on distinction, which formerly I thought to win at an easy rate; but now I see that long years of labor must be given to secure

even the *'succes de societe,'*—which, however, shall never content me."
She said that although she wished to combine in herself "genius,"
"grace," and "the power of pleasurable excitement," certain "obstacles"
stood in her way. "I am wanting in that intuitive tact and polish, which
nature has bestowed upon some, but which I must acquire. And, on the
other hand, my powers of intellect, though sufficient, I suppose, are not
well disciplined. Yet all such hindrances may be overcome by an ardent
spirit. If I fail, my consolation shall be found in active employment."[5]

Hers was no doubt a daunting schedule, but the tone of her report is
buoyant. Much later, in a depressed mood, she was to write otherwise
about her father's educational regimen:

> Thus I had tasks given me, as many and various as the hours would
> allow, and on subjects beyond my age; with the disadvantage of reciting
> to him in the evening, after he returned from his office. . . . I was often
> kept up till very late; and as he was a severe teacher, both from his
> habits of mind and his ambition for me, my feelings were kept on the
> stretch till the recitations were over. Thus frequently, I was sent to bed
> several hours too late, with nerves unnaturally stimulated. The conse-
> quence was a premature development of the brain, that made me a
> "youthful prodigy" by day, and by night a victim of spectral illusions,
> nightmare and somnambulism, which at the time prevented the har-
> monious development of my bodily powers and checked my growth,
> while, later, they induced continual headache, weakness, and nervous
> affections, of all kinds. As these again re-acted on the brain, giving un-
> due force to every thought and every feeling, there was finally produced
> a state of being both too active and too intense, which wasted my con-
> stitution and will bring me,—even although I have learned to under-
> stand and regulate my now morbid temperament,—to a premature
> grave (*M*, I, 15).

Hallucinations, nightmares, and somnambulism were lifelong terrors. But Robert N. Hudspeth has reminded us of "the observation that
Henry Hedge made many years later: Margaret Fuller, he said, had a
normal education. She had what most boys of any promise had, and
pretty much under the same grueling conditions. New England was
never easy on its bright children" (*L*, I, 21–22). Although Fuller felt that
her father's pedagogy wrecked her childhood, the point "is less that
Margaret's father wished she were a boy"—as Ann Douglas has observed—"than that he treated her with as much seriousness as if she

---

5 *The Letters of Margaret Fuller*, ed. Robert N. Hudspeth (Ithaca: Cornell University Press,
    1983–1995), I, 151–152. Hereafter, quotations from the *Letters* of Fuller will be cited as *L*,
    in parentheses, in the text.

were one." As Fuller was also to acknowledge, her father "taught her what almost none of her feminine peers possessed: 'self-respect,' 'self-reliance.'"[6] In any case, Timothy Fuller's educational regimen prepared her for a life of literature and criticism. Among women she had few intellectual equals in the 1830s and 1840s.

II

In her youth, like many transcendentalists, Margaret Fuller proclaimed an Emersonian self-reliance that endeared her to her women students but that made her seem arrogant to very nearly every male acquaintance. This was in part what William Wetmore Story, her sculptor friend in Rome, meant by saying that she was her own "worst enemy." According to Hawthorne, Emerson had "apotheosized her as the greatest woman . . . of ancient or modern times, and the one figure in the world worth considering."[7] But she could stun Emerson himself by announcing matter-of-factly that "I now know all the people worth knowing in America, and I find no intellect comparable to my own"; and she could casually observe that "I myself am more divine than any I see" (*L*, I, 327). Such doting on herself would have charmed Whitman, and it clearly reflects Emerson's exhortations in "Self-Reliance." But celebrations of herself like these repelled Hawthorne and his sister-in-law, Elizabeth Peabody, as well as Thoreau and James Russell Lowell, the latter satirizing, in *A Fable for Critics*, Margaret's "I-turn-the-crank-of-the-Universe air."[8]

Emerson took note of this egotism—only to underplay it—in the *Memoirs* in remarking that "It is certain that Margaret occasionally let slip, with all the innocence imaginable, some phrase betraying the presence of a rather mountainous *me*, in a way to surprise those who knew her good sense. She could say, as if she were stating a scientific fact, in enumerating the merits of somebody, 'He appreciates *me*'" (*M*, I, 234, 236). An index of the size of her ego is suggested in her blithely announcing to Carlyle "I accept the Universe," to which he retorted, "By Gad, she'd better."[9] Thus one may see that in buying wholesale Emerson's claim that perfection is attainable, that we are all gods, that no-

---

6 Ann Douglas, *The Feminization of American Culture* (New York: Alfred A. Knopf, 1977), pp. 264–265. Hereafter, quotations from this volume will be cited as *FAC*, in parentheses, in the text.

7 Nathaniel Hawthorne, *The American Notebooks*, ed. Claude M. Simpson (Columbus: Ohio State University Press, 1972), p. 371.

8 *Poetical Works of James Russell Lowell* (Boston: Houghton Mifflin, 1904), IV, 63–64.

9 Quoted in *Margaret Fuller: American Romantic*, ed. Perry Miller (Garden City, N.Y.: Anchor Books, 1963), p. ix.

thing is at last sacred but the integrity of one's own mind, and that humility and submission to superior authority are vices, Fuller appeared presumptuous and exposed herself to ridicule.

The transcendental doctrine, with its emphasis on consciousness and the unity of one soul (any soul) with another, was in my view a dangerous doctrine for New England youth in that it downplayed, if it did not deny, those elements of identity that are a part of what the mature Emerson would later ruefully acknowledge to be fate. I mean here one's sex, race, social class, educational background, and so forth. Even one's own physical body, as young Emerson claims in *Nature,* is part of the NOT-ME. It might be one thing for Emerson, who was possessed of his own soul, as well as of his own body, to enunciate this doctrine. But it had confusing effects on some his younger disciples. In any case, we find in Fuller a bizarre gender confusion that permeates her journals and letters. Emerson reported that "she had a feeling that she ought to have been a man, and said of herself, 'A man's ambition with a woman's heart, is an evil lot'" (*M,* I, 229). This led her to posit a universal androgyny, observing that "There is no wholly masculine man, no purely feminine woman." Fuller therefore split herself into masculine and feminine identities, associating passion and feeling with her womanhood, and the life of the intellect with a masculine self: "Man partakes of the feminine in the Apollo, Woman of the masculine as Minerva." [10] Scattered throughout *Woman in the Nineteenth Century* we find evidences of this bifurcation of powers. If "the intellect, cold, is ever more masculine than feminine," its counterpart, "the electrical, the magnetic element in woman," gives her special gifts:

> The especial genius of woman I believe to be electrical in movement, intuitive in function, spiritual in tendency. She excels not so easily in classification, or re-creation, as in an instinctive seizure of causes, and a simple breathing out of what she receives that has the singleness of life, rather than the selecting and energizing of art (*WNC,* 103, 115).

But although she wanted to be a man, fate had given her a woman's body. "I love best to be a woman," she lamented in her early thirties, "but womanhood is at present too straitly-bounded to give me scope. At hours I live truly as a woman; at others, I should stifle; as, on the other hand, I should palsy, when I would play the artist" (*M,* I, 297). Yet this wanting to be a man was not the usual androgynous sensibility, formerly acclaimed in feminist criticism, but evidence of a deeply dis-

---

10 Margaret Fuller, *Woman in the Nineteenth Century and Kindred Papers,* ed. Arthur B. Fuller (1845; reprinted New York: Greenwood Press, 1968), p. 116. Hereafter, quotations from this work will be cited as *WNC,* in parentheses, in the text.

turbed psychosexual maladjustment.

Doubtless her troubled view of herself as a woman arises in part out of her father's giving her the education of a boy. But partly it had to do with that body and that face which Margaret was fated to be given. One must concur with Elizabeth Hardwick that we cannot understand Margaret without understanding the physical impression she made on others.[11] The minister Frederick Henry Hedge, her closest friend from her adolescence and the founder of the Transcendental Club, wrote of her:

> With no pretension to beauty then [at thirteen], or at any time, her face was one that attracted, that awakened a lively interest, that made one desirous of a nearer acquaintance. . . . It was a face that fascinated, without satisfying. Never seen in repose, never allowing a steady perusal of its features, it baffled every attempt to judge the character by physiognomical induction (*M*, I, 91–95).

Emerson said of her appearance, on first meeting her, that it was "nothing prepossessing. Her extreme plainness—a trick of incessantly opening and shutting her eyelids—the nasal tone of her voice—all repelled; and I said to myself, we shall never get far" (*M*, I, 202–203). They did of course go very far, as Emerson began to see past her plainness. But something about her look and mannerisms called attention to her physical presence. Poe, who knew her in the world of New York journalism, fixated (as he would) on her upper lip, which "as if impelled by the action of involuntary muscles, habitually uplifts itself, conveying the impression of a sneer."[12] Her good friend William Henry Channing took note of the shape of her neck, as did many others, finding its curve "swan-like when she was sweet and thoughtful, but when she was scornful or indignant it contracted, and made swift turns, like a bird of prey."[13] These are curious impressions, delivered by *friends*. Those *not* her friends were less friendly. James Russell Lowell called her "a pythoness." And Oliver Wendell Holmes wrote a novel, *Elsie Venner*, based in part on her ophidian look and manner. This was an effect that Margaret had on some people—especially on a number of men who were not her intellectual equal.

Emerson remarked that "When she was twelve, she had a determination of blood to the head." I am not sure what this is meant to

---

11 Elizabeth Hardwick, "The Genius of Margaret Fuller," *New York Review of Books*, April 10, 1986, pp. 14–15.

12 *The Complete Works of Edgar Allan Poe*, ed. James A. Harrison (reprinted New York: AMS Press, 1979), XV, 82–83.

13 Quoted in Hardwick, "Genius of Margaret Fuller," p. 15.

diagnose, though it may be simply acne. In any case, Margaret wrote that "My parents . . . were much mortified to see the fineness of my complexion destroyed. My own vanity was for a time severely wounded; but I recovered, and made up my mind to be bright and ugly" (*M*, I, 228–229). Bright and ugly she certainly was, though not without a sexual and intellectual magnetism that drew several men to her. As her letters disclose, she was extremely close, a soul mate in fact, to James Freeman Clarke, a distant cousin. She was romantically drawn to George T. Davis, but he broke her heart. By age twenty-two she had resolved on celibacy; her letters make various references to being a nun and allude to the Vestal Virgins of ancient Rome as models of a pure life of intellectual devotion and commitment. To James Freeman Clarke she remarked in 1832:

> 'T is true, the time is probably near when I must live alone, to all intents and purposes,—separate entirely my acting from my thinking world, take care of my ideas without aid,—except from the illustrious dead, —answer my own questions, correct my own feelings, and do all that hard work for myself. How tiresome 't is to find out all one's self-delusion! I thought myself so very independent, because I could conceal some feelings at will, and did not need the same excitement as other young characters did. And I am not independent, nor never shall be, while I can get anybody to minister to me. But I shall go where there is never a spirit to come, if I call ever so loudly (*L*, I, 78).

Yet she was never fated to be celibate, although it was not yet clear to her what, sexually, she was fated to be.

Fuller's "crushes" on Anna Barker, Caroline Sturgis, and several of the girls she taught—feelings in part founded on the dubious transcendental notion that souls exist well nigh independent of bodies, sexual bodies—illuminate the plight of an American intellectual woman trying, in a milieu of secrecy about sex, to find herself. In her private journal she remarked that "It is so true that a woman may be in love with a woman, and a man with a man. I like to be sure of it, because undoubtedly it is the same love we shall feel when we are angels. . . ."[14] Of course, angels do not have bodies, but the implication is that she was experimenting, trying out love with a woman so as to experience something angelic or divine, transcending the drag of heterosexual flesh. To be sure that a woman could love a woman meant abandoning her usual "refuge in the All" (*L*, II, 126), but the risks seemed instructive.[15] Her

---

14 Quoted in *The Woman and the Myth: Margaret Fuller's Life and Writings*, ed. Bell Gale Chevigny (Old Westbury, N.Y.: The Feminist Press, 1976), pp. 112-113.
15 Hawthorne captures this in Coverdale's remark that the transcendental ethos at Blithedale,

passionate involvement with some of the girls in her class produced such perfervid and rapturous effects that the saintly Emerson later uneasily recorded that her female friendships were "not unmingled with passion, and had passages of romantic sacrifice and of ecstatic fusion, which I have heard with the ear, but could not trust my profane pen to report." So tinged with erotic seduction was Fuller's teaching that one of her female students later remarked: "Had she been a man, any one of those fine girls of sixteen, who surrounded her here, would have married her: they were all in love with her, she understood them so well" (*M*, I, 281–282). Ultimately Fuller came to realize that such incipient lesbianism, even if not practiced, would destroy her, and after a tempestuous breakup with her friend Caroline Sturgis, they reconstructed a relationship which Fuller described as "redeemed from the search after Eros" (*L*, II, 105, 117).[16]

III

Yet Eros was in my view *the* driving, the very nearly uncontrolled energy in this woman; and the absence of a proper love object, of a man who might fulfill her, produced in Margaret extreme anxiety and sexual frustration. One of the great catastrophes of Margaret Fuller's life was rejection in love by Samuel Ward, who decided to marry Anna Barker, a mutual friend for whom Margaret also had a passionate erotic attachment. With her ready command of foreign languages, she read the French for a sexual understanding not available in the Anglo-American tradition. She marveled at George Sand's insight into "the life of thought" and concluded, "She must know it through some man" (*M*, I, 247). Emerson said he liked Sand's occasional "authentic revelations of what passes in man & in woman," but he objected to Sand's "sickness of the French intellect."[17] He made it clear that he wanted a purer model for Margaret. But in this great work of instruction he did not propose himself for the job.

---

a transparent description of Brook Farm, "seemed to authorize any individual, of either sex, to fall in love with any other, regardless of what would elsewhere be judged suitable or prudent." See Nathaniel Hawthorne, *The Blithedale Romance*, eds. Seymour Gross and Rosalie Murphy (New York: W. W. Norton, 1978), p. 67.

16 The most risible new critical claim is that Fuller's tormented and masochistic relationships with other young women prove the superiority of lesbianism. See Lillian Faderman's stupefying *Surpassing the Love of Men: Romantic Friendship and Love Between Women from the Renaissance to the Present* (New York: William Morrow, 1981), pp. 160–161, and Mary E. Wood's bizarre essay "'With Ready Eye': Margaret Fuller and Lesbianism in Nineteenth-Century American Literature," *American Literature*, 65 (March 1993), 1–18.

17 *Letters of Ralph Waldo Emerson*, ed. Ralph Rusk (New York: Columbia University Press, 1939), II, 235.

A continuing refrain of her letters in the 1830s is her yearning for someone who could give her this insight. She told F. H. Hedge that she longed "to pour out my soul to some person of superior calmness and strength and fortunate in more accurate knowledge. I should feel such a quieting reaction" (*L*, I, 224). Only Goethe, she thought, had a mind equal to her own and the requisite sexual vitality, for his frank openness to passion and his amorous liaisons had stimulated a desire aching within her. To James Freeman Clarke, in May 1833, she wrote:

> We cry, "help, help," and there is no help—in man at least. How often I have thought, if I could see Goethe, and tell him my state of mind, he would support and guide me! He would be able to understand; he would show me how to rule circumstances, instead of being ruled by them; and, above all, he would not have been so sure that all would be for the best, without our making an effort to act out the oracles; he would have wished to see me [as?] what Nature intended (*L*, I, 182).

Margaret begged all the men she knew for more information about Goethe's affairs, ostensibly for a biography of the German writer. To Hedge she wrote on July 12, 1837:

> But what I most want to say is this— Will you, Henry, can you tell me all the scandal about Goethe—about his marriage and so forth? I have asked Mr Emerson and others whom I thought might know, but the little they can tell only puzzles and disturbs me. In all the books I have had sent me there is nothing which enables me to know what I am about on this subject and I ought, before I go any further, in my business— Will you write me in a few days any thing you know of his first residence at Weimar and about his living so many years with the person he afterwards married— How could that be at so decorous a court and under the eye of the Grand Duchess— I hope you will be able to give me light, but if not, I intend writing to Madame Jameson— Say nothing to Miss P. if she is with you or, indeed, to any one— Write when you can to a poor, lonely *'female'*—Afftly M.F." (*L*, I, 292–293).

Margaret Fuller never completed the biography. Such intimate details as she wished to learn from the men she knew could not be openly disclosed to an unmarried New England girl. For most of her contemporaries, Goethe was sexually dangerous, and his open sensuality excluded him from their esteem. As Perry Miller has said about Margaret's essay on Goethe, however, "Here Margaret brashly defends *Werther* against the prevailing American opinion that it was a foul corrupter of youth; and she praises *The Elective Affinities*, which American men regarded as the nadir of sensual depravity. . . . Viewed in this perspective, Margaret's essay is a basic document in the history of intellectual freedom in the United States." Miller's position, a gross exaggeration, nevertheless seems to be that, in defending Goethe, Margaret struck a blow for liberated sensuality. Whether the fears of American men about Goethe's influence were to be realized in her case only the Roman years would later reveal.[18]

IV

Emerson, though an ex-minister, a married man, and a father, was next best to Goethe, as "the most pivotal mind of his time." And Fuller intrigued to meet him, remarking that Emerson was "that only clergyman of all possible clergymen who eludes my acquaintance" (*L*, I, 210). By 1835 she was remarking that "I am flattered that Mr Emerson should wish to know me. I fear it will never be but 'tis pleasant to know that he wished it—I cannot think I should be disappointed in him as I have been in others to whom I had hoped to look up, the sensation one experiences in the atmosphere of his thoughts is too decided and peculiar" (*L*, I, 224). Their friendship, when once they met, was fated to be tense and complex, in part because of those qualities in Margaret that she confessed to James Freeman Clarke in 1834: "I am not a reasonable woman and must needs be putting more of feeling into my intercourse with others than is any wise necessary or appropriate" (*L*, I, 206).

In her relationship with Emerson, Margaret was not reasonable, moderate, balanced, or judicious. In fact, in my view she tried desperately to seduce Emerson, at least intellectually. Her energy in pursuit of him went beyond the romantic cult of friendship—although *that* was the decorous context within which their relations were always circumscribed. In the fall of 1840 both she and Caroline Sturgis, in a bizarre triangle, pursued Emerson to the brink of Eros. She visited with him at length, often for up to a month, monopolizing the man and shutting out his wife, as Lydian Emerson thought, from her proper place at his side. As the letters and journals of the principals make plain, Fuller's time spent with Waldo—in the privacy of his study, on long walks in the woods, and the like—drove Lydian to a scene of jealous despair.[19] The drama here must have been intense and can only be reconstructed from faint clews and indirections. Margaret wanted Emerson's exclusive at-

---

18 Miller, *Margaret Fuller: American Romantic*, p. 79.

19 Fuller justified her dismissal of Lydian in her journal: "As to my being more his companion that cannot be helped, his life is in the intellect not the affections. He has affection for me, but it is because I quicken his intellect. —I dismissed it all, as a mere sick moment of L's." Quoted in Chevigny, *Woman and the Myth*, p. 128.

tention, to be his most intimate friend, to be a friend whose closeness transcended mere external relationships like the legal institution of marriage. Emerson invited her into his "chicken coop" (as he called it), challenged her to be the fullest kind of friend, and then seemed taken aback when she proved foxy and demanding of more than he had to give. What was it she wanted? In their conversations, Emerson pleaded confusion of her motives, ignorance of their direction, his own limitations. But in his journals he was more candid in reconstructing this conversation, which they must have had about this time:

> You would have me love you. What shall I love? Your body? The supposition disgusts you. What you have thought and said? Well, whilst you were thinking and saying them, but not now. I see no possibility of loving anything but what now is, and is becoming; your courage, your enterprize, your budding affection, your opening thought, your prayer. I can love, but what else?[20]

It was always that "what else" that Fuller required. Frustrated by Emerson's lofty ministerial reserve, she complained of his "use" of the instincts "rather for rejection than reception," and his failure to offer her "the clue of the labyrinth of [her] own being" (*L*, II, 159). Thinking that she wanted power over him, he had to call a temporary halt to their relationship.

Emerson's reserve with Margaret Fuller must be understood in the light of his theory of self-reliance and its connection to the notion of friendship. Nothing could have been farther from his thought than the idea that two souls could merge in some sort of ecstatic fusion, as either lovers or friends. His essay "Friendship" seems intended to address the importunate appeal that friends such as Margaret Fuller were making to him. (She and Caroline Sturgis were not the only women who found Emerson personally attractive.) The essay is marked by the expected observations about the ennobling power of friendship—its capacity to transcend differences of individual character, relation, age, sex, and circumstance, and its foundation on truth. But there are idiosyncratic formulations, distinctively Emersonian in concept, which Margaret Fuller was not prepared to understand in 1840. Here is a sampling of observations—culled in no particular order from "Friendship"—that accounts for why the Platonic Emerson resisted Margaret Fuller and others who pressed him too closely:

> "Friendship, like the immortality of the soul, is too good to be believed.

---

20 *Emerson in His Journals*, ed. Joel Porte (Cambridge: Harvard University Press, 1982), p. 246.

The lover beholding his maiden, half knows that she is not verily that which he worships; and in the golden hour of friendship, we are surprised with shades of suspicion and unbelief. We doubt that we bestow on our hero the virtues in which he shines and afterwards worship the form to which we have ascribed this divine inhabitation. In strictness the soul does not respect men as it respects itself. In strict science all persons underlie the same condition of an infinite remoteness. . . ." "O friend, . . . thou art not my soul but a picture and effigy of that. . . ." "A friend, therefore, is a sort of paradox in nature. I who alone am, I who see nothing in nature whose existence I can affirm with equal evidence to my own, behold now the semblance of my being, in all its height, variety, and curiosity, reiterated in a foreign form; so that a friend may well be reckoned the masterpiece of nature. . . ." "The soul environs itself with friends, that it may enter into a grander self-acquaintance or solitude. . . ." "We seek our friend not sacredly, but with an adulterate passion which would appropriate him to ourselves. In vain. We are armed all over with subtle antagonisms, which, as soon as we meet, begin to play and translate all poetry into stale prose. Almost all people descend to meet. All association must be a compromise. . . ." "Bashfulness and apathy are a tough husk, in which a delicate organization is protected from premature ripening. . . ." "Let us buy our entrance to this guild by a long probation. . . ." "Respect so far the holy laws of this fellowship as not to prejudice its perfect flower by your impatience for its opening. We must be our own before we can be another's."

Emerson held that friendship is so demanding a relation that it seldom affords satisfaction. "The higher the style we demand of friendship, of course, the less easy to establish it with flesh and blood. We walk alone in the world. Friends, such as we desire, are dreams and fables." Since he held friendship to be a purer relation than that of love and marriage, he remarks: "I do not wish to treat friendships daintily, but with roughest courage. When they are real, they are not glass threads or frostwork, but the solidest thing we know." Friendship was ideally a relationship between two large formidable natures who were "mutually beheld, mutually feared." The friend was to be "to thee for ever a sort of beautiful enemy, untamable, devoutly revered, and not a trivial conveniency to be soon outgrown and cast aside." The relationship with this beautiful enemy is to be entirely spiritual: "It is foolish to be afraid of making our ties too spiritual, as if so we could lose any genuine love." In another place he writes, "Leave this touching and clawing. Let him be to me a spirit. A message, a thought, a sincerity, a glance from him, I want, but not news nor pottage." But in fact too close a relation is dangerous: "though I prize my friends, I cannot afford to talk with them and study their visions, lest I lose my own. It would indeed give me a certain household joy to quit this lofty seeking, this spiritual astronomy, or search of stars, and come down to warm sympathies with you; but then I know well I shall mourn always the vanishing of my mighty gods." Emerson was fully aware that Margaret and others considered him aloof, and he concludes the essay with an admonition about what to do if a friend is aloof:

> Why should I cumber myself with regrets that the receiver [of my friendship] is not capacious? It never troubles the sun that some of his rays fall wide and vain into ungrateful space, and only a small part of the reflecting planet. Let your greatness educate the crude and cold companion. If he is unequal, he will presently pass away; but thou art enlarged by thy own shining, and, no longer a mate for frogs and worms, dost soar and burn with the gods of the empyrean. It is thought a disgrace to love unrequited. But the great will see that true love cannot be unrequited. True love transcends the unworthy object, and dwells and broods on the eternal.

Finally, in one of his most remarkable statements, he observes that it is "better to be a nettle in the side of your friend than his echo. The condition which high friendship demands is ability to do without it."[21]

This view of friendship seemed cold to Margaret and emotionally unsatisfactory. Consequently, when, some months later, they resumed their conversation, there was an inevitable tension. His idea that *"O my friends, there are no friends"* was to her "a paralyzing conviction" (*L*, I, 294). Emerson notes the tension between them in his journal for October 12, 1842, where he describes his reaction after a visit from Margaret: "I would that I could, I know afar off that I cannot give the lights & shades, the hopes & outlooks that come to me in these strange, cold-warm, attractive-repelling conversations with Margaret, whom I always admire, most revere when I nearest see, and sometimes love, yet whom I Freeze, & who freezes me to silence, when we seem to promise to come nearest."[22]

Fuller's reaction against Emerson's view of friendship is expressed most clearly in her letter to Channing in about July 1841:

---

21 "Friendship," in *Ralph Waldo Emerson: Essays and Lectures*, ed. Joel Porte (New York: Library of America, 1983), pp. 341–354.
22 *The Heart of Emerson's Journals*, ed. Bliss Perry (Boston: Houghton Mifflin, 1926), pp. 166–167.

It is very noble but not enough for our manifold nature. Our friends should be our incentives to Right, but not only our guiding but our prophetic stars. To love by sight is much, to love by faith is more; both are the entire love without which heart, mind, and soul cannot be alike satisfied. We love and ought to love one another not merely for the absolute worth of each but on account of a mutual fitness of temporary character. We are not merely one another's priests or gods, but ministering angels, exercising in the past the same function as the Great Soul in the whole of seeing the perfect through the imperfect nay, making it come there.

She did not like Emerson's lines beginning "Have I a lover / Who is noble and free / I would he were nobler / Than to love me." She told Channing not to pity her "where I love, but where I do not. The soul pines to know the All well enough to love all, happy where there is any outlet for the tide of thought and love. The tragedy is deep in proportion to the character, but it is only in time." Channing apparently told her to fix upon the possible and sublimate her passions in work. She replied that she had "no powers except so far as inspired by high sentiment, if I economized I should be naught. . . . You often say still I must exaggerate. *I do not.* You do not yet understand me" (*L,* II, 214–215).

Eventually Margaret came to understand Emerson's distance as not a rejection of herself and her friendship but an acting out of his most deeply held principles, as well as a reflection of his unique personality, and thus an expression of the consistency of his thought and conduct. In a letter to Channing the following year, she gives a history of her changing relationship to Emerson:

> After the first excitement of intimacy with him,—when I was made so happy by his high tendency, absolute purity, the freedom and infinite graces of an intellect cultivated much beyond any I had known,—came with me the questioning season. I was greatly disappointed in my relation to him. I was, indeed, always called on to be worthy,—this benefit was sure in our friendship But I found no intelligence of my best self; far less was it revealed to me in new modes; for not only did he seem to want the living faith which enables one to discharge this holiest office of a friend, but he absolutely distrusted me in every region of my life with which he was unacquainted.

But now she was, she said, "better acquainted with him. His 'accept' is true; the 'I shall learn,' with which he answers every accusation, is no less true." Emerson had confessed to her his limitations. He felt, he said, "shut up in a crystal cell," from which only "a great love or a great task could release me," and he hardly expected either from what remained of his life. She found that his limitations "fitted him for his peculiar work," and she could "no longer quarrel with them; while from his eyes looks out the angel that must sooner or later break every chain." And she concluded her letter by protesting: "What did you mean by saying I had imbibed much of his way of thought?" (*L*, III, 91–92).

V

Margaret Fuller was not, like Emerson, one for the contemplative life: she was a born talker and a born teacher. Consequently she organized and conducted "Conversations" for the women of Boston each fall and spring between 1839 and 1844. In a letter perhaps to Sophia Ripley on August 27, 1839, she outlined the aims and purposes of her program. The meetings would supply "a point of union to well-educated and thinking women" and provide a place where "many of mature age" could find "stimulus and cheer" and could "state their doubts and difficulties with hope of gaining aid from the experience or aspirations of others." She saw her role as that of suggesting topics "which would lead to conversation of a better order than is usual at social meetings." But, she added,

> my own ambition goes much farther. Thus to pass in review the departments of thought and knowledge and endeavor to place them in due relation to one another in our minds. To systematize thought and give a precision in which our sex are so deficient, chiefly, I think because they have so few inducements to test and classify what they receive. To ascertain what pursuits are best suited to us in our time and state of society, and how we may make best use of our means for building up the light of thought upon the life of action.

For Margaret, the women would tackle "the great questions. What were we born to do? How shall we do it? which so few ever propose to themselves 'till their best years are gone by" (*L*, II, 86–87).

These gatherings were judged by the participants to be highly successful (except for the one time when men were invited to attend). Fuller led the discussions, frequently attired in an exotic costume felt to be vaguely oriental. Those attending included many of Fuller's former students, friends, women writers and reformers, and the wives of writers such as Hawthorne and Emerson, plus socially prominent women in Boston. Occasionally she held the gatherings elsewhere, for example "at Brook Farm, where I gave *conversations* on alternate evenings with the husking parties" (*L*, III, 97). Some of the orthodox Christian and politically conservative Bostonians had reservations, as Sarah Clarke noted: "there had been some fear expressed about town that it was a kind of infidel association, as several noted transcendentalists were engaged in it" (*L*, II, 89n).

Occasionally notes were taken of the conversational proceedings, and while there is testimony to the effect of the importance to the participants, not all the accounts are wholly commendatory, and there is not a full body of evidence on which to judge their intellectual content.[23] One reason why they might not have been completely satisfactory to all women is that Fuller often conducted a monologue in which she appeared to be dissociated from the audience, even in something like a trance. Her eloquence was described as mesmeric, oracular and prophetic, and she came to have the reputation of a local sybil, or seeress, especially in view of that exotic costume. This mode of communication must certainly have seemed like the transcendentalist opening herself up to the monitions of the Oversoul and letting herself be filled by the divine afflatus that inspires genius, as Emerson had exclaimed. It is probably this style of trancelike speaking that led Henry James to make Verena Tarrant, in *The Bostonians,* an oracular spokeswoman for feminist liberation.

In *The Feminization of American Culture,* Ann Douglas remarks that Margaret Fuller required

> no reading of the participants in the "Conversations." . . . This gave an air of insubstantiality to many of the discussions, which ranged loftily but vaguely over vast topics and ideas. The nature of the Greek religion, the meaning of "life," were questions that apparently could be debated on the spot with no external aids or preparation. During one of the 1841 Conversations, Fuller told her class "she could keep up no intimacy with books. She loved a book dearly for a while but . . . she was sure to take a disgust to it, to outgrow it." Having gleaned what an author had to give, she "tired" of him—even in the case of Shakespeare.

Further, Douglas remarks, "The revolt against books, against the role of reader, which she enacted for her feminine pupils and herself, was a symbolic protest against the derivative lives to which their society consigned them; they, Fuller insisted, were *originals*" (*FAC,* 270).[24]

---

23 For a transcription of one Conversation, probably taken down by Caroline Sturgis, see *The American Transcendentalists,* ed. Perry Miller (Garden City, N.Y.: Doubleday, 1950), pp. 102–103. See also Chivigny, *Woman and the Myth,* pp. 224–231.

24 It should be remarked that the inadequacy, even the tiresomeness, of books, compared to original inspiration, is a distinctly unoriginal Fullerian idea, derived as it is from Emerson's "The American Scholar."

During this period, Fuller also attained an enduring reputation in American literary history as the first editor of *The Dial.* She also published some important early work there, particularly "The Great Lawsuit: Man versus Men, Woman versus Women." This essay evolved into *Woman in the Nineteenth Century.* Though it lasted only four years and never had a large readership, *The Dial* was an important outlet of transcendental thought; and Margaret worked hard to make it a good magazine. She cajoled authors to produce manuscripts, improved the contributors' fuzzy prose, and oversaw the design and proofing of the magazine. After two years she turned the task over to Emerson, who edited it between 1842 and 1844, when it folded. Even so, she made a very great contribution to it during its final phase.

VI

Resigned to being bright and ugly, and fascinated by Mary Magdalene, George Sand, Goethe's mistresses, and Madame de Staël's Corinne, Fuller abandoned New England, where men, she said, seemed full of "petty intellectualities, cant and bloodless theory" (*L*, III, 143). Her circumstances had not changed since she had told Almira Barlow that "I am more and more dissatisfied with this world, and *cannot* find a home in it" (*L*, I, 209). Fuller's departure for New York, to write for Horace Greeley's newspaper, was seen in Concord as a dangerous test of constraining ethical standards, and her social work with "fallen women" in Sing Sing Prison seemed a doubtful project in political journalism for a woman who had shown no interest whatsoever in the New England abolition movement then raging.[25] The Englishwoman Harriet Martineau expressed this criticism most acidulously in her *Autobiography,* where she contrasted herself and Fuller on the issue of antislavery:

> The difference between us was that while she was living and moving in an ideal world, talking in private and discoursing in public about the most fanciful and shallow conceits which the transcendentalists of Boston took for philosophy, she looked down upon persons who acted instead of talking finely, and devoted their fortunes, their peace, their repose, and their very lives to the preservation of the principles of the republic.[26]

But abolition was not Fuller's issue, a fact that seemed paradoxical to

---

25 On her work at the *Tribune,* see Madeline B. Stern's *The Life of Margaret Fuller* (New York: E. P. Dutton, 1942), pp. 336–375.

26 *Harriet Martineau's Autobiography,* ed. Maria Weston Chapman (Boston: James R. Osgood, 1877), II, 381.

her antislavery friends, who tended to support all the liberal ventures in what was called the "Sisterhood of Reforms": temperance, women's rights, educational reform, the eight-hour day, child-labor laws, and so on. Still, Margaret Fuller *was* moving more and more toward a philosophy of social criticism allied to some kind of nascent activism.

For a time it seemed this activism might center on the condition of women. Her theoretic position was clearly enunciated in *Woman in the Nineteenth Century*. Published in 1845 in New York, the book was an outgrowth of "The Great Lawsuit" article in *The Dial*, and it went some way toward defining her true direction as a social critic. Most urgent to Fuller was a serious redefinition of the role of women in society, and she was unwilling to postpone it until after the emancipation of blacks. Making an Emersonian claim for the full development of both men and women, Fuller remarks that "a broader protest is made in behalf of Woman. As men become aware that few men have had a fair chance, they are inclined to say that no women have had a fair chance" (*WNC*, 24). Education for them was deficient and unrelated to their duties. Arguing that women should be self-dependent, she remarks that the remedy of bad institutions (like marriage) is the development of woman's character. "I believe that, at present, women are the best helpers of one another." She said she "would have Woman lay aside all thought, such as she habitually cherishes, of being taught and led by men." Women, she argued, needed "a much greater range of occupation than they have." And "if you ask me what offices they may fill, I reply—any. I do not care what case you put; let them be sea captains, if you will" (*WNC*, 172, 119, 174). In view of Margaret's later career in Italy, her remarks on the subject of masculine women who defy convention or take lovers outside the bond of marriage seem interesting:

> But women like Sand will speak now and cannot be silenced; their characters and their eloquence alike foretell an era when such as they shall easier learn to lead true lives. But though such forebode, not such shall be parents of it. Those who would reform the world must show that they do not speak in the heat of wild impulse; their lives must be unstained by passionate error; they must be severe lawgivers to themselves. They must be religious students of the divine purpose with regard to man, if they would not confound the fancies of a day with the requisitions of eternal good. Their liberty must be the liberty of law and knowledge. . . . Wherever abuses are seen, the timid will suffer; the bold will protest. But society has a right to outlaw them till she has revised her law; and this she must be taught to do by one who speaks with authority, not in anger or haste. . . (*WNC*, 77).

Doubtless this claim for the purity of the woman who would reform society accounts for why Hawthorne, in *The Scarlet Letter*, does not allow the fallen Hester to become a prophetess of the new feminist order.

Unfortunately, the style of *Woman in the Nineteenth Century* is digressive, incoherent, and repetitive. The argument continually dissolves into personal reminiscence. Arcane mythological references parade her learning but obscure her intent. Repeatedly, sentences written with force and economy, like the first two below, dissipate into the transcendental gas:

> We would have every arbitrary barrier thrown down. We would have every path laid open to Woman as freely as to Man. Were this done, and a slight temporary fermentation allowed to subside, we should see crystallizations more pure and of more various beauty. We believe the divine energy would pervade nature to a degree unknown in the history of former ages, and that no discordant collision, but a ravishing harmony of the spheres, would ensue (*WNC*, 37).

Such a ravishing harmony was not imminent in New England, nor was it likely even in New York. Some of those who knew Fuller thought they understood very well the source of her feminism—the frustrations of Eros. Sophia Hawthorne wrote to her husband:

> What do you think of the speech Queen Margaret Fuller has made from the throne? It seems to me that if she were married truly, she would no longer be puzzled about the rights of woman. This is the revelation of woman's true destiny and place, which never can be *imagined* by those who do not experience the relation. . . . Had there never been false and profane marriages, there would not only be no commotion about woman's rights, but it would be Heaven here at once. . . . I do not believe any man who ever knew one noble woman would ever speak as if she were an inferior in any sense: it is the fault of ignoble women that there is any such opinion in the world.[27]

Emerson also thought that Margaret's unmarried state was disabling to her, especially after he read her journal of the 1830s in preparation for writing the *Memoirs:*

> The unlooked for trait in all these journals to me is the Woman, poor woman: they are all hysterical. She is bewailing her virginity and languishing for a husband. "I need help. No, I need a full, a godlike

---

27 Quoted in Julian Hawthorne, *Nathaniel Hawthorne and His Wife: A Biography* (Boston: James R. Osgood, 1885), I, 257.

embrace from some sufficient love." &c. &c. .... This I doubt not was all the more violent recoil from the exclusively literary & "educational" connections in which she had lived. Mrs Spring told me that Margaret said to her, "I am tired of these literary friendships, I long to be wife and mother."[28]

Her friend the editor Horace Greeley, who sympathized with her liberal viewpoint, likewise felt that her feminism issued from the frustrations of her personal life: "noble and great as she was, a good husband and two or three bouncing babies would have emancipated her from a great deal of cant and nonsense."[29] This viewpoint, common enough among those who knew her, suggests that she gave clear, if unconscious, indications that her feminism was rooted in emotional deprivation.

This argument is plausible. During the period of journalism in New York, she met and fell in love with James Nathan, a European Jewish businessman with whom she had a Platonic relationship for the next several months. What Nathan made of her radical feminism, mixed, as it was, with transcendental spirituality, must be largely imagined. No doubt he was impressed by the severity of her strictures against the in-stitution of marriage, but he must have been confused by her vague talk of the ethereal love that the bodiless angels feel. In any case, it is clear that he took her to be a liberated woman and propositioned her, and, as she was unwilling to translate their love into a sexual affair, he gradually withdrew from her. Her appeals in the love letters to him are poignant revelations of how much she wished their love to be divine as well as human; but as he transferred his interest to a young girl in his charge, who may have been living with him all along, Fuller's pleas began to echo in the void.

Today it is of course anathema to suggest that radical feminism may have a source in a woman's personal failure in intimate relationships with men. (Even so, this intuition led Hawthorne, in *The Blithedale Ro-mance,* to make frustrated love the origin of the feminism of Zenobia.)[30] But if this is the case with Margaret Fuller, it is no discredit to her, since she was indeed more than worthy of love itself and worthy of the kind of remarkable man she sought. In any case, Margaret at this time cavalierly dismissed marriage as a woman's true destiny and place in the world. But did she see herself as leading the vanguard? Where *was* the woman to lead the transition into a better state of relations between

---

28 *Emerson in His Journals,* p. 414.

29 Horace Greeley, *Recollections of a Busy Life* (New York: J. B. Ford, 1868), p. 178.

30 The speed with which Margaret Fuller dropped feminism, once she had found Giovanni Ossoli, has disappointed some of her admirers, but it suggests that Hawthorne may have been right.

men and women? "And will not she soon appear? The woman who shall vindicate their birthright for all women; who shall teach them what to claim, and how to use what they obtain?" (*WNC,* 177). She was not the woman. For feminism was not her complete focus. Like most of the transcendental crowd, she had no vocation. A vocation was self-limitation; to be a feminist was to be constricted, as a farmer or lawyer is constricted: the vocation limits the whole man, or woman. As Ann Douglas remarks, "If Fuller was clear during her transcendental period about what she was rejecting, she was much less sure about what she was putting in its place. No one can read the accounts of the Conversations, not to speak of the correspondence with Emerson, and escape the realization that Fuller did not yet know her true direction" (*FAC,* 270). Even so, the *Herald* articles on such subjects as prison, labor, and slavery (which now began to interest her) show that she was becoming more preoccupied with wealth, power, and political oppression. Living in New York with the Greeleys, she came in contact with the currents of radicalism fermenting in the metropolis, and she began to romanticize the working classes and socialism. Writing for Greeley's paper on capital and labor, she intoned:

> There is no peace. . . . It would appear that the political is being merged in the social struggle: it is well. Whatever blood is to be shed, whatever altars cast down, those tremendous problems MUST be solved, whatever be the cost! . . . To you, people of America, it may perhaps be given to look on and learn in time for a preventive wisdom. . . . You may learn the real meaning of the words FRATERNITY, EQUALITY: you may, despite the apes of the past who strive to tutor you, learn the needs of a true democracy. You may in time learn to reverence, learn to guard, the the the true aristocracy of the nation, the only real nobles—the LABORING CLASSES.[31]

Ann Douglas has remarked that Fuller "had never been more rhetorically impressive than when she passionately redeemed the legacy of the founding fathers by translating it in terms of the socialism which had become her creed" (*FAC,* 285). But the rhetoric here, overblown and strident, is no more impressive than the socialism it espouses. It is a socialism tainted with class hatred, the romance of the proletariat, and the threat of violence against independent merchants and owners. And, despite what Professor Douglas here commends, Fuller's view was far more corrupting to liberal democracy and American politics than

---

31 Margaret Fuller, *At Home and Abroad,* ed. Arthur B. Fuller (1851; reprinted Port Washington, N.Y.: Kennikat Press, 1971), pp. 305–306.

"redeeming." The founding fathers would have shuddered to hear her, but then they were, well, the apes of the past.

In any case, the ordinary relation of New York workingmen and their bosses seemed to resolve itself with little Jacobin violence and bloodshed. And when Nathan left for Europe, Margaret managed to break free herself and headed for London and Paris. Ostensibly she was to write articles for the *Tribune,* but it seems evident to me that—like many American expatriates—she was in search of a personal (if not a sexual) liberation only available at the fountainhead of European socialist thought.[32]

VII

The final stamp of what Margaret Fuller was to become, for better or worse, occurred in the convergence in her life of three new European acquaintances: George Sand, whose conduct and whose novels had already shown her the image of a woman in whom sexual passion and social commitment could continually interact; Giuseppe Mazzini, the Italian revolutionary in exile whose politics now offered her the socialist cause she needed; and Adam Mickiewicz, the Polish poet and patriot in exile, who immediately diagnosed the causes of her felt ineffectuality and frustration. After reading *Woman in the Nineteenth Century,* he told her: "For you the first step in your deliverance and of the deliverance of your sex (of a certain class) is to know, whether you are permitted to remain a virgin" (*L,* V, 176n).[33]

What should be the position of a woman in a time of political revolution or social reorganization? Does the revolutionary condition itself—or merely a belief in radical politics—require that a woman jettison her sexual upbringing and act on the notion of free love? Mickiewicz implied that Margaret would have to give up her virginity if she wanted to be free. How ready are these radical men to seduce and corrupt the sexual innocent on the ground of politics! The sixties communes reeked of the idea that if you wanted to free your mind, you had

---

32 For a different interpretation of Fuller's expatriation, the reader may wish to consult Charles Capper's *Margaret Fuller: An American Romantic Life—The Private Years* (New York: Oxford University Press, 1993). While only the first of the projected two-volume life has yet appeared, Capper reconstructs Fuller's life on the doubtful paradigm of the American intellectual who, in a state of social alienation (not sexual frustration), is driven toward personal involvement in some immense historical or political world crisis.

33 On the Mickiewicz relationship, see Leopold Wellisz, *The Friendship of Margaret Fuller D'Ossoli and Adam Mickiewicz* (New York: Polish Book Importing Co., 1947), and Paula Blanchard, *Margaret Fuller: From Transcendentalism to Revolution* (New York: Delacorte Press, 1978), pp. 284–295.

to sleep around. Was it Bobby Seale, the Black Panther, who said that the only position for a woman in the black liberation movement was prone? In Fuller's time, it was the master himself, Charles Fourier, who had endorsed this sexual anarchy. He taught that in a properly constituted harmonic society (that is, in one of his associationist phalanxes) members could remain virginal if they wished, become monogamously involved with a single spouse, simultaneously embrace several spouses in polygamy, or take a string of changing sexual partners seriatim. Only homosexuality was forbidden. Fourier's sexual ideas were largely suppressed in public discussions of how to reorganize society in New England, but committed Associationists, like Fuller, knew very well what the embrace of socialism was likely to involve.

In any case, once Margaret Fuller left New England; left the moral milieu of men like Emerson, James Freeman Clarke, and W. H. Channing; once she had left the protective milieu of her mother and the women of her family; she answered Mickiewicz's question for herself. Once she decided that it was not permitted for her to remain a virgin, she was, in a manner of speaking, fated—fated to travel to Rome, to fall in with Giovanni Angélo Ossoli, to go to bed with him, and (since we live in a world of moral cause and effect) to become pregnant with his child during the most tumultuous months of violence in that failed revolutionary endeavor. It hardly mattered that Ossoli spoke no English, was a hopeless intellectual inferior, had no idea of who she was, and offered no means of supporting her and the child. Once she became committed to the social reorganization of Italy through violent revolution, her sexual attitudes became fully radicalized.

In Italy, Margaret Fuller passed on from transcendental individualist and feminist to the role of enthusiastic socialist. During the revolutions of 1848 she became an ardent champion of the Risorgimento, claiming Mazzini, Mickiewicz, and other revolutionaries as her friends. All that was known in America was that Margaret was living in Rome, espousing the republican cause, and writing a history of the unfolding political and military events. [34] Her politics might have been doubtful to New England conservatives. But a scandal more troubling was in the wind. For the news about Margaret, reported back to Concord, was that she had taken a lover. She called him her husband, but there was some question whether she and Giovanni Ossoli, ten years her junior, had ever really been married. Perhaps even worse, it was discovered they already had a child. Family and friends were stunned.

---

34 For a biographical treatment of this tumultuous period, see Joseph Jay Deiss, *The Roman Years of Margaret Fuller* (New York: Thomas Y. Crowell, 1969).

Strangely enough, for one who is held by modern feminists to have been sexually liberated, Margaret Fuller concealed from her friends and family in New England her relationship with Ossoli and their child, even as she became more strident, in her ongoing *Tribune* articles, about her socialist politics. When the news of her "husband" and child broke, her friends and family wanted to believe that the worst was not true, that Margaret must have married Ossoli, that the child had to be legitimate. But Margaret's explanation as to why she had kept this decisive relationship secret for almost two years, in order to spare her mother worry, confused more than explained it. In fact, she had no intention of explaining herself, even at the price of social ostracism, telling one friend:

> If you decide to meet with me as before, and wish to say something about the matter to your friends, it will be true to say that there have been pecuniary reasons for this concealment. But *to you* in confidence I add, this is only half the truth; and I cannot explain or satisfy my dear friend farther—I should wish to meet her independent of all relations; but as we live in the midst of "society," she would have to inquire for me now as *Margaret Ossoli*; that being done, I should like to say nothing farther on the subject.[35]

Such explanations offered no explanation at all. Margaret's friends were left in an impossible position by her scandalous or at least baffling behavior. Sarah Clarke even complained to Margaret that "the world" had been saying "injurious things of which we were not authorised to deny. . . ." Things looked bad. Emerson offered to help her find an American publisher for her history of the Italian revolution, mainly in order to keep her from coming back to Massachusetts. Rebecca Spring put it most decisively: "Much as we should love to see you, and strange as it may seem, we, as well as all of your friends who have spoken to us about it, believe it will be undesirable for you to return at present" (*M&M*, 328).

Of course there were certain reasons why the Ossolis might have wanted their relationship kept secret. Ossoli's brothers were conservative Catholics who opposed the revolution; Ossoli stood to inherit a small amount of money from his elderly father, which he would lose if it came out that he was a revolutionist married to an American socialist. But somehow these facts did not seem to explain everything satisfactorily. And Margaret was perversely mum. Biographers have found no documented evidence that a marriage ever occurred. During the revolution-

---

35 Quoted in Joan von Mehren, *Minerva and the Muse: A Life of Margaret Fuller* (Amherst: University of Massachusetts Press, 1994), p. 315. Hereafter, quotations from this work will be cited as *M&M*, in parentheses, in the text.

ary chaos, of course, many records were destroyed. But it is questionable whether a priest would have married Ossoli, a Catholic, and Fuller, a Protestant. And marriage by a Protestant clergyman would not have been sanctioned by Ossoli's religion. But why had Margaret concealed this information from her family until well after the child was born? Did she not wish them to know that she was an adulteress, that she had an illegitimate child? Had Margaret married, or did she think such ceremonies irrelevant? Had she concealed news of her marriage because there was no marriage or because a marriage ceremony would have been seen as a betrayal of her feminist principles? Boston wanted to know. Margaret refused to answer questions, simply declaring, in the most moving way, her love for her husband and child.

Emerson insisted that her criticism of marriage as an institution was merely theoretic and that, when she returned, a license would be produced. "When it came to be a practical question to herself, she would feel that this was a tie that ought to have the solemnest sanction; that against the theorist was a vast public opinion, too vast to brave."[36] But others, such as Channing were not so sure, seeing Margaret as a George Sand willing to risk being outlawed by society for the sake of making an attack on marriage. Since Italy was dangerous and they had no source of income, Margaret decided to return to Boston and support her family through journalism. When this became known, tongues wagged in Boston. How would Margaret be received? As a wife and a married mother or as an adulteress with a natural child?

The month-long return voyage in the *Elizabeth* seemed doomed from the start. The captain contracted smallpox and immediately died; the baby Angelo also became infected; yet unexpectedly, the child recovered from the disease. At the end the ship was under the command of an inexperienced mate, Henry Bangs, who was driven off course in a storm and wrecked the ship on a sandbar off Fire Island. It took the ship a great many hours to break up and sink. A number of passengers and crew members threw themselves into the surf and made it to shore. Others drowned in the attempt. Some (like the Ossolis) hung back and so perished when the ship went under. Of course the shipwreck destroyed any evidence that might have resolved the question of whether Margaret and Ossoli had married. Thoreau was sent to Fire Island to recover the Ossolis' bodies and their belongings, but only the child Angelo was washed ashore, together with one box of Margaret's papers. Some of the witnesses of the shipwreck—only sixty rods off-shore—said that Margaret had seemed to hold back from a leap into the

---

36 Quoted in Chevigny, *Woman and the Myth*, p. 415.

surf that might have saved them. This has raised the specter of her wanting to commit suicide. Surely confronting her friends and family in Boston, after the stupefactions of what she had done in Italy, would have been daunting. But in my view she had sufficient courage and self-reliance to weather the ostracism. In any case, Thoreau did not salvage the manuscript of her history of the Italian revolution, nor did he find the marriage license they all desperately wanted to see.

Hawthorne's reaction to Margaret Fuller's Italian experience was the most condemnatory, and he has accordingly been denounced by feminists as perfidious. His final view of her was indeed harsh. But his reaction must be understood as coming from a man who reverenced moral purity in women, who were to redeem man from his fallen sensuality and to find their fulfillment in love and the sacrament of marriage and family. Feminist critics of the institution of marriage were, in his view, enemies of the holiest relation possible between men and women. Convinced that the Ossoli business was the final evidence of Fuller's collapse into sensuality and adultery, he interviewed the Joseph Moziers in Florence, who had supported Margaret financially, nursed her in illness, and met Ossoli after the revolution. Mozier had apparently become disillusioned with Fuller's "licentiousness," and his report to Hawthorne brought out those traits of Puritan character that Hawthorne concedes in the Custom House chapter of *The Scarlet Letter.* In his *Italian Notebooks,* Hawthorne writes:

> He [Ossoli] was the handsomest man Mr. Mozier ever saw, but entirely ignorant even of his own language, scarcely able to read at all, destitute of manners; in short, half an idiot, and without any pretensions to be a gentleman. . . . He could not possibly have had the least appreciation of Margaret; and the wonder is, what attraction she found in this boor. . . . As from her towards him, I do not understand what feeling there could have been, except it was purely sensual; as for him towards her, there could hardly have been even this, for she had not the charm of womanhood.

Hawthorne felt that Margaret "had a strong and coarse nature," which she had never succeeded in refining. He remarked that she had "not left in the minds of those who knew her any deep witness to her integrity and purity. She was a great humbug; of course with much talent, and much moral reality, or else she could not have been such a great humbug." Mozier told him that he doubted that Margaret had any manuscripts or papers dealing with the Italian revolution. And Hawthorne concluded:

Thus there appears to have been a total collapse in poor Margaret, morally and intellectually; and tragic as her catastrophe was, Providence was, after all, kind in putting her and her clownish husband, and their child, on board that fated ship. . . . [She had] a strange, heavy, unpliable, and in many respects, defective and evil nature. . . . On the whole, I do not know but I like her the better for it;—the better, because she proved herself a woman after all and fell like the lowest of her sisters.

That he might have liked her better for her fall suggests how ridiculous Hawthorne found the transcendentalists' belief in the possibility of perfection, their godlike condition, their orphic inspirations and vatic pronouncements. Margaret's fall humanized her and thus drew her back into the realm of errant humanity, where the rest of us live. *The Scarlet Letter* (1850), with its portrait of the fallen Hester, was begun the year of Margaret's death, and his feminist suicide Zenobia, in *The Blithedale Romance* (1852), was composed while Emerson, Channing, and Clarke were interviewing her friends, reviewing her correspondence and journals, taking notes about her family history, and drawing together the materials for her *Memoirs*. The real Margaret and the fictional Hester and Zenobia were all cautionary instances of the fate of sexual irregularity in the transcendental woman who thought she could be "her own Redeemer, if not her own Creator."[37] Holmes's *Elsie Venner,* James's *The Bostonians* and *The Portrait of a Lady,* and Hawthorne's *The Scarlet Letter* and *The Blithedale Romance* all owe something to the memory of this extraordinary woman, the American Corinne, the intellectual wonder and the sexual terror of her age.

How can we define her today? Was she the Murphy Brown of her time, the single professional woman who claimed for herself a sexual freedom that justified even the bearing of a child out of wedlock? Margaret, of course, was different from the Murphy Browns of our time: she considered herself *married* to Ossoli and intended even to support him and live with him in America in a traditional family arrangement. But in forewarning her mother that Giovanni was ten years her junior and that he might not forever be satisfied with her, she was perhaps letting her mother know that theirs was "a Fourierist marriage"—viz., one without a ceremony. (That is, no marriage at all.) This much seems suggested in one of Margaret's letters to her mother in which she remarks, "In earlier days, I dreamed of doing and being much, but now I am content with the Magdalen to rest my plea hereon, '*She has loved much*'" (*M&M*, 290). Out of such as this came Hawthorne's Hester Prynne.

---

37 Nathaniel Hawthorne, *The French and Italian Notebooks,* ed. Thomas Woodson (Columbus: Ohio State University Press, 1980), pp. 154–157.

As I review Fuller's letters and journals, her journalism and her travel writing, not to speak of *Woman in the Nineteenth Century*, it is impossible for me to resist the conclusion—shared by none of her biographers—that Margaret Fuller is more compelling as an instance of radical thought and sexual confusion than as an important nineteenth-century writer. Emerson, James Freeman Clarke, and W. H. Channing tried to tidy up the prose in her letters and journals in the 1852 *Memoirs of Margaret Fuller Ossoli*. This service led Donna Dickenson to claim that these male editors produced a Fuller style that was "frilly, namby-pamby, prissy and florid, quintessentially 'a woman's way of writing.'"[38] This is of course nonsense. It is the sad case that Margaret Fuller wrote before the invention of the American vernacular style. Her prose, absent any editing, is heavy, leaden, weighted with ill-digested historical and mythological allusions, at times prissy and florid, and always literary in the worst sense of the word. Margaret Fuller mesmerized her contemporaries, but, in later years, Emerson was to say that Fuller represented only "an interesting hour & group in American cultivation."[39] This is indeed dismissive, but then he felt that she left no lasting books. We of course cannot hear this brilliant talker talk; we cannot hear this "moral improvisatrice" (as Henry James called her) weave her audible spell. We are left with her books, and they, however admirable in intent, fail of pleasing aesthetic form. Even so, the "Margaret-ghost," as Henry James observed in *William Wetmore Story and His Friends*, still haunted the corridors of the New England mind a half-century later. Despite the ongoing decline of moral values and all the modern Murphy Browns loosed upon the world, it still does.

---

38 Donna Dickenson, *Margaret Fuller: Writing a Woman's Life* (New York: St. Martin's Press, 1993), p. 10.
39 *Emerson in His Journals*, p. 429.

The Marrying
Kind: James's
The American

Henry James's *The American* is a novel of manners juxtaposing the mores of an aristocratic French society with the comparative vulgarity of the American traveler in Paris, specifically a Western businessman who has amassed a sudden fortune and has come abroad to cultivate aesthetic interests and, as it turns out, to find a wife.[1] A great deal has been written about this "international theme"—by Leon Edel, Oscar Cargill, Kermit Vanderbilt, and others—so that it is perhaps not necessary here to belabor these oft-discussed matters.[2]

But there are one or two matters relevant to the way that the international theme exploits the concept of marriage that have not been sufficiently elucidated in the criticism. One of them has to do with the antithetical social ambition of the American, Christopher Newman, and that of Noémie Nioche. The central marriage theme is developed simultaneously on two fronts: both Newman and Noémie are each in search of a spouse. But significantly different intentions animate these two characters. In the case of Noémie, James deploys the familiar theme of

---

1 For a fuller discussion of this theme, see James W. Tuttleton, *The Novel of Manners in America* (New York: W. W. Norton, 1974), pp. 48–85.

2 Quotations from *The American* and from several essays mentioned herein, are (unless otherwise indicated) taken from *Henry James's The American*, ed. James W. Tuttleton (New York: W. W. Norton, 1978). Hereafter, quotations from the novel and the cited essays will be indicated by the abbreviation *A*, in parentheses, in the text. See Edel, "A Portrait Rich in National Ambiguities," in *A*, pp. 415–426; Cargill, "*The American*," in *A*, 426–441; Kermit Vanderbilt, "James, Fitzgerald, and the American Self-Image," *Massachusetts Review*, 6 (1965), 289–304; Christof Wegelin, *The Image of Europe in Henry James* (Dallas: Southern Methodist University Press, 1958); and Frederick J. Hoffman, "Freedom and Conscious Form: Henry James and the American Self," *Virginia Quarterly Review*, 37 (1961), 269–285.

marriage as an avenue to greater wealth and upward social mobility. In novels where love is obstructed by class barriers, money is of course crucial, and James gives it its due in the dilemma faced by father and daughter over her dowry. M. Nioche puts the matter succinctly: "Ah, monsieur, one doesn't get a husband for nothing. Her husband must take her as she is; I can't give her a sou. But the young men don't see with that eye." Newman may advance an American viewpoint in suggesting that "your young men are very shabby. . . . They ought to pay for your daughter, and not ask money themselves" (*A*, 53–54), but the custom of the country, in France, was the necessary *dot*. In reply to Newman's generous offer of money to provide the dowry, in exchange for a half-dozen execrable copies of well-known paintings, however, Noémie remarks: "What sort of husband can you get for twelve thousand francs? . . . Grocers and butchers and little *maîtres de cafés!* I will not marry at all if I can't marry well" (*A*, 64).

Newman's sage counsel—"I would advise you not to be too fastidious"—doubles back upon him with sharp irony when we come to consider the height of his own marital ambitions. But the trajectory of the plot with Noémie Nioche is established in this exchange, and her subsequent conduct, however vulgar or immoral, is directed to the end of escaping the poverty of the *petite bourgeoisie*—if not as a rich man's wife, then at least as an aristocrat's mistress. In the end she comes closer to her goal than Newman to his, she having successively brought in tow both a French count and an English lord.

The plot line associated with Newman, however, does not deal with the usual theme of upward social mobility, greater wealth, or improved social status. For one thing, Newman is already immensely rich—much richer, in fact, than the Bellegardes, the aristocratic family with which he becomes involved. Second, he has no interest in their social status. His aim is not to enter the sacred circle of the Faubourg St. Germain but rather to possess Claire de Cintré, the flower of the Bellegarde family, to draw her out of its narrow confines, and to offer her, in recompense, the whole wide world. This indifference to their social status is indicated in his telling the young marquise that he really does not want to come into the family by way of marriage: "I only want to take Madame de Cintré out of it" (*A*, 144). In this respect the book therefore differs from those novels of manners in which the energies of the *nouveau riche* protagonist are directed toward gaining an entry into polite society. Newman has no interest in the Bellegardes' social status because he has no interest in "society," and, as an American democrat, he thinks he is as good as anybody. In fact, he has picked up the phrase in the political palaver of American democrats and he here applies it to himself: he is "nature's nobleman."[3] Instead of the usual motive of moving up, then, James defines Newman's intention in terms of acquisition.

As a businessman, Newman has risen to the top of the financial world through making and selling washtubs and leather, through stock deals and like transactions, some apparently rather cutthroat. He has made a pile high enough to enable him to renounce the bloodthirstiness of Gilded Age business practices and to "assimilate" Europe. Practically speaking, he believes that "Europe was made for him, and not he for Europe. . . . The world, to his sense, was a great bazaar, where one might stroll about and purchase handsome things; but he was no more conscious, individually, of social pressure than he admitted the existence of such a thing as an obligatory purchase" (*A*, 66).

The principal purchase in question is of course a wife. And there is no mistaking the acquisitiveness evident in Newman's whole courtship of Claire de Cintré. He is the businessman par excellence. He has a shrewd sense of what being rich ought to entail. He studies the market. He knows the worth of things and appearances, and he is ready to take moderate risks. He has made a complete inventory of every *objet d'art* in his collection. But as he remarks to Mrs. Tristram, "To make it perfect, as I see it, there must be a beautiful woman perched on the pile, like a statue on a monument. She must be as good as she is beautiful, and as clever as she is good. . . . I want to possess, in a word, the best article in the market" (*A*, 44). This degree of fastidiousness, in view of the commercial advice he gives to Noémie Nioche, is bound to reverberate with irony as the story goes along. For while he believes that any desire can be realized—with enough determination, energy, and cash—he obviously does not know the height of exclusiveness of which the snobbish Bellegardes are capable. I suggest that it is this detached commercial acquisitiveness that renders Newman ineffective as the dynamic lover his American reviewers wanted him to be. His failure to sweep Claire off her feet, whatever the piddling impediments of French snobbishness, has always seemed a problematic aspect of his characterization.[4] His desire for a wife is in fact willed, for he is not a sufficiently passionate

---

3 On Newman's "nobility," see H. R. Hays, "The Limitations of Christopher Newman," in *Henry James: The American*, ed. Gerald Willen (New York: T. Y. Crowell, 1972), pp. 402–413; Constance Rourke's splendid *American Humor: A Study of the National Character* (New York: Harcourt, Brace, 1931), p. 200; and Charles Sanford, *The Quest for Paradise: Europe and the American Moral Imagination* (Urbana: University of Illinois Press, 1961).

4 *The Nation* reviewer correctly observed that if Newman had really wanted to marry Claire, "all the mothers and brothers in Christendom would have been no more guard for Madame de Cintré than half a dozen cobwebs"; likewise the *Scribner's* reviewer remarked that "it was an imperative condition that he should have tried to marry the woman he loved, and if he must fail, that his failure should be in no wise weak and spiritless" (*A*, 392, 399). But for many readers it was.

man. He is not a great lover. And in this respect Urbain may be right in calling Newman's persistence in trying to retrieve Claire a mere "audacious pertinacity."

I

In the service of the plot parallels involving Newman's and Noémie's matrimonial ambitions, James strikes off an impressive array of marital symbols derived from the visual arts, literature, music, and mythology. These have been the subject of some critical notice, although a full-scale treatment of James's allusive technique remains to be done.[5] On one level, the world of art—the great masters, the magnificent museums—is sketched in by James in order to underline the bewilderment of a businessman who had just discovered "a very rich and beautiful world," one that "had not all been made by sharp railroad men and stockbrokers" (*A*, 75). What should be made of this dazzling discovery is enough to give our hero an "aesthetic headache" (*A*, 17). But for the reader it is an additional pleasure to observe the uses to which specific paintings are put by the author in order to complicate the question of matrimony.

The motif of marriage is continually reinforced by a network of allusions to paintings by Titian, Raphael, Murillo, Veronese, and others. Murillo's beautiful moon-borne Madonna is the first painting to come under Newman's scrutiny in the Louvre, although, "baffled on the aesthetic question" (*A*, 19), he admires Noémie's copy as much as the original. That James should have set up, at the outset of the novel, a symbol resonant with the notion of divine motherhood, innocence, and purity suggests two things: both Newman's aspiration to a certain kind of wife, and a contrast (yet to become apparent) with Noémie, who passes in the course of the action from the condition of a coquette to that of a tawdry prostitute. James's symbolic intent is suggested with a brilliant economy of means in a sentence near the end of Chapter 1: "Mademoiselle Noémie had collected her accessories, and she gave the precious Madonna in charge to her father, who retreated backwards out of sight, holding it at arm's-length and reiterating his obeisances" (*A*, 25). This comment crystallizes in a single sentence the notion of chaste

---

5 The best work in this aspect of James criticism has been done by Edwin T. Bowden in *The Themes of Henry James: A System of Observation Through the Visual Arts* (New Haven: Yale University Press, 1956), by Viola H. Winner in the impressive *Henry James and the Visual Arts* (Charlottesville: University Press of Virginia, 1970), and by Adeline Tintner in *The Museum World of Henry James* (Ann Arbor: UMI Research Press, 1986) and in her latest work *Henry James and the Lust of the Eyes: Thirteen Artists in His Work* (Baton Rouge: Louisiana State University Press, 1993).

virtue, the father's responsibility for preserving it, his inability to do so, and his fawning obsequiousness. Later, when she destroys one of her copies by painting two crimson daubs on it, so as to create "the rough indication of a cross," we have been alerted to James's motif of appearance and reality: she is a poor imitation of the Madonna. Her remark about the cross ("It is the sign of truth" ([A, 133]) is spoken without any deep understanding of the truth of virtue and self-sacrifice implicit in the Christian faith.

Another work of art—Paul Veronese's portrait of the marriage feast at Cana—is put to a like use in the opening of Chapter 2. In this scene Newman sits before the depiction of Christ's first miracle and finds that the painting "satisfied his conception, which was ambitious, of what a splendid banquet should be" (A, 26). James observes what it is that attracts Newman: "In the left-hand corner of the picture is a young woman with yellow tresses confined in a golden head-dress; she is bending forward and listening, with the smile of a charming woman at a dinner-party, to her neighbour. Newman detected her in the crowd, admired her, and perceived that she too had her votive copyist—a young man with his hair standing on end. Suddenly he became conscious of the germ of the 'collector'" (A, 26). This scene too adumbrates, in a symbolic way, several matters to follow. The recognition of a beautiful woman, the votive attention, the marriage, the splendid banquet, wifely charm at a dinner party, the wife as an object of the collector's mania; —all of these take on full form as the plot unfolds but are here simply noted with a symbolic compression that suggests how rapidly James's art had matured since *Roderick Hudson*.

Both of these artworks depict the Holy Family or the subject of marriage in the context of the Gospels and therefore radiate sacred associations. What are we to make of them? I do not believe that James was a religious symbolist along the lines suggested by Quentin Anderson's *The American Henry James*. But the multiplication of other artworks sacred to the Christian faith does beguile the critic's curiosity. The allusion to Noémie's study of the "Madonnas and St. Johns" (A, 60), in the context of Newman's question about her being a coquette, reminds us that if the Madonna is an image of virgin purity and Noémie will come to a bad end, St. John lost his head through the betrayal and sexual treachery of Salome, even as Valentin loses his life in part as a consequence of Noémie's machinations. In the context of this conversation about her imputed immorality, Noémie proposes, as a commission, a copy of the *Marriage of St. Catherine*. That Newman's marriage to Claire will be sanctified by her saintliness seems to be authenticated as we get to know Claire. Indeed, as Newman later says, "She is my dream realised" (*A*, 106). But more than a little irony inheres in James's choice of St. Catherine's marriage when, after the Bellegardes have broken faith, Urbain remarks, "I think my mother will tell you that she would rather her daughter should become Soeur Catherine than Mrs. Newman" (*A*, 250). Catherine of Siena (1347–1380) is well known in the hagiographies for her piety and asceticism. Claire's renunciation of the world, not to speak of her renunciation of marriage to Newman and of the motherhood of his children, is therefore interestingly implied by the reference. From Saint to Sister is, indeed, Claire's direction in the novel.[6]

Yet, as it turns out, Catherine is not the name elected by this beautiful woman who takes the veil. In the last chapter of the novel, we and Newman discover, from Mrs. Tristram, that on her twenty-seventh birthday Claire "took the name of her patroness, St. Veronica. Sister Veronica has a lifetime before her!" (*A*, 304). Veronica, we are reminded, was the holy woman of Jerusalem who gave to Christ, on his way to Calvary, a handkerchief. Ever afterward, it is said, the handkerchief bore his image. (Indeed, any cloth so bearing an image of Christ is called a veronica.) While her fiancé's name is Christopher, or Christ-bearer, no elaborate one-for-one parallels should be sought in these religious allusions. It is enough to say that they are consciously dropped in passing for associative value and that they suggest notions of purity, virtue, and asceticism associated with Claire (the antithetical associations being pertinent to Noémie) and notions of betrayal and emotional agony associated with Newman.

The alteration of the religious name from Catherine to Veronica may associate the anguish of Newman with the passion of Christ, but these matters cannot be carried too far. Otherwise we would have to do something improbable with Newman's use of the language of Pontius Pilate, when, in speaking to Valentin of M. Nioche, he says, "If the old man turns out to be a humbug, you may do what you please [with Noémie]. I wash my hands of the matter" (*A*, 136). James, as an inheritor of some of Hawthorne's moral interests, knew enough to avoid his predecessor's overdevelopment of images and allusions. An "abuse of the fanciful element" was not consistent with James's sense of realism in fiction, and in the biography *Hawthorne* (1879), soon to be published, James criticized Hawthorne on this very point. In *The American*, as elsewhere, James merely indulges the liberty of a free irony in playing with the latencies of suggested meaning.

That Newman is not meant to be a religious figure is suggested by

---

6 For another reading of the allusion, see Kathleen A. Sherflick, "Claire de Cintré in Henry James's *The American* and St. Clare of Assisi," *Henry James Review*, 12 (1991), 117–119.

the symbolism of two other *objets d'art* alluded to in the novel. The first is a fan which is nervously opened by old Madame de Bellegarde in the scene where Newman threatens to stage an engagement party at his hotel featuring the singer Madame Frezzolini and "all the first people from the Théâtre Française" (*A*, 170). As she pales before this prospect, the old marquise opens an antique fan on which is painted "a *fête champêtre*—a lady with a guitar, singing, and a group of dancers round a garlanded Hermes" (*A*, 171). The old lady's horror at an uncivil public revel—to which will be invited the likes of Miss Kitty Upjohn, Miss Dora Finch, General Packard, and C. P. Hatch—with Newman, the King of Leather and Washtubs, as an American avatar of the garlanded Hermes, Greek god of commerce—is wittily suggested by the latent implications of this old fan.

The second symbolic artwork is the expensive gift that Newman purchases for the Reverend Mr. Babcock, an uptight New England minister, who has come to France on funds supplied by his congregation for moral and cultural self-development but who finds Europe to be "impure" and his traveling companion Newman to be wanting in a sufficient "moral reaction" to their sightseeing. In response to Babcock's long letter charging him with hedonism, Newman purchases for him "a grotesque little statuette in ivory, of the sixteenth century, which he sent off to Babcock without a commentary. It represented a gaunt, ascetic-looking monk, in a tattered gown and cowl, kneeling with clasped hands and pulling a portentously long face. It was a wonderfully delicate piece of carving, and in a moment, through one of the rents of his gown, you espied a fat capon hung round the monk's waist." That James intends us to see a latent meaning in this gift, as well as in the other *objets d'art* mentioned in the novel, is suggested by the curious questions posed by the author:

> In Newman's intention what did the figure symbolise? Did it mean that he was going to try to be as "high-toned" as the monk looked at first, but that he feared he should succeed no better than the friar, on a closer inspection, proved to have done? It is not supposable that he intended a satire upon Babcock's own asceticism, for this would have been a truly cynical stroke. He made his late companion, at any rate, a very valuable little present (*A*, 73).

These alternatives open up several interpretive possibilities; in doing so they reflect Hawthorne's familar trick of giving a multiple interpretation of symbolic objects and actions and so saturating a work in polysemous meaning. But, at the same time, James's suggested possibilities cloud the issue of what might be the most plausible motive in Newman's giving the gift. In fact, as the narrative voice of the tale, James suddenly abjures omniscience: he can tell us what the gift did not symbolize (perhaps it symbolized nothing), but he cannot tell us what it did mean. James thus avoids the excesses of allegory and symbolism for which he would later criticize his most important American predecessor.[7]

II

A number of literary allusions, fairy tales, folk legends, and myths complement these symbolic artworks so as to suggest, without developing, other layers of meaning pertinent to the theme of marriage. One of the most textually significant is the allusion to *Faublas*, a book which Newman reads to avert insomnia at the Croix Helvétique, where Valentin lies dying. This recondite title alludes in shortened form to *Les Amours du Chevalier Faublas* published by Jean Baptiste Louvet de Couvray in Paris in 1821. The full title is a more suggestive gloss associating the loves of Valentin and Newman. But by 1907, when the New York Edition was prepared, James had concluded that the abbreviated allusion was too obscure and that the full title was too cumbersome and explicit, with the effect that he altered the name of the book, in revision, to *Les Liaisons Dangereuses*, the work by Choderlos de Laclos published in 1782, the title of which provided a more evident, expressive ironic association.

Not so textually significant, but an allusion nevertheless suggestive of the improbable romanticism of Newman's courtship, is the duchess's remark that Newman's "real triumph . . . is pleasing the countess; she is as difficult as a princess in a fairy tale" (*A*, 190). At the engagement party, as Urbain introduces Newman to his peers, James remarks that "If the marquis was going about as a bear-leader, if the fiction of Beauty and the Beast was supposed to have found its companion-piece, the general impression appeared to be that the bear was a very fair imitation of humanity." Despite the civilities of the aristocracy, Newman is obliged to ask himself, "Am I behaving like a d—d fool?" (*A*, 191). Much of the time, unfortunately—in that salon and on that occasion—he is.

That Newman will not prove to be the prince who can carry off the princess is suggested by another fairy-tale allusion. At one of the dinner

---

7 James's critique is summed up in his remark that "the faults" of *The Scarlet Letter* "are, to my sense, a want of reality and an abuse of the fanciful element—of a certain superficial symbolism." See James's *Hawthorne* (1879; reprinted New York: Collier Books, 1966), p. 101. On the matter of Newman's "reading" the several "texts" of the Paris world, see Michael Hobbs's "Reading Newman Reading: Textuality and Possession in *The American*," *Henry James Review*, 13 (1992), 115–125.

parties Newman arrives at the hôtel de Bellegarde just in time to hear Claire de Cintré finish reading a story to her young niece: "'But in the end the young prince married the beautiful Florabella . . . and carried her off to live with him in the Land of the Pink Sky. There she was so happy that she forgot all her troubles, and went out to drive every day of her life in an ivory coach drawn by five hundred white mice. Poor Florabella,' she explained to Newman, 'had suffered terribly'" (*A*, 137–138). F. Y. Bernard has astutely argued, on the basis of other evidence, that the Land of the Pink Sky is America.[8]

But Newman is not to be the princely deliverer who will transport Claire from suffering in Paris to the joys of San Francisco. And the dénouement of the plot is appropriately adumbrated in Claire's remark a few minutes later: "I have very little courage; I am not a heroine. . . . I could never have gone through the sufferings of the beautiful Florabella . . . not even for her prospective rewards" (*A*, 138). In this admission Newman's fate is sealed.

Valentin's allusion to King Cophetua and the beggar-maid puts additional emphasis on the impossible fairy-tale courtship of Newman. In discussing the exalted character of the family, which descends from the ninth century, Valentin remarks that the young women had, with only a few exceptions, always married into old families. Best of the exceptions was the ancestor in the middle ages who had "married a beggar-maid, like King Cophetua. That was really better," Valentin remarks: "It was like marrying a bird or a monkey; one didn't have to think about her family at all. Our women have always done well; they have never even gone into the *petite noblesse*. There is, I believe, not a case on record of a misalliance among the women" (*A*, 103). This remark, like Claire's observation that she is no heroine, aptly suggests the disappointment of the hero at the end. The allusion, however, is charged with an ironic paradox. For it is Newman who has the kingly wealth, of course, while the Bellegardes are financially "forlorn"; but it is the Bellegardes whose aristocratic status will effectively deprive Newman, nature's nobleman, of an opportunity for kingly "condescension."

The American hovers on the borderline between high comedy and tragedy while ultimately descending into a doubtful melodrama. James was to address this mixture of styles many years later, when he came to write the preface. But that James, early in the book, wanted to invest the forthcoming dénouement with tragic overtones is suggested in Mrs.

---

8 F. Y. Bernard, "James's Florabella and the 'Land of the Pink Sky,'" *Notes and Queries*, 13 (1966), 70. This otherwise astute identification is marred by his attempt to adduce this allusion as a proof supporting John A. Claire's doubtful claim that Claire is the daughter of Mrs. Bread. See Claire's "*The American*: A Reinterpretation," *PMLA*, 74 (1959), 613–618.

Tristram's comparing Claire to Desdemona in *Othello.*[9] Just after New-man has met Claire for the first time, and she has not foreclosed further meetings, Mrs. Tristram congratulates Newman and remarks of Madame de Cintré: "No woman was ever so good as that woman seems. . . . Remember what Shakespeare calls Desdemona: 'a supersubtle Venetian.' Madame de Cintré is a supersubtle Parisian. She is a charming woman, and she has five hundred merits; but you had better keep that in mind" (*A*, 117). One is struck with that *seems*. It alerts us to a pos-sible discrepancy between the appearance and the reality of Claire's goodness. And her suggestion that Newman keep in mind Claire's su-persubtlety forewarns us that Madame de Cintré may be entirely capable of commanding the resolution of the impending conflict. Implicit in the Desdemona allusion is also the notion of the betrayal of a lover. Des-demona is entirely innocent of treachery to Othello, of course, but Madame de Cintré's decision to enter a convent, however victimized she is by her family, represents a failure of courage which effectively betrays and repudiates Newman's love for her.

The destructiveness of women who victimize men and prevent the fulfillment of love is suggested in Mrs. Tristram's allusion to Keats's "La Belle Dame sans Merci," on the occasion when she tells Valentin that he reminds her of the "knight-at-arms, / Alone and palely loitering." Valentin replies with elaborate facetious courtesy but suggests that "it is good manners for no man except Newman to look happy" (*A*, 192). The linking of Newman and Valentin with the beautiful ladies without mercy not only forecasts how both will suffer in love but constitutes a part of the subtext of feelings and associations negative to marriage.

The setting for Valentin's confession to Newman that he has come within an inch of "taking that girl Noémie *au sérieux*" (*A*, 198) is a per-formance of Mozart's *Don Giovanni*. Both of these men are putative Don Juans but wind up unsuccessful in love. The conversation among the principals about the plot of the story sets up a series of parallels among the characters of the opera and of the novel, in which, above all, Newman is the ostensible Don Juan whose pursuit of Claire as Donna Elvira will be obstructed by Urbain as the man of stone, with the ironic

---

9 Whether James is a comic, a tragic, or a melodramatic novelist, or some combination of all three, continues to vex his critics. Richard Poirier in *The Comic Sense of Henry James* and Ronald Wallace in *Henry James and the Comic Form*, among others, argue the first; Frederick Crews in *The Tragedy of Manners* poses the second; and Leo B. Levy in *Versions of Melodrama*, Jacques Barzun in "James the Melodramatist" (*Kenyon Review*, 5 [1943], 508–521), and Peter Brooks in *The Melodramatic Imagination* see James as essentially melodramatic. For a study of tragic implications of the *Othello* reference, see Agostino Lombardo's "Henry James, *The American* e il mito di *Otello*," *Friendship's Garland: Essays Presented to Mario Praz. . . . 2 vols. (Roma: Edizioni di Storia e Letteratura, 1966).

reversal that Newman will be the one forsaken, not Donna Elvira. James is not content to let the reader draw the parallels in this scene but points to them himself. In this overt authorial interpretation, there is, I believe, a failure of the young writer's trust in his readers. But the operatic analogues are in any event unmistakable and constitute another adumbration of the end of the novel.

III

William Dean Howells complained to James that in his stories previous to *The American* the promised marriages had had a way of evaporating. Indeed they did, for marriage in *The American,* as in previous works, seems hardly a consummation devoutly to be wished. A brief look at the several marriages in the novel is enough to trouble the reader at the negativism with which James presented the estate of wedlock. Most criticism, however, has tended to center only on Newman's loss of Claire.

First, with respect to the Tristrams, it takes little reading between the lines to discover how incompatible this couple is. Mrs. Tristram virtually detests her boorish husband, hankers after Newman, and, as the novel develops, suffers a good deal of jealousy over Claire's managing to take him away from her. James writes that "it was only a tenderly perverse theory of his hostess of the Avenue d'Iena [Mrs. Tristram] that he was faithless to his early friendships. She needed the theory to explain a certain moral irritation by which she was often visited; though, if this explanation was unsound, a deeper analyst than I must give the right one. Having launched our hero upon the current which was bearing him so rapidly along, she appeared but half-pleased at its swiftness" (*A,* 116–117). The "moral irritation" is plainly jealousy arising out of discontent at her marriage to a boor and out of a sense of loss represented by Newman's abandoning the confidences of her parlor *tête-à-têtes* for Claire's drawing room.

That wives detest their husbands, that marriage partners may be cold, faithless, and unsympathetic, seems to be the latent subtext of this novel. Certainly the young marquise has little use for Urbain, although she is powerless before his familial authority. Still, she, like Mrs. Tristram, sees Newman as a likely romantic diversion. She asks him, "'What do you think of my husband?'—confessing, 'It's a strange question, isn't it? But I shall ask you some stranger ones yet'" (*A,* 144). She urges him to form "an alliance, offensive or defensive," with her (*A,* 145) and repeatedly tries to induce him to take her to the Bal Bullier, the "ball in the Latin Quarter, where the students dance with their mistresses" (*A,*

202). Newman eventually comes to pity her, especially

> since she was a silly, thirstily-smiling little brunette, with a suggestion of
> an unregulated heart. The small marquise sometimes looked at him
> with an intensity too marked not to be innocent, for coquetry is more
> finely shaded. She apparently wanted to ask him something or tell him
> something; he wondered what it was. But he was shy of giving her an
> opportunity, because, if her communication bore upon the aridity of
> her matrimonial lot, he was at a loss to see how he could help her. He
> had a fancy, however, of her coming up to him some day and saying
> (after looking round behind her) with a little passionate hiss: "I know
> you detest my husband; let me have the pleasure of assuring you for
> once you are right. Pity a poor woman who is married to a clock-image
> in *papier-mâché!*" (*A,* 183).

In this passage James may be drawing upon the reputation of the French
for what Matthew Arnold had called their "lubricity." In any event, the
scene marks one more marital failure in the book.

Madame de Bellegarde, the younger, is merely an aristocratic version, however, of Madame Nioche, Noémie's mother. If Noémie is a
"*franche coquette,*" according to her father, "she comes honestly by it.
Her mother was one before her!" Madame Nioche is described as having
deceived her husband under his very nose, "year after year. I was too
stupid, and the temptation was too great. But I found her out at last. I
have only been once in my life a man to be afraid of; I know it very well:
it was in that hour! Nevertheless I don't like to think of it. I loved her—I
can't tell you how much. She was a bad woman." And in alluding
ominously to his "dark days, and my explosion with Madame Nioche,"
the old man remarks, "She was my purgatory, monsieur!" (*A,* 57).

While we may wish to consider the dubious source of these confidences about marriage, that the institution may be purgatorial for
either or both parties is implied for very nearly every couple. Certainly
it is for Claire as the wife of M. de Cintré. Married off at eighteen to an
odious but wealthy man of sixty, whose money she renounced during a
lawsuit brought by his family in which scandalous evidence tended to
incriminate him in a fraud, Claire washed her hands of the money—and
of marriage—"forever." Such is the disagreeableness of matrimony, in
this novel, that it is hard to disagree with Valentin, who says of Claire
that he does not see "why a widow should ever marry again. She has
gained the benefits of matrimony—freedom and consideration—and
she has got rid of the drawbacks. Why should she put her head into the
noose again? Her usual motive is ambition; if a man can offer her a
great position, or make her a princess or an ambassadress, she may

think the compensation sufficient" (*A*, 108).

The ultimate horror of married life is implied in the relationship of Claire's parents, the old marquis and marquise. That the wife should have murdered her husband in order to prevent his barring Claire's marriage to the odious thief Cintré translates mere marital discord, which, as we have seen, is horrific enough, into heinous criminality. Babcock's classmate, who had studied architecture in Paris and who had "had a love affair with a young woman who did not expect him to marry her" (*A*, 69), begins to sound less scandalous than the marriages that are sketched in here by James.

It may be tempting to ascribe these marital disasters to the European custom of the *mariage de convenance* in which the girl is "sold" for the dowry, or in which her title, if she is an impoverished noble, is traded for wealth. That much is suggested by Mrs. Tristram, who remarks of Claire: "She has been sold once; she naturally objects to being sold again." Newman cannot believe that "helpless [French] women are bullied into marrying men they hate." But Tristram reminds Newman, to no avail, that "a great deal of that kind goes on in New York. . . . Girls are bullied or coaxed or bribed, or all three together, into marrying nasty fellows. There is no end of that always going on in the Fifth Avenue, and other bad things besides. The Mysteries of the Fifth Avenue! Someone ought to show them up" (*A*, 79–80).

All these disastrous marriages may of course be seen as James's attempt to create the context that will prepare us for the ending (and, secondarily, to express his sympathy for the marriageable girl). But James's biographers have speculated suggestively on other possible reasons that led James to break off Newman's marriage. Leon Edel remarks that "having ruled out marriage for himself," James "found it genuinely difficult to offer it to those of his heroes with whom he was in some way identified. The marriage tie, to Henry's vision, was a tie which enslaved: and women represented a threat to man's sovereignty. . . . To accept them as mates was to court . . . disaster" (*A*, 422). But the rejection of the life of celibacy in the service of the imagination, James's choice of the so-called "high priesthood of art," seems less likely a way of putting it than a downright aversion to an institution so implicitly full of duplicity, infidelity, and heartache—both for the women and for the men.

This objection, however, is insufficient for Fred Kaplan, James's most recent biographer. In *Henry James, The Imagination of Genius: A Biography*, Kaplan has found in the author's supposed homosexuality (or at least homoeroticism) a sufficient ground for James's aversion to marriage and his dismal characterization of the institution. Kaplan's James is, by selective quotation, completely "outed" as homosexual by nature but unfortunately repressed by personal, familial, and cultural circumstance. Kaplan's James has an eye for handsome young Italian boys, for white-flanneled youth on the Oxford sward, for Paul Joukowsky and Hendrik Anderson, for Jocelyn Persse and Morton Fullerton, and so forth. But if Kaplan's James is a man "surrounded by sensuality," he is nevertheless "afraid of his own sensual nature" and therefore reluctant to face what is obvious, or at least obvious to Professor Kaplan.[10]

James's parents were of course much concerned about wedlock for their children. Henry Senior held that marriage was essential to the expression of rightly directed sexuality; and the novelist's mother told Henry Junior that she knew he would make "the most loving and loveable and happiest of husbands" and he would "thrive in every way" if he were to be more favorably disposed toward "the divine institution of marriage." Of all the children, dear Harry was the tenderest or most "sentimental" (*K*, 150, 29). Why didn't he marry?

It is Kaplan's view that James, well into his forties, still "did not think of himself as homosexual," but he "had no doubt about what men did in bed together," because "homosexual activities were widespread," however "muted, private, disguised, mostly out of the public eye." I do not know how Kaplan knows what Henry knew, but James is said to have had "a dim sense of his own homoeroticism" (*K*, 300–301) which grew apace over the years. And this key to his identity (the love that dare not speak its name) is invoked to explain the "homosexual themes" of "The Author of Beltraffio," "The Pupil," and other stories and novels.

If as Professor Kaplan remarks, "there was seemingly no end to his artistic cunning, his obsessive imaginative inventiveness, in dramatizing the interconnections between his life and his art" (*K*, 458), we are entitled to ask whether, seen through the homoerotic lens, James emerges as a more powerful novelist, a greater artist. Kaplan's psychoanalytical readings, like many of Edel's, do not inspire confidence. Edel's James had a lifelong sibling rivalry with his brother William, but Kaplan finds in Henry an "uneasy passion" *even for William* that manifests itself in "explicitly homoerotic" stories like "A Light Man." We are told that *The Aspern Papers* is a tale in which the homoerotic sensibility that allows the narrator to love Jeffrey Aspern makes him recoil from marriage to Tina—a rather ghoulish motif, it seems to me, since Aspern, if a love object, has long been deceased. Maisie, we learn, "knew everything about sexual relationships and activities" but "did not know that they

---

10 Fred Kaplan, *Henry James, The Imagination of Genius: A Biography* (New York: William Morrow, 1992), p. 107. Quotations from this volume will hereafter be indicated by *K*, in parentheses, in the text.

were immoral"—a reading that effectively robs the novel's epistemological theme of its moral content (*K*, 91, 319, 418).

Kaplan makes little of the marriage theme in *The American*, but if
we turn to marriage in more substantial fictions, Kaplan tells us that in
The Portrait of a Lady Henry's passion for William has now turned into
an allegory of revenge in which William is the model for the sinister
Gilbert Osmond and Isabel is a portrait of the novelist. I confess I do
not know what to do with Kaplan's interpretation of the most famous
osculation in all of James's fiction, the scene in which Caspar Goodwood
passionately kisses the married Isabel Archer: "Her marriage is a disaster,
a projection of the fear of marriage and erotic consummation that James
felt. Her sexuality is stifled by inner anxieties and outer circumstances,
an effective representation of James's sense of his own erotic impulses.
He would like to press against his body and lips the hard form and passionate kiss that Caspar Goodwood presses against Isabel's body and
lips, his kiss 'like a flash of lightning'" (*K*, 241–242). It is not clear to me
how Kaplan is able to read James's mind here. In writing this scene, was
James really imagining himself being kissed by a virile stud like Goodwood? Is this what homosexual novelists do when they write scenes of
heterosexual love—transpose the sexes? Moreover, are all of James's
women characters now to be understood as merely dear old Harry in
drag? And if Isabel is Henry, and Kaplan can read the novelist's mind,
why can't Kaplan name the real-life model of Goodwood, the hankered-
for object of James's supposed perverse longing? This facile biographical
device of sex-switching produces "sexual inversion" with a vengeance
and, to me at least, makes a freak of the drama of love and power, registered by both men and women readers, in the story of Isabel Archer. To
be frank about it, "James" is no more and no less to be identified with
Isabel than with Caspar Goodwood, Osmond, Henrietta Stackpole, or
Lord Warburton.

The evidence is in fact abundant that James was, over the years, extremely close to a number of women. He fell in love with Minnie
Temple, who died young; he cherished what she had meant to him for a
lifetime, and in *The Wings of the Dove* he undertook to "lay the ghost"
by "wrapping it" in "the beauty and dignity of art."[11] For a time he was a
daily companion of, and even traveled with, the unchaperoned "*she*-
novelist" Constance Fenimore Woolson, to the scandal of his sister-in-
law Alice and some others in their circle (*K*, 328). Edel even insinuated
that James had amorous evidence to hide in rushing down to Venice,

---

11 *Henry James: Autobiography*, ed. Frederick W. Dupee (Princeton: Princeton University
Press, 1983), p. 544.

after Woolson's suicide, to destroy his letters to her. Other extremely close but not sexually intimate women friends included Grace Norton, Lizzie Boott, Fanny Kemble, and Henrietta Reubell. But in treating these relationships Kaplan in my view appallingly effeminizes James, remarking about his lifelong friendship with Grace Norton: "They found a comfortable way to be spinsters together" (*K*, 401).

If James did not marry, perhaps more weight should in fact be placed upon his conviction that "Life is, in fact, a battle" in which "evil is insolent and strong; beauty enchanting but rare; goodness very apt to be weak; folly very apt to be defiant; wickedness to carry the day; imbeciles to be in great places, people of sense in small, and mankind generally unhappy" (*K*, 170). He told Grace Norton that "one's attitude toward marriage" was "part of one's attitude toward life"; and that if he married he would be guilty in his own eyes of an inconsistency: "I should pretend to think just a little better of life than I really do" (*K*, 228).[12] Yet if James never married on principle, he did idealize beauty in men and women; and this is the cause, late in his life, for his mawkish affection for Hendrik Andersen and Jocelyn Persse. But as far as overt homosexuality was concerned, James was always repulsed by it and disgusted by evident expressions of "unmanliness." When Joukowsky revealed himself as queer, he became repellent to James. Pater and the flamboyant aesthetes surrounding him were likewise repugnant. Oscar Wilde was "repulsive" and a "fatuous cad." J. A. Symonds's self-revelations were "almost insane." And when the avowed homosexual Horace Walpole propositioned James, the latter was appalled and rejected his advances.

IV

In his preface to *The American,* James conceded in 1907 that the

> way things happen is frankly not the way in which they are represented as having happened, in Paris, to my hero. . . . The great house of Bellegarde, in a word, would, I now feel, given the circumstances, given the whole of the ground, have comported itself in a manner as different as possible from the manner to which my narrative commits it. . . . They would positively have jumped then, the Bellegardes, at my rich and easy American, and not have "minded" in the least any drawback.

To the aristocrats' original crimes of mendacity and murder, that is to

---

12 Yet not having his own children, like his brother William, made him say that "I have simplified, though doubtless also (in a sense) impoverished my life in remaining unmarried" (*K*, 306–307).

say, James now added that of greed and, by way of explanation, remarked that "such accommodation of the theory of a noble indifference to the practice of a deep avidity is the real note of policy in forlorn aristocracies—and I meant of course that the Bellegardes should be virtually forlorn" (*A*, 34–36). Had he really known the French aristocracy in the 1870s, he would have had the Bellegardes accept Newman and milk him for every sou they could get.

James's feeling that he had misunderstood the deep avidity of the French nobility led him to discourse at some length, in the preface, between the "kinds," or modes, of realism and romance. I refer the reader to his extended discussion of the two, which has its own interest independent of the novel. But here I should like to argue a claim about his presentation of marriage that I have not seen sufficiently advanced in the criticism of the book: namely, that if there is in James's words an "affront to verisimilitude" in the novel, it is not in the Bellegardes' eventually rejecting Newman; it is in their initially consenting to entertain his courtship for Claire at all. Commoners have in real life of course married into the French aristocracy; that is not the point. It is *fictional* consistency in characterization that is my point. Throughout the book as he wrote it, James was at great pains to characterize Urbain and the old marquise as exceptionally proud, haughty, arrogant, mechanically polite, but intensely snobbish aristocrats. The family descend from the ninth century; they perpetuate the royalist tradition; there has never, as Valentin remarks, been a misalliance among the women. The conduct of Urbain and his mother is entirely consistent with their aristocratic caste, their familial pride, and their passion of blood—except in one respect: they weaken momentarily and countenance Newman's courtship of Claire. In my view, this lapse, the lapse from the putative hauteur of the family, is the point that fails of realism. How such a family, as James conceived them, could have permitted themselves even for a moment to suffer the lounging, slangy, socially illiterate American manufacturer of washtubs and leather goods is a nice question—one that James does not really wish us to ask. In fact, all of his prefatory remarks have the effect of leading us away from this central problem in the consistency of his characterization. I for one do not, therefore, find the Bellegardes' rejection of Newman a lapse into romance at all. Rather, the rejection redeems the novel from the fairy-tale conclusion toward which Newman's engagement was heading. The young James was closer to the truth than the elder when he told William Dean Howells in 1877 that the demands of realism required a breaking off of the match:

> *Voyons;* it would have been impossible: they would have been an im-

possible couple. . . . We are each the product of circumstances and there
are tall stone walls which fatally divide us. I have written my story from
Newman's side of the wall, and I understand so well how Mme. de
Cintré couldn't really scramble over from *her* side! If I had represented
her as doing so I should have made a prettier ending, certainly; but I
should have felt as if I were throwing a rather vulgar sop to readers who
don't really know the world and who don't measure the merit of a novel
by its correspondence to the same.[13]

James's 1907 preface nails the unmitigated "romance" of the book to
the Bellegardes' rejection of Newman. In my view this is one of the
Master's diversions; it obscures the more obvious affronts to realism. I
refer to the elaborate trappings of the Gothic mode implied by the concealed murder, the deathbed accusation, the incriminating note surfac-
ing after many years, the duel of "honor," and the incarcerated heroine,
whose imprisonment behind the walls of the Carmelite nunnery
(together with the vow of silence!) strikes the American Protestant imagination as the ultimate horror. Here is romance aplenty. Walpole,
Radcliffe, and Monk Lewis could not have done better. I point to this
whole assemblage of materials as another signal instance of James's attempt to transform the sow's ear of sentimental romanticism into the
silk purse of the "new realism." But the effort is not wholly successful,
and James was surely right in remarking that the book has a hole in it
almost large enough to sink it.

V

One other aspect of the novel's truth to life seems worthy of remark. I
refer to James's late discovery that at the time of composition he had
been "*plotting arch-romance without knowing it*" (*A*, 25; my italics).[14]
Whatever distinctions James intended in distinguishing between
"realism" and "romance," my interest here is in what appears to be
James's recovered affection for the romantic mode. In rereading the
book at the time of revision, and in discovering the novel's "emblazoned
flag of romance," he found that the novel yielded him "no interest and
no reward" comparable to the recognition of how "romantic" he had
been. By 1907, of course, the "war over realism," fought by Howells and
James, Twain and DeForest, Howe, Eggleston, and many others, had
been won. And, as the handbooks say, the realism of the 1870s had been

---

13 *Henry James: Letters*, II, 104–105.
14 See also George Knox's "Romance and Fable in James's *The American*," *Anglia*, 83 (1965),
    308–323.

succeeded by the starker naturalism of Norris, Crane, and others. There is therefore something poignant in the mature James's losing himself "at this late hour, I am bound to add, in a certain sad envy of the free play of so much unchallenged instinct" as he found in the youthful *The American.* James disclosed more than a little regret at the extent to which, throughout his career, the demands of "verisimilitude" had contained, if not restrained, his imagination. "One would like to woo back such hours of fine precipitation. They represent to the critical sense . . . the happiest season of surrender to the invoked muse and the projected fable" (*A,* 25).

But the elderly James could no longer "invent" with the free, instinctive, "thoughtless" indifference to critical questions that had characterized his youth. Nor did he really wish to. His "whole faculty" had awakened, and he could no longer write so spontaneously. Why, then, we may ask, did James not rewrite *The American* totally? Why did he not go beyond the level of the sentence, the phrase, the word—so as to eliminate the romantic elements of the book? Why did he not get rid of the Gothic banalities? In my judgment, the task was simply too formidable and would have involved not just revision but a complete rewriting, perhaps in the vein of *The Ambassadors,* perhaps under the constraints of verisimilitude that characterize the story of Lambert Strether.

The best that James could do was therefore to mount, in his preface, a defense of the novel as one of the "mixed genre" varieties and to celebrate the kind of imagination capacious enough to interfuse both modes—realism and romance. He wrote in 1907 that he doubted "if any novelist . . . ever proposed to commit himself to one kind or the other with as little mitigation as we are sometimes able to find for him." He remarked that the interest of a great writer's genius is the greatest "when he commits itself in both directions; not quite at the same time or to the same effect, of course, but by some need of performing his whole possible revolution, by the law of some rich passion in him for extremes." And in contemplating those writers of genius who had worked both the realistic and romantic veins, "the men of largest responding imagination before the human scene," he singled out Scott, Balzac, and "the coarse, comprehensive, prodigious Zola" as writers for whom "the deflexion toward either quarter has never taken place," with the effect that the writer of genius in mixed modes "remains therefore extraordinarily rich" and washes us "successively with the warm wave of the near and familiar and the tonic shock, as may be, of the far and strange" (*A,* 31).

The warm wave of the near and familiar unquestionably came through *The American* as originally written. Its source was that "high probity of observation" that made James a superb portraitist of realistic social types engaged in the matrimonial dance. But, clearly, James was enchanted by the discovery of the latent romanticism of his youthful vision, and he wished to preserve it intact—not to rewrite it out of the novel—and so to represent himself (along with Scott, Balzac, and Zola) as committed in both directions simultaneously, by the law of some rich passion in him for extremes.

Yet James did try to salvage the novel by making claims for Newman, in the preface, that neither the early nor the late form of the novel can support. These claims tend in the direction of making Newman out to be one of the supersubtle fry, a person with an "intenser consciousness." James insisted in the preface that the interest of everything is all in Newman's "vision, his conception, his interpretation: at the window of his wide, quite sufficiently wide, consciousness we are seated, from that admirable position we 'assist.' He therefore supremely matters; all the rest matters only as he feels it, treats it, meets it" (*A*, 37).

Newman surely is the focus of the book, and we are sympathetic to his plight. But this astonishing remark attempts to transform Newman and his drama into something like that of Strether in *The Ambassadors,* of whom the remark could be said to be literally true. Yet a protagonist of Strether's civility and sensitivity could never have come from Civil War battlefields, Western campfires, and the manufactory of washtubs. And certainly we cannot narrow our experience of the novel to Newman's "vision, his conception, his interpretation." If we do so, we forfeit the wit and social comedy that are directed at him—not only by the other characters but by James himself. For Newman is above all else an incarnation of what James, in his essay "Americans Abroad" (1878), called that "profound, imperturbable, unsuspectingness on the part of many Americans of the impression they produce in foreign lands." And much of the comedy of the novel occurs because "the impression produced is a good deal at variance with European circumstances" (*A*, 360).

But the elderly James, in the process of sounding and "dragging" the depths of his own creative past in order to reconstruct his intention, in using "the long pole of memory" to "fish up such fragments and relics of the submerged life and the extinct consciousness" as could be retrieved and pieced together, forgot how comic he had originally conceived Newman to be (*A*, 26). In reading the early version of the novel, that comedy clearly shines forth to us.

Propriety and Fine Perception: James's The Europeans

Henry James's *The American* (1877) offered an exquisite satire on the vulgarity of the American businessman, a sudden millionaire, elevated into a new culture icon. In consequence, the novel aroused both fierce nationalism at home and supercilious amusement abroad. James's definition in this novel of the "national type" so dismayed some of his American reviewers that James reopened the vexed question of international social relations in an essay entitled "Americans Abroad," published in *The Nation* in October 1878. The point of view James espoused in this essay is identical with that expressed in Emerson's essay "Manners," namely, that "defect in manners is usually the defect of fine perceptions."[1]

Commenting on American national self-consciousness in Europe, together with the American's complete unawareness of the impression he produces abroad, James observed:

Americans in Europe are outsiders; that is the great point, and the point thrown into relief by all zealous efforts to controvert it. As a people we are out of European society; the fact seems to us incontestable, be it regrettable or not. We are not only out of the European circle politically and geographically; we are out of it socially, and for excellent reasons. We are the only great people of the civilized world that is a pure democracy, and we are the only great people that is exclusively commercial. Add the remoteness represented by these facts to our great and painful

---

1 *Ralph Waldo Emerson: Essays and Lectures*, ed. Joel Porte (New York: Library of America, 1983), p. 523.

geographical remoteness, and it will be easy to see why to be known in Europe as an American is to enjoy an imperfect reciprocity.[2]

James himself had suffered this "imperfect reciprocity" from almost the beginning of his European expatriation, having complained that although he had gone "reeling and moaning thro' the streets" of Rome "in a fever of enjoyment," he still felt "how Europe keeps holding one at arm's length": "Sometimes I am overwhelmed with the pitifulness of this absurd want of reciprocity between Italy itself and all my rhapsodies about it."[3] That Americans *were* outsiders accounts for the frequency with which he came to stage his conflicts, in the later works, between Americans traveling abroad and expatriate Americans who had formed Europeanized colonies. In fact, James's essay "Americans Abroad" is a reply to an extremely witty article about just such a group. In "The American Colony in France," which had appeared the previous April in *The Nation*, "I. M." (Frederick Sheldon) had observed that too conspicuous on the European scene were American

> single ladies who have come to study for prima donnas or for "general culture," with no visible means of support; married ladies without their husbands (many American families, like their mercantile houses, having branches on this side); widows of the class called *vedova pericolante* in Italy, sometimes alone, sometimes with a daughter pretty, dressy, not bashful, *qui s'habille et babille*; and young girls travelling together without chaperonage or duennage, *sans puer* and all, of course, *sans reproche*; but no amount of conscious rectitude will get them the respect of other people who are accustomed to draw certain inferences from certain appearances.

Although by 1878 he had lived some time in Italy and France, James had been very little exposed to the native aristocracies of Europe. He was an unknown; they did not pay him court; the reciprocity had been imperfect. The portrait of the de Bellegardes, in *The American*, was faked, derived largely from Balzac and the Théâtre Français. He had not understood the aristocrat, as he later conceded in the preface to the New York edition of the novel. Sheldon's essay had the effect of suggesting to James the dramatic possibilities of American colonies abroad. In his subsequent fiction, he would substitute these colonies for the foreign aristocrats (whom he did not know), aristocrats who were accustomed

---

2 Henry James, "Americans Abroad," *The Nation*, 27 (October 3, 1878), 208–209.
3 *Henry James: Letters*, ed. Leon Edel (Cambridge: Harvard University Press, 1974), I, 160, 428. Hereafter, quotations from this edition of the letters of James will be cited as *HJL*, in parentheses, in the text.

to drawing certain inferences from certain appearances. Sheldon's description of the unattended girl abroad and the "Colonie Américaine," with its "idle, aimless existence," its tea and gossip, its "little gradations of rank and its *grandes dames*" who "unite in sneering at those they call 'low Americans'" is so suggestive a model for Mrs. Costello's American colony in Rome that it clearly provoked James to imagine the experience narrated in *Daisy Miller* (1879).[4]

The irritation of Europeanized Americans, in their insular little colonies, is directed at what James in "Americans Abroad" called the "profound, imperturbable, unsuspectingness on the part of many Americans of the impression they produce in foreign lands." He was capable of appreciating American "naturalness" in behavior. But he observed that "it may sometimes provoke a smile, when the impression produced is a good deal at variance with European circumstances." Of conscious and unconscious Americans in Europe, he remarked:

> The great innocence of the usual American tourist is perhaps his most general quality. He takes all sorts of forms, some of them agreeable and some the reverse, and it is probably not unfair to say that by sophisticated Europeans it is harshly interpreted. They waste no time in hair-splitting; they set it down once for all as very vulgar. It may be added that there are a great many cases in which this conclusion hardly seems forced.[5]

Christopher Newman had been one such case; Daisy Miller was about to be another: a conclusion as to their vulgarity seems hardly forced. But what James's subtle art asks us to do is to split hairs on precisely this point: to weigh the unsuspecting innocence of Americans traveling abroad against the conviction of Europeans (and Europeanized Americans) that innocence counts for less than rigid adherence to the custom of the country. And to drive home the point to European readers, he reversed the situation in *An International Episode* (1879), a nouvelle in which the "unsuspectingness" of a pair of Englishmen in America is made the point of his satire.

I

James's intention, in writing *An International Episode*, was more complex than the exchange of essays in *The Nation* might suggest. In fact, *An International Episode* is partly a response to Laurence Oliphant's little

---

4 I. M. (Frederick Sheldon), "The American Colony in France," *The Nation*, 26 (April 18, 1878), 258.
5 James, "Americans Abroad," pp. 208–209.

satire on American manners in New York City called *The Tender Recollections of Irene Macgillicuddy*, which was serialized in *Blackwoods' Magazine*, published in book form, and reviewed by James for *The Nation* on May 30, 1878. It dealt with what Oliphant believed to be the chief feature of New York fashion, "the eagerness and energy displayed by marriageable maidens in what is vulgarly called 'hooking' a member of the English aristocracy." James was exasperated with Oliphant's treatment of the *haut monde* of New York, but he felt that *Irene Macgillicuddy* did disclose that "it is possible, after all, to write tales of 'American society.'" He concluded that perhaps there were American social types, perhaps there was a good deal of local color, and "a considerable field for satire." But why, he asked,

> should it be left to the cold and unsympathetic stranger to deal with these things? Why does not native talent take them up—anticipate the sneers of foreign irony, take the wind from its sails and show us, with the force of real familiarity, both the good and the evil that are to be found in Fifth Avenue and on Murray Hill? Are we then so dependent upon foreign labor that it must be left to the English to write even our "society stories"?[6]

Clearly not.

In *An International Episode* James rewrote Oliphant's story from an American viewpoint. The tale comes down to an American girl's rejection of marriage to an English lord. English readers who had taken pleasure in James's satire on the American girl in *Daisy Miller* bristled at this reversal of the expected. Mrs. F. H. Hill, whose husband edited the London *Daily News*, protested in print "against the manners of Lord Lambeth and Mr. Percy Beaumont . . . being received as typical of the manners of English gentlemen. As individual characters we take them on their merits and judge them accordingly, but true as types they certainly are not." She also took occasion to criticize the manners of James's English ladies: "Perhaps he does not consider that English manners are pretty, and we have no doubt that he has had ample means of judging."[7]

This last cut James could not ignore. It insinuated that he had used his entrée into English society to gather material for satire. Having met Mrs. Hill in the drawing rooms of London, James broke a long-standing habit of ignoring reviewers and denied to her, in a letter of March 21, 1879, that he had meant to make "a résumé of my view of English man-

---

6 Henry James, Review of *The Tender Recollections of Irene Macgillicuddy*, in *The Nation*, 26 (May 30, 1878), 357.

7 Quoted in Howells Daniels, "Henry James and 'An International Episode,'" *Bulletin of the British Association for American Studies*, 1 (1960), 26.

ners. My dear Mrs. Hill—the idea is fantastic!" He defended the accuracy of his characterization of Lord Lambeth and Beaumont; and of
his English women he remarked:

> The two ladies are a picture of a special case, and they are certainly not
> an over-charged one. They were very determined their manners should
> not be nicer; it would have quite defeated the point they wished to
> make, which was that it didn't at all suit them that a little unknown
> American girl should marry their coveted kinsman.

What is extraordinary about James's exchange with Mrs. Hill is the
intensity of his reaction. James's letters are often marked by "the mere
twaddle of graciousness," but here he is at white heat: "One may make
figures and figures without intending generalizations—generalizations
of which I have a horror. I make a couple of English ladies doing a disagreeable thing—*cela c'est vu:*—excuse me!—and forthwith I find myself
responsible for a representation of English manners!" He complained of
the bother of being an American when English novelists of manners like
Trollope, Thackeray, and Dickens "were free to draw all sorts of unflat-
tering English pictures, by the thousand. But if I make a single one, I am
forthwith in danger of being confronted with a criminal conclusion—and sinister rumors reach me as to what I think of English
society."[8] And he expressed considerable annoyance that English readers
like Mrs. Hill saw no harm in his pictures of disagreeable Americans,
saw in fact a "natural fitness" in them.

From the violence of his reaction it is clear that this episode considerably angered James. It also induced in him a great deal of anxiety
over the extent to which the English reading public might react nega-
tively to his satiric portraits of them. He feared, in short, the loss of his
audience. James told his mother that he had been

> very delicate; but I shall keep off dangerous ground in future. It is an
> entirely new sensation for them (the people here) to be (at all delicately)
> ironised or satirised, from the American point of view, and they don't at
> all relish it. Their conception of the normal in such relation is that the
> satire should be all on their side against the Americans; and I suspect
> that if one were to push this a little further one would find that they are
> extremely sensitive.[9]

James's desire to defend the American against the European sneer

---

8 *Selected Letters of Henry James,* ed. Leon Edel (London: Rupert Hart-Davis, 1956), pp.
106–107.
9 See *The Letters of Henry James,* ed. Percy Lubbock (New York: Scribner's, 1920), I, 68. Extremely sensitive they certainly were, but no more so than the outraged Americans who

had the effect, then, in *An International Episode*, of risking the loss of his English audience. Yet how to take away from the Oliphants our American "society stories" without at the same time risking the favor of his American audience as well? *The American* and *Daisy Miller* had come dangerously close to that edge. Clearly a balance had to be struck, a perspective had to be achieved, a vantage point discovered, from which the folly of "unsuspectingness" in both American and European travelers could be posed. James's conclusion was the neutral ground of cosmopolitanism: it offered much safer footing than the "dangerous ground" on which he had been standing. In *The Europeans* he found the safe footing he sought.

II

The American, Daisy Miller, and *An International Episode* had all, in the failures of their various love matches, veered toward the tragic. (In fact, they are melodramas.) For tragedies, James told his editor, William Dean Howells, "arrest my attention more" and "say more to my imagination." But Howells and the public did not want another tale of an "evaporated marriage" (*HJL*, I, 105), another New World defeat at the hands of the Old. Consequently James promised Howells a four-number hymeneal comedy for the *Atlantic Monthly,* "a very joyous little romance" set in Boston in the 1830s.

The scenario, as James described it to Howells, provides an interesting commentary on his original intention and suggests how extensively he was to recast *The Europeans* in the process of actually writing it. He wished to satirize some features of New England, but he armed himself against criticism by setting the tale a half-century in the past:

> I shall probably develop an idea that I have, about a genial, charming youth of a Bohemianish pattern, who comes back from foreign parts into the midst of a mouldering and ascetic old Puritan family or his kindred (some imaginary locality in New England 1830) and by his gayety and sweet audacity smooths out their rugosities, heals their dyspepsia and dissipates their troubles. *All* the women fall in love with

---

could not see the American girl in the portrait of Daisy Miller. As James was to observe, through Captain Lovelock the next year in *Confidence* (1879): "You know the Americans are so deucedly thinskinned—they always bristle up if you say anything against their institutions. The English don't care a rap for what you say—they've got a different sort of temper, you know. With the Americans I'm deuced careful—I never breathe a word about anything. While I was over there I went in for being complimentary. I laid it on thick, and I found they would take all I could give them. I didn't see much of their institutions after all; I went in for seeing the people. Some of the people were charming—upon my soul, I was surprised at some of the people." See *Confidence* (London: Macmillan, 1921), pp. 200–201.

him (and he with them—his amatory powers are boundless); but even for a happy ending he can't marry them all. But he marries the prettiest, and from a romantic quality of Christian charity, produces a picturesque imbroglio (for the sake of the picturesque I shall play havoc with the New England background of 1830!) under cover of which the other maidens pair off with the swains who have hitherto been starved out: after which the beneficent cousin departs for Bohemia (*with his bride, oh yes!*) in a vaporous rosy cloud, to scatter new benefactions over man—and especially, woman-kind!—(Pray don't mention this stuff to any one. It would be meant, roughly speaking, as a picture of the conversion of a dusty, dreary domestic circle to epicureanism. But I may be able to make nothing of it. The merit would be in the amount of color I should be able to infuse into it.) But I shall give you it, or its equivalent, by November next (*HJL*, I, 106).

What James actually sent Howells was "its equivalent"; the tale is considerably different from the story here projected. It comes down to the Baroness Münster, whose morganatic marriage to Prince Adolph of Silberstadt-Schreckenstein is about to be dissolved, and her brother Felix Young, a penniless artist with a magazine commission for an illustrated newspaper, voyaging to America to seek their fortune among their Boston cousins, the Wentworths. Eugenia, the baroness, hopes to forestall her divorce until she can secure a rich husband in America. Robert Acton almost proposes marriage to her but does not, and she returns to Europe to hold the prince to his vows. Felix, however, wins the hand of Gertrude, and the novel concludes with their marriage and three other weddings as well: her sister Charlotte's marriage to the Unitarian minister Mr. Brand; her brother Clifford Wentworth's marriage to Lizzie, Robert Acton's sister; and Acton's reported marriage to "a particularly nice young girl."[10]

As described in the scenario, the novel was to have contrasted epicureanism and puritanism. But the new tale became instead what James called a "study" of the differences between cultural thinness and thickness; between spontaneity and the inhibitions produced by a rigid moral code; between openness to the opportunities of life and a narrow sense of duty; between the bright and the grey views of life. As embodied, the contrasts inhere in the opposition between Europe and America; between Felix and Eugenia; and between Gertrude and the Wentworths. The change in intention arose from the unresolved issues

---

10 Henry James, *The Europeans: A Sketch*, in *Henry James: Novels, 1871–1880*, ed. William T. Stafford (New York: Library of America, 1983), p. 1038. Hereafter, quotations from this work will be cited as *E*, in parentheses, in the text.

we have traced in James's previous essays and novels with respect to the "unsuspectingness" of the foreigner seeking to "hook" a well-placed mate. It also grew out of James's analysis of the social conditions of "provincial" New England in the 1830s and 1840s, as he researched the American Notebooks for his biography *Hawthorne* (1879).

Even so, the full contrast fails to balance. *The Europeans* is set wholly in Boston and its rural environs; there are no complementary pictures of European life. It is largely in Eugenia that the richness of Old World culture and the complexity of its social existence are suggested. If the American landscape "seemed to be all foreground" and the "foreground . . . inferior to the *plans reculés*," Europe is only by implication more picturesque, the "middle distance" setting off the further ranges. If the public coachmen in Boston wear straw hats, we are reminded in passing that "at Silberstadt Madame Münster had had liveries of yellow and crimson" (*E*, 904). If Boston reminded her of "a fair in a provincial town," she "found herself alternately smiling and shrinking." American manners are conspicuous by their general absence. To Eugenia it is "anomalous" that "at the hour at which ladies should come out for an airing and stroll past a hedge of pedestrians, holding their parasols askance," there are "no indications of this custom" in Boston (*E*, 884). Felix tells Eugenia that the Wentworth style has "the *ton* of the golden age" (*E*, 902), but she wishes to know whether they have nothing golden but their *ton*. This reminds us of Christof Wegelin's observation that if New England is a place where morality is flaunted and wealth concealed, in Europe the reverse is true.

Mr. Wentworth and his family are convinced that "this country is superior in many respects" to England and Holland (*E*, 907), and if Eugenia is the wife of a prince, Mr. Wentworth is satisfied to observe that "we are all princes here" (*E*, 915). Yet New England life is bare, colorless, and lacking in romance (Gertrude has sought escape in the *Arabian Nights* when Felix mysteriously materializes before her), while Europe is by implication rich in picturesque colors softened by the passage of time. Felix holds her enthralled with gay tales of having played with a band of provincial musicians and performed in a troupe of strolling actors. His account of his European life transports her into "a fantastic world; she seemed to herself to be reading a romance that came out in daily numbers" (*E*, 937). Imagining the world that Hawthorne must have known, James creates a family of New Englanders who lack the forms of civilized existence. They do not know how to take compliments, for example, except with the silence "of modesty and expectation." The behavior of the Europeans, however, is marked by the civility and *politesse* of an old civilization. They are smooth.

But it would be a mistake to assume that in *The Europeans* James wholly abandoned his gentle "ironisation" of Europeans so as to avoid losing his audience abroad. Nor is his point the safer ridicule of American cultural thinness, which had got him into trouble at home. Setting the novel in a remote and bygone era, transposing it into an historical romance, partly delivered him from the ire of contemporary critics who would defend the current state of the American culture. *The Europeans* does not fully enlist our sympathies with one side or the other. When James wrote to his mother of moving to safer ground, he meant the high ground of cosmopolitanism, from which those damaging charges of nationalism could not be heard. No, indeed. To oversimplify in such a way is to make the mistake of Oscar Cargill, who claimed that the ideal of "concentrated patriotism"[11] which led James to write *The American* was "still burning with white intensity" when he wrote *The Europeans,* so that the result was a novel in which "a pair of 'corrupt' Europeans, brother and sister, are immersed in an American experience, purifying in inverse ratio to their 'cosmopolitanism.'"[12] Nothing could be farther from the truth. At least two considerations need to be examined if we are to understand the complexity of James's treatment of the international theme in this work: the "Europeanism" of Eugenia and Felix, and the differences in their ways of looking at life.

III

Eugenia and Felix are not identified with any specific country. Both are utterly deracinated from any *patria* or native land. They are children of Americans; their father was born in Sicily, but of American parents; their mother was a Bostonian. Felix was born in France, Eugenia in Vienna. Felix, in fact, admits to having lived in "every city in Europe" (*E,* 897). They are nephew and niece of Mr. Wentworth, and their American relatives constitute the familial basis for their visit to the United States. It is not merely because James needs a motive to get them to Boston that he makes them the children of Americans. His aesthetic intent goes beyond that. That they are the children of "Europeanized Americans" constitutes the significant element in James's obfuscation of their national origins. Their Europeanness is not of a provincial variety. T. S. Eliot, another expatriate, once observed that "it is the final perfection, the consummation of an American, to become, not an Englishman, but a European—something which no born European, no person

11 James, "Occasional Paris" (1877), in *Portraits of Places* (London: Macmillan, 1883), p. 75.
12 Oscar Cargill, *The Novels of Henry James* (New York: Macmillan, 1961), p. 62.

of any European nationality, can become."[13] The Europeanizing process requires the deliberate abandonment of attitudes, values, and manners that are distinctively national to the countries where they originate: France, England, Italy, and so on. It requires, in other words, the erasure from one's character and conduct of whatever might conceivably be called provincial. (Provincialism, it is well to remember, was, according to James, Hawthorne's principal attribute. This remark led the critic Wentworth Higginson, conceivably the model for Mr. Wentworth, to retort that American literature needed more such provincial writers.)[14] "If you have lived about," James wrote in the same year *The Europeans* was published, you

> have lost that sense of the absoluteness and the sanctity of the habits of your fellow-patriots which once made you so happy in the midst of them. You have seen that there are a great many *patriae* in the world and that each of these is filled with excellent people for whom the local idiosyncrasies are the only thing that is not rather barbarous. There comes a time when one set of customs, wherever it may be found, grows to seem to you about as provincial as another.[15]

James's preoccupation, in this passage and in the novels of this period, is with the conflict that arises when Americans encounter incomprehensible European customs, reject them, or imperfectly assimilate them; and when "Europeanized Americans" return to a provincial America incapable of appreciating their denationalized Old World manners. "You are a foreigner of some sort," says Gertrude, trying to fix Felix's identity more specifically. But James is not interested in our understanding Felix or Eugenia in terms of a national provincialism; he wishes us to understand them as simply foreign, foreign to Boston, as intruders with a disturbing and differing view of the world. In this sense "Europe" constitutes a metaphor for the romance of the strange and far away, the rich and ambiguous, the mysterious and indefinite: "Of some sort—yes; I suppose so. But who can say of what sort? I don't think we have ever had occasion to settle the question. You know there are people like that. About their country, their religion, their profession, they can't tell" (*E*, 897). The Europeanness of these two strangers prevents us from establishing a provincial identity for them as French, German, or Italian.

13 T. S. Eliot, "On Henry James," in *The Question of Henry James*, ed. F. W. Dupee (New York: Henry Holt, 1945), p. 109.
14 Wentworth Higginson so consistently criticized James's preference for European social forms, in reviews and essays, that James complained to Howells that the "Higginsonian fangs" had bespattered his "gore" throughout the pages of many American periodicals.
15 James, *Portraits of Places*, pp. 75–76.

James's technique is thus a way of reinforcing the mystery of personality, one of the principal themes in Hawthorne's best work, as James remarked in his biography. Hawthorne, as James observed there, cared for the deeper psychology.

Both Eugenia and Felix, who suddenly and mysteriously appear before the Wentworths, seek their fortunes, one literally and the other figuratively. In the contrast between them James not only establishes the relationship between fineness of manners and fineness of perception but also embodies in Felix the proper norm of social and moral conduct, as he understood it. It is surprising, then, that so acute a critic as Richard Poirier has argued vigorously for the centrality of Eugenia in *The Europeans*. He observes that her exclusion from the Wentworth society at the end of the novel, far from being a just and satisfying defeat of her selfish calculations, is a trenchant criticism of the angularity and in-sularity of a society that cannot assimilate her. [16] Eugenia is without question an intelligent and stylish addition to the unadorned circle of the Wentworths. But, at the same time, to emphasize her story over-much is to neglect the moral dimension in James's drama of "finely mingled motives." The meaning of her "rejection" (in fact she returns to Europe voluntarily) can only be clarified by discriminating between her view of the relation between morals and manners and that of her brother.

Eugenia has come to America to size up her cousins, to estimate, in terms of their wealth, her chance to make a better situation for herself if her morganatic marriage fails. She is ambitious, even cynical in the can-dor with which she weighs the Wentworths in the future she plans for herself. Felix too has come in search of his fortune, but for him fortune is a metaphor for the wealth that experience brings. Eugenia insists on the Wentworths' being rich; that is all she insists on. Felix agrees that it will be pleasanter if they are rich, but he counts upon their being "powerful, and clever, and friendly, and elegant, and interesting, and generally delightful!" (*E*, 882). If Eugenia has an eye on the main chance, Felix has his eyes open to bright possibilities of every kind. He has accompanied Eugenia to America, at her suggestion, in search of opportunities for enlarged consciousness, freely receptive to impressions and experiences as they open up before him. Felix does a good deal of clowning, which continually exasperates the baroness, and to some readers he has seemed a light vehicle for the serious statement about manners and morals which James intended him to communicate. Full of

---

16 Richard Poirier, *The Comic Sense of Henry James* (New York: Oxford University Press, 1967), p. 123. Hereafter, quotations from this work will be cited as *CS*, in parentheses, in the text.

high spirits and comic wit, he is often called frivolous and consents so to be described. But the vocabulary of those who characterize him in this way is inadequate to account for Felix's sense of delight: he finds life worth living. If Eugenia thinks of America as "horrible," Felix thinks it "comical," "delightful," "charming." If she thinks American girls too visible in public, too bold, and devoid of polite manners, he cannot see too much of them, is charmed by their loveliness, and thinks them "just right." The difference between their conceptions of the world and be-tween their attitudes toward the "proprieties" is rather like that between Urbain and Valentin de Bellegarde in *The American*, and James's rhetorical strategy always is to manipulate the reader's sympathies in favor of Felix.

The spectacle of Eugenia's attempt to adapt herself to the Wentworth society is rich in wit; it cuts both ways, James "ironising" the calculated artifice she employs as well as the studied plainness of New England so-cial life, which renders her arts ineffectual. Her behavior is an utter enigma to everyone. That Mr. Wentworth "was paralyzed and bewil-dered by her foreignness" (*E*, 929) is a measure of the dazzling figure she cuts in her new situation. The absence of any basis for comparison in estimating her gives Eugenia "a feeling of almost illimitable power" (*E*, 924), and she permits herself an extravagance of style stupefying to the Wentworth household. She decorates the cottage that Mr. Went-worth gives her with *portières* suspended in doorways, wax candles dis-tributed about in unexpected places, and "anomalous draperies" dis-posed over the arms of sofas and backs of chairs. Charlotte and Gertrude are bewildered by Eugenia's "copious provision of the element of costume": "India shawls suspended, curtain-wise, in the parlor door, and curious fabrics, corresponding to Gertrude's metaphysical vision of an opera-cloak, tumbled about in the sitting places." The effect of so "obtrusive" a "distribution of her wardrobe" almost provokes Charlotte to offer to help Eugenia to "put her superfluous draperies away." But on Gertrude the effect of Eugenia's "most ingenious," "most romantic in-tention" is to awaken her to the charm of conscious art as a means of enriching an otherwise colorless existence. "'What is life, indeed, without curtains?' she secretly asked herself," and James comically remarks of her dawning perception that she had been "leading hitherto an existence singularly garish and totally devoid of festoons." What is significant here is not the actual properties of Eugenia's scenic design. Indeed, the India shawl, the curious fabrics, and the "remarkable band of velvet, covered with coarse, dirty-looking lace" (*E*, 921) are actually rather pathetic elements in Eugenia's closet of stage props. What is sig-nificant is Gertrude's awakening "metaphysical vision," her perception (it is an insight of the imagination) of the meaning of Eugenia's refinement of nature, her rearrangement of the world in terms of artful design, a response to life which James nearly always associates with Europe. (This association is evident, for example, in Mary Garland's having been "brought up to think a great deal of 'nature' and nature's innocent laws," in *Roderick Hudson,* only to discover, through Rowland Mallet's instruction, "the need of man's spirit to refine upon them," a discovery that produces in Mary, as well as in Gertrude, "a well-nigh tragic tension."[17])

This tension involving nature and art provoked by Eugenia's flamboyant style also reminds us of the effect on Christopher Newman of the exquisite manners of Claire de Cintré, whom Eugenia, at her most refined, resembles. Newman wonders where Claire's good manners end and her sincerity begins. Can the art of social expression, polite manners, be an instrument of insincerity? Newman worries about it. Although the reader never doubts the perfect correspondence, in *The American,* between Claire's inner intention and the outward form of her manners, the Wentworths are rightly troubled about Eugenia. She is bored; she is openly irritated at a manner of life so unadorned that it provides her no materials to work with. But Gertrude's awakening instinct for the difference between Eugenia's social and their moral reality allows her to interpret Eugenia to her baffled cousins. Gertrude's first discovery occurs at the moment of their introduction, when Eugenia remarks on the Wentworth girls' "handsomeness." This compliment pleases Gertrude, though she cannot say why, for she knows it to be untrue. Later she perceives that flattery has been employed; however "untrue," it creates beneficence, a good feeling which can never be actualized in the airless atmosphere of absolute truth.

Eugenia acts unconsciously on the assumed value of flattery, and it irritates her to discover that these Americans do not also recognize the value, even the necessity, as one of the graces of civilized living, of an occasional fib spoken with a fine intention. When Robert Acton introduces her to his mother, an invalid steeped in the high-minded essays of Emerson, Eugenia declares that Robert has told her a great deal about his mother: "Oh, he talks of you as you would like, . . . as such a son *must* talk of such a mother!" The remark is a graceful one; it is meant to please. But it simply is not true. Acton has never even mentioned his mother. Mrs. Acton

> sat gazing; this was part of Madame Münster's "manner." But Robert
> Acton was gazing too, in vivid consciousness that he had barely men-

---

17 Henry James, *Roderick Hudson,* ed. Leon Edel (New York: Harper and Row, 1960), p. 224.

tioned his mother to their brilliant guest. He never talked of this still maternal presence—a presence refined to such delicacy that it had almost resolved itself, with him, simply into the subjective emotion of gratitude. And Acton rarely talked of his emotions. The Baroness turned her smile toward him, and she instantly felt that she had been observed to be fibbing. She had struck a false note. But who were these people to whom such fibbing was not pleasing? If they were annoyed, the Baroness was equally so; and after the exchange of a few civil inquiries and low-voiced responses she took leave of Mrs. Acton (*E*, 953).

In this passage one may observe James's double point of view, his sympathy with both positions. To Mrs. Acton, who knows that her son is not the kind to speak gracefully about his mother, Eugenia's flattery has passed over into mendacity. But the passage also implies a judgment on a society so absolutist in its respect for "truth" that graceful but meaningless civilities are unacceptable. It is one of those many instances in the novel where a conflict arises "between people who believe in manners and artfulness, which often pass for deception, and those who are suspicious of them." Insofar as the angular puritan community cannot appreciate the good intention beneath the slight prevarication, James directs our sympathies to Eugenia. But why her art does not count for much in Boston deserves fuller consideration, particularly in the light of Poirier's claim that "at the end of the novel James's compassion and admiration are given more to Eugenia than to her American friends" (*CS*, 115, 144).

To the extent that Eugenia may rectify what James believed to be an active deficiency in the culture of New England, she is a positive force in the novel. She brings color, civility, charm, and conscious art to a community that is plain, dull, and barren of sophistication and grace. Or rather, she can have this effect if she wishes to. But Eugenia's manners are often used to conceal her true feelings. Even worse, her studied politeness is often intended to be impolite, suggesting a failure of feeling on her part, "a defect of fine perceptions," a radical incapacity to sympathize with the condition of a foreign society into which she herself is the intruder. This is clear in the perplexity of the Wentworth girls over how to show all proper attention to Madame Münster without, at the same time, being intrusive. These untutored American girls show a nice perception of the problem of whether or not to visit the distinguished guest living across the road. Eugenia has no such reciprocal perception of the significance of American customs, like that of "dropping in": "'One goes into your house as into an inn—except that there are no servants rushing forward,' she said to Charlotte. And she added that that was very charming. Gertrude explained to her sister that she meant just the reverse; she didn't like it at all." Gertrude gradually grows conscious of Eugenia's trick of the insulting remark balanced by the insincere compliment. Without any knowledge of the world, however, they have no way of penetrating to the real significance of Eugenia's attitudes. "Charlotte inquired why she should tell an untruth, and Gertrude answered that there was probably some very good reason for it which they should discover when they knew her better. 'There can surely be no good reason for telling an untruth,' said Charlotte. 'I hope she does not think so'" (*E*, 924–925).

In general, Eugenia's imperial manners on occasions like this are meant to express by indirection an upper-class derogation of a provincial style that she feels to be *infra dignitatem*. Her behavior is a means of holding the Wentworth girls at arm's length, of preventing intimacy, of asserting (through irony) her intellectual superiority, of preventing them from understanding her even while she is irritated at not being perfectly understood. In this sense one may agree with Poirier that Eugenia's manners constitute the means by which the baroness protects her "own inner freedom." But it is not clear in what sense her manners "allow others the least difficulty and the least fear in fully expressing themselves" (*CS*, 115). The opposite is in fact true: Eugenia's strategy prevents the Wentworths from fully expressing their wish for a nearer relation to so distinguished a guest, of yielding to the very *voix du sang* that Eugenia has invoked in throwing herself on the charity of her American cousins. As James observes through Marcellus Cockerel in "The Point of View" (1882), "As for manners, there are bad manners everywhere, but an aristocracy is bad manners organized. (I don't mean that they may not be polite among themselves, but they are rude to every one else.)"[18] In his search for "reciprocity," the novelist had personally suffered that kind of rudeness. In this novel he gets, with Eugenia, his innings.

Eugenia fails to make her fortune in the New World because, for all her potential for graceful conduct, she is not above using her social arts to realize a doubtful matrimonial ambition. Robert Acton declines to propose because he fears that she is not fully honest, that her gift for the polite fib conceals something more deeply deceitful. His intuition is accurate. For she tells Acton that she has renounced her marriage (and by implication is therefore free to accept his proposal) while she tells Felix that she has not done so. It is not possible for the reader to know which

---

18 Henry James, "The Point of View," in *The Complete Tales of Henry James*, ed. Leon Edel (Philadelphia: Lippincott, 1962–1964), IV, 515.

of these statements is the truth; and probably it does not matter. But it is inescapably true that Eugenia is lying to one of them and, whichever it is, the lie is too serious to warrant her enjoying our full esteem. In fact, James's handling of the point of view, so sophisticated and self-effacing in the later novels, is nowhere more intrusive than in his directing us to a negative response, even while he seeks to soften the judgment which must be made upon Eugenia's cynical opportunism:

> As I have had the honor of intimating, she had come four thousand miles to seek her fortune; and it is not to be supposed that after this great effort she could neglect any apparent aid to advancement. It is my misfortune that in attempting to describe in a short compass the deportment of this remarkable woman I am obliged to express things rather brutally. I feel this to be the case, for instance, when I say that she had primarily detected such an aid to advancement in the person of Robert Acton, but that she had afterwards remembered that a prudent archer always has a second bowstring (*E*, 976).

Clifford Wentworth, the callow son who has been rusticated from Harvard for drinking, is Eugenia's conception of a second bowstring. In her final breach of good faith, and taste, she undertakes to make Clifford, the heir to the Wentworth fortune, fall in love with her—under the pretext of civilizing him, of giving him a set of polite manners. In presenting Eugenia's motivation in this case, James is extraordinarily subtle; he is under the difficult obligation of making her motive clear without suggesting that she is vulgar, of putting us in possession of essential fact without at the same time suggesting that this remarkable woman is disgusting:

> Eugenia was a woman of finely-mingled motive, and her intentions were never sensibly gross. She had a sort of esthetic ideal for Clifford which seemed to her a disinterested reason for taking him in hand. It was very well for a fresh-colored young gentleman to be ingenuous; but Clifford, really, was crude. With such a pretty face he ought to have prettier manners. She would teach him that, with a beautiful name, the expectation of a large property, and, as they said in Europe, a social position, an only son should know how to carry himself (*E*, 976).

It is part of the beauty of James's characterization that while Eugenia is an adventuress, we cannot call her simply that. While she does scheme at "hooking" young Clifford (she is thirty-three), she yet has a disinterested social ideal which, in any case, is worth his realizing.

The fullness of James's characterization of Eugenia thus prevents the novel from becoming the sinister melodrama it otherwise might be.

Nevertheless she fails, even at hooking Clifford. Why she should have regarded her expedition to America a failure, James observes with a fine irony, is not exactly apparent, since "she had been treated with the highest distinction for which allowance had been made in American institutions." But under the circumstances her social powers, in the severely truthful democratic milieu, are ineffectual; and she chooses to return to the Old World. Her irritation, James observed, came at bottom from the sense

> that the social soil on this big, vague continent was somehow not adapted for growing those plants whose fragrance she especially inclined to inhale and by which she liked to see herself surrounded—a species of vegetation for which she carried a collection of seedlings, as we may say, in her pocket. She found her chief happiness in the sense of exerting a certain power and making a certain impression; and now she felt the annoyance of a rather wearied swimmer who, on nearing shore, to land, finds a smooth straight wall of rock when he had counted upon a clean firm beach. Her power, in the American air, seemed to have lost its prehensile attributes; the smooth wall of rock was insurmountable (*E*, 996).

IV

If for Eugenia the American shore represents a solid rock wall, for Felix it is a smooth sandy beach leading up to a spacious sunny house of charming hospitality. He is hardly the amorous figure that James sketched in the scenario, but he is charming, gracious, good-tempered, and generous. In the dialectic of the novel's concern with conduct and values, Felix Young immediately suggests both youth and happiness. In this we have a vestige of the Hawthornean technique; our readiness to accept its allegorical basis will make Felix's didactic function much more accessible. Felix has a vivid moral sense, he joyfully affirms life (here Hawthorne's gloom is turned on its head), and he has a sophisticated and adaptable mode of behavior. These qualities create a paradigm of the ideal relation, as James understood it, between manners and morals. James's characterization of Felix thus constitutes, in its way, an antithesis to that of Eugenia:

> Never was a nature more perfectly fortunate. It was not a restless, apprehensive, ambitious spirit, running a race with the tyranny of fate, but a temper so unsuspicious as to put Adversity off her guard, dodging and evading her with the easy, natural motion of a wind-shifted flower.

Felix extracted entertainment from all things, and all his faculties—his imagination, his intelligence, his affections, his senses—had a hand in the game (*E*, 921–922).

He is innocent of precisely those "moral lapses" and "social oversights" that alienate the community from Eugenia. If it is he who suggests, for instance, that Eugenia civilize Clifford Wentworth, Felix is manifestly preoccupied with "the work of redemption." He is certainly not prepared for the construction Eugenia places on his suggestion, and the idea of her trying to ensnare Clifford in *matrimony* suddenly looms before him: "The idea in prospect had seemed of the happiest, but in operation it made him a trifle uneasy. 'What if Eugenia—what if Eugenia'—he asked himself softly; the question dying away in his sense of Eugenia's undetermined capacity" (*E*, 963). The worst we can say of Felix is that he has an insufficient appreciation of the capacity of human beings for what Hawthorne called the bosom serpent of egotism.

Yet it is Felix who first begins to wake Gertrude from the trance she has been in, to open her up to the delight of self-knowledge, to the naturalness of being herself. It is Felix who guides Mr. Brand to a conscious recognition that he really loves and ought to marry Charlotte, not Gertrude. And it is Felix who reveals to Mr. Wentworth the secret that joy and a sense of duty may coexist harmoniously. This is manifestly illustrated in Felix's discreet courtship. He knows that to take advantage of his position as a guest in the home of his uncle, in order to make love to Gertrude, would be a breach of good conduct. For this reason he behaves toward her with extraordinary circumspection—in utter contrast to the hooking Eugenia. When he can no longer resist declaring his love, he approaches Gertrude's father to ask for her hand and to apologize for his impropriety. His interview with Mr. Wentworth is one of the most scintillating bits of social comedy in the novel, particularly in Felix's attempt to absolve himself of his presuming to court her:

> "Have you never suspected it, dear uncle?" Felix inquired. "Well that proves how discreet I have been. Yes, I thought you wouldn't like it."
>
> "It is very serious, Felix," said Mr. Wentworth.
>
> "You think it's an abuse of hospitality!" exclaimed Felix, smiling again.
>
> "Of hospitality?—an abuse?" his uncle repeated very slowly.
>
> "That is what Felix said to me," said Charlotte, conscientiously.
>
> "Of course you think so; don't defend yourself!" Felix pursued. "It *is* an abuse, obviously; the most I can claim is that it is perhaps a pardonable one. I simply fell head over heels in love; one can hardly help that. . ." (*E*, 1025).

Felix's belief that he has been guilty of bad manners is utterly lost on Mr. Wentworth, who is fixated on the moral gravity of a marriage proposal. He is incapable of understanding Felix's unexpected offer in light of the postulated social offense he is supposed to have felt.

The marriage of Felix and Gertrude, as F. W. Dupee has observed, resolves a potentially disastrous situation in the Wentworth household.[19] For at the beginning of the narrative Gertrude is on the brink of a profound rebellion against her puritanical world for reasons which she cannot understand. In Felix's educating Gertrude to a totally new way of looking at life, one of the happiest configurations of the plot is achieved. It grows out of Felix's definition of the distinctive defect of New England society: "There is something the matter with them; they have some melancholy memory or some depressing expectation" (*E*, 902–903). He wishes that "they were not all so sad" (*E*, 923). He tells Gertrude that he believes them to be too unhappy and to take "a painful view of life, as one may say" (*E*, 935). He adjures her to enjoy life, which may be considerably different from giving parties, going to the theatre, reading novels, and keeping late hours, her naive view of "enjoying oneself."

> "I don't think it's what one does or doesn't do that promotes enjoyment," her companion answered. "It is the general way of looking at life."
>
> "They look at it as a discipline—that's what they do here. I have often been told that."
>
> "Well, that's very good. But there is another way," added Felix, smiling: "to look at it as an opportunity."
>
> "An opportunity—yes," said Gertrude. "One would get more pleasure that way" (*E*, 936).

This conversation constitutes the turning point in Gertrude's moral transformation. It frees her to be herself, to express freely her love of the strange, the mysterious, the formal, and the decorative. The Wentworths had described her as "frivolous," but "spontaneous" or "natural" might be a fairer term. Her new perception leads Gertrude far beyond the Reverend Mr. Brand, who tries to get her back onto what he believes is the straight and narrow. (In his attempt to manipulate her life he is clearly one of Hawthorne's Ethan Brand figures.) To him she cries out passionately:

> "I am trying for once to be natural! . . . I have been pretending, all my life; I have been dishonest; it is you that have made me so!" Mr. Brand stood gazing at her, and she went on, "Why shouldn't I be frivolous, if I

---

19 F. W. Dupee, *Henry James* (New York: Sloan, 1951), p. 102.

want! One has a right to be frivolous, if it's one's nature. No I don't care for the great questions. I care for pleasure—for amusement. Perhaps I am fond of wicked things; it is very possible!" (*E*, 972).

In this case we are doubtless meant to interpret Gertrude's final remark in the light of Mr. Brand's very great provocation. Gertrude, a good girl, is hardly about to scuttle down the road to perdition, though it is pertinent to remark that Emerson's "Self-Reliance" had conceded that the self to be actualized might turn out to be evil. Although Gertrude may come to "live for pleasure" and be fond of "wicked things," it is not probable. For among the forms of beauty adored by Felix, who has awakened her, is what he calls "the beauty of virtue."

The Europeans thus dramatizes the triumph of Felix Young's view of life as an opportunity to be actualized and refined through the artifice of elaborate form, and to be enjoyed for the intricate moral and social arrangements which constitute its beauty. Although Felix is gaily idealized and constitutes an allegorical type, he serves several purposes. He is the necessary foil both to the "unsuspecting" baroness, in his union of cosmopolitan social grace and moral sensitivity, and to the Wentworths, in his commitment to spontaneity, amusement, and the natural self. R. P. Blackmur once unaccountably said that since *The Europeans* suggested "no overmastering theme, no vision or psychology of life," and "no great shaping power of artistic form, in the technical sense," it need not "be read for anything but pleasure." [20] Compared with the works of the "major phase," *The Europeans* is a light performance, a gracile tribute to Hawthorne, our greatest romancer. Yet it is one of the most serious of the early comedies of manners, as well as a pleasure to read. As a tale of "American society" it finds the sought-for local "field for satire," and, by dint of "native talent" it reflects "the force of real familiarity." It balances, in a unique way, the strengths and limitations of a safely denationalized European culture, offensive to no specific audience. And it gently exposes to purifying ridicule the too serious moralism, still vestigial, of old New England in its plain living and high thinking. In doing so, it finds the field of satire to be the high, safe ground of cosmopolitanism.

---

20 R. P. Blackmur, "Introduction," in *Washington Square* and *The Europeans* (New York: Dell, 1959), p. 5.

William Dean
Howells and the
Uses of Criticism

It seems only yesterday that Lionel Trilling reported that he had created a sensation, in the cafeterias at Columbia University, by assigning to his students the work of William Dean Howells. What could Professor Trilling have conceivably found of interest—his students wanted to know—in this Victorian purveyor of old-fashioned realism in American fiction? Howells seemed too commonplace to be admitted to the company of Lawrence, Joyce, Proust, Mann, Kafka, and the other masters of modernist fiction.

This question Trilling brilliantly answered in "William Dean Howells and the Roots of Modern Taste." Anyone who takes the trouble to look up that essay, in *The Opposing Self: Nine Essays in Criticism,* will find a remarkable description of Howells's concern with the quotidian and a moving defense of his central subject—the actualities of middle-class family life. Howells is important, Trilling argued, because he concerned himself with the question of the heroic in relation to the ordinary problems of existence, like searching for a place to live, as Basil March does, at length, in *A Hazard of New Fortunes* (1890), or struggling with the problem of how to rear one's children, as Silas and Persis do in *The Rise of Silas Lapham* (1885). Trilling observed that we do not find such ordinary life-experience dealt with in the modernists because "the prototypical act of the modern intellectual is his abstracting himself from the life of the family." And nowhere is this indifference to, or rejection of, the family as a theme more evident than in much modernist fiction. But Trilling called it an act of presumption to think that such matters are beneath the dignity of the artist and critic. Even for the intellectual, "it is a fact of spirit that it must exist in a world which requires it to engage in so dispiriting an occupation as hunting for a house."[1] Howells appreciated these stubborn facts of the quotidian, and, in the process of dramatizing them, he disclosed an important reality for us today—the extent to which such facts require us to moderate our radical sentiments and our passion for alienation.

Trilling's essay was a lively and provocative work of criticism, but I have the impression that he convinced few enough of his students and virtually none of our intellectuals. It was Trilling's attention to writers like Howells and his concern with the moderation of the will that led Joseph Frank, in "Lionel Trilling and the Conservative Imagination," to accuse Trilling of confusing "even the most casual bourgeois convention" with "the most sacrosanct conditions of life itself," and to "endow social passivity and quietism *as such* with the halo of aesthetic transcendence."[2] I believe it is still commonly felt by our critics and writers today that any sympathetic attention, in the literary art, to a realist portrayal of ordinary middle-class family problems is really trivial, and perhaps even a pandering to the political status quo. The subjects that interested Howells and Jane Austen, Trollope and George Eliot seem to have evaporated in a thirst for novels of adventure and word-induced agitations. True literary excitement, we often hear, derives from more radical critiques of society or portraits of individuals at the point of some passionate extreme—as reflected, for instance, in adultery, incest, and murder; in nihilism, radicalism, and terrorism; or in drug-induced hallucinations, paranoid conspiracies, and intellectual crime and sadistic punishment—all of those aberrations, in short, that deviate from the ordinary life. Since the rise of modernist and antirealist fiction in our century, and of its champions, Howells has been the symbol of everything to be rejected about the realist school and the genteel tradition.

I

Howells was no stranger to controversy in his own time and in fact must be understood as a subversive figure in Genteel Era literary and social thought.[3] His outrageousness came in part from his temerity in founding a "new school" of fiction writing that had scant use for the aris-

---

1 Lionel Trilling, *The Opposing Self: Nine Essays in Criticism* (New York: Viking, 1955), p. 93.
2 Joseph Frank, "Lionel Trilling and the Conservative Imagination," in *The Widening Gyre: Crisis and Mastery in Modern Literature* (New Brunswick, N.J.: Rutgers University Press, 1963), p. 266.
3 This aspect of Howells's unconventionality is wonderfully captured in Robert L. Hough's *The Quiet Rebel: William Dean Howells as Social Commentator* (Lincoln: University of Nebraska Press, 1959), pp. 111–112.

tocratic prejudices of English authors or the formal clumsiness of British writers who were widely thought to be his betters. Some literary nationalism inheres in his critical thinking. But his call for a more realistic portrait of the conditions of American life brought him under the censure of a wide range of nineteenth-century British and American critics and writers who believed that fiction ought to present not what *was* or *is* but what should be, that fiction must present an idealization of life so as to form a model for our emulation—and that the model ought distinctly to be English. Howells's dismissal of the romantic distortions of life by the domestic sentimental writers of his time was matched by a shocking devaluation of some of the most popular English favorites in America:

> The art of fiction [he wrote in 1882] has, in fact, become a finer art in our day than it was with Dickens and Thackeray. We could not suffer the confidential attitude of the latter now, nor the mannerism of the former, any more than we could endure the prolixity of Richardson or the coarseness of Fielding. These great men are of the past—they and their methods and interests; even Trollope and Reade are not of the present. The new school derives from Hawthorne and George Eliot rather than any others; but it studies human nature much more in its wonted aspects, and finds its ethical and dramatic examples in the operation of lighter but not really less vital motives. The moving accident is not its trade; and it prefers to avoid all manner of dire catastrophes. It is largely influenced by French fiction in form; but it is the realism of Daudet rather than the realism of Zola that prevails with it, and it has a soul of its own which is above the business of recording the rather brutish pursuit of a woman by a man, which seems the chief end of the French novelist. This school, which is so largely of the future as well as of the present, finds its chief exemplar in Mr. James; it is he who is shaping and directing American fiction, at least (I, 322).[4]

Imagine writing off the English masters in favor of the French (even the less pornographic French), or calling Henry James—who had just insulted the national character (in *The American*) and American girlhood (in *Daisy Miller*)—"a very great literary genius" whose style "is, upon the whole, better than that of any other novelist I know" (I, 323). The

---

4 All citations from the criticism of Howells, unless otherwise indicated, will refer to one of the following works and will be indicated by volume and page numbers, in parentheses, in the text: *W. D. Howells: Selected Literary Criticism.* (Bloomington: Indiana University Press, 1993)—Volume I, 1859–1885; Volume II, 1886–1897; Volume III, 1898–1920. This three-volume edition represents the valuable collaboration of several literary and textual critics: Ulrich Halfmann, Christoph K. Lohmann, Don L. Cook, David Kleinman, Donald Pizer, and Ronald Gottesman.

American Anglophiles were outraged, as were the British.

The firestorm Howells touched off was instantaneous, bitter, and prolonged. Exponents of the genteel tradition, like Hamilton Wright Mabie, spurned the new school of realism and clamored for idealization in art. "Realism," Mabie said of *The Rise of Silas Lapham*, "is crowding the world of fiction with commonplace people; people whom one would positively avoid coming in contact with in real life; people without native sweetness or strength, without acquired culture or accomplishment, without that touch of the ideal which makes the commonplace significant and worthy of study." [5] Another group, exponents of the romance genre, proclaimed, like Robert Louis Stevenson in "A Humble Remonstrance," that, since all art is ruthlessly selective, no fiction can ever be truly realistic: "The novel, which is a work of art, exists, not by its resemblances to life, which are forced and material, . . . but by its immeasurable difference from life." [6] Yet the defenders of realism were quick on the counterattack, claiming that the "scientific detachment" and "clinical observation" of masters like Howells and James had killed once and for all sentimental distortion in fiction and the idealism of the romance mode. This prolonged controversy over the merits of literary realism signaled a paradigmatic shift in the history of fiction and criticism in this country.

Howells's comment about the lubricity of many French novels also points to another ground for the attack against him. If the genteel tradition thought realism was too graphic, if not photographic, some younger writers who had benefited from the greater openness achieved through Howells's efforts attacked him as *insufficiently* realistic, especially in dealing with sex. Frank Norris—in "A Plea for Romantic Fiction"—spoke for many young naturalists, who were influenced by Zola, in condemning the realist "drama of a broken teacup, the tragedy of a walk down the block, the excitement of an afternoon call, the adventure of an invitation to dinner." The younger naturalists claimed a freedom to explore what Norris flamboyantly called "the unplumbed depths of the human heart, and the mystery of sex, and the problems of life, and the black, unsearched penetralia of the soul of man." [7] Mencken, in "The Dean," likewise mocked the prudish Howells as an "Agnes Repplier in pantaloons," and Sinclair Lewis, in "The American Fear of Literature,"

---

5 Hamilton Wright Mabie, "A Typical Novel," in *The War of the Critics over William Dean Howells*, eds. Edwin H. Cady and David L. Frazier (Evanston: Row, Peterson, 1962), pp. 40–41.

6 Robert Louis Stevenson, *Essays by Robert Louis Stevenson*, ed. Will D. Howe (New York: Scribner's, 1918), p. 259.

7 Frank Norris, *The Responsibilities of the Novelist and Other Literary Essays* (New York: Doubleday, Page, 1903), p. 215.

lampooned him before the Swedish Academy as "one of the gentlest, sweetest and most honest of men" who "had the code of a pious old maid whose greatest delight is to have tea at the vicarage."[8]

The young can be especially cruel—and are often quite wrong. As Elizabeth Stevens Prioleau has shown in *The Circle of Eros: Sexuality in the Work of William Dean Howells*, Howells's novels were in fact regarded as quite racy by his contemporaries, especially since he deployed so effectively fictive techniques of indirection and veiled allegory. Though he will seem tame to readers brought up on Updike, Burroughs, Mailer, and Erica Jong, Ms. Prioleau is quite right in observing that Howells dealt so richly and suggestively with the erotic life that graphic details are indeed superfluous.[9] Anyone with any doubt about this matter should look again at Howells's *A Modern Instance*, from which Freud could have learned a thing or two about the Electra complex and the forms of its symbolic displacement.

II

We come back, then, to the paradox of Howells's contemporary radicalism and to his current reputation as a spokesman for genteel values, for an old-fashioned realism, and for themes and topics that have seemingly lost their importance for intellectuals. To justify any new attention to Howells, to explain this controversial writer and his significance for today, may require some background. Born in 1837 in Martin's Ferry, Ohio, Howells grew up in what was then the Western Reserve. As a boy he worked on the family's newspapers in Ashtabula and Columbus, setting type and later reporting, writing, and reviewing. It was there in the West that he absorbed the democratic sympathies that mark every novel he ever wrote. Howells never had the benefit of a college education, since the family business needed him too much, and like many writers of that time—Twain, Crane, and Dreiser, for example—the composing room was his Harvard and Yale College. Howells's youthful literary ambition included poetry, for which he had little talent, and the drama, which was never to be his forte. It was in criticism and fiction that Howells was eventually to make his mark.

A literary tour of the East in 1860 brought him introductions to Emerson, Hawthorne, Oliver Wendell Holmes, James Russell Lowell

---

8 H. L. Mencken, "The Dean," in *Prejudices: First Series* (New York: Alfred A. Knopf, 1919), p. 57; see also Sinclair Lewis, "The American Fear of Literature," in *The War of the Critics over William Dean Howells*, p. 153.

9 Elizabeth Stevens Prioleau, *The Circle of Eros: Sexuality in the Work of William Dean Howells* (Durham: Duke University Press, 1983).

(editor of the *Atlantic*), and the publisher James T. Fields. Boston was then the literary capital of the nation, and these Brahmins recognized in the boy literary ambition, personal charm, and utter seriousness, if not yet the signs of greatness. Perhaps not altogether seriously, they gave this young Westerner reason to believe that if he applied himself, he too could become one of their exalted number.[10] After he left Boston for Columbus, young Howells had the audacity to write to Fields: "I look forward to living there some day—being possibly the linchpin in the hub."[11]

A campaign biography of Lincoln, who ran for president in 1860, won Howells a government post in the consulate in Venice, where he spent the Civil War years. This Italian period was improved by extensive study of ancient and modern languages and literatures, and of European life and culture. He read widely, wrote criticism, and composed his first travel book, the charming *Venetian Life* (1866). His essays "Recent Italian Comedy" and "Modern Italian Literature," for the *North American Review*, were well received, and Lowell electrified Howells by remarking, "You have enough in you to do honor to our literature. Keep on cultivating yourself" (I, xv).

Yet the spectacle of aristocratic politics in Europe dismayed Howells, and the moral quality of its life appalled. He left Italy because, he said, he was finding himself "almost expatriated, and I have seen enough of uncountryed Americans in Europe to disgust me with voluntary exile, and its effects upon character."[12] Yet Europe did not turn out to be, in his thinking, a total loss. In Italy Howells discovered the brilliant realist comedies of the eighteenth-century playwright Carlo Goldoni, whose work redirected Howells toward a fiction based on what he called the "critical observance of books and men in their actuality."[13]

Back in the United States, between 1866 and 1870, Howells got the job of assistant editor at the *Atlantic Monthly*, where his hard work, erudition, charm, and congeniality made him a favorite of Longfellow, Lowell, Holmes, Agassiz, and the others. Between 1871 and 1881 he was the chief editor of the *Atlantic*—the linchpin of the hub indeed; and in that most influential post he reshaped the direction of American fiction by launching an all-out attack on the domestic sentimental writers (now

---

10 Kenneth S. Lynn, *William Dean Howells: An American Life* (New York: Harcourt, Brace, Jovanovich, 1970), p. 96.

11 W. D. *Howells: Selected Letters*, eds. George Arms, *et al.* (Boston: Twayne Publishers, 1979–1983), I, 58.

12 *The Life in Letters of William Dean Howells*, ed. Mildred Howells (Garden City, N.Y.: Doubleday, Doran, 1928), I, 85.

13 Quoted in Clara M. and Rudolf Kirk, *William Dean Howells* (New Haven, Conn.: College and University Press, 1962), p. 46.

being revived by feminists) and by publishing the new regionalists and realists—Mark Twain, Bret Harte, John Hay, Sarah Orne Jewett, Henry James, John W. DeForest, Mary Noailles Murfree, and others.

At the same time he launched his own career as a novelist and attained popular esteem with *Their Wedding Journey* (1872), *A Chance Acquaintance* (1873), *A Foregone Conclusion* (1875), *Doctor Breen's Practice* (1881), *A Modern Instance* (1882), *A Woman's Reason* (1883), and *The Rise of Silas Lapham* (1885). Henry James thought he stood a fair chance of becoming "the American Balzac." "That's a great mission," he told Howells; "go in for it!" [14] By 1885, indeed, Howells was widely regarded as perhaps the most distinguished living American writer.

In later years he was to be called "The Dean of American Letters," for he consolidated his impressive reputation with other novels of comparable quality and interest—so many of them, in fact, that only a few may be listed here: *Indian Summer* (1886), *Annie Kilburn* (1888), *A Hazard of New Fortunes* (1890), *The Landlord at Lion's Head* (1897), and *The Leatherwood God* (1916). Between 1886 and 1892, moreover, he conducted a column, the "Editor's Study," at *Harper's Monthly*, in which he called the public's attention to important new books and enunciated the new principles of realism. Thereafter his later criticism was regularly featured in *Harper's Weekly* (1895–1897), *Literature* (1898–1899), the *North American Review* (1900–1912), and other magazines. Some of his periodical essays, dealing with the art of fiction, were gathered into a collection called *Criticism and Fiction* (1891), which became the rallying point for those who saw themselves enrolled under the banner of realism—writers like James, Hamlin Garland, Stephen Crane, Mary Wilkins Freeman, E. W. Howe, and H. H. Boyeson.

The movement of American literary realism was an amalgam of many elements and personalities. "No one invented realism," Howells told Thomas Sergeant Perry in 1886; "it came." [15] Still, Howells and his ideas were the most important formative influences. Edwin H. Cady has remarked that Howells

> was in fact almost incredibly informed, sophisticated, and many-sided; in his time an absolute insider, an old professional, long a standard-bearer of the *avant garde*, the friend and ally of the great, the sponsor and patron of the gifted young and friendless, the despair of the entrenched and ancient. [16]

Howells's critical practice suggests how catholic and wide-ranging were

14 *Henry James: Letters*, ed. Leon Edel (Cambridge: Harvard University Press, 1975), II, 268.
15 *W. D. Howells: Selected Letters*, III, 153.
16 Edwin H. Cady, *W. D. Howells as Critic* (London: Routledge and Kegan Paul, 1973), p. 2.

his literary interests and how perceptive and generous were his sympathies. Even when he did not like a specific kind of book, or the book itself that illustrated the type, he usually managed to find something to say about its merits while disposing of it. I have the impression that he read nearly everything by everybody who was anybody and much inferior work by a great many writers once popular but now unknown. The greatest writers of his time—Hawthorne, Poe, Melville, Whitman, Twain, Rossetti, Browning, Dickens, Thackeray, Turgenev, Tolstoy, Zola, James, Wilkins, Hardy, Dunbar, Ibsen—all are subjects of his critical reflection; and it is remarkable to witness his unfolding grasp of a writer—like a James or a Dickens—over the nearly sixty years of his commentary on the literary life of his time. He had a perceptive eye, a quick grasp of a writer's essence, but a remarkable ability to change his mind as writers deepened in importance over time or as the defect of his initial response became apparent to him. It was no accident that generations of readers came to feel that Howells was a reviewer whose judgments could be trusted.

III

Criticism, he remarked in *My Literary Passions* (1895), "ever since I filled myself so full of it in my boyhood, I have not cared for, and often I have found it repulsive." It was, he thought, the "idlest" thing in the world; it was "absolutely useless to art of any sort"; and he told Thomas Bailey Aldrich in 1901 that "I hate criticism. . . . I never did a piece of it that satisfied me."[17] How remarkable, then, that he became one of America's greatest literary critics. This ranking he attained because most of the time he saw reviewing as a "stern and responsible duty: the exercise of discernment between the good and the bad, the false and the true, the sincere and the sham." True criticism, he held,

> consists of a calm, just, and fearless handling of its subject, and in pointing out in all honesty whatever there is hitherto undiscovered of merit, and, in equal honesty, whatever there has been concealed of defect. This function is entirely distinct from the mere trade-puff of the publisher, the financial comments of the advertiser, or the bought-and-sold eulogium of an ignorant, careless, or mercenary journalist. It is equally removed from the wholesale and baseless attacks of some rival publication house, or from the censure which is inspired by political, personal, or religious hatred. So commonly, however, especially in

---

17 W. D. Howells, *My Literary Passions* (New York: Harper's, 1895), p. 235; I, xvii; *W. D. Howells: Selected Letters*, IV, 265.

America, is this high function of literary criticism degraded to base uses that we can hardly wonder at the popular incredulity as to its aim and scope (I, 60–61).

He saw the public as gaining from an accurate description of the form and content of the work under review. And he saw it as the reviewer's task to try to correct the taste of the age. The realism which Howells espoused evolved, over a considerable period of time, out of his editorial work with young writers and his extensive reading and reviewing of the established. His general principles have been conveniently summarized as follows:

> He advocated modest honesty and clear and truthful adherence to reality, fidelity to the authentic, the experienced, the observed instead of romanticistic abstraction, sentimentality, and pretense. His criticism was built on respect for the common as the naturally human *par excellence*. In adhering to principles and techniques of narration which serve these ends, it valued the prevalence of character revelation over plot invention, "dramatic" presentation over authorial intrusion and didacticism, and organic over superimposed structure (I, xx).

Howells's principles suggest a reaction against the prevailing romanticism that so disfigured earlier nineteenth-century fiction. Art was for him, as for Aristotle, a mimetic representation of phenomenal reality, a speaking picture of character in relation to the external conditions of life. The test of art was thus its verisimilitude, the measure of its realism, its capacity to mirror existence with fidelity, and to reflect it with a balance that is representative of the range and variety of existence. The test of the novel for him, as he remarks in *Criticism and Fiction* (1891), is this: "Is it true?—true to the motives, the impulses, the principles that shape the life of actual men and women?" (II, 327). His several reviews and essays dealing with his two close friends, Mark Twain and Henry James, are typical of his thinking in their stress on the writer's fidelity to the observed facts of human experience. In his 1887 piece on "The Truthfulness of Mark Twain's Fiction," the brilliance of *Innocents Abroad* and *Roughing It* inspires him to this exhortation:

> Let fiction cease to lie about life; let it portray men and women as they are, actuated by the motives and the passions in the measure we all know; let it leave off painting dolls and working them by springs and wires; let it show the different interests in their true proportions; let it forbear to preach pride and revenge, folly and insanity, egotism and prejudice, but frankly own these for what they are, in whatever figures and occasions they appear; let it not put on fine literary airs; let it speak

the dialect, the language, that most Americans know—the language of unaffected people everywhere—and we believe that even its master-pieces will find a response in all readers (II, 49).[18]

Above all Howells stood for the art that conceals art, for impersonal narration, and for the presentation of character by dramatic and indirect means. Ivan Turgenev was his model: "Tourguenief's method is as far as art can go. That is to say, his fiction is to the last degree dramatic. The persons are sparely described, and briefly accounted for, and then they are left to transact their affair, whatever it is, with the least possible comment or explanation from the author." He said that when he "remembered the deliberate and impertinent moralizing of Thackeray, the clumsy exegesis of George Eliot, the knowing nods and winks of Charles Reade, the stage-carpentering and lime-lighting of Dickens, even the fine and important analysis of Hawthorne, it was with a joyful astonishment that I realized the great art of Tourguenief."[19]

But however much Howells's criticism was founded on an aesthetic of realism, *mimesis* was never an end in itself. The moral function of literature, to teach as well as to delight, was also important. Art instructs by means of enjoyment. The pleasure of a realistic portrait is the aesthetic bait that hooks the reader, even as the novelist simultaneously "teaches" him about the condition of the world and our manifold experience. Howells told Thomas Wentworth Higginson, "I should be ashamed and sorry if my novels did not unmistakably teach a lenient, generous, and liberal life: that is, I should feel degraded merely to amuse people." [20] And he criticized Ralph Keeler's *Vagabond Adventures* in saying that "a book has no business to be merely literature; and such a book as this especially ought to teach something,—ought to disenchant youth with adventure, and show Poverty in her true colors" (I, 178). Even so, Howells's point of view does not endorse overt didacticism in literature, as his criticism of George Eliot's mini-sermons may suggest. The instruction of any good novel, in teaching us how to live, derives from its fidelity to life itself. In *Literary Friends and Acquaintance* (1900), he remarked of realist fiction that "truth to life is suffered to do its unsermonized office for conduct."[21]

He faced a more serious problem, however, with how conduct might be corrupted by the experience of reading fiction. American novels that

---

18 Howells thought so well of this formulation that he repeated it, with slight variations in *Criticism and Fiction* (1891); see II, 327–328.

19 From Howells's *My Literary Passions*, quoted in *The Rise of Realism*, ed. Louis Wann (New York: Macmillan, 1949), p. 524.

20 *W. D. Howells: Selected Letters*, II, 238.

21 Howells, *Literary Friends and Acquaintance*, p. 102.

romanticized seduction and illicit love nearly always provoked his ire, not because the illicit is uncommon or alien to the experience of life but because the audience for fiction, in the America of his time, consisted largely of young unmarried girls, for whom representations of immoral sexuality, like that in *Madame Bovary* and *Anna Karenina,* could be ethically disorienting.

> If the novel were written for men and for married women alone, as in continental Europe, it might be altogether different. But the simple fact is that it is not written for them alone among us, and it is a question of writing, under cover of our universal acceptance, things for young girls to read which you would be put out-of-doors for saying to them, or of frankly giving notice of your intention, and so cutting yourself off from the pleasure—and it is a very high and sweet one—of appealing to these vivid, responsive intelligences, which are none the less brilliant and admirable because they are innocent (II, 342).

If he valued the moral purity of his young readers, he acceded to the conditions under which he was obliged to work; in any case, no American magazine editor would have printed a Flaubertian story of seduction and adultery—much less a coarser treatment of the theme such as could be found in Zola. Howells thus drew a line beyond which his realism would not go. There could not be, he said, any "palpitating divans" in his novels. Writing to John Hay in 1882, Howells noted that his son John was "at this moment curled up on the lounge reading [Howells's novel] *Dr. Breen's Practice.* For this reason, if for no other, I could not have palpitating divans in my stories; my children are my censors, and if I wished to be wicked, I hope they would be my safeguards. . . . I am a great admirer of French workmanship, and I read everything of Zola's that I can lay hands on. But I have to hide the books from the children!" [22] The restrictions imposed on him by "Mrs. Grundy"—which no Continental writer had to suffer—irritated Howells at times, as it did James. Even so, both writers were circumspect and reserved by temperament. They have been wrongly condemned for this—by those who accord no moral function to art (or who have a lower moral standard)—as sissies or pious old maids.

In his reviews and essays, Howells is quite explicit about how adventure stories and other romances may corrupt the reader. Romantic novels hurt, he tells us, "because they are not true—not because they are malevolent, but because they are idle lies about human nature and the social fabric, which it behooves us to know and to understand, that we

---

22 *Life in Letters of William Dean Howells,* I, 311.

may deal justly with ourselves and one another" (II, 44). Justice is a recurrent theme in his criticism, especially with respect to social and class relations. As a Western democrat from Ohio and an outsider with the Boston elite, he was hypersensitive to the arrogance and snobbishness of the privileged class, which nevertheless was charmed by his talents.

Realism in his view was meant to affirm the native dignity of every person, no matter how socially despised—hence his celebration of Twain and others who made the Huck Finns and Hank Morgans their protagonists. The romanticization of lords and ladies, the "aristocratic spirit," he thought, was passing away in fiction. "Democracy in literature is the reverse of all this. It wishes to know and to tell the truth, confident that consolation and delight are there; it does not care to paint the marvellous and impossible for the vulgar many, or to sentimentalize and falsify the actual for the vulgar few" (II, 353). Thomas Sergeant Perry was right in remarking in 1882 that

> there is truly a national spirit in the way Mr. Howells shows . . . the emptiness of convention and the dignity of native worth. . . . After all, what can realism produce but the downfall of conventionality? Just as the scientific spirit digs the ground from beneath superstition, so does its fellow-worker, realism, tend to prick the bubble of abstract types. Realism is the tool of the democratic spirit, and Mr. Howells's realism is untiring. It is, too, increasingly good-natured. We feel that Mr. Howells is scrutinizing the person he is writing about with undisturbed calmness, and that no name and no person can impose upon him by its conventional value.[23]

So confident was Howells, in the 1870s and early 1880s, of the triumph of economic progress and political egalitarianism that he saw everywhere in America a genial present and a sublime future. His essay on Dostoevsky in 1886 expresses this "good nature" in remarking that a novel like *Crime and Punishment*

> is to be praised only in its place, and its message is to be received with allowances by readers exterior to the social and political circumstances in which it was conceived. It used to be one of the disadvantages of the practice of romance in America, which Hawthorne more or less whimsically lamented, that there were so few shadows and inequalities in our broad level of prosperity; and it is one of the reflections suggested by Dostoïevsky's book that whoever struck a note so profoundly tragic in

---

23 Thomas Sergeant Perry, "William Dean Howells," *Century Magazine*, 23 (March 1882), 680–685.

American fiction would do a false and mistaken thing—as false and as mistaken in its way as dealing in American fiction with certain nudities which the Latin peoples seem to find edifying. Whatever their deserts, very few American novelists have [like Dostoevsky] been led out to be shot, or finally exiled to the rigors of a winter at Duluth; . . . and in a land where journeymen carpenters and plumbers strike for four dollars a day the sum of hunger and cold is certainly very small, and the wrong from class to class is almost inappreciable. We invite our novelists, therefore, to concern themselves with the more smiling aspects of life, which are the more American, and to seek the universal in the individual rather than in the social interests. It is worth while, even at the risk of being called commonplace, to be true to our well-to-do actualities. . . (II, 336).

There is a great deal of truth is this remarkable statement. America *did* offer greater opportunities for freedom and advancement than any other nation in the world—hence the massive immigration seen in those years. Yet the comment has always been held against Howells as evidence that he had no sense of social evil, that he had sold out and was toadying to the the Gilded Age "establishment."

IV

The paradox in this remark about the "smiling aspects of life" is that it does not really represent what Howells then in fact really thought. He had just recently suffered a nervous breakdown. Such breakdowns always have many causes, but the fact is that the disparities between the rich and poor had overwhelmed him. Massive immigration, unemployment, laissez-faire economics, and violence between capital and labor had begun to horrify him. The Haymarket Riot in Chicago in 1886 was a turning point in his life. On that occasion a bomb was thrown at a labor rally; many were injured, and some policemen were killed or wounded. A group of workingmen was arrested for throwing the bomb, though the evidence connecting them to it seemed tenuous. When the Supreme Court confirmed the verdict of guilty, Howells wrote many open letters and essays condemning the forthcoming "civic murder" of these laborers, and urging clemency. In doing so he ran counter to the establishment and risked his position as an arbiter of American life and letters. *The Rise of Silas Lapham* (1885), *The Minister's Charge* (1887), *A Hazard of New Fortunes* (1890), and *The World of Chance* (1893) all reflect Howells's darkening mood. To save his own soul he embraced the personal creed of Christian socialism. It was compounded of the

Gospels and the writings of Laurence Gronlund, the English Fabians, William Morris, and others; he commended it to his readers.

Central to this phase of his literary criticism was the example of Tolstoy, the great novelist and Russian aristocrat who had rejected his worldly fame and accomplishments in order to become peasantlike, striving to serve the lowliest of the low, in the manner of Christ. Tolstoy's "My Confession," "My Religion," and "What to Do?" transformed Howells's life and taught him, he wrote, "to hope that the world may yet be made over in the image of Him who died for it, when all Caesar's things shall be finally rendered unto Caesar. . . . He taught me to see life . . . as a field for endeavor towards the happiness of the whole human family; and I can never lose this vision, however I close my eyes, and strive to see my own interest as the highest good" (II, 264–265). This transformation was stupefying to many of the Boston literati; Howells had caught a case of the "Russian measles," many of them thought; and, as for the Haymarket rioters, Whittier said that the ruffians were well hanged.[24]

A Hazard of New Fortunes has its moments as a realist portrait of those economic inequalities in the 1880s. But when ideology overtakes a writer, mere verisimilitude is rarely felt to be adequate to the task of converting people to socialism. Howells's later novels became more and more talky and didactic, overtly religious and socialistic. Finally, in *A Traveler from Altruria* (1894) and *Through the Eye of the Needle* (1907), he abandoned realism altogether for the utopian fantasy of socialist brotherhood—where private property and money do not exist, where the good of others in Altruria is central, all have the means of subsistence, and perfect equality is the basis of life. All of this sounds very Edenic, but Howells, despite having opened up the *Atlantic* to many essays on free silver, taxation, specie payment, and other such topics, knew next to nothing about how capital is formed or wealth is created. In these romances he failed to describe how America might get from the Gilded Age to Altruria—without, that is, bloody conflict over the confiscation of private property. But this humanitarian sympathy always endeared him to the left, though his failure "to provide contemporary critics with a sufficiently militant brand of liberalism" has led to the charge that "he lacked moral intensity."[25] Howells's willingness to mod-

24 Edwin H. Cady, *The Realist at War: The Mature Years, 1885–1920, of William Dean Howells* (Syracuse: Syracuse University Press, 1958), p. 71.

25 George N. Bennett, *William Dean Howells: The Development of a Novelist* (Norman: University of Oklahoma Press, 1959), p. 214. More recent radicals, like the *Partisan Review* crowd, disillusioned with Stalinist communism, came to express little but contempt for "the 'middle-brow'-progressive mentality," of which Howells was said to be preeminently representative. It was a mark of Trilling's drift away from them toward neoconservatism

erate the tendencies of political radicalism may account, in part, for why Trilling thought him beneficial to modern readers.

The socialist romances were rather a blip in Howells's lifelong commitment to realism, which he resumed after the turn of the century. Even so, as he advanced in years, such esteem as he enjoyed with the American public was that of an elder statesman and congenial man of letters whom the modern world seemed largely to have passed by. Howells continued to write contemporary reviews—on Arnold Bennett, Robert Herrick, Charles Chesnutt, the later James, and Hamlin Garland—as the multivolume selected criticism, in the Indiana edition, will attest. But much of his late criticism is memorial in character, dealing with writers whom he had loved or at least long known—Twain, Zola, Tolstoy, Eliot, and Poe. It is nonetheless acute for being quite naturally retrospective, but Howells was poignantly aware that he had been superseded by younger writers. As he told Henry James a few years before his death, "I am comparatively a dead cult with my statues cut down and the grass growing over them in the pale moonlight."[26]

On the occasion of his seventy-fifth birthday party in 1912, Henry James sent him from London a magnificent tribute, "A Letter to Mr. Howells," in which he praised Howells's fiction and put on record his sense of

> that unfailing, testifying truth in you which will keep you from ever being neglected. The critical intelligence—if any such fitful and discredited light may still be conceived as within our sphere—has not at all begun to render you its tribute. . . . You may remember perhaps, and I like to recall, how the great and admirable Taine, in one of the fine excursions of his French curiosity, greeted you as a precious painter and a sovereign witness. But his appreciation, I want you to believe with me, will yet be carried much further, and then . . . your really beautiful time will come.[27]

There is always recurrent talk of a Howells revival, but it has never really come. And Howells's case of "Russian measles" may make him seem even more outdated, now that we see the Soviet Union defunct and socialism in its death throes. His claim for the realistic social novel seemed likewise passé in the 1950s, when the avant-garde offered its

---

that he continued to admire Howells. See Daniel Aaron's *Men of Good Hope: A Story of American Progressives* (New York: Oxford University Press, 1961), pp. 301–302. On the matter of Trilling's neoconservatism at the end, see Diana Trilling, *The Beginning of the Journey: The Marriage of Diana and Lionel Trilling* (New York: Harcourt, Brace, 1993).

26 *Life in Letters of William Dean Howells*, II, 250.

27 Henry James, "A Letter to Mr. Howells," *North American Review*, 195 (April 1912), 558–562; reprinted in *Henry James: Essays on Literature, American Writers, English Writers*,

obituary for the novel. Moreover, throughout the 1960s and 1970s we passed through a troubling era for the modern writer in which reality itself was called into question. As the fabulist Ronald Sukenick complained at the time, "Reality doesn't exist, time doesn't exist, personality doesn't exist. God was the omniscient author, but he died; now no one knows the plot, and since our reality lacks the sanction of a creator, there's no guarantee as to the authenticity of the received version."[28] How could there be a faithful portrait of reality if it doesn't exist? Moreover, in the 1980s antirealism seemed to be the only game in town for intellectuals and writers who had been seduced by Derrida and the deconstructionists' claim that there is such a yawning abyss between language and reality that no representation of the latter is in fact possible. The fabulations of Barthelme, Barth, Burroughs, Coover, Hawkes, Pynchon, McElroy, and Sorrentino, for example, seemed to be the only thing that interested our literary critics. And this kind of writing was produced, and praised, even though the attempt to overturn consciousness of the objective world, to abolish ordinary language, and to destroy the canons of representational realism condemned the antirealists to social marginality and ensured their unimportance to most readers. (Only Barthelme had a hint of how insignificant antirealist novels had become even as the reviewers and creative writing departments were still singing their praises. In his *City Life*, everyone is a dwarf next to the museum's gigantic statues of Tolstoy.)[29]

It is sometimes said that TV and the movies have now displaced the realist novel in giving images of social actuality. But it is my impression that Henry James was right in remarking—in "The Future of the Novel" (1899)—that the novel will likely never die out because there are still neglected and unexploited too many sources of interest—"whole categories of manners, whole corpuscular classes and provinces, museums of character and condition, unvisited."[30] We still want the novelist who will visit them and, as Howells recommended, give us a faithful portrait of what he sees. All it takes is a sharp eye for the way we live now. In the meantime we have Howells's novels, which continue along; he is never quite forgotten though he has never attained a revival like that of Henry James or Kate Chopin.

---

ed. Leon Edel (New York: Library of America, 1984), p. 510.

28 Quoted in Arthur M. Saltzman's *The Fiction of William Gass* (Carbondale: Southern Illinois University Press, 1986), pp. 3–4.

29 For a splendid analysis of contemporary antirealist fiction, see John Kuehl's *Alternate Worlds: A Study of Postmodernist Antirealist Fiction* (New York: New York University Press, 1989).

30 Henry James, "The Future of the Novel," in *The Future of the Novel: Essays on the Art of Fiction*, ed. Leon Edel (New York: Vintage, 1956), p. 40.

Yet a contemporary writer with a sharp eye for social categories of the kind that absorbed Howells and James is Tom Wolfe, who predicted in *The New Journalism* (1973) that the novel of the future would be a detailed reportorial realism that would portray the individual in intimate and inextricable relation to the society around him. Of course this kind of novel, which is exactly that espoused by Howells, has been written all along in our century, in, for instance, the admirable work of John O'Hara, James Gould Cozzens, John Cheever, John Updike, and Louis Auchincloss. But Wolfe wanted something more on the vast social scale of Balzac or the Tolstoy of *Anna Karenina,* something broader in its canvas than Cheever's Westchester County or Auchincloss's Park Avenue *milieux.* Wolfe did not get it from the contemporary writers he challenged in the mid-1970s. So he wrote the novel himself, in *The Bonfire of the Vanities* (1987).

The Bonfire of the Vanities is, in my view, a brilliant novel that perfectly illustrates the principles of realism for which Howells stood. But of more importance, in relation to Howells, is Wolfe's essay "Stalking the Billion-Footed Beast," which appeared afterward in *Harper's* in November 1989. This essay was nothing less than a manifesto for social fiction in which Wolfe called for a return to long, reportorial, realistic novels, Balzacean fiction with a broad social canvas, like the work of Lewis, Faulkner, Hemingway, Buck, Styron, and Steinbeck. Howells was not mentioned in that essay, as I recollect it, but he is clearly—in books like *A Hazard of New Fortunes*—the American precursor of this type of social fiction. And if there is to be a resurgence of this kind of fiction, if it experiences the great revival Wolfe calls for, then perhaps Howells's beautiful time will have come at last.

The Elusive
Stephen Crane

"It has been a theory of mine ever since I began to write, which was eight years ago, when I was sixteen, that the most artistic and the most enduring literature was that which reflected life accurately." [1] So remarked young Stephen Crane (1871–1900), author of *Maggie: A Girl of the Streets* (1893) and *The Red Badge of Courage* (1895), to the editor of *Demorest's Family Magazine* in 1896. The conviction evident in this remark is a measure of how far writers have since departed from the representational function of art, from the view of art as a reflection of reality. Crane came to his majority at a time when verisimilitude in literature was a value worth trying to realize. To mirror reality in art, to tell it "the way it was"—in Hemingway's memorable locution—is no longer, it seems, a predictable intention of the serious novelist. John Hawkes, for one, has even claimed that the conventional elements of realist fiction—plot, character, setting, and theme—are "the true enemies of the novel." [2] Crane, however, at least in much of his prose, belonged to the school of Aristotelian mimesis; he placed his faith in the representation of observed reality. He remarked that he had always tried

> to observe closely, and to set down what I have seen in the simplest and most concise way. I have been careful not to let any theories or pet ideas of my own be seen in my writing. Preaching is fatal to art in literature. I try to give to readers a slice out of life; and if there is any moral or les-

---

1 *The Correspondence of Stephen Crane,* eds. Stanley Wertheim and Paul Sorrentino (New York: Columbia University Press, 1988), I, 230. Hereafter, quotations from this text will be given as *CSC,* in parentheses, in the text.

2 See John Enck, "John Hawkes: An Interview," *Wisconsin Studies in Contemporary Literature,* 6 (1965), 149.

son in it I do not point it out. I let the reader find it for himself (*CSC*, I, 230).[3]

A slice of life Crane certainly gave his readers—especially in his portraits of the Bowery underworld. But the moral significance of his work has been a problem for interpretation ever since he burst onto the literary scene in 1895. For Crane was wonderfully self-effacing in his fiction and had little of that reflexive self-consciousness that has lately, and almost fatally, disfigured the fictional art. Nor was he much more self-revelatory in his letters and journals. It was particulars of the visual field, precisely rendered in fiction, that counted for him, not a factitious relation to them. And if readers were dismayed at the seamy particulars of his representation, or if they disliked the irony that undercut his characters' doubtful gestures of heroism, he could take the flak. "I understand that a man is born into the world with his own pair of eyes," he once remarked. "To keep close to my honesty is my supreme ambition" (*CSC*, I, 195–196). With his "particular pair of eyes" and fierce honesty, Crane was acclaimed at the *fin de siècle* as a boy wonder in art, a juvenile genius with the pen, our own native Chatterton, perhaps our own Rimbaud. These sentimental estimates gained even greater currency in later years, for Crane's death from tuberculosis in 1900, at the tender age of twenty-nine, ended a striking career which was marked by the ordeal of a difficult fame and continual public controversy. Amy Lowell summed up one popular myth: Crane was "a boy spiritually killed by neglect."[4] But the facts are otherwise. In life he attracted a great deal of attention, more in fact than he could conveniently handle. Less public attention would very probably have prolonged his life.

Myths of neglected genius ought at least to be accompanied by tales of profitless labor unacknowledged by editors, publishers, and readers. That certainly was not—at least after *Maggie*—the case with Crane. If his career as a *published* writer spanned just seven years, his death gave final shape to what is in fact a rather substantial published *oeuvre*. It includes, in addition to *Maggie* (1893) and *The Red Badge* (1895), *George's Mother* (1896), *The Little Regiment and Other Episodes of the American Civil War* (1896), *The Third Violet* (1897), *The Open Boat and Other*

---

3 It should be remarked that Howellsian realism and *tranche de vie* naturalism were in fact temporary phases in Crane's development. As Crane intensified his parodic experiments, he added to his repertoire not only expressionistic symbolism and pictorial or chromatic impressionism (as in *The Red Badge*) but also absurdist existentialism (as in "The Open Boat"). These modes are often blended with irony and interwoven into a single tale (as in "The Blue Hotel").

4 See Amy Lowell, "Introduction," *The Work of Stephen Crane* (New York: Alfred A. Knopf, 1926), VI, xxix.

Tales of Adventure (1898), *Active Service* (1899), *The Monster and Other Stories* (1899), *Whilomville Stories* (1900), and *Wounds in the Rain: War Stories* (1900). To this list we must add his remarkable collections of verse, some of it memorable—namely, *The Black Riders and Other Lines* (1895), *A Souvenir and a Medley: Seven Poems and a Sketch* (1896), and *War Is Kind* (1899).

Moreover, so celebrated a public figure was Steven Crane in life, and so poignant was he in death, that nearly every scrap he wrote was subsequently collected, edited, printed, and sometimes reprinted—in such volumes as *Great Battles of the War* (1901), *Last Words* (1902), *The O'Ruddy: A Romance* (1903)—completed by Robert Barr, *Et Cetera: A Collector's Scrap-Book* (1924), combat journalism in *A Battle in Greece* (1936), a play called *The Blood of the Martyr* (1940), *The War Dispatches* (1964), *New York City Sketches and Related Pieces* (1964), his *Notebook* (1969), and *Crane in the West and Mexico* (1970). And in recent years the University Press of Virginia reedited, under the supervision of Fredson Bowers, all of his works, preparing the *University of Virginia Edition of the Works of Stephen Crane* (1969–1975) according to modern, if sometimes controversial, bibliographical methods. All these texts have played a role in the continuing apotheosis of Stephen Crane as an "infant precocious," the marvelous boy, a genuine American *Wunderkind*.

Stephen Crane, it must be said, had the bad luck to have Thomas Beer, the novelist, write the first biography.[5] Wilson Follett, who knew Beer and who prepared a twelve-volume edition of Crane's works between 1925 and 1927, was convinced that "many of the letters and other documents" on which Beer based his life "may never have existed" and that parts of Beer's biography of Crane were "fictional" (*CSC*, I, 7). Recent research confirms this suspicion. Beer's highly impressionistic biography, as much invented as factual, concocted scenes, characters, and comments by Crane that later students have simply been unable to authenticate or verify. Nevertheless, Beer's questionable work shaped the dominant image of Crane and has contaminated nearly every subsequent biography and edition of his letters. The poet John Berryman, for example, produced an eccentric Freudian biography of Crane in 1950.[6] Heavily dependent on Beer, it made psychoanalytic hay out of Beer's invented letters and accepted, as true, "facts" that were already under suspicion. The scholar R. W. Stallman tried to clean up the situation by editing (with Lillian Gilkes) the letters and composing a massive new

---

5 Thomas Beer, *Stephen Crane: A Study in American Letters* (New York: Alfred A. Knopf, 1923). Beer's inventions are repeated in his *Hanna, Crane, and the Mauve Decade* (New York: Alfred A. Knopf, 1941).
6 See John Berryman, *Stephen Crane* (New York: Sloane, 1950).

biography of Crane in 1968. But he too relied overmuch on Beer's quotations from the mysteriously "lost letters" and even included them in his own edition of the correspondence. In consequence, a reliable biography of Crane's life, always the stuff of myth and mythmaking, remains to be written.[7] Some facts, however, are beyond dispute.

I

Stephen Crane was born on November 1, 1871, in Newark, New Jersey, the fourteenth and last child of Jonathan Townley Crane, a very distinguished Methodist clergyman, and Mary Helen Peck Crane, the daughter of a clergyman and the niece of the reverend Bishop Jesse T. Peck. After the death of Crane's father in 1880, the mother and children moved to Asbury Park, a resort town on the Atlantic, where young Stephen grew up. At sixteen he was sent to the Claverack College and Hudson River Institute, a military high school—"the happiest period of my life," Crane later said, "although I was not then aware of it" (*CSC*, I, 212). In 1890 he spent a term at Lafayette College but dropped out and then transferred to Syracuse University for a term. Academic studies, however, were not his forte. More interesting was his job as a stringer for the *New York Tribune*, which took him into the Putnam County police court where he interviewed prostitutes and criminals. He followed up these investigations in the Bowery, where he became well known to the local pimps, drifters, thieves, and hookers. Meanwhile he wrote stories about life at the Jersey shore, camping in upstate New York, and sketches of the urban underworld—all written, he would later say, in "my clever Rudyard-Kipling style" (*CSC*, I, 63).

The turning point in Crane's life as a writer occurred while covering a lecture by Hamlin Garland for the *Tribune* in 1891. In conversations with this older writer, the youth was initiated into Garland's theory of "veritism" in fiction and heard for the first time about William Dean Howells's call for realism in the novel. Their contempt for Genteel Era sentimentalism, their advocacy of the ordinary, and their call for a precise representation of observed American reality—these struck a responsive chord and transformed Garland and Howells into what Crane called his new "literary fathers." And, in 1893, he told Lily Brandon

---

7 See Robert W. Stallman and Lillian Gilkes, eds., *Stephen Crane: Letters* (New York: New York University Press, 1960). Two rather full and imaginative lives are those of Robert W. Stallman, *Stephen Crane: A Biography* (New York: George Braziller, 1968), and Christopher Benfy, *The Double Life of Stephen Crane* (New York: Alfred A. Knopf, 1992). For a more straightforward factual account of the life, see Stanley Wertheim's valuable *The Crane Log: A Documentary Life of Stephen Crane, 1871–1900* (New York: G. K. Hall, 1994).

Munroe, an older married woman with whom he was having an affair, that he had

> renounced the clever school in literature. It seemed to me that there must be something more in life than to sit and cudgel one's brains for clever and witty expedients. So I developed all alone a little creed of art which I thought was a good one. Later I discovered that my creed was identical with the one of Howells and Garland and in this way I became involved in the beautiful war between those who say that art is man's substitute for nature and we are the most successful in art when we approach the nearest to nature and truth, and those who say—well, I don't know what they say. They don't, they can't say much but they fight villianously [sic] to keep Garland and I out of the big magazines. Howells, of course, is too powerful for them (*CSC*, I, 63).

Out of his Bowery experience, reshaped by the canons of the new realism, came Crane's first novel, *Maggie: A Girl of the Streets* (1893). Brief, blunt, and ironic, *Maggie* laconically narrated the seduction of an innocent young slum girl, her rejection and eviction by the outraged family, and her descent into prostitution, culminating in suicide. The material itself was raw stuff for genteel America, despite the contemporaneous wave of sociological reportage like Jacob Riis's *How the Other Half Lives: Studies Among the Tenements of New York* (1890). Particularly objectionable was Crane's nonjudgmental presentation of the heroine; this was beyond the pale—too much like the filthy Zola of *Nana*. Crane knew that no respectable publisher would touch it, and he was obliged to have *Maggie* privately printed, at his own expense, under the pseudonym "Johnston Smith"—a nondescript name deliberately chosen so as to keep his pious family in the dark and to prevent the authorities from tracking him down and prosecuting him for obscenity.

It would be pleasant to report that the correspondence of Stephen Crane during this period throws a vivid light on his relation to the theme, form, and style of *Maggie*. But we gain from the letters little new insight into the workings of his imagination. Unfortunately, Crane was neither a distinguished correspondent nor an especially reflective writer. His letters are dashed off, urgently practical, directed mainly at the recipient. They do not rise to the level of the epistolary art, even if they are indispensable to an understanding of his life. His flyleaf comment on *Maggie*, repeated in several verbatim book-gift inscriptions, does disclose, however, an acute awareness of the moral tone of the time, his attitude toward his forbidden subject, and the impact on his thinking of naturalistic theories of environmental determinism:

It is inevitable that you will be greatly shocked by this book but continue, please, with all possible courage, to the end. For, it tries to show that environment is a tremendous thing in the world and frequently shapes lives regardless. If one proves that theory, one makes room in Heaven for all sorts of souls, notably an occasional street girl, who are not confidently expected to be there by many excellent people. It is probable that the reader of this small thing may consider the author to be a bad man, but, obviously, that is a matter of small consequence to The Author (*CSC,* I, 5).

Sympathy and compassion for the fallen woman are evident in this comment, together with an aversion to the genteel morality of Crane's Methodist household. But its asserted environmental determinism is at odds with what the novel in fact portrays. Readers who assent to the naturalistic proposition that environment shapes lives regardless may wonder how Maggie could grow up in the violent slum world of Rum Alley and yet turn out to be the flower that "blossomed in a mud puddle."[8] Her mother is a violent alcoholic, her brother a young tough, and the neighborhood a violent battleground of posturing thugs and and menacing growlers. How could she have managed to preserve her innocence so long into young womanhood?[9]

And if we read the book closely, it seems likewise evident that she is largely a victim of self-deception rather than of her brutal environment, since she prefers to see her seducer-boyfriend Pete as a knight in shining armor rather than as the coarse thug he is. Maggie, in short, lives in the world of her fantasies, a state of illusion substantially of her own making (though stimulated by the Bowery melodramas that she attends, where heroes and villains are readily stereotyped, easily recognized, and cheered or hissed accordingly). The novel in fact comes close to illustrating Crane's observation, recorded in one of those Beer letters that have disappeared, that

> I do not think much can be done with the Bowery as long as the . . .
> [blurred] . . . are in their present state of conceit. A person who thinks
> himself superior to the rest of us because he has no job and no pride
> and no clean clothes is as badly conceited as Lillian Russell. In a story of
> mine called "An Experiment in Misery" I tried to make plain that the

---

8 Stephen Crane, *Maggie: A Girl of the Streets,* ed. Thomas A. Gullason (New York: W. W. Norton, 1979), p. 16.

9 Donald Pizer has offered the most convincing argument that *Maggie* fails to fulfill the naturalistic tenet of environmental determinism. See "Stephen Crane's *Maggie* and American Naturalism," *Criticism,* 7 (1965), 168–175; reprinted in *Stephen Crane's Career: Perspectives and Evaluations,* ed. Thomas A. Gullason (New York: New York University Press, 1972), pp. 335–343.

root of Bowery life is a sort of cowardice. Perhaps I mean a lack of ambition or to willingly be knocked flat and accept the licking. . . . I had
no other purpose in writing "Maggie" than to show people to people as
they seem to me. If that be evil, make the most of it (*CSC,* II, 671).

Crane seems to have "picked up" ideas about realism or naturalism then
in the air but not rigorously to have thought them through before
launching his next experiment. In any case, since the first edition of
Maggie had no publicity, distribution, or sales, it had zero impact on his
fortunes as a writer. Howells, whom he had come to know by 1893,
might have championed the book, but even he—at the time—must have
been dismayed by its coarse language and unremitting attention to the
frowning aspects of American life.[10]

Crane's fortunes, however, dramatically improved in 1895 when his
second novel, *The Red Badge of Courage,* was syndicated in several
newspapers and published by D. Appleton. The story of a raw recruit's
psychological terror in his first exposure to combat, Crane's tale was a
demonstration of the young man confronting an existential test. In exploring the anatomy of cowardice, Crane created a protagonist whom
Joseph Conrad—no doubt remembering his own Lord Jim—elevated
into "the symbol of all untried men."[11] Vivid in its impressionistic
vignettes, the book was widely acclaimed in both England and America
as a superb treatment of the Civil War, perhaps the best war novel of all
time. Reviewers compared Crane with Tolstoy and Zola, often to Crane's
advantage. The book was a best-seller and went through fourteen print-
ings in the first year; the twenty-four-year-old author was an instant
national celebrity. His success made possible a reissue in 1896 of *Maggie*
(in a less profane, rather expurgated form) and brought him feature-
writing assignments in the West and Mexico, a commission to report on
the Cuban insurrection of 1896, a war correspondent assignment in the

---

10 Howells told Cora Taylor in 1900 that, while he was "slow in getting at it," he had in fact
 liked the novel when he first read it. (See *Stephen Crane: Letters,* eds. R. W. Stallman and
 Lillian Gilkes [New York: New York University Press, 1960], p. 306.) And shortly after
 Crane's death, in 1902, he concluded that *Maggie* was "the best thing he did" because the
 tenement world "was essentially his inspiration, the New York of suffering and baffled and
 beaten life, of inarticulate or blasphemous life; and away from it he was not at home, with
 any theme, or any sort of character. It was the pity of his fate that he must quit New York,
 first as a theme, and then as a habitat. . . ." This relegation of *The Red Badge* to secondary
 status was doubtless based on the war novel's "literary" origin in history books, its less
 realistic, more impressionistic style, and on its inutility in reforming the socioeconomic
 conditions. See William Dean Howells, "Frank Norris," *North American Review,* 175
 (December 1902), 770–771.
11 Joseph Conrad, *Last Essays* (New York: Doubleday, Page, 1926); reprinted in *The Red Badge
 of Courage: Text and Criticism,* eds. Richard Lettis, Robert F. McDonnell, and William E.
 Morris (New York: Harcourt, Brace and World, 1960), p. 129.

Greco-Turkish War of 1897, and a *New York World* commission to cover the Spanish-American War of 1898. All these journalistic adventures led to an immense amount of reportage, most of it, it must be said, entirely uninspired hackwork. Still, out of Crane's far wandering came a handful of stories by which he will always be remembered—particularly "The Open Boat," "The Bride Comes to Yellow Sky," and "The Blue Hotel."

II

While Crane's great productivity is striking, his career as a serious literary artist virtually ended, it seems to me, in 1895—the year of *The Red Badge of Courage* and *The Black Rider and Other Lines.* The last five years of his life reflect a dismaying decline into pathetic and ineffective potboiling, with only an occasional short-story success. This slide was largely the consequence of his brilliant talent for self-destruction, particularly in the management of his personal life and his private affairs. As the record circuitously suggests, Crane reacted to the piety of his Methodist upbringing as many children of clergymen will do—by becoming the "black sheep" of the family and cultivating the forbidden. Alienated from the moral world represented by his family and religion, which he was ready to write off as mere hypocrisy, Crane descended into the Bowery underworld of thieves and prostitutes, ostensibly to report on "conditions." He fell afoul of the New York City police in 1895 by publicly defending a known prostitute, Dora Clark, against false arrest. In quixotically undertaking to defend this streetwalker, who had been picked up in his company for public solicitation, the chivalric Crane exposed himself to slander and vilification—the police insinuating that he was an alcoholic, a drug addict, or worse. [12] Police Commissioner Theodore Roosevelt had liked *The Red Badge of Courage,* but thenceforth he shunned the young novelist-reporter. And the outraged New York City police lay in wait and harassed him wherever he went.

Crane had, quite frankly, a genius for getting involved with impossible women. After the collapse of his affair with Mrs. Munroe, to whom he gave the manuscript of *Maggie* (her husband burned it in a rage),

---

12 Crane's bizarre defense of this supposed "Mary Magdalene" has led Edwin Cady, strangely enough, to call it an expression of Crane's "most enduring and fundamental ideal: the Christian gentleman." It is quite true that the Gospels commend a compassion for the socially despised, but Crane's aversion to piety and preference for the *demimonde* do not suggest any special concern for the ethics of the Christian gentleman, at least as Methodists and other Christians of his time would have understood it. What is clear, however, is that he resented authority figures, resisted the imposed enforcement of morals, and despised hypocrisy. See Edwin Cady, *Stephen Crane* (New Haven, Conn.: College and University Press, 1962), pp. 75ff.

and after the failure of his seduction of Nellie Crouse (a particularly conventional girl from Akron), Crane became involved in a sticky affair with Amy Leslie, the brilliant but unstable theatre critic for the *Chicago Daily News*, from whom he had borrowed money. She appears to have told him that she was pregnant with his child. Thus, with the New York City police hounding him and with Amy Leslie demanding money or marriage, the Cuban insurrection that November offered Crane the perfect way out of his troubles: he ran. In moments of crisis, in fact, flight was his characteristic gesture. As he remarked to Ripley Hitchcock, his Appleton publisher, in March 1896, "I cannot help vanishing and disappearing and dissolving. It is my foremost trait" (*CSC*, I, 213).

In Jacksonville, Florida, where Crane was awaiting a boat for Cuba that fall in 1896, he expressed his undying love to Amy Leslie, and, perhaps anticipating death, enjoined his literary executor Willis Brooks Hawkins "to help Amy in what is now really a great trouble." Most students of Crane's life have inferred that he got her into trouble, but one witness reports that Amy Leslie had "framed Crane, saying she was pregnant, in an effort to get Crane to marry her" (*CSC*, I, 262). The truth of the matter we shall perhaps never know. But the Jacksonville letters of December 1896 show Crane simultaneously reassuring Amy Leslie while scoring a new romantic conquest in one Cora Taylor. This appears to have been an easy enough score, especially for the handsome and famous author of *Maggie* and *The Red Badge*, whom Ford Madox Ford would later describe as "an Apollo with starry eyes."[13] But it had long-range and, in my view, disastrous implications.

Cora Taylor, née Howorth, was the veteran madam of one of the swankest whorehouses in Jacksonville—a "pleasure resort" called the Hotel de Dream. At the time Cora met Crane she had gone through two husbands but was still married to Captain Donald William Stewart, the younger son of an English baronet. No one knows where she met Stewart or how, after her marriage broke up, she got from London to Florida. Why she took the name Taylor is also a question. But by 1896 she had accumulated quite a little property and ran a class-A establishment—or so said the clerk at the St. James Hotel, who kept "a list of the better houses of ill fame for the intelligent guidance of guests of the hotel."[14] Cora, it would appear, was not without erotic competition, for Crane knew other madams along "the line" (as the red-light district in

13 Quoted in Miranda Seymour, *A Ring of Conspirators: Henry James and His Literary Circle, 1895–1915* (Boston: Houghton Mifflin, 1988), p. 25.

14 Lillian Gilkes, *Cora Crane: A Biography of Mrs. Stephen Crane* (Bloomington: Indiana University Press, 1960), p. 26. Hereafter, quotations from this work will be given as *CC*, in parentheses, in the text.

Jacksonville was called). He gave away his novels to a number of his new friends along this "line," and in fact generously inscribed a copy of *Maggie* to Lyda de Camp, one of the more notorious Jacksonville whoremistresses, in February 1897. But, according to habitués of the district, Cora (who had come from a respectable Boston family) "had class" and so she captured the youth.[15]

Lillian Gilkes, Cora Taylor's biographer, was of the opinion that Cora belonged

> in the tradition of those European women—authors and courtesans —who, with their intellectual curiosity, wit, and immense personal charm, achieved renown in the salons over which they more or less unconventionally presided: the Aphra Behns, Ouidas, George Sands, de Staëls, and Récamiers.[16]

This, it seems to me, is putting a pretty face on a tawdry matter. Cora, despite her affectation of nobility in calling herself "Lady Stewart," was not a Mme. Récamier. Six years older than Crane and remarkably big-bosomed and stout of thigh, she was more a maternal figure to the errant writer than a grand intellectual or literary inspiration. But in Crane's infatuation she had a good thing going, and she played her cards very shrewdly. (Perhaps getting wind of this new liaison, Amy Leslie meanwhile sued Crane for the recovery of her loan—creating a public ruckus in New York that did nothing for his reputation.)

Cora Taylor and the world of letters nearly lost the brilliant young novelist on the morning of January 2, 1897. En route to Cuba to report on the insurrection, his filibustering steamer the *Commodore*—carrying men and munitions to the Cuban rebels—mysteriously exploded and went down. Struggling with heavy seas in a small dinghy for thirty hours, the captain, Crane, and two others eventually washed up on the Daytona beach. As Wertheim and Sorrentino rightly note, "For Crane, this struggle for survival with the elements and its irrational denouement [the oiler Higgins, the best swimmer in the group, was drowned in the surf] confirmed his view of the essential conditions of life itself and was fictionalized, with very little alteration of the actual circumstances, in his finest story, 'The Open Boat'" (*CSC*, I, 261).

---

15 See the letter of January 22, 1934, in which E. W. McReady, one of Crane's friends, describes the "hostess" Cora and her clientele at the Hotel de Dream: "Fact is, she was a cut above us in several ways, notably poise and surety of command of herself & others. If she had any false notes I was then all too unskilled in recognizing authentic 'class,' or lack of it, to detect any. . . . Stephen took her in his stride—and, as it turned out, in some very solid respects, the gray mare proved to be the best horse. . . ." Quoted in *Stephen Crane: Letters*, p. 340.

16 Gilkes, *Cora Crane*, p. 29.

Back in Jacksonville, Crane was provided by Cora with such price-less consolations that, when he was commissioned to cover the Greco-Turkish war that spring, he wangled for her a commission as the first female war correspondent, and together they sailed for Greece. Richard Harding Davis, a journalist who also covered this war, mentioned Cora in a letter from Athens, as "a Lady Stuart [sic] who has run away from her husband to follow Crane." He described her as "a commonplace dull woman old enough to have been his mother and with dyed yellow hair" (*CC*, 76, 92). Curiously, Crane's first dispatches about this little "bathtub war" were highly lyrical: he beat the military drum (*CC*, 85). But hardly had the war's sobering reality begun to impress him when it ended abruptly, after a month, with the rout of the Greeks. After some local sightseeing (they of course had to visit a harem in Constantine), Crane and Cora decided to settle in England. After all, Stephen could not take the madam of a Jacksonville whorehouse back to his Methodist family in New Jersey. The police in New York might also be a problem. Where could they live? In England, Crane's fiction was immensely popular; and there, they thought, the unconventionality of their liaison would be more acceptable. To simplify matters, in England, they always repre-sented themselves quite respectably as "Mr. and Mrs. Crane."

III

Stephen Crane's life with Cora in England was, it must be said, the stuff of sheer bohemian excess. Settling at Ravensbrook, Oxted, Surrey, in June 1897, they fell in with the writers Harold Frederic, Ford Madox Heuffer (later Ford), and H. G. Wells, all of whom were then living nearby with women not their wives. Joseph and Jessie Conrad were also neighbors, and the then-struggling Polish author became one of Crane's closest friends. (To Conrad, Crane confided that his firsthand ex-perience of the war in Greece proved to him that *The Red Badge* was "all right" [*CSC*, I, 283].) Even Henry James, living nearby in Rye, was drawn into the bizarre social life, which often resembled a three-ring circus, of the young "Mr. and Mrs. Crane." So many people descended on them from London—the idle, admirers, the curious, people with a cause, out-and-out sponges—that Crane nearly went bankrupt in en-tertaining them and could do little work. According to Ford Madox Hueffer, the Cranes attracted "the most discreditable bums any city can ever have seen" (quoted in *CC*, 129). In December 1897 Cora remarked to Sylvester Scovel that "Stephen is fat, for him, and works hard. He is content and good quite the old married man" [sic] (*CSC*, I, 316). But she obviously missed the signs of his growing discontent. More an adventurer than a husband, Crane found it lucky for him when the Spanish-American War broke out in 1898. Pulling a disappearing act, he abandoned Cora for the attractions of that bully little war. As he told his brother William, "I am a wanderer now and I must see enough."[17]

Crane's adventures in Cuba provoked yet another of the great public scandals of his life: the uproar that occurred when, literally, he dropped from sight. Very possibly he had grown tired of Cora or become embarrassed by the alliance he had contracted with her. Perhaps he was tired of domestic life and—in the age of rough rider heroes—wanted more adventure than was offered even in his unconventional arrangement with Cora. Perhaps he simply wanted escape from guests and groupies and sought the peace and freedom to write. In any case, he became a runaway. He stopped writing to Cora and disappeared in Havana. Not knowing where he was and unable to communicate with him, Cora became utterly frantic. With no money of her own, the bills piled up, solicitors threatened, tradesmen sued, and the domestic situation at Ravensbrook began to collapse. To make ends meet, Cora tried to sell his juvenilia to publishers and promised them manuscripts that Crane had not yet written. She wrote hysterical letters and fired off cables, desperately trying to find her husband. All the war correspondents in Cuba were mobilized for the search. To John Hay, the U.S. ambassador in London, Cora addressed a desperate appeal for help in finding him, noting that Crane

> was watched, I understand, by the spanish police. He was stopping quietly at Hotel Pasaje—and disappeared about Sep 8*th*. I am almost distracted with grief and anxiety. I am sure you will personally ask the President to instruct the American commission to demand Mr. Crane from the Havana police (*CSC*, II, 370–371).

She likewise cabled Crane's family in America, who were stunned by the bombshell that Stephen not only had disappeared but now had a wife. Those who knew let it be known in America that Madam Cora, still married to Stewart, was no wife to Stevie. Tongues wagged on both sides of the Atlantic: Crane had done it again. Eventually the Hearst press tracked him down and reported that Crane was "hiding" in a Havana boardinghouse, holed up, writing. Apparently oblivious to what had been going on, Crane was angered and humiliated by the public fuss. "For a mild and melancholy kid," said James Gibbons Huneker, "he certain had fallen completely into the garbage can of gossip" (quoted in *CC*, 175).

---

17 See R. W. Stallman, *Stephen Crane: An Omnibus* (New York: Alfred A. Knopf, 1952), p. 663.

It is commonly said of *The Red Badge of Courage*, as Wertheim and Sorrentino put it, that the novel "exposed the futility of war and expressed an extremely cynical attitude toward heroism" (*CSC*, I, 285n).[18] But Crane's attitude toward the military, his attraction to warfare, and his behavior in wartime seem utterly inconsistent with this common critical estimate of the novel. Is *The Red Badge* an antiwar novel or was Crane in fact drawn to violence in battle and the opportunities it occasioned for virile heroism? This contradiction—evident in both the fiction and in the author's life—deserves further exploration.[19]

First, we must remember that he was sent to Claverack because, as his sister-in-law, Mrs. George Crane, later put it, "He loved to play at soldiers from his earliest childhood." "Most of his playthings were in the form of toy soldiers, guns and the like," she remarked, and "his fondness for everything military induced his mother to send him to the Claverack Military Academy" (*CSC*, I, 27). During the Greco-Turkish war he wrote his brother William from Athens that he hoped

> to get a position on the staff of the Crown Prince. Wont that be great? I am so happy over it I can hardly breathe. I shall try—I shall try like blazes to get a decoration out of the thing but that depends on good fortune and is between you and I and God (*CSC*, I, 285).

He failed, of course, to get that commission. But when the war later broke out with Spain, Crane tried to enlist in the U.S. Navy. Physically unfit, the journalist nevertheless covered the landings at Guantanamo and distinguished himself for bravery far beyond that expected of even a combatant. He repeatedly exposed himself to withering Spanish gunfire and was later praised by many officers for his coolness under fire. A commission, decorations, heroism—all these he appeared to want for himself, however much his fiction appears to undercut the idea of glory in combat. Some of the other journalists in Cuba thought that Crane had a death wish and was trying to get himself killed. Struggling with guilt, couldn't this minister's son face a return to Cora? Or had his in-

---

18 The editors explain this discrepancy by remarking that "Crane's vainglorious boasts must be evaluated in the perspective of his guilt feelings over his youthful bohemianism and his desire to ingratiate himself with William, the stern paterfamilias, seventeen years his senior and a community leader and magistrate in Port Jervis, who was always known as Judge Crane." But Crane's predictable excitement, wherever the action was, seems not sufficiently accounted for by this explanation.

19 The question of whether Henry Fleming in *The Red Badge of Courage* is initiated though battle into manhood, or whether the self-deluded youth is still in a state of confusion at the end, has vexed critics for nearly a century. In my view Crane's multiple and abbreviated ironies and the incoherence of the final pages of the novel prevent us from attaining, through a mere *explication de texte*, any clear answer. Nor will reading comparable stories, like "The Veteran" or "The Mystery of Heroism," resolve the ambiguity of the novel.

cipient tuberculosis become manifest and spurred him on to these feverish last-minute heroics? The answer to these questions is difficult, in part because we do not have Crane's letters to Cora, which are mysteriously missing.[20] In any case, Crane's feelings about returning to Cora can be only inferred from his behavior and from a certain reading between the lines.

With respect to this enigma, the poem "Intrigue" may be illuminating. While it ostensibly eroticizes Death as the lover, certain lines appear to refer to Cora. "Tell me why," he asks in one lyric, "behind thee / I see always the shadow of another lover?" In another poem he writes: "He had your picture in his room / A scurvy traitor picture / And he smiled / — Merely a fat complacence / Of men who know fine women— / And thus I divided with him / A part of my love." And another reads:

Thou art my love,
And thou art the ashes of other men's love,
And I bury my face in these ashes,
And I love them—
Woe is me.[21]

Was he overwhelmed with jealousy about her past—or morbidly in love with it? Was she in fact faithful to him—or turning tricks on the side? Was the possessive Cora suffocating to the youth—or did he relish humiliation? Did this errant son of Methodism yet have a lingering conscience—or was he a moral masochist soliciting his own degradation? It is hard to tell. For whatever reason, Crane lingered in North America after the war and, during the nine months of his separation from Cora, he again tried (unsuccessfully) to revive his affair with Lily Brandon Munroe. Meanwhile there is no clear answer to the question Conrad posed to the frantic Cora: "What kind of trouble is Stephen in? You make me very uneasy. Are you *sure* you can bring him back?" (*CSC*, I, 383).

Eventually Crane did come back to Cora, with explanations we can only imagine, for there is no extant documentary evidence. But he took up life with her at a new establishment in England, Brede Place. This

---

20 Wertheim and Sorrentino remark that they were denied access to some collections, one of which may contain Crane's letters to her. In their search for Crane letters, Stallman and Gilkes remark that "Writing to Thomas Beer in 1932, John Northern Hilliard claimed ownership of 150 Crane letters held in storage with some Crane-inscribed books. All this is untraced and presumably now lost. Hilliard's daughter says that she cannot recall any such library in her father's possession. Perhaps Hilliard was exaggerating his holdings; but who knows?" See *Stephen Crane: Letters*, p. xii.

21 *The Complete Poems of Stephen Crane*, ed. Joseph Katz (Ithaca: Cornell University Press, 1972), pp. 117, 113, 111.

huge manorial hall, further from London, nevertheless lured even more unwelcome visitors ("lice," Crane called them). Cora was visibly relieved to have him back, but the maintenance of this new household, with its caretaker, horses and dogs, and the steady stream of visitors, cost "Baron Brede," as Crane was called, a pretty penny. Much of the expense was owing, it would seem, to Cora's extravagance and love of luxury. "I have lived five years in one all my life," Cora once noted in her diary; "I have never economized in sensation, emotion. I am a spendthrift in every way." Crane, on the financial side, was little better. "In one way Steve and I are the same person," Cora told one of his friends. "We have no sense about money at all" (*CC*, 46, 130).

IV

To pay for the cases of wine and champagne, the game pies, the sides of beef and cartloads of vegetables for this establishment, Crane had to write, write, write. The burden of his correspondence in the last two years of his life is invariably money. To Paul Revere Reynolds, his American agent, and James B. Pinker, his English agent, and to various newspaper editors and publishers the theme is always the same—send as much as possible, immediately. The appeals became increasingly desperate and ugly. He canned Revere because the checks were not frequent enough, and he likewise threatened to fire Pinker (the distinguished agent of James, Conrad, and other important writers). Meanwhile, Crane ground out the copy—journalistic essays, mediocre short stories, abortive novel manuscripts—almost all of dubious quality. Throughout this period Cora also bombarded his agents, sending promises of more "stuff" to come, demands for immediate payment, appeals for advances on yet unwritten manuscripts, expressing fear of their immediate eviction. In *The Critic* in 1900, Karl Harriman remarked that Crane once

> remained in his room for three days, sleepless and complaining when Cora tiptoed in with food on a tray that even the slight sound, breaking his concentration, was like a brick hurled through a window. In that time he poked four stories under the door, and Cora ran them off on the typewriter for Pinker (quoted in *CC*, 203).

At this point in Crane's life, only the word count, not the quality of his prose, seemed to matter to them.

Such slapdash work was not easy to sell, and Crane repeatedly complained of editors' indifference and the critics' continual comparison of his new stuff with what he called "the damned book 'The Red Badge.'" Couldn't they see that "the high dramatic key of The Red Badge cannot be sustained"? Invariably they could not. Many of his stories were rejected, and published works—such as *The Third Violet* and *Active Service*—produced critical dismay. Crane knew that his recent prose was "pretty rotten work" and said, "I used myself up in the accursed 'Red Badge'" (*CSC*, I, 161). He became so imperious about money that Pinker was obliged to write Crane on October 24, 1899:

> I confess that you are becoming most alarming. You telegraphed on Friday for £20; Mrs. Crane, on Monday, makes it £50; today comes your letter making it £150, and I very much fear that your agent must be a millionaire if he is to satisfy your necessities a week hence. . . . There is a risk of spoiling the market if we have to dump too many short stories on it at once (*CSC*, II, 539–540).

A disappointment of Crane's correspondence, so concerned as it is with money, is that Crane rarely reflects on what his writing means to him; nor does he have much to say about the distinguished English writers with whom he was so frequently in contact. The best of this literary material is never very felicitous in expression. A few instances, however, may be revealing. On November 11, 1897, Crane told Conrad that *The Nigger of the Narcissus* was

> simply great. The simple treatment of the death of Waite [James Wait] is too good, too terrible. I wanted to forget it at once. It caught me very hard. I felt ill over that red thread lining from the corner of the man's mouth to his chin. It was frightful with the weight of a real and present death. By such small means does the real writer suddenly flash out in the sky above those who are always doing rather well (*CSC*, I, 310).

Conrad reciprocated by praising Crane's "A Man and Some Others" and by saying that he was horribly envious of him. "Confound you—you fill the blamed landscape—you—by all the devils—fill the sea-scape." "The Open Boat" he called "immensely interesting. I don't use the word in its common sense. It is fundamentally interesting to me. Your temperament makes old things new and new things amazing. I want to swear at you, to bless you—perhaps to shoot you—but I prefer to be your friend" (*CSC*, I, 315).

In response to some direct questions from Thomas Hutchinson, Crane observed in 1899 that

> I am not carnivorous about living writers. I have not read any of the books that you ask me to criticize except that of Mr. Howells, and it has disappointed me. My tastes? I do not know of any living author whose works I have wholly read. I like what I know of Anatole France, Henry

James, George Moore and several others. I deeply admire some short stories by Mr. Bierce, Mr. Kipling and Mr. White. Mr. Hardy, since you especially inquire about his work, impresses me as a gigantic writer who "over-treats" his subjects. I do not care for the long novels of Mr. Clemens, for the same reason. Four hundred pages of humour is a little bit too much for me. My judgment in the case is not worth burning straw, but I give it as portentously as if kingdoms toppled while awaiting it under anxious skies (*CSC*, II, 566).

This occasional wit does not shine on every page but is welcome when we encounter it. Crane told Henry Sanford Bennett that he was wrong about Ford Madox Hueffer: "I admit he is patronizing. He patronized his family. He patronizes Conrad. He will end up by patronizing God who will have to get used to it and they will be friends" (*CSC*, II, 497). As one used to consorting with prostitutes in the red-light districts, Crane naturally complained of "tea at James's. My God how does he stand these bores who pester him. Mrs. Humphry Ward was there. What an old cow! She has no more mind than a president. Nice to us, though" (*CSC*, II, 507). That James had even invited the Cranes to tea was a testament to his admiration of the young writer and an act of remarkable tolerance—for ugly rumors had begun to spread in Surrey that Cora was not Crane's wife, and James had limited tolerance for brazen disregard of social conventions.

In respect to Oscar Wilde, whose recent homosexual entanglements had landed him in Reading Gaol, Crane was rather blunt. "About Wilde and his troubles," he observed,

a mere stranger and runaway dog like me can't be supposed to care. I met him once. We stood and looked at each other and he bleated like a sheep. With those bad manners that are so awfully much mine I laughed in his face. He tried to borrow money from Dick Davis when he was being tried after insulting Davis all across London. Something pretty poor in him. And I owe my brothers too much money to bother about helping with subscriptions for a mildewed chump like Wilde. Blood, etc. If Harris and the rest of Wilde's friends really want to help him they ought to send him express to Weir Mitchell [a physician-novelist specializing in the treatment of literary neurasthenics] or some specialist in his kind of malady. Perhaps it is because I lived on borrowed money and ate in lunch-wagons when I was trying to be someone that these magnified sinners in good duds bore me so. That isn't what Conrad would call a sentiment of generosity but it is mine (*CSC*, II, 507).

Such are the literary remarks we invariably find in his letters. If they fail of any great insight and tend toward gossip, he might have had better teachers than the newspapermen with whom he was clearly more comfortable.

The beginning of the end for Crane occurred in the winter season of 1899 when he and Cora decided to throw a huge four-day Christmas party. This bizarre extravaganza required the redecoration of the whole manor hall at Brede Place and the renovation of the bedrooms for some fifty-odd invited house guests. The festivities were highlighted with the performance of a silly play dealing with the legend of the Brede Hall ghost, Sir Goddard Oxenbridge. While Crane wrote most of "The Ghost," he solicited copy (of almost any kind) from Henry James, Joseph Conrad, Wells, George Gissing, H. Rider Haggard, and other writer friends—so as to feature them as authors on the printed program. If H. G. Wells thought the party a lark, the neighbors called it a Babylonian orgy. Drinking and dancing and games went on apace. But the gaiety ended abruptly on December 29, after the grand ball, when Crane collapsed with a lung hemorrhage, and his doom was sealed.

Desperate to save him, Cora got the best medical attention she could, but, as Crane's condition deteriorated, Dr. Mitchel Bruce recommended his removal to the Black Forest for the Nordrach treatment, a regimen for tuberculosis that included rest, overeating, and mild exercise. Broke and in debt to Pinker, who had advanced money on yet unpublished stories, Cora appealed desperately to Crane's family and friends for financial assistance, but little was forthcoming. Rather surprisingly, the tenderest expression of affection for Crane came from Henry James, who told Cora:

> It is a shock to me that Crane is less well—I was full of hope, & had been, in that hope, assuming that a good effect had come to him from his move: cheerful theories much disconcerted! I think of him with more sympathy & sorrow than I can say. . . . I won't pretend to utter hopes about Crane which may be vain—or seem to you now, & thereby only irritating or, at least, distressing: but I constantly think of him & as it were pray for him. I feel that I am not taking too much for granted in believing that you may be in the midst of worries on the money-score which will perhaps make the cheque, for Fifty Pounds, that I enclose, a convenience to you. Please view it as such & dedicate it to whatever service it may best render my stricken young friend. It meagrely represents my tender benediction to him (*CSC*, II, 658–659).

But the convalescence in the Black Forest was to no avail. Stephen Crane died on June 5, 1900.

For those interested in the fate of Cora Crane, it may be remarked that she lost out to the Crane family in a contest over the right to Crane's literary estate and returned to Jacksonville, Florida. Crane had been, Lillian Gilkes remarks, "the instrument, thus far, of her salvation, which appeared to Cora—romanticist that she was—in the twin guise of redemption and social rehabilitation" (*CC*, 267). But with the loss of his estate, redemption and social rehabilitation no longer seemed to interest her. And there in Jacksonville, in a mysteriously short time, she accumulated a good deal of property, opened up another whorehouse, "The Court," and in 1905 married one Hammond P. McNeil, a young saloonkeeper of twenty-five (she was forty-one). Furious at her attentions to a Harry Parker (age nineteen), McNeil murdered Parker in cold blood but was acquitted because it was "a husband's crime of honor." He then sued Cora for divorce, claiming he had been deceived as to her character and did not know she kept a "disorderly house" (*CC*, 341). Her name became a public joke and a byword. And of course these widely publicized events did Crane's posthumous reputation no good. When Cora Crane died in 1910 she was cohabiting with a businessman named Ernest Budd, said to be estranged from his wife. It was rumored in Jacksonville that their "adopted" child was really hers, fathered by Budd. But her biographer Lillian Gilkes was unable to verify this tale (*CC*, 356–357, 371).

On learning of Crane's death, Henry James wrote to Cora, "I feel I can say nothing to you that you haven't been saying again and again to yourself. What a brutal, needless extinction—what an unmitigated unredeemed catastrophe! I think of him with such a sense of possibilities and powers." [22] If James felt a tenderness to Crane's memory, his final judgment of Cora was less forgiving: "She is indeed, clearly, an unprofitable person," he told Pinker, "and I judge her whole course and career, so far as it appeared in this neighbourhood, very sternly and unforgivingly. I sent her a contribution which reached her at the moment of Crane's death . . . and yet I learn that the young local doctor here, who gave almost all his time to them, quite devotedly, during Crane's illness, and took them to the Black Forest, has never yet, in spite of the money gathered in by her at that time, received a penny, and doesn't in the least expect to. It's really a swindle." [23] When Cora, in 1907, took a sentimental trip back to Surrey and appeared for a visit at Lamb House, James sent back a curt note saying, "I am at present in London, so that a call at Lamb House will not find yours truly" (quoted in *CC*, 345).

---

22 *Henry James: Letters,* ed. Leon Edel (Cambridge: Harvard University Press, 1984), IV, 145.
23 Quoted in Seymour, *A Ring of Conspirators,* p. 203.

Possibilities and powers Crane did indeed have, in abundance. Had his circumstances been more propitious, had his domestic arrangements been less financially ruinous, he might have more brilliantly realized those possibilities. As it is, we find it hard to disagree with the editors of his correspondence that "the constantly reiterated demand for money, money, money in Crane's letters to his publishers and literary agents and his final deterioration into hackwork suggest what his future might have been had he survived his twenty-ninth year" (*CSC,* I, 2). We are left then with *Maggie, The Red Badge,* a few distinguished stories, and a handful of striking poems. These do not add up to a substantial *oeuvre.* But they do sufficiently testify to Crane's brilliant, if meteoric, literary talent. And to a great extent they redeem him from the charge of relentless hackwork and surely elevate him above the level of those who were merely doing rather well.

The Perils of
Solitude:
Kate Chopin's
The Awakening

One vindication of the revision of the canon in American literature today, or so it is frequently claimed in the academy, is the recent discovery and elevation into preeminence of Kate Chopin (1850–1904). She is indeed very "hot" at the moment, for remarkable reasons (not always literary in kind) that I shall presently discuss. Barbara C. Ewell has remarked of Mrs. Chopin's best novel, *The Awakening* (1899), that "the recognition of its revolutionary achievement took some sixty years.[1] In fact, however, Mrs. Chopin's work has been long known to those with a serious interest in the literature of the period, and every university of any standing (in the South at least) has, from afar back, assigned her stories to students. I myself vividly remember reading them in the 1950s in Chapel Hill, along with such other regionalists as Sarah Orne Jewett, Mary Wilkins Freeman, Grace King, and Thomas Nelson Page. So Mrs. Chopin cannot be claimed as a "lost" author newly discovered by the recent race-gender-class canon-busters.

It is true that her reputation languished in the decades just after her death in 1904. (Perhaps this is the fate of most writers.) But *The Awakening* was republished in 1906, and Daniel Rankin revived interest in her with his 1932 biography.[2] In 1969 Per Seyersted added fresh information to the portrait in *Kate Chopin: A Critical Biography*, and in

---

1 Barbara C. Ewell, *Kate Chopin* (New York: Ungar, 1986), p. 158.
2 Daniel Rankin, *Kate Chopin and Her Creole Stories* (Philadelphia: University of Pennsylvania Press, 1932).

the same year he also edited her complete works.[3] Well before 1970, moreover, a number of serious American critics had addressed the issues raised in her work[4] —all of this before the present Chopin "revivalists" arrived on the scene.

During her lifetime and for some time thereafter, Mrs. Chopin was principally known as a Louisiana local colorist, a writer in the vein of George Washington Cable and Grace King. But she was generally thought to be, at her best, distinctly better than King and perhaps better than Cable, even though she never wrote anything of the ambitious scope and exotic romanticism of Cable's *The Grandissimes* (1880). No one questioned that Mrs. Chopin was a Southern regionalist: the setting, subjects, and characters of her short stories in *Bayou Folk* (1894) and *A Night in Acadie* (1897), and in her novels *At Fault* (1890) and *The Awakening* (1899), confirmed that. Simply to list some of her titles ("The Bênitous' Slave," "Désirée's Baby," "Mamouche," "Nég Créol," and "Tante Cat'rinette") will immediately suggest that exotic milieu of Cajuns and Creoles, as well as a strange and faraway world of magnolia trees, Spanish moss, secluded lagoons, and mysterious bayous.

Local-color writing was, in my student days, in disfavor in the academy, and perhaps rightly so. For regionalist prose was largely a collection of sentimental tales of local peculiarities of character—tales typified by "the-most-unforgettable-character-I-ever-met" stories that used to appear, and perhaps still do, in the *Reader's Digest*. Few serious critics paid much attention then to Bret Harte, Thomas Nelson Page, Joel Chandler Harris, and the others. Now, however, the critical situation is different. Local-color writing offers a new pretext for criticism: if the local colorists are women, they may be ransacked for evidence that they were real or protofeminists and accordingly exalted. If they don't give evidence of nascent feminism, all is not lost: they can always be elevated as repressed victims of the "male critical establishment."

I

Mrs. Chopin is nowadays most often invoked as a brilliant critic of the institution of marriage, as a portrayer of the oppressed condition of women under the "patriarchy," and as a writer whose acute perceptions transcend the representation of trivial regional idiosyncrasies. The re-

---

3 *The Complete Works of Kate Chopin,* ed. Per Seyersted (2 vols., Baton Rouge: Louisiana State University Press, 1969).

4 Among the men who shaped Mrs. Chopin's modern reputation were Fred Lewis Pattee, Arthur Hobson Quinn, Joseph J. Reilly, Carlos Baker, Clarence Gohdes, Van Wyck Brooks, Kenneth Eble, Edmund Wilson, Warner Berthoff, Lewis Leary, and Larzer Ziff.

valuation of her work along feminist lines may be illustrated by considering "The Story of an Hour." In this brief but stunning tale, a Mrs. Mallard, "afflicted with heart trouble," is told that her husband Brently, who "had never looked save with love upon her," has been killed in a train wreck. Mrs. Chopin writes that Mrs. Mallard "did not hear the story as many women have heard the same, with a paralyzed inability to accept its significance. She wept at once, with sudden, wild abandonment, in her sister's arms." Then she goes to her room alone. There she stares out the window, awaiting "something [that] was coming to her." She does not know what it is, but something remarkable is striving "to possess her." Suddenly it comes to her and, in a state of increasing excitement, she begins to whisper "free, free, free!" and envisions "a long procession of years to come that would belong to her absolutely":

> There would be no one to live for her during those coming years; she would live for herself. There would be no powerful will bending hers in that blind persistence with which men and women believe they have a right to impose a private will upon a fellow-creature. A kind intention or a cruel intention made the act seem no less a crime as she looked upon it in that brief moment of illumination.

Kate Chopin writes that Mrs. Mallard had loved Brently—at times—and that he had loved her. But that her husband might have loved her, or she him, counts for naught "in face of this possession of self-assertion which she suddenly recognized as the strongest impulse of her being."

Yet just as suddenly, Brently Mallard walks through the doorway: the report of his death has been a mistake—he is alive! And the shock of his reappearance causes Mrs. Mallard to collapse. Kate Chopin ends the story quite tersely: "When the doctors came they said she had died of heart disease—of the joy that kills."[5] The story concludes in a remarkable reversal, yet its trick ending, of a kind made so popular in the 1890s by O. Henry, is saved from mere facility by its ambiguity. What is it, exactly, that kills Mrs. Mallard?

It is easy to say (as feminists often do) that Mrs. Mallard's oppression in marriage dissolves into a moment of freedom but that, when this is robbed of her, she expires in a fatal disappointment.[6] She is thus seen

---

5 Kate Chopin, "The Story of an Hour," in *A Vocation and a Voice: Stories by Kate Chopin*, ed. Emily Toth (New York: Penguin Books, 1991), pp. 76–79. This volume is a new collection, never published in her lifetime, of twenty-three stories that Mrs. Chopin was putting together at the time of her death.

6 Mary E. Papke claims that "what murdered her" was "the birth of individual self," and "the erasure of that joy when her husband and, necessarily, her old self returned." See "Chopin's Stories of Awakening," in *Approaches to Teaching Chopin's The Awakening*, ed. Bernard Koloski (New York: Modern Language Association, 1988), p. 75.

to be a martyr to the cruelty of marriage, which Mrs. Chopin is at pains to criticize for its unfairness to women. The view that Mrs. Chopin had it in for marriage is common in the criticism of her work, and the oppression of men in marriage is also frequently advanced as her distinctive theme—especially with respect to Edna Pontellier's affliction in *The Awakening.* The assumption is thus common that Mrs. Chopin held convictions commonly found in contemporary feminism. But was Mrs. Chopin in fact opposed to marriage as such? Her life may hold a clue.

The older biographies of Rankin and Seyersted have, in certain respects, now been superseded by Emily Toth's recent life, *Kate Chopin.*[7] It is a labor of love, a remarkable work of twenty years of research. It is distinctly a work of the current moment in our culture, when feminist imperatives dictate how the tensions in intimate relationships shall be viewed. Thus Professor Toth writes: "Chopin's fictional wives are often discontented, and attracted to other men; some of them yearn for the freedom of their single days. . ." (*KC,* 30). This much is true. It is Mrs. Chopin's great distinction to have been first to describe the inner frustrations of women and to bring out into the open the intensity of female sexual feeling. But her knowledge that people—both men and women—have sexual feelings and long for freedom from emotional bonds should not blind us to her deeper preoccupation—the *effect* of that wish, those feelings, on the self, not an attack on the institution of marriage as such. The feminist reading of "The Story of an Hour," doubtless suggested by the tale itself, does not do entire justice, it seems to me, to Mrs. Chopin's remarkable irony.

We might just as easily note that Mrs. Chopin locates the desire for power over another in both men *and* women: "that blind persistence with which men and women believe they have a right to impose a private will upon a fellow-creature." Mrs. Mallard's strongest impulse in the story, released by the news of her husband's death, is a desire to assert herself. Had she wished to assert herself over her husband when he was alive? Does she wish to assert herself over others now that she is free? With her husband now dead, this last possibility seems within her grasp. If her husband who "lived for her" was cruel in (it is suggested) bending her to his will, should Mrs. Mallard be praised for likewise wishing now to assert herself over others?

This is, among other things, a story about a woman who feels as a *burden* the love of another person who lives for her; it is about the wish to escape from that burden, not a tale about the usual kind of spousal

---

7 See Emily Toth, *Kate Chopin: A Life of the Author of The Awakening* (New York: William Morrow, 1990). Hereafter, quotations from this work will be given as *KC,* in parentheses, in the text.

victimization. Perhaps the joy that kills is the ecstasy of mistakenly believing that one can be free from the bond created by spousal care and concern. Perhaps it is the belief that, under different circumstances, one is at liberty to assert oneself over others. These possibilities are at least suggested by Mrs. Chopin herself, in a letter to the *Natchitoches Enterprise*, where she remarks in another connection: "It were an unspeakable calamity if anyone should think he has the right to impose a private will on others. That is a part of a striker, an assassin."[8] If a woman believing that she has "a right to impose a private will upon a fellow-creature" may herself be considered an assassin, perhaps Mrs. Mallard is slain by the check that reality gives to her own now-liberated will to power. However we choose to see it, "The Story of an Hour" should make plain that Mrs. Chopin *is* more than a local colorist; her sense of psychological complexities runs deep into the recesses of human character.

II

Kate Chopin, despite the evident Frenchness of her name, was not exactly a French woman, a Creole, or a Louisianian. She was born in St. Louis, Missouri, in 1850, to Thomas O'Flaherty, a slaveholding Irish businessman. But St. Louis had been founded by French explorers and contained many old French families, and O'Flaherty's marriage to Eliza Faris allied him to a society of wealthy families whose names resonate with the city's distinguished social history—the Chouteaus, Gratiots, Benoists, Gareschés, and Charlevilles. Her father was killed in a train accident when she was five; Kate O'Flaherty's principal influences were, therefore, her mother and her grandmother, Victoire Charleville, who apparently instilled in the child a passion for independence, a love of all things French, and a deep skepticism about "those Americans." But if the blood of the O'Flahertys ran deep in her veins, it was her mother's social standing that gave her entrée into the city's most exclusive social circles. Kate read German and spoke French fluently, and—as she grew up—she read the latest Continental literature. With respect to her schooling, Kate attended the Sacred Heart Academy, where she had a conventional Catholic education intended to confirm young women in the faith and to prepare them to be Christian wives and mothers. But she was an unconventional girl, and at her debut this "Irish beauty" was described as one of the loveliest young women of St. Louis. Clearly she was one of the brightest.

---

8 Kate Chopin, "At Fault: A Correction," *Natchitoches Enterprise*, December 18, 1880, p. 3.

Some sense of Kate Chopin's personality is suggested by the journal she kept during her adolescence. Discussing the social life of the city on Holy Thursday of 1869, she writes:

> In three more days Lent will be over—and then commence again with renewed vigor—parties, theatres, and general spreeing. I feel as though I should like to run away and hide myself; but there is no escaping. I am invited to a ball and I go.—I dance with people I despise; amuse myself with men whose only talent lies in their feet; gain the disapprobation of people I honor and respect; return home at day break with my brain in a state which was never intended for it; and arise in the middle of the next day feeling infinitely more, in spirit and flesh like a Lilliputian, than a woman with body and soul.—I am diametrically opposed to parties and balls; and yet when I broach the subject—they either laugh at me—imagining that I wish to perpetrate a joke; or look very serious, shake their heads and tell me not to encourage such silly notions.

These are the ruminations of a young woman who has found the vivid social life of St. Louis a vexation of the spirit, as well as of the flesh, and who finds its enforced conformity at odds with her own predilections. Again in her diary she observes:

> You are the only one, my book, with whom I take the liberty of talking about myself. I must tell you a discovery I have made—the art of making oneself agreeable in conversation. Strange as it may appear it is not necessary to possess the faculty of speech; dumb persons, provided they be not deaf, can practice it as well as the most voluble. All required of you is to have control over the muscles of your face—to look pleased and chagrined, surprised indignant and under *every* circumstance—interested and entertained. Lead your antagonist to talk about himself—he will not enter reluctantly upon the subject I assure you—and twenty to one—he will report you as one of the most entertaining and intelligent persons,—although the whole extent of *your* conversation was but an occasional "What did *you* say?—What did *you* do?—What do *you* think?"—On that principle you see, my friend, you are very entertaining. . . (*KC*, 91–92).

What is disclosed here is nothing less than a solitary identity, a deep sense of human egotism, and an awareness of how one's own vanity deceives one in judging others.

Such a girl, belonging to such a social class, was automatically slated for marriage to a young man from one of the best families, but Kate was too bright and independent for most of her beaux. Her attitude toward men as suitors is suggested by her remark that a friend

who knows me as well as anyone is capable of knowing me—a gentleman of course—told me that I had a way in conversation of discovering
a person's characteristics—opinions—and private feelings—while they
knew no more about me at the end than they knew at the beginning of
the conversation. Is this laudable? Bah! I'll not reason on it, for whatever my conclusion I'll be sure to follow my inclination.

These remarks are indications of her feelings of intense personal privacy,
her temperamental reserve, and her fiercely independent spirit. These
attitudes herald the incipient writer who will penetrate the secret lives of
actual men and women in order to create the turbulent inner lives of
fictional characters. Even so, Kate O'Flaherty seems to have accepted the
academy's view of woman's role in marriage very seriously, and she
copied out—and underlined—this passage from a book she had been
reading:

> If a house with fair possibilities for home comfort is thoroughly com-
> fortless . . . , [if] the gentlemen of the family are prone to be "out of
> evenings"—who is to blame? Almost invariably, the women of the fam-
> ily. The men make or mar its outside fortunes; but its internal comfort
> lies in the women's hands alone. And until women feel this—recognize
> at once their power and their duties—*it is idle for them to chatter about
> their rights.*[9]

On "the happiest day of my life," as she recorded it in her journal for
June 9, 1870, she was married to Oscar Chopin, a handsome young man
whose familial connections reached down into Louisiana. There is every
evidence that they loved each other very much. Oscar was, as she put it
in her diary, "the right man." [10] After a honeymoon in Europe, they
settled in New Orleans, where Oscar became a cotton factor. No one
knows very much about the nine years of their life there, except that
Kate bore Oscar Chopin six children: Jean Baptiste, Oscar Charles,
George Francis, Frederick, Felix Andrew, and Lélia. Given the resentment in some feminist criticism at the constraints of marriage, particularly when the wife is said to be reduced to a "baby factory," such a
bright woman, who bore six children in eight years, must have been
miserable—no?

The interview testimony of those who knew the couple, gathered by
earlier biographers like Rankin and Seyersted, suggests otherwise. Ac-

---

9 Dinah Craik, *The Woman's Kingdom* (New York: Harper and Brothers, 1869), p. 89.
10 Per Seyersted, *Kate Chopin: A Critical Biography* (Baton Rouge: Louisiana State University
   Press, 1969), p. 31. Hereafter, quotations from this work will be cited as *PS,* in parentheses,
   in the text.

cording to their informants, the typical view was that "Kate was devoted to Oscar and thought him perfect." Mrs. John S. Tritle, a family friend, remembered that "Kate was very much in love with her Oscar" (*KC,* 131). And Seyersted remarks that Kate and Oscar "always preferred each other to other company" (*PS,* 38). I make this point because some careless readers of *The Awakening,* who know nothing of the author, have been ready to characterize Edna Pontellier, the protagonist, as a self-portrait of the author. Nothing could be farther from the case. One of the vexing aspects of Chopin criticism is the readiness of some critics to see the novel as if Edna were an autobiographical portrait.[11]

Oscar Chopin was not successful in his New Orleans business; consequently in 1879 the family moved inland to Cloutierville, a village in Natchitoches Parish, where the Chopin clan had large landholdings. Oscar managed a general store there and was apparently liked by all the townspeople. Mrs. L. Tyler, a frequent visitor in their household, later told Rankin something that makes him sound very different from Léonce Pontellier: "Oscar, ever jovial and cheerful and fun-loving and really very stout, liked to romp with the children through the house and about the gardens. 'I like disorder when it is clean' was his favorite saying" (*KC,* 131).

But Oscar Chopin was so injudicious in his dealings and so liberal with credit that, when he suddenly died of malaria in 1882, he left his wife and children saddled with a $12,000 debt. Kate Chopin ran his store for a while, collected from his debtors, and eventually paid off the bills. Like a good wife she had followed her husband, but now she was exiled in a rural *milieu* with decidedly provincial gallic in-laws. Her own family was in Missouri. In 1884 she returned to St. Louis with her children and, after her mother's death the following year, maintained them reasonably well, in a happy household, from her real estate and rental income.

Kate Chopin is such an expert witness of the tensions in marriage (as well as in other relationships) that Emily Toth is fain to force a theory, in her recent biography, that the Chopins themselves had marital troubles in Cloutierville, and that Kate found solace in the attentions of Albert Sampite, a wealthy landowner in the village. This affair is said to be pertinent to the plot of *The Awakening* and therefore deserves some consideration. On what does Toth's theory rest? The tale was bruited

---

11 Even Seyersted cannot resist the temptation to see Edna Pontellier as Kate: "the author—on the unconscious level—identified herself deeply both with Edna's struggle and with her torment." But reading a deceased author's unconscious mind can be tricky: Phanor Breazeale, Kate's brother-in-law, said that she had modeled Edna on a well-known Creole woman of New Orleans. See *PS,* pp. 173, 137.

about many years later by the Sampite children and grandchildren that Kate Chopin had broken up the Sampites' marriage. Sampite and his wife did become estranged, and the marriage ended in divorce. But the legal records suggest another reason: Albert Sampite drank and beat his wife; she and the children left him. There is no documentary evidence of Kate's having had a relationship with Sampite, a striker; and certainly there was never a charge by Loca Sampite of an alienation of affections or of adultery.

The basis for Professor Toth's claim for such an affair involves several other dubious items. First, the old Cloutierville villagers made Kate an item of gossip. But how could they not? This beautiful red-headed New Orleans (nay, *St. Louis*) woman, descended from the Irish O'Flahertys, wore plumed hats, rode astride, liked to flirt, played cards, and smoked Cuban cigars. She must have been the most spectacular woman in the parish; but this flamboyance and her indifference to backcountry mores do not translate into adultery. Other bits of evidence adduced by Professor Toth: Edna Pontellier's lovers, in *The Awakening,* are *Alcée* and *Robert,* the first and last syllables of whose names can be combined to make up Albert Sampite's first name; finally, some Chopin stories, such as "The Storm," deal with infidelity. The evidence is thus quite thin.

That the Sampite family might find it convenient to blame an out-sider, to find a scapegoat for the marital estrangement, seems less plausible to Toth than the gossip she heard from third-generation de-scendants nearly a century later. It is worth objecting, incidentally, that Professor Toth picks to pieces every male friendship that Kate Chopin ever had for evidence of sexual liaisons, as if her fictional treatment of infidelity could not have derived from the observation of others, from literary sources, or from a vivid imagination, but must be a reflection of Kate Chopin's sleeping around. At work in this latest biography is some unarticulated assumption that since Kate was beautiful and bright, she must have been "sexually liberated" in the modern sense—that is, will-ing to give herself to whomever she pleased (like Edna Pontellier)—in short, to be an adulteress.

There is no question that Kate Chopin was sexually alluring. Rankin interviewed a number of men who acknowledged in this beautiful and brilliant widow "a quality of sex that is inexplicable." Some had been in love with her and had wanted to marry her. One admirer reported to Rankin that "she seemed to reply to their silent declarations: 'I have seen other days of life and know the mystery and lure of another's love. You cannot touch my heart.'" Moreover, Seyersted, who interviewed Rankin at length before his death, reports that "Rankin heard nothing but 'data beyond reproach' about the author's personal life." In fact, a friend of Kate's reported that "one reason why she did not remarry was her feeling that she could not be as close with anyone as she had been with Oscar" (*PS*, 61–62, 72).

Looking at her life—as reported by Rankin, Seyersted, and now Toth—one is inclined to think that none of the men identified as possible lovers could conceivably have competed with Oscar Chopin or his memory. And it may have been the case that—after having been married to him and borne him six children—Kate was through with all that. Kate's daughter-in-law suggested as much in remarking that, after her return to St. Louis, she was wholly devoted to her writing. In any event, with no documentary evidence for any supposed affairs, gossip must be seen for what it is—simply gossip; and the attempt to sensationalize Kate Chopin's love life falls flat.

There is, however, one comment of hers, later in life, after she had become a well-known writer, that gives us a clue to her view of marriage; and it calls into question the modern ideal of the liberated writer expressing herself sexually with whomever she chooses. Speaking of the death of loved ones, after she had become a well-known author, Mrs. Chopin wrote:

> I cannot live through yesterday or tomorrow. It is why the dead in their character of dead and association with the grave have no hold upon me. I cannot connect my mother or husband or any of those I have lost with those mounds of earth out at Calvary cemetery. I cannot visit graves and stand contemplating them as some people do, and seem to love to do. . . . If it were possible for my husband and my mother to come back to earth, I feel that I would unhesitatingly give up every thing that has come into my life since they left it and join my existence again with theirs. To do that, I would have to forget the past ten years of my growth—my real growth. But I would take back a little wisdom with me; it would be the spirit of a perfect acquiescence (*KC*, 241).

The wisdom of the spirit of perfect acquiescence, acquiescence in her relationship as a daughter and wife—these are not the sentiments of Edna Pontellier or of modern feminists who complain that a woman is "characteristically defined as someone's daughter, someone's wife, someone's mother, someone's mistress." [12] If Mrs. Chopin understood herself in this way, so must we all in our relations. In fact, this moving

---

12 Margaret Culley, "Edna Pontellier: 'A Solitary Soul,'" in *Kate Chopin's* The Awakening: *An Authoritative Text, Contexts, Criticism,* ed. Margaret Culley (New York: W. W. Norton, 1976), p. 228. Hereafter, quotations from this edition of *The Awakening* will be cited as *A*, in parentheses, in the text.

assertion of love in an existence joined with her husband and six children (a love also suggested in a number of Mrs. Chopin's poems) may indicate that, in *The Awakening*, not the Pontelliers but the fruitful Ratignolles reflect the Chopins' marriage: "The Ratignolles understood each other perfectly. If ever the fusion of two human beings into one has been accomplished on this sphere it was surely in their union" (*A*, 56 [correction insert]).

III

After Kate Chopin's return to St. Louis in 1884, she created something of a salon attended by locals with some rather advanced, though not very radical, opinions. Of this circle only the journalist William Marion Reedy, of the *St. Louis Mirror*, is memorable. [13] In St. Louis, Kate resumed her place in the most respectable social circle, was well known to Mrs. Charlotte Stearns Eliot (the poet's mother), and, since she belonged to the *haut monde* of St. Louis, the society columns of the city newspapers regularly reported her comings and goings, her club activities, the ubiquitous teas and card parties, her presence at operas and dances, her fiction reading and book publications. And it was in St. Louis that she wrote her greatest novel, *The Awakening*.

In the Norton Critical Edition of this novel, the editor, Margaret Culley, appends to it a number of contemporary book excerpts and newspaper articles from the *New Orleans Daily Picayune* and elsewhere commenting at length on the "woman question." These articles all tend to assert the unhappiness of women in marriage. The journalist Dorothy Dix, in particular, condemns the self-sacrificing attitude of women and remarks that "women have awakened to the fact that they have been overdoing the self-sacrifice business." Is that what Edna Pontellier awakens to? Moreover, in "A Strike for Liberty," Dix warns that

> There comes a time in the life of almost every woman when she has to choose between a species of slavery and freedom, and when, if she ever expects to enjoy any future liberty, she must hoist the red flag of revolt and make a fight for her rights. It counts for nothing that the oppressor is generally of her own household and is blissfully unconscious of being a tyrant.

Chief among the wife's "oppressors," for Dix, are "the children": "In her desire to be a good mother, and to do everything possible for her child's

---

13 See John L. Idol's "William Marion Reedy and Kate Chopin," *Missouri Historical Society Bulletin*, 30 (October 1973), 57–58.

welfare, the average mother permits herself to be made a martyr before she realizes it" (*A*, 128, 131–132). Is Léonce Pontellier a domestic tyrant, and are Edna's children really oppressors?

The implication of printing these articles alongside the novel is to suggest that they might have shaped Kate Chopin's view of marriage or influenced the composition of her novel. At the very least they are meant to provide an "historical context" for understanding the novel, perhaps as a work of social protest against the oppression of women in marriage. Yet it should be pointed out that these articles appeared in the New Orleans newspaper *long after* Mrs. Chopin had returned to St. Louis. No effort is made by Culley to demonstrate that Mrs. Chopin might have read them. Culley concedes that "Kate Chopin was not a feminist, and *The Awakening* is not a political novel. . . ." Nevertheless, she argues that "it is important to understand the political and social context in which it appeared" (*A*, 119). But *this* context is reductive, as the following paragraphs undertake to show, for it reduces the novel to precisely the kind of Ibsenist social protest writing that Kate Chopin said she did not endorse.[14]

In the most recent biography, Emily Toth is likewise fain to point out that

> The rights of women were constantly discussed in intellectual circles in the 1890s. Kate Chopin's women friends all supported suffrage, as did William Marion Reedy, editor of the St. Louis *Mirror*. Being antisuffrage was seen as reactionary (although the Missouri General Assembly would not give women the right to vote until 1919).

Yet after all of this Toth is vexed to have to report that "Kate Chopin never directly recorded her opinion of women's suffrage. . ." (*KC*, 184). Indeed she did not. We do know, however, what her opinion was. Kate's son Felix explicitly defined his mother's relation to the feminist political movement of that time: "She was not interested in the woman's suffrage movement. But she belonged to a liberal, almost pink-red group of intellectuals, people who believed in intellectual freedom and often expressed their independence by wearing eccentric clothing" (*PS*, 63–64).

---

14 It should be noted that a recent survey revealed that feminist members of the Modern Language Association prefer Culley's edition because they "like the Norton's inclusion of political and social documents of the 1890s, especially the passages from Dorothy Dix and Thorstein Veblen." No doubt a major reason is that these appended articles permit student indoctrination in feminist tenets. As Barbara C. Ewell has exulted, "The stories of Edna and her author are the real stuff of consciousness-raising." See *Approaches to Teaching Chopin's The Awakening*, pp. 3, 86. This seems to be the case even though the Norton text was badly edited and is full of textual errors. (It has since been emended, but the new text appeared too late to take into account here. And the doutbtful essays remain.)

It is worth pausing a few moments to consider this lack of interest in a cause—women's liberation—which *The Awakening* is often said to endorse. Professors Culley and Toth are not alone, I believe, in longing—in spite of the evidence—to make Mrs. Chopin out to be in the vanguard of the woman's movement.[15] Now, there is no doubt that the newspapers of the day covered the suffragist movement and that it was a continual topic of conversation in intellectual circles. Kate's friend Billy Reedy *was* sympathetic to the movement, up to a point, and he also published articles on marriage and its problems. The following is from one of his columns in the *Mirror,* published while Chopin was writing *The Awakening:*

> Woman's latest discovery is that the husband is a drag. . . . The woman generally is becoming more and more individualized in matrimony. Woman has evolved from a doll into a human being. . . . A certain amount of independence for a woman is a very good thing. Old ladies will tell any one that it is good for the marital institution for women not to be too pliant and submissive to their husbands, just as they maintain that it is mistaken policy to try to prolong the honeymoon indefinitely, instead of getting away from each other occasionally. . . . Women who submit to complete obliteration in matrimony will find, in time, that they will not need to obliterate themselves, for they will be ignored. . . . Woman's truest duties are those of wife and mother, but those duties do not demand that she shall sacrifice her individuality (*KC,* 308–309).

It is reasonable to assume that Mrs. Chopin, in the salons frequented by St. Louis intellectuals, discussed or heard opinions like these. And her political sympathy may indeed have been in accord with that of Reedy and those attired in eccentric costumes. [16] Nonetheless, it must be strenuously asserted, since the evidence is compelling, that Mrs. Chopin always cast a skeptical eye on visionary social activists. In fact, in respect to one lady reformer who wished to "make life purer, sweeter, better worth living," Kate commented: "It is well that such a spirit does not ever realize the futility of the effort. A little grain of wisdom gained from the gospel of selfishness—what an invaluable lesson" (*PS,* 65–66). Furthermore, it is worth registering that Kate Chopin resigned from the Wednesday Club, which was filled with feminist reformers, and even satirized them—as "idealists who think they have a right and a mission

---

15 Seyersted, perhaps again reading the author's unconscious mind, suggests, despite his own evidence to the contrary, that Mrs. Chopin had "secret emancipationist urges" (*PS,* 173).

16 Even so, I do not believe I am wrong in saying that Reedy's view of "woman's truest duties" would be dismissed by many modern feminists as still "imprisoning" women in the domestic role.

to reform others"—in her short story "Miss McEnders" (*PS*, 97). This is a tale, needless to say, that is not popular with consciousness-raising professors.

Why was Mrs. Chopin averse to feminist protest fiction? The answer is clear. To have become an ideologist for the political causes of the day would have condemned her art to its own time and deprived it of a later audience after the cause had been won. Criticizing Hamlin Garland for devoting his fiction to a cause—promoting the single-tax theory of Henry George so as to effect an economic revolution—Kate Chopin objected that Garland "undervalues the importance of the past in art and exaggerates the significance of the present." She went on to say that

> Human impulses do not change and can not so long as men and women continue to stand in relation to one another which they have occupied since our knowledge of their existence began. It is why Aeschylus is true, and Shakespeare is true to-day, and why Ibsen will not be true in some remote to-morrow, however forcible and representative he may be for the hour, because he takes for his themes social problems which by their very nature are mutable. And, notwithstanding Mr. Garland's opinion to the contrary, social problems, social environments, local color and the rest of it are not *of themselves* motives to insure the survival of a writer who employs them.[17]

In this remark, Mrs. Chopin puts her finger on the central problem, for the writer, of the *roman à thèse*. But she also identifies the defect, today, of an ideological criticism reductive of the artwork to a political issue of past or contemporary social relevance. About this matter Mrs. Chopin was quite decided. One of her newspaper interviewers, for example, reported that she had "great respect for Mrs. Humphry Ward's achievements"; but he paraphrased her as saying that "Mrs. Ward is *au fond* a reformer, and such tendency in a novelist she [Kate Chopin] considers a crime against good taste."[18] The choice of the term "taste" here is decisive: it bears upon solidly formulated aesthetic judgments. Mrs. Chopin did not wish to create fiction out of the partisan politics of her time, nor did she wish to have it used *as such* by ideologues of a *later* time. She was first and last an artist, and it was according to standards of taste and judgment in art that she wished to be evaluated, not on her political correctness. But this is to get ahead of ourselves.

---

17 Review of Hamlin Garland's *Crumbling Idols*, in *St. Louis Life*, October 6, 1894; quoted in Rankin, p. 143; Seyersted, pp. 86–87.

18 "Marcella," *Providence Sunday Journal*, April 15, 1894, p. 13; quoted in *KC*, p. 244.

IV

Once back in St. Louis, Kate Chopin began to write. Although she was prolific, most of the national magazines repeatedly rejected her fiction (they found her stories plotless, morbid, or ethically repugnant), and most of it appeared in local newspapers or marginal magazines such as *Youth's Companion*. When her novel *At Fault* was rejected, she was obliged to have it printed at her own expense by a St. Louis printing company. Circulation was small. Some of her tales appeared in *Vogue* and the *Atlantic*, but she never attained anything like the national reputation of a Howells, a Garland, or a Henry James.

With the publication of *The Awakening* in 1899, however, Mrs. Chopin attained a greater measure of celebrity, if not notoriety, than any of the stories had brought her. This novel, set in New Orleans and at the Grand Isle coastal resort, recounts the life of Edna Pontellier, wife of a Creole husband Léonce and mother of two young children. During a holiday at the sea, she feels estranged from her husband and uncertain of her future. Her children disturb her, and she measures herself against Mme. Adèle Ratignolle, the "perfect wife" and "mother-woman" who is everything as a familial presence that Edna cannot be. During the summer Edna begins to neglect her husband and children, then abandons them and undertakes to live the free life of the artist in her own little cottage—the "pigeon house." The pianist Mlle. Reisz, whose music (especially the Chopin *Impromptu*) is that of a profound and dedicated keyboard artist, sizes up Edna perfectly: she does not have the strength or discipline to become a serious artist; her wings are too weak to soar above the ordinary life. Mlle. Reisz remarks:

> To be an artist includes much; one must possess many gifts—absolute gifts—which have not been acquired by one's own effort. And, moreover, to succeed the artist must possess the courageous soul. . . . The brave soul. The soul that dares and defies (*A*, 63).

Failed as an artist, Edna takes the two lovers Alcée Arobin and Robert LeBrun, rejects the one and is abandoned by the other, and finally—all avenues of transcendence having failed her—she swims out into the sea and drowns: "Today it is Arobin; to-morrow it will be someone else. . . . There was no human being whom she wanted near her except Robert; and she even realized that the day would come when he, too, and the thought of him would melt out of her existence, leaving her alone" (*A*, 113).

The novel is spare and terse, brilliantly interwoven with an intricate symbolism, and it is remarkably deep in its psychological analysis and understanding. The Creole milieu is expertly recreated, and Mrs. Chopin's narrative self-effacement forces the reader to do nearly all the work of interpretation and understanding. In 1899, in America, a frank presentation of adultery was taboo, unless euphemistically and evasively handled—and then morally denounced by the author. Anything else was wallowing in the trough of Zolaism. But Mrs. Chopin was not obliged to live by her art, and she was obviously indifferent to the standards of Genteel Era criticism. Her literary models were in fact European: Flaubert (especially in *Madame Bovary*), Tolstoy (whose *Anna Karenina* had dealt with the deeper aspects of the man-woman relationship), Turgenev (the model writer for throwing a group of characters together to see what would happen), George Sand, Mme. de Staël, the Goncourts, Paul Bourget, Victor Hugo, and Alphonse Daudet.[19]

But especially in the work of Guy de Maupassant, whose stories she loved enough to translate, she found the way to focus her terse, ironic, penetrating, and even morbid representations of human psychology. In praising Maupassant, Mrs. Chopin wrote:

> About eight years ago there fell accidentally into my hands a volume of Maupassant's tales. These were new to me. I had been in the woods, in the fields, groping around; looking for something big, satisfying, convincing, and finding nothing but—myself; a something neither big nor satisfying, but wholly convincing. It was at this period of my emerging from the vast solitude in which I had been making my own acquaintance, that I stumbled upon Maupassant. I read his stories and marvelled at them. Here was life, not fiction; for where were the plots, the old-fashioned mechanism and stage trapping that in a vague, unthinking way I had fancied were essential to the art of story making. Here was a man who had escaped from tradition and authority, who had entered into himself and looked out upon life through his own being and with his own eyes; and who, in a direct and simple way, told us what he saw. When a man does this, he gives us the best that he can; something valuable for it is genuine and spontaneous (*KC*, 205).

As a result of the convergence of these literary influences, working on her own powers of observation and ironic understanding, together with her sense of that "vast solitude" in which she had been making her own

---

19 Seyersted is not sure that Kate Chopin knew the novels by Flaubert and Tolstoy, but given her wide reading and their currency in critical discussions of the time it is improbable that she could have missed them. Tolstoy was then publishing a novel (*The Resurrection*) that, in its serial form, in *Cosmopolitan*, was called *The Awakening*. Whether Mrs. Chopin knew of the original title is not known. See also Thomas Bonner, Jr., "Kate Chopin's European Consciousness," *American Literary Realism*, 8 (1975), 281–284.

acquaintance, *The Awakening* appeared. It was a novel of such deep understanding of human psychology and such aesthetic distinction that it deserves to be read more widely than it is.

V

Yet at its publication, *The Awakening* was pointedly criticized for its subject and treatment, both in St. Louis and throughout the nation. The *St. Louis Post-Dispatch* reviewer wrote that "Like most of her work . . . , 'The Awakening' is too strong drink for moral babes, and should be labeled 'poison.'" The reviewer of the *Providence Sunday Journal* wrote that "the purport of the story can hardly be described in language fit for publication. We are fain to believe that Miss Chopin did not herself realise what she was doing when she wrote it. . . . [It] fairly out Zolas Zola." And there was this from the *New Orleans Times Democrat*:

> This unhappy Edna's awakening seems to have been confined entirely to the senses, while reason, judgment, and all the higher faculties and perceptions, whose office it is to weigh and criticise impulse and govern conduct, fell into slumber deep as that of the seven sleepers. It gives one a distinct shock to see Edna's crude mental operations. . . . The assumption that such a course as that pursued by Edna has any sort of divine sanction cannot be too strongly protested against. . . . Certainly there is throughout the story an undercurrent of sympathy for Edna, and nowhere a single note of censure of her totally unjustifiable conduct (*KC*, 347–348).

Emily Toth thinks that "*The Awakening* can be read as a cautionary tale about the promises of men," and she complains that "*The Awakening* was published to an overwhelming chorus of male disapproval" (*KC*, 333, 21). Seyersted likewise complains of "the male censors who killed her literary creativity" (*PS*, 183).[20] It should be insisted that neither *The Awakening* nor Mrs. Chopin's later work was ever censored, though some of the reviews were *censures*. In fact both men *and* women reviewers both praised *and* condemned the novel. One of the most striking attacks is that by Frances Porcher (under the pen name of Fanny S. Roper) in the *St. Louis Mirror*: "There is no fault to find with the telling of the story; there are no blemishes in its art, but it leaves one sick of human nature and so one feels—*cui bono?*"[21]

---

20 See Toth for a correction of Seyersted's gross exaggeration of the effect of the reviews on Mrs. Chopin—especially the claim that she stopped writing after *The Awakening*. As Toth shows, she continued to write until her death.
21 Frances Porcher, "Kate Chopin's Novel," *St. Louis Mirror*, 9 (May 4, 1899), 6; see *A*, p. 145.

Willa Cather was equally tough on Kate Chopin and her "Creole Bovary." She said that she would not try to say

> why Miss Chopin has devoted so exquisite and sensitive, well-governed a style to so trite and sordid a theme. She writes much better than it is ever given to most people to write, and hers is a genuinely literary style; of no great elegance or solidity; but light, flexible, subtle, and capable of producing telling effects directly and simply. . . . [Women of the Bovary type expect] the passion of love to fill and gratify every need of life, whereas nature only intended that it should meet one of many demands. They insist upon making it stand for all the emotional pleasures of life and art; expecting an individual and self-limited passion to yield infinite variety, pleasure, and distraction, to contribute to their lives what the arts and the pleasurable exercise of the intellect gives to less limited and less intense idealists. . . . They have staked everything on one hand, and they lost. . . . Edna Pontellier, fanciful and romantic to the last, chose the sea on a summer night and went down with the sound of her first lover's spurs in her ears, and the scent of pinks about her. And next time I hope that Miss Chopin will devote that flexible iridescent style of hers to a better cause.[22]

Such criticism by women reviewers diminishes the claim that Mrs. Chopin's art was attacked only by men. Given Mrs. Chopin's adulterous subject and her refusal to pass an explicit judgment on her heroine, there even developed a legend, given currency by Seyersted and widely circulated in Chopin literary criticism, that *The Awakening* was banned in St. Louis, removed from the library shelves, and that Mrs. Chopin was herself ostracized by the women of her clubs.[23] Thanks to Professor Toth, we now know that none of these dire events occurred. Kate remained an intimate of the ladies in St. Louis despite her satire on reformist predilections; perhaps if the book was not available in the St. Louis libraries, it was because the copies were always checked out.

And why shouldn't the novel have been checked out? Kate Chopin was famous in St. Louis, it was an excellent novel, and critics in St. Louis had praised it—for example, this male reviewer for the *St. Louis Post-Dispatch* on May 20, 1899:

> There may be many opinions touching other aspects of Mrs. Chopin's novel, "The Awakening," but all must concede its flawless art. The delicacy of touch, of rare skill in construction, the subtle understanding of motive, the searching vision into the recesses of the heart—these are

---

22 Cather, "Books and Magazines," *Pittsburgh Leader*, July 8, 1899, p. 6; *A*, pp. 153–155.
23 See Seyersted's misleading chapter "A Daring Writer Banned," pp. 164–185.

known to readers of "Bayou Folk" and "A Night in Acadie." But in this new work power appears, power born of confidence. There is no uncertainty in the lines, so surely and firmly drawn. Complete mastery is apparent on every page. Nothing is wanting to make a complete artistic whole.[24]

Responding to her negative critics, Mrs. Chopin remarked on her heroine in Book News:

Having a group of people at my disposal, I thought it might be entertaining (to myself) to throw them together and see what would happen. I never dreamed of Mrs. Pontellier making such a mess of things and working out her own damnation as she did. If I had had the slightest intimation of such a thing I would have excluded her from the company. But when I found out what she was up to, the play was half over and it was then too late.[25]

This evasive remark is typical of Kate Chopin's playful and ironic way of mystifying her intention, which is best ascertained in an attentive reading of the novel itself.

In much contemporary criticism, Kate Chopin's reference to Edna's "damnation" is dismissed as so much ironic badinage. The novel is commonly held out to us as a work in which a woman, oppressed by marriage and motherhood, makes a sublime existential gesture of protest against the patriarchy by taking her own life. It is accordingly praised as "a hymn to aloneness as a source of strength and power," "a call to self-discovery and a celebration of personal freedom" (KC, 21).[26] But what view of aloneness is conveyed? What kind of self is discovered? What use of freedom is it to destroy herself? And on what grounds can self-destruction be a "privileged" resolution? Since the suicide is central to our interpretation of Edna's "awakening," to Mrs. Chopin's view of her heroine, and to the meaning of the novel, some demystifications may be in order.

VI

The doubtful view that Edna Pontellier is a heroic figure whose final gesture of suicide is a noble act of protest against the conditions of female life originated with Per Seyersted. His analysis, written in the

---

24 C. L. Deyo, "The Newest Books," St. Louis Post-Dispatch, May 20, 1899, p. 4; see A, p. 147.

25 Kate Chopin, "Aims and Autographs," Book News, 17 (July 1899), 612.

26 See also Toth's "Kate Chopin's The Awakening as Feminist Criticism," Louisiana Studies, 15 (1976), 241–251.

1960s when the existentialism of Sartre and Beauvoir was all the rage, claims that Edna is "a symbol of womankind"—surely a doubtful proposition. He sees the novel as an illustration of "the process of existential individuation": Edna "has a real existence only when she gives her own laws, when she through conscious choice becomes her own creation with an autonomous self." Seyersted argues that Edna "insists on an individual, authentic existence and wants a freedom to exert a conscious choice which can bring out her own essence," and that "it is less important to her to live than to have a self." Since, for Mrs. Chopin, "in the patriarchy, man would not willingly relinquish the role of conqueror, nor woman that of the conquered," Edna's fate is sealed: "Her death is not so much a result of outer forces crowding her in as a triumphant assertion of her inner liberty"; it is "the crowning glory of her development from the bewilderment which accompanied her early emancipation to the clarity with which she understands her own nature and the possibilities of her life as she decides to end it. Edna's victory lies in her awakening to an independence that includes an act of renunciation" (*PS*, 158, 144, 147–148, 149–150). Renunciation, indeed!

This stirring assertion is on a par with several other attempts to exalt Edna as an existential rebel, a tragic heroine, or even a goddess. For Eleanor B. Wymard, Edna's death is a "defiant act of will,"[27] although that description hardly seems to square with the heroine's affectless drift. Kenneth Eble claims that Edna is a classical Phaedra, whose suicide is an immersion in Eros that gives her "the power, the dignity, the self-possession of a tragic heroine."[28]

The longing to make Edna the heroine of a modern feminist drama of free sexuality and emancipation from family responsibility leads to other, sometimes risible interpretations. One of the most intriguing new maneuvers is to deny that there *is* a suicide and to insist that, since Edna is a goddess or myth figure, the final swim must be understood in symbolic terms. "We do not actually 'see' Edna drown," Cristina Giorcelli proposes, "but see her instead surrounded by and bathed in symbols of fertility and immortality (the sea, the sun, bees)."[29] Sandra Gilbert and Susan Gubar pull out all the stops and, on no credible evidence, apotheosize Edna. Readers of the novel are surprised to learn from them that *The Awakening* is "a feminist myth of Aphrodite/Venus as an alter-

27 Eleanor B. Wymard, "Kate Chopin: Her Existential Imagination," *Southern Studies*, 19 (1980), 375.

28 Kenneth Eble, "A Forgotten Novel: Kate Chopin's *The Awakening*," *Western Humanities Review*, 10 (1956), 261–269; reprinted in *A*, p. 170.

29 Cristina Giorcelli, "Edna's Wisdom: A Transitional and Numinous Merging," *New Essays on The Awakening*, ed. Wendy Martin (Cambridge: Cambridge University Press, 1988), p. 109.

native to the patriarchal western myth of Jesus." In entering the ocean, Edna sinks "not into death but back into her own life, back into the imaginative openness of her childhood." Professors Gilbert and Gubar claim that the last swim "may not seem to be a suicide—that is, a death—at all, or, if it is a death, it is a death associated with a resurrection, a sort of pagan female Good Friday that promises an Aphroditean Easter."[30] Such words have no relation to the novel. Sleeping Beauty, Snow White, Venus, Persephone, Icarus, Psyche—the list of mythic figures, seized upon to allegorize the ending as something other than a poignant woman's resort to suicide, grows apace.[31] But poor Edna, sunk in a new sense of absolute solitude as "her position in the universe as a human being," trying to get shut of Raoul and Etienne so as to escape every vestige of human relatedness, is hardly adequate to the modern need for a triumphant heroine.[32]

These extraordinary critical pronouncements, undertaking to "valorize" illicit passion, adulate suicide, and even to deny that it happened, collide with the evident fact that, whatever Edna may think of her husband and children, she is not enslaved in her domestic role. Her husband Léonce, though possessed of a mild Creole sexism, is as loving and attentive as any husband of the time and place might be. Edna, it should be remembered, "was forced to admit that she knew of none better." Their children, Raoul and Etienne, are not monsters demanding exceptional attention—especially in view of the large number of servants Edna is provided: a cook, a maid, a mulatto servant, and a quadroon woman to care for the children. Adèle Ratignolle's marriage and her many children are pointedly introduced as an example of what kind of elemental passion and fulfillment a woman—not averse to living for others—may find in wife- and motherhood. Edna bizarrely pities Mme. Ratignolle for her "colorless existence which never uplifted its possessor beyond the region of blind contentment," for never having experienced "life's delirium." But Mrs. Chopin pointedly remarks that Edna herself doesn't know what she means by "life's delirium," and it is clear that the

---

30 Sandra M. Gilbert and Susan Gubar, *No Man's Land: The Place of the Woman Writer in the Twentieth Century.* Vol. II: *Sexchanges* (New Haven: Yale University Press, 1989), p. 109.

31 On Persephone, see Giorcelli, pp. 128–139; on Icarus, see Lawrence Thornton's "Edna as Icarus: A Mythic Issue," in *Approaches to Teaching Chopin's* The Awakening, pp. 138–143; on Sleeping Beauty, see Suzanne Wolkenfeld's "Edna's Suicide: The Problem of the One and the Many," in *A*, p. 222; on Psyche, see Rosemary F. Franklin, "*The Awakening* and the Failure of Psyche," *American Literature*, 56 (1984), 510–526.

32 So vexing is Edna's failure to be the heroine feminists want her to be that Suzanne W. Jones claims that the suicidal ending is a mistake. We are stunned to learn that "Edna's confusion only mirrors her creator's," and that the novel ends in suicide because of poor Kate Chopin's "inherited notions." See Jones's "Two Settings: The Islands and the City," in *Approaches to Teaching Chopin's* The Awakening, pp. 124–125.

Ratignolles have a rich, vivid, and exciting sexual, family, and social life, and that it is Edna who is sunk in ennui (*A*, 56 [correction insert]).

The idea that Edna's awakening can be reduced to the discovery of sex accords to Eros a value that the novel, I believe, does not finally sustain. Edna's love affair with Alcée Arobin is merely carnal, and Robert's departure from Grand Isle seems motivated by his discovery that chivalric attentions of a flirtatious kind, to Edna, however common in Creole culture, have gotten out of hand—as Adèle Ratignolle predicted in telling Robert that she is not "one of us" (*A*, 21).

Seyersted is right in thinking that, to make a suicidal death positive, one would have to redefine it as a philosophical act. But his recourse to the sixties existentialism of Sartre and Beauvoir, superimposed on the novel after the fact, does not answer to the story's rich complexity. Stoicism might also offer a philosophical justification for suicide, but there is nothing in the novel, or in Chopin's letters, journals, or essays, that discloses an interest in the stoic rationalization of suicidal death. Mrs. Chopin, however, did admire Whitman, who expresses a longing for reunion with the divine, with "sane and sacred death." In "Out of the Cradle Endlessly Rocking," Whitman celebrates the message of the sea as the seductive lisp of "death, death, death, death, death." Whitman, in fact, has been claimed as the literary source of the pervasive ocean imagery of the novel.[33] But is Whitman the analogue for Edna's longing? Does she have, like him, the desire to be reunited with the origin of being, the divine spirit, symbolized in the sea—to be, that is, "laved in the flood of thy bliss O death"?[34] It seems unlikely.

Granting Mrs. Chopin's admiration for Whitman's nature poetry, it is difficult to see this student of Darwinian science as a transcendentalist or to read the novel as "Kate Chopin's *Leaves of Grass*" (*PS*, 162). And nothing in the novel suggests a transcendentalist psychology in the narrative voice or in Edna herself. In fact, I suspect that Mrs. Chopin would have agreed with Melville, who notes in *Moby-Dick* that the desire to merge with the universe can produce a horrific surprise: self-annihilation by drowning. In "The Mast-Head" chapter, Melville criticizes the transcendentalist view of nature in the figure of the sailor atop the mast who sinks into an idealist reverie, "loses his identity" in "the blending cadence of waves with thoughts," "takes the mystic ocean at his feet for the visible image of that deep, blue, bottomless soul, pervading mankind and nature":

---

33 Lewis Leary, *Southern Excursions: Essays on Mark Twain and Others* (Baton Rouge: Louisiana State University Press, 1971), pp. 169–174.

34 The phrase is from "When Lilacs Last in the Dooryard Bloom'd."

There is no life in thee, now, except that rocking life imparted by a gently rolling ship; by her, borrowed from the sea; by the sea, from the inscrutable tides of God. But while this sleep, this dream is on ye, move your foot or hand an inch; slip your hold at all; and your identity comes back in horror. Over Descartian vortices you hover. And perhaps, at midday, in the fairest weather, with one half-throttled shriek you drop through that transparent air into the summer sea, no more to rise for ever. Heed it well, ye Pantheists!"[35]

Edna's is not in my view a pantheist reverie; hers is a continuing daydream of wish fulfillment. Yet the connection between the sea, the abyss of solitude, and the labyrinth of subjectivity which leads to death is the same as in Melville: "The voice of the sea is seductive," Mrs. Chopin writes, "never ceasing, whispering, clamoring, murmuring, inviting the soul to wander for a spell in abysses of solitude; to lose itself in mazes of inward contemplation" (*A*, 15). The longing for death implies, in fact, not the triumph of Eros but of Thanatos.

VII

Let us leave the cogitations of those daft academics for whom a woman's suicide is a noble protest against ordinary reality and consider the novel in terms of Mrs. Chopin's remarkable grasp of human psychology. The first point to be made is that the title *The Awakening* is not her own; it was attached to the novel by her publisher, who did not like the title *A Solitary Soul*. This point is important, because its major theme *is* solitude. And insofar as it deals with an authentic awakening, it is an awakening to a total solitude that Edna feels to be her essential condition. Far from a "hymn to aloneness," the novel deals with the self-destructive consequences of that feeling. *The Awakening* thus reflects a theme Mrs. Chopin had encountered in two of Maupassant's works, "Solitude" and "Suicide," both of which she translated and published in St. Louis. In the sketch called "Solitude," two friends leave a dinner party and walk out into the evening. One of them remarks:

> For a long time . . . I have endured the anguish of having discovered and understood the solitude in which I live. And I know that nothing can end it; nothing! Whatever we may do or attempt, despite the embraces and transports of love, the hunger of the lips, we are always alone.

---

35 Herman Melville, *Moby-Dick*, ed. Charles Feidelson, Jr. (Indianapolis: Bobbs-Merrill, 1964), pp. 214–215.

> I have dragged you out into the night in the vain hope of a moment's escape from the horrible solitude which overpowers me. But what is the use! I speak and you answer me, and still each of us is alone, side by side but alone.

So far as love is concerned, "after each embrace the isolation grows." Especially "after the rapturous union" of sex, which blends "two souls into one being," does the speaker feel "more than ever" that he is "alone—alone!"[36] In one of her solipsist reveries, Edna entitles one of Mlle. Reisz's pieces "Solitude" and envisions "the figure of a man standing beside a desolate rock on the seashore. He was naked. His attitude was one of hopeless resignation as he looked toward a distant bird winging its flight away from her" (*A*, 26–27). Hopeless resignation at the impossibility of transcending one's own subjectivity, a naked despair at the widening abyss that separates each individual life, despite a transient sexual union, is the theme of both tales. "Suicide" likewise deals with "a solitary existence left without illusions" culminating in a self-inflicted death. In this tale the narrator reflects on the reasons for suicide given in a letter left by a friend whose outward existence revealed "nothing of the great catastrophes which we invariably seek as motives for such acts of despair." The explicit reasons seem trivial: the weather, his digestion, the odor of his room, the monotony of a daily routine like shaving. But these add up to a "slow succession of life's little miseries" and produce "the fatal disorganization of a solitary existence left without illusions." Especially noteworthy, in view of *The Awakening*, is the suicide's "loss of unquestioning faith" and his sense of himself as the plaything of "stupid and engaging illusions." Recollecting his former lovers and the advancing years brings home to him the specter of "old age; hideous, solitary; approaching infirmities; no one near me; the end, the end, the end." In this condition of inner destitution and solitude, overcome by what the letter calls "the misery of all things," "the inutility of effort," and "the vanity of endeavor," the suicide succumbs to "the absolute nothingness of life" and turns a revolver on himself.[37] Robert D. Arner claims that Edna's "sense of obligation to [her children] is what drives her to commit suicide to escape that obligation."[38] But this will not square with Edna's profound indifference, with that deep Maupassantian lassitude of

---

36 Maupassant, "Solitude," in *The Kate Chopin Companion: With Chopin's Translations from French Fiction*, ed. Thomas Bonner, Jr. (New York: Greenwood Press, 1988), pp. 195–196. Mrs. Chopin's translation of this tale first appeared in *St. Louis Life*, 13 (December 28, 1895), 30.

37 Maupassant, "Suicide," in *The Kate Chopin Companion*, pp. 203–205.

38 Robert D. Arner, "Kate Chopin's Realism: 'At the 'Cadian Ball' and 'The Storm,'" *Markham Review*, 2 (February 1970), [3].

spirit that settles over her. She succumbs to "the old ennui,"

> the hopelessness which so often assailed her, which came upon her like
> an obsession, like something extraneous, independent of volition. It was
> something which announced itself; a chill breath that seemed to issue
> from some vast cavern wherein discords wailed. There came over her
> the acute longing which always summoned into her spiritual vision the
> presence of the beloved one, overpowering her at once with a sense of
> the unattainable (*A*, 88).

What is most striking about the portrait of Edna is Mrs. Chopin's expert grasp of the psychology of infinite loneliness and of the *anomie* that issues from it. Ennui, depression, and hopelessness are the facts of her psychic life which she tries to banish with daydreams of a beloved (the soldier, the tragedian, Robert) only to go under in the recognition that they are illusions and that, even if available, none could banish the despair of solitude which is her lot. As Edna grows more and more affectless and dissociated from human relationships, she of course seizes upon their imperfections as the cause of her condition—even as Maupassant's suicide "explains" his act as arising from shaving, the weather, or "the people whom I formerly met with pleasure" but who are now tiresomely predictable and fixed in "the same ideas, the same joys, the same habits, the same beliefs, the same disgusts."[39] Dissatisfaction with marriage and motherhood, with lovers and friends, with art and her social life are merely the "explanations" that do not explain Edna's deteriorating psychic life. The original title of the novel was *A Solitary Soul*, and Mrs. Chopin's theme is a pathological withdrawal from life, as Edna, like the Maupassant characters, becomes obsessed with her own separateness; it is as pronounced here as it is in Melville's *Bartleby, the Scrivener* or in Eliot's Ugolino in the tower in *The Waste Land*.

None of Edna's desperate distractions—living for herself alone, committing adultery, and dabbling in painting—has a chance of lifting her out of the abyss of solitude, the profound indifference to life, into which she is descending. Edna's breakdown and suicide have their mysterious origins in a lost psychology of childhood, which Mrs. Chopin only intriguingly and ambiguously hints at—in the memories of her father, the grassy meadow at the farm, and the soldier's spurs. Whatever these elliptical allusions may mean—and they may be beyond any interpretive certainty—neither Edna Pontellier nor Kate Chopin is a convincing martyr to the oppression of men in marriage. If Mrs. Chopin

---

39 *The Kate Chopin Companion*, p. 204.

was a very private person—a "solitary soul" herself (or, as her son Felix put it, a "lone wolf")—she differed from her character Edna in this: when Kate entered that "vast solitude" in which she was to make her own acquaintance, she found there a convincing self and it was well worth living—living in intimate familial and avid social interconnectedness; Edna found nothingness. Suzanne Wolkenfeld is right in saying that "Edna's suicide is not a conscious choice reached through her achievement of self-awareness"; it is "a defeat and a regression, rooted in a self-annihilating instinct, in a romantic incapacity to accommodate herself to the limitations of reality." And Cynthia Griffin Wolff has convinced me that "we must see Edna's final suicide as originating in a sense of inner emptiness, not in some finite failure of love."[40]

---

40 Suzanne Wolkenfeld, "Edna's Suicide: The Problem of the One and the Many," in *A*, pp. 222, 220; Cynthia Griffin Wolff, "Thanatos and Eros: Kate Chopin's *The Awakening*," *American Quarterly*, 25 (October 1973), 449–471; in *A*, p. 215.

Radical Bewilderment: The Case of Jack London

In 1897 Jack London went up to the Klondike in that great feverish stampede and tried, like thousands of others, to make his fortune by mining for gold. Scurvy sent him back to California the following year, his health a wreck and his pockets all but empty of the coveted yellow dust. But if, like Mark Twain, he did not strike it rich, London did discover there a new kind of material for fiction—the tough gold miners and trappers of the Far North. His violent and chilling stories of the Yukon—so charged with perilous adventure and alien in tone to the proprieties of the Genteel Era—constitute the best of his fiction. This is so despite the social consciousness and militant activism that made London an ardent spokesman for various left-wing causes. In fact, as Kenneth Lynn has rightly remarked of London's tales of the Far North, "Except for the similar sensation caused by the appearance of Mark Twain's mining-camp humor in the midst of Victorian America, nothing more disturbing to the forces of gentility had ever happened to our literature, and it decisively changed the course of American fiction."[1]

The Klondike, however, did more than just provide American literature with a new kind of material. Prospecting in the Far North opened London's eyes to the violence of life itself. "It was in the Klondike I found myself," he wrote. "You get your perspective. I got mine."[2] His

---

1 Kenneth Lynn, "Disturber of Gentility," *New York Times Book Review,* February 14, 1965, p. 20.

2 Joan London, *Jack London and His Times: An Unconventional Biography* (Seattle: University

perspective is tersely dramatized in "The White Silence," a tale in *The Son of the Wolf* (1900), the first volume of what came to be his ongoing "Northland Saga." Snowbound in the frozen waste, the Malamute Kid, his friend Mason, and Mason's Indian wife, Ruth, have just made camp. The Kid battles to whip into submission his starving dogs, who have gone out of control and broken into the food supply.

> The dogs had broken the iron rule of their masters and were rushing the grub. He joined the issue with his rifle reversed, and the hoary game of natural selection was played out with all the ruthlessness of his primeval environment. Rifle and axe went up and down, hit or missed with monotonous regularity; lithe bodies flashed, with wild eyes and dripping fangs; and man and beast fought for supremacy to the bitterest conclusion.[3]

The Kid overpowers the dogs, but, later, he cannot nullify the fate that destroys his friend Mason, who is crushed by a falling tree. Of this apparent accident, London writes: "For generations it had stood there, and for generations destiny had had this one end in view,—perhaps the same had been decreed of Mason" (*SS*, I, 145). Whatever fatality had produced this bad timing (it is impossible to know whether London means it as an act of fate or of chance), "with the temperature at sixty-five below zero," even a well man "cannot lie many minutes in the snow and live." Ruth is numb with despair at what must inevitably follow for "her white lord," as Mason is called, "the first white man she had ever seen,—the first man whom she had known to treat a woman as something better than a mere animal or beast of burden" (*SS*, I, 142). After she pushes off with the dogs, the Kid waits a decent interval and then, with his rifle, puts Mason out of his misery.

Death is often a mercy. London's North is a world of inhuman cold, with blinding snow and sudden blizzards that obscure the trail. At sixty-five below the silence is eerie. The mouth rimes over with frozen breath and spittle freezes before it hits the ground. "This is a cold so ominous and relentless that it takes on a personality," as Eugene Burdick has rightly remarked.[4] In this domain of ice and snow, the gnarled prospectors, grizzled Mounties, Innuit guides, and strong half-breed women have exceptional spirit and primitive grit. It is an especially

---

of Washington Press, 1968), p. 146.

3 *The Complete Short Stories of Jack London*, eds. Earle Labor, Robert C. Leitz, III, and I. Milo Shepard (Stanford, Calif.: Stanford University Press, 1993), I, 148. Hereafter, citations from this text will be given as *SS*, in parentheses, in the text.

4 Eugene Burdick, "Introduction," in *The Best Short Stories of Jack London* (Greenwich, Conn.: Fawcett, 1962), p. vi.

ruthless world for the women, who exist there for one purpose: to breed. After the squaw has reared her young, "Her task was done. But a little while, on the first pinch of famine or the first long trail, and she would be left . . . in the snow, with a little pile of wood. Such was the law" (*SS*, I, 447). It is the law that only the strong and cunning survive, and only if luck smiles.

If inhuman nature were not enough, London's stoic survivors often face the ravenous wolves, encircling the campfire, patiently waiting to rush, always ready to feast. In "The Law of Life," the order of existence prescribes the death of the old chief Koskoosh—now blind, feeble, and helpless. He cannot keep up with his traveling kinsmen and is left behind when they break camp.

> He did not complain. It was the way of life, and it was just. He had been born close to the earth, close to the earth had he lived, and the law thereof was not new to him. It was the law of all flesh. Nature was not kindly to the flesh. She had no concern for that concrete thing called the individual. Her interest lay in the species, the race. This was the deepest abstraction old Koskoosh's barbaric mind was capable of, but he grasped it firmly (*SS*, I, 446–447).

At the end of the tale, his ears straining to hear the approach of the wolves, blind Koskoosh has a childhood memory flash before his vacant eyes—and old moose brought down by "the flashing forms of gray, the gleaming eyes, the lolling tongues, the slavered fangs" (*SS*, I, 450).

London's is a frankly naturalistic view of existence, a "materialistic monism," as he called it, jerry-rigged from bits of Darwin, Huxley, Spencer, Haeckle, and other contemporary skeptical scientists. As the passage about the falling pine tree suggests, London believed that there was "no such thing as free will. Environment determines absolutely. The individual moves along the line of least resistance." This is a view wildly at odds with his sense of the power of the superman, who successfully imposes his irresistible will upon the malleable world.[5]

The pitilessness of nature in the frozen North is also projected in some seventy-seven other stories published in collections such as *The God of His Fathers* (1901), *Children of the Frost* (1902), and *The Faith of Men and Other Stories* (1904).[6] Especially memorable are "The Devil's Dice Box," "The White Silence, "To the Man on the Trail," "To Build a Fire," and "An Odyssey of the North." These are wonderfully written

---

5 London is quoted here in Carolyn Johnston, *Jack London—An American Radical?* (Westport, Conn.: Greenwood Press, 1984), p. 50.

6 Earle Labor, "Jack London," *American Realists and Naturalists*, eds. Donald Pizer and Earl N. Harbert (Detroit: Gale, 1982), p. 356.

stories of stupefying courage and epic endurance, of strange customs and primitive justice. But the mere *range* of London's novels and stories is also impressive. Not just the rigors of the Klondike but political venality, boxing, sailing, suicide, industrial labor, the slums, South Pacific island life, penal reform, romance, and revolutionary socialism are thematized in London's prolific imaginative world.

I

It is a critical cliché that none of London's stories is as remarkable as the story of his own life. It certainly *was* the stuff of romance; and he fictionalized his experience with a kind of directness and vitality that made him preeminently—with Melville, Twain, Hemingway, Mailer, and Jack Kerouac—a devotee of the cult of experience, that is, a writer who seeks out physical adventure with a view to writing it up. Born in San Francisco in 1876, London was evidently the illegitimate son of an astrology professor named William Henry Chaney and Flora Wellman, a socially ambitious but very unhappy spiritualist. She made a marriage of convenience with the widower John London, who had children of his own and whose name the writer adopted. London said in *John Barleycorn* that, from his ninth year onward, his youth was one of unremitting toil.[7] And so it was. The boy mowed lawns, delivered newspapers, swept saloon floors, set up pins in the bowling alley, and picked up every odd job he could find. For a while he worked eighteen hours a day in a pickle cannery. At age fifteen, with borrowed money, he bought the ship *Razzle-Dazzle* and became an oyster pirate on San Francisco Bay. Then, because jail was too great a risk, this "Prince of Thieves," as he was called in the underworld, became a deputy for the California Fish Patrol, himself chasing the oyster thieves.

After a stint in 1893 as an able-bodied seaman aboard the *Sophia Sutherland*, bound for Japan, London went underground as a tramp and gratified his appetite for adventure by riding the rods with hoboes—an experience he recounted in *The Road* (1907). When he first read Nietzsche is a much debated question, but there is no doubt that early on he saw himself "raging through life without end like one of Nietzsche's *blond beasts*, lustfully roving and conquering by sheer superiority and strength."[8] At other times he was drawn to the solidarity of the homeless drifters who shared with each other their cigarettes, grub, and whiskey. London's aimless wandering in search of adventure led to

---

7 London, *John Barleycorn*, ed. Arthur Calder-Marshall (London: Bodley Head, 1964), p. 51.
8 London, *War of the Classes* (New York: Macmillan, 1905), p. 270.

his arrest for vagrancy in 1894 and a thirty-day jail sentence in upstate New York. He was later to say—quite implausibly—that "I have often thought that to this training of my tramp days is due much of my success as a short-story writer." This was the case, he felt, because

> in order to get the food whereby I lived, I was compelled to tell tales that rang true. At the back door, out of inexorable necessity, is developed the convincingness and sincerity laid down by all authorities on the art of the short-story. Also, I quite believe it was my tramp-apprenticeship that made a realist out of me. Realism constitutes the only goods one can exchange at the kitchen door for grub.[9]

One of the short-story authorities by whom London set great store at this period was Herbert Spencer, whose "The Philosophy of Style" taught him, he said,

> to transmute thought, beauty, sensation and emotion into black symbols on white paper; which symbols, through the reader's eye, were taken into his brain, and by his brain transmuted into thoughts, beauty, sensations and emotions that fairly corresponded with mine. Among other things, this taught me to *know* the brain of my reader, in order to select the symbols that would compel his brain to realize my thought, or vision, or emotion. Also, I learned that the right symbols were the ones that would require the expenditure of the minimum of my readers' brain energy, leaving the maximum of his brain energy to realize and enjoy the content of my mind, as conveyed to his mind.[10]

This passage has a whiff of *fin-de-siècle* mind-science to it. But embedded in the neurological economics is the writer's conviction that literature is a system of significations intended for symbolic representation. What fiction represents is the cognitive and affective disposition of the author. The reader—possessed of kindred faculties of perception and cognition—can recognize any valid correspondence between the author's world and his own. In the process of transmuting the author's inward view of the world to a language that disseminates it to the reader, what identifies genuine art is its economy of symbolic representation.

On a more mundane level, the hobo's life, London went on to say, transformed him into a socialist and impressed him with the need for more education. In 1895 he returned to Oakland, took some high school classes, and then went to the University of California for a term. English classes inflamed him with the creative passion, but Franklin

---

9 Jack London, *The Road*, ed. I. O. Evans (London: Arco, 1967), p. 142.
10 Quoted in Charmian London, *The Book of Jack London* (New York: Century, 1921), II, 50.

Walker is right to have said that London is "to a considerable degree a self-made writer."[11] In recollecting his apprenticeship in *John Barleycorn,* London remarked:

> Heavens, how I wrote! . . . I wrote humorous verse, verse of all sorts from triolets and sonnets to blank verse tragedy and elephantine epics in Spenserian stanzas. On occasion I composed steadily, day after day, for fifteen hours a day. At times I forgot to eat, or refused to tear myself away from my passionate outpouring in order to eat.[12]

Then gold was found in the Klondike, and greed for the yellow dust materialized everywhere. It discovered its check in the inhuman wilderness, where London's imagination found at last a significant form.

II

I shall return to London's Klondike in a moment. But here it should be remarked that, after the great success of his early Yukon tales, the "boy Socialist" ran for mayor of Oakland in 1901. He lost decisively in his first political venture, but the experience brought him national publicity and a lifelong avidity for speechmaking, social activism, and public applause. London's celebrity got him many platform commissions and book proposals. In 1902 he went off to England in order to conduct an examination of poverty in the London slums. In some ways 1903 was an *annus mirabilis* for him. In that year he published two quite different books—*The People of the Abyss* (a muckraking exposé of English ecomic conditions) and *The Call of the Wild* (the tale of a dog's regression to lupine savagery). The appearance of these two works in the same year points to a never-resolved contradiction in London's mind between, on the one hand, his belief in the Darwinian-Nietzschean view of life as a struggle for survival in which only the blond beast or the *Übermensch* survives; and, on the other hand, his belief in a violent revolutionary socialism, to be followed by an era of collectivization and cooperation. The fictional works that express the Nietzschean view include *The Sea Wolf* (1904), the tale of a brutal sea captain, Wolf Larsen, who delights in torturing his crew; *The Game* (1905), in which the bloody fistfight in the boxing ring is London's metaphor for life; *Before Adam* (1907), in which prehistoric hominids bludgeon each other with clubs; and of course the many Klondike tales in *The Complete Short Stories of Jack London.*

---

11 Franklin Walker, *Jack London and the Klondike* (San Marino, Calif.: The Huntington Library, 1966), p. 206.
12 Jack London, *John Barleycorn,* pp. 146–147.

The works that furnish a Marxian view of existence include *The People of the Abyss, War of the Classes* (1905), *The Human Drift* (1917), and tales like "The Apostate," "Goliah, "The Slot," and "The Dream of Debs." These detail the horrors of urban industrialism, the avarice of capitalists, the virtue of the proletariat, and the economic rivalry between political empires that make the workers' lives a horror. In "The Apostate" (based on London's stint in the cannery), mere manual labor is said to transmogrify a strapping young boy into a "work beast," an atavistic figure who "did not walk like a man," who "did not look like a man," who was "a travesty of the human," a "twisted and stunted and nameless piece of life that shambled like a sickly ape, arms loose-hanging, stoop-shouldered, narrow-chested, grotesque and terrible" (*SS*, II, 1128–1129). London was a remarkable narcissist in love with his own good looks and muscular physique. His several bodybuilding photographs, for some of which he stripped down to his BVDs, suggest that he saw himself as having the lithe grace of a Greek god and the sinewy brawn of a Viking warrior. But when he came to write about manual labor of the kind that had developed his own physique, the Victorian Gospel of Work was turned on its ideological head and denounced as ruthless and oppressive. In *The People of the Abyss*, the English, thanks to capitalist exploitation, are "sodden and forlorn creatures, uncouth, degraded, and wretched below the beasts of the field." He claimed that "the chief trouble with these poor folk is that they do not know how to commit suicide, and usually have to make two or three attempts before they succeed."[13] Marie L. Ahearn has acclaimed London's English book as a predecessor to Tom Wolfe's "New Journalism," but the work is in fact a grotesque reduction of England's working men and women to subhuman existence and a work of cumbersome propaganda dependent on the formulaic locutions of Marx and Engels.[14]

Over the years socialists have pretended, as Philip Foner puts it, that London "showed a basic misunderstanding of the tenets of Socialism, which rejected all terrorist, anarchistic, individualistic policies. . . ."[15] But it is a mistake to think that socialism is in principle averse to violence. Certainly there were many socialists in London's time ready to foment class war. In fact, as Carolyn Johnston has demonstrated, London's political speeches clearly show that he "identified ideologically with the

---

13 Jack London, *The People of the Abyss*, ed. I. O. Evans (1903; reprinted New York: Archer House, 1963), pp. 164, 166.

14 Marie L. Ahearn, "*The People of the Abyss*: Jack London as New Journalist," *Modern Fiction Studies*, 22 (Spring 1976), 73–83.

15 Foner's bizarre claim, produced after World War II in order to paper over the left's prewar subversions, is taken up by the editor in *Curious Fragments: Jack London's Tales of Fantasy Fiction*, ed. Dale L. Walker (Port Washington, N.Y.: Kennikat Press, 1975), p. 87.

left wing of the party, with his emphasis on revolutionary class struggle, enthusiasm for the Russian Revolution, and his acceptance of violence as an acceptable strategy."[16] In a speech in New York in 1905 London told his audience:

> You have mismanaged the world, and it shall be taken from you! . . . Look at us! We are strong! Consider our hands! They are strong hands, and even now they are reaching forth for all you have, and they will take it, take it by the power of their strong hands; take it from your feeble grasp.[17]

This is proletarian class hatred pure and simple; it threatens class warfare. What London implied here is that if he and his radical friends had their way, the barricades would be thrown up, guns would be produced, the "enemies of the people" would be stripped of their possessions, and a great many Americans would be eliminated if they tried to defend their homes and belongings. London was drawn to the idea of a revolution for the sheer bloodlust of it. Some socialists registered this, saw London as a loose cannon, and warned party leaders that his threats of violence were alienating the American public.[18] But a different viewpoint was held by butchers like Lenin and Trotsky. Having engineered a bloodbath in Russia—involving the "liquidation" of millions of peasants, Mensheviks, monarchists, and just plain folks like you and me—Trotsky knew how useful men like London can prove once a revolution is triggered. Jack London, Trotsky said, "saw incomparably more clearly and farther than all the social-democratic leaders of that time taken together."[19]

In accounting for the ideological split between Darwinism and socialism in London's stories, we note that London was an autodidact who simply worked up, in some degree, Malthus, Mill, Kropotkin, Henry George, Marx, and Engels. Lecturing on socialism at various colleges, he claimed that "It is no longer a question of whether or not there is a class struggle. The question now is what will be the outcome of the class struggle."[20] He welcomed Upton Sinclair's forgotten novel *The Jungle*

---

16 Carolyn Johnston, *Jack London*, p. 115.
17 Quoted in Joan London, pp. 308–309.
18 The Socialist leader Eugene Debs said that London "was a romantic mind, an adventurous spirit, and that combination cannot be expected to sink itself into the grooves of logic and practicability." See Ray Ginger, *The Bending Cross: A Biography of Eugene Victor Debs* (New Brunswick, N.J.: Rutgers University Press, 1949), p. 426.
19 Trotsky is quoted in Joan London, *Jack London and His Times*, p. 314. Lenin appreciated London too: on his deathbed, he asked his wife to read him London's "Love of Life." See Carolyn Johnston, *Jack London*, p. 186.
20 Philip S. Foner, *Jack London: American Rebel* (New York: Citadel Press, 1947), p. 459.

(1905) as "the book we have been waiting for these many years. The Uncle Tom's Cabin of Wage Slavery." [21] With dangerous simple-mindedness he offered the American people an either-or choice: either socialism or continued "capitalization of labor and the enslavement of the whole population." Luckily for us today, the vast majority of American readers at the turn of the century paid no attention to London's political ideas, even while they consumed his fiction with gusto. [22] They consumed it even when London mounted the soapbox and, in novels like *The Iron Heel* (1907), foretold the fascist horrors in store for us if we *didn't* capitulate to the socialists. This novel, like "Goliah," portrays the collapse of capitalism from "the weight of its own iniquities," the apocalypse of civil war, and the rise of a fascist tyranny—all of which is finally superseded by the golden age of collectivism. For nearly a half-century American socialists pointed to this novel as proof that fascism had an American face. It could happen here—and was going to, if we didn't collectivize immediately. But in fact *The Iron Heel* was a false alarm. [23]

Jack London in reality knew little enough about how entrepreneurs venture capital, manufacture products, or manage a business. Very simply he had been traumatized by his early years of manual labor; he detested it, and his "strongest ambition was to escape the working class himself." [24] He never got over the fact that his first *Atlantic Monthly* short story, "An Odyssey of the North," paid him the equivalent salary of four months of manual labor. He later told Cloudesley Johns that "certes, if they wish to buy me, body and soul, they are welcome—if they pay the price. I am writing for money. . . ." Artistic distinction seemed irrelevant, but, as for fame, he said, "If I can procure fame, that means more money." [25] In vowing "to become a vender of brains" rather than brawn, London wrote mainly to make a living, though he occasionally

---

21 London's 1906 review of *The Jungle* is reprinted in *No Mentor but Myself: A Collection of Articles, Essays, Reviews, and Letters, on Writing and Writers,* ed. Dale L. Walker (Port Washington, N.Y.: Kennikat Press, 1979), p. 104.

22 Despite London's tedious pounding the drum for socialism, between 1900 and 1915 he was the most popular writer in America, thanks in part to the fact that his wild "private life was front-page copy for every major newspaper in the country." See Earle Labor, *Jack London* (New York: Twayne Publishers, 1974), preface, n.p.

23 London rather perplexedly confessed of *The Iron Heel:* "I *didn't* write the thing as a prophecy at all. I really don't think these things are going to happen in the United States." He said that he hoped "the increasing socialist vote" would prevent class war. "But I will say that I sent out, in *The Iron Heel,* a warning of what I think *might* happen if they don't look to their votes. That's all." See Charmian London, *The Book of Jack London,* II, 139.

24 Carolyn Johnston, *Jack London,* p. 19.

25 *The Letters of Jack London,* eds. Earle Labor, Robert C. Leitz, III, and I. Milo Shepard (Stanford, Calif.: Stanford University Press, 1988), I, 164. Hereafter, citations from this collection will be given as *L,* in parentheses, in the text.

achieved much more than that.[26] What is poignant, in any case, is to see the materialist writer degrade literary art to a mere cash nexus.

For all his socialist propagandizing and detestation of the bourgeoisie, London longed for wealth and yearned to be an aristocrat living in the grand style. By dint of nonstop fiction writing and reams of newspaper articles, he eventually amassed enough money to buy a yacht, a good many thoroughbreds, and a huge estate in California. His expenditures for fine stud horses, Spanish tiles, imported eucalyptus trees, and the like were legendary.[27] At the end he and his wife Charmian were traveling with a retinue of five or six servants.[28] If there is a paradox in this proletarian socialist's becoming "one of the first American writers to earn a million dollars through his writing,"[29] it must be understood in relation to the fact that London squandered the money almost as fast as he made it.

The Darwinian-Nietzschean and the Marxian-socialist viewpoints are almost entirely contradictory, and his attraction to both indicates how thoroughly self-divided Jack London really was. He seems in *The Sea Wolf, The Iron Heel,* and other such stories to be a pessimistic naturalist glorifying force, brutality, the superman who survives all opposition—the individualist who triumphs over both nature and his social inferiors. But in *Martin Eden, The People of the Abyss,* and other such works he seems to be glorifying cooperation and the unity of the masses as an antidote to "rapacious individualism" in politics, business, and the like. In an essay called "The Class Struggle" (1903), London argued that laborers should reject the idea of the survival of the fittest and refuse to be the "'glad perishers' so glowingly described by Nietzsche"; and in "Wanted: A New Law of Development" (1902), he claimed that "all the social forces are driving man on to a time when the old selective law will be annulled."[30]

But who could *annul* a force so cosmic and impersonal as the law of natural selection? The idea is ridiculous, but London wanted to believe that a socialist polity could cancel out individualism and that forced economic redistributions, by the state, would set at naught the law of competition.[31] Wanting, however, does not make it so. There was still

26 Jack London, "What Life Means to Me," printed in *Revolution and Other Essays* (New York: Macmillan, 1912), p. 301.

27 John Perry, *Jack London: An American Myth* (Chicago: Nelson-Hall, 1981), p. 270.

28 The marriage itself is the focus of Clarice Stasz's *American Dreamers: Charmian and Jack London* (New York: St. Martin's Press, 1988).

29 Carolyn Johnston, *Jack London,* p. 163.

30 Foner's *Jack London* reprints both essays; see pp. 459, 433.

31 The factionalist infighting among the several socialist parties that were active at the turn of the century—not to speak of their contentiousness with other radical groups including the

that troublesome notion of the Nietzschean will to power, which London saw as deeply implanted in the primordial self and as the instrument of human survival. He waffled so much that some modern critics doubt London's commitment to socialism. In *Jack London—An American Radical?*, Carolyn Johnston concludes that "because London was so attracted to the elitist view of the heroic leader, he feared that socialism might also impede individuality and lead to degeneration by eliminating competition. He never resolved his dilemma. . . ."[32] Andrew Sinclair has likewise remarked that "in his confident moments, Jack could claim in his compelling way that some sort of logic held together all his contradictions," but that logic has escaped most of his critics. At times it deserted even London himself, who would occaionally confess, "No, I am not a revolutionist or Marxist" because "I've read too much Spencer for that."[33] In *Martin Eden* he has his autobiographical hero looking

> to the strong man, the man on horseback to save the state from its own rotten futility. Nietzsche was right . . . the world belongs to the strong— the strong who are noble as well . . . the world belongs to the true noblemen, to the great blond beasts, to the non-compromisers, to the "yes sayers."[34]

London's socialist fiction—like that of William Dean Howells, Edward Bellamy, and Upton Sinclair—is largely propaganda and has been effectively swept by political events into the dustbin of history. His fiction is most compelling when it taps London's own blood consciousness, expresses his sense of the primordial, and dramatizes the struggle for survival in nature—especially in the Yukon. His enduring theme, for most readers, is the strength, cunning, and intelligence it takes to come through and succeed in the ordeal of existence. And when he lets himself go, imaginatively, in the creation of stories like "To Build a Fire," "Love of Life," and "Odyssey of the North," he can be riveting. So decisively was his imagination aroused by the idea of the struggle for survival and by the Nietzschean strongman that London complained that his indictment of capitalist individualism was not being grasped by readers of his fiction. They just didn't get it, though his message, he thought, was clear enough. "I have again and again written books that failed to get across," he told Mary Austin in 1915.

---

syndicalists, Nationalists, and communists—ought to have made London question the very premise of peaceful cooperation under a leftist regime.

32 Carolyn Johnston, *Jack London*, p. 77.

33 Andrew Sinclair, *Jack: A Biography of Jack London* (New York: Harper and Row, 1977), pp. 76–77.

34 Quoted in Patrick Bridgwater's *Nietzsche in Anglosaxony: A Study of Nietzsche's Impact on English and American Literature* (Bristol: Leicester University Press, 1972), p. 169.

Long years ago at the very beginning of my writing career, I attacked Nietzsche and his super-man idea. This was in *The Sea Wolf*. Lots of people read *The Sea Wolf*, no one discoverd that it was an attack upon the super-man philosophy. Later on, not mentioning my shorter efforts, I wrote another novel that was an attack upon the super-man idea, namely my *Martin Eden*. Nobody discovered that this was such an attack. At another time I wrote an attack on ideas brought forth by Rudyard Kipling, and entitled my attack "The Strength of the Strong." No one was in the slightest aware of the point of my story (*L*, III, 1513).

A more self-conscious writer might have quizzed himself about the reader's so-called blindness. For the glorification of primitive individual strength is not only visible in the work; it often totally eclipses the socialist sloganeering. At times it even devolves into a "thrilling" sadism, as is suggested by the mere titles of many of his works—*White Fang* (1906), *The Iron Heel* (1907), *The Strength of the Strong* (1911), and *The Abysmal Brute* (1913). But, as Gunilla Bergsten has quite charitably remarked, "Ideas were not his strong point, and he had no sure sense of consistency in questions dealing with philosophy."[35]

Darwin had proposed that, while no *telos* or purpose in life is evident in the operation of natural selection, life evolves from simplicity to complexity, from savagery to civilization. And, taking a rosy view of where we were going, Herbert Spencer deduced in *First Principles* that "evolution can end only in the establishment of the greatest perfection and most complete happiness."[36] But London came to see that, if evolution has no purpose in life, the process might just as easily reverse itself and produce atavism and a human regression to bestiality. This is the meaning of stories like "Love of Life" and *The Call of the Wild*, where the protagonist's primitive biological ancestry lures him back from domesticity and civilization into a feral nature red in tooth and claw. It could happen any time: civilization is a thin veneer of constraints papered over the eruptive animal appetites. In *Before Adam*, by a strange "freak of heredity," a modern man is not "called" backward but rather begins to experience the memories of a "Big-Tooth," his "other self," the prehistoric hominid he "once was." He recollects the savage conflict for preeminence among rival anthropoid groups. In particular he recalls a savage member of his clan called Red-Eye who was "an atavism." As he was "more primitive than any of us," he "tended to destroy the horde by his unsocial acts. He was really a reversion to an earlier type, and his

35 See Gunilla Bergsten, "Jack London—Lone Wolf and Social Critic," trans. J. O. Nilsen, in *Jack London Newsletter*, 8 (1975), 107.
36 Herbert Spencer, *First Principles* (London: Williams and Norgate, 1870), p. 517.

place was with the Tree People [an apelike group] rather than with us who were in the process of becoming men."³⁷ Men, London would have us believe, could at any time experience the Red-Eye within.

"Competition was the secret of Creation," a character says in *A Daughter of the Snows* (1902). "Battle was the law and way of progress. The world was made for the strong, and only the strong inherited it, and through it there ran an eternal equity." ³⁸ Equity obscurely implies a rough justice in the fact of the preeminence of the strong. But the basis of that justice is not set forth. In *White Fang*, however, London empties evolution of all its ostensible equity or human meaning whatsoever and reduces the world to "a place wherein ranged a multitude of appetites, pursuing and being pursued, hunting and being hunted, eating and being eaten, all in blindness and confusion, with violence and disorder, a chaos of gluttony and slaughter, ruled over by chance, merciless, plan-less, endless." The intent of the novel is to define life as meat. "Life itself was meat. Life lived on life. There were the eaters and the eaten. The law was; EAT OR BE EATEN."³⁹ This is a purely animalistic view of existence, of course, but London's imagination thrilled to the action possibilities of such stark moral reductions. Notable is the dominance of chance in the order of existence, as London defines it here, the planlessness of crea-tion. Whether we are to understand the blindness and confusion of the world as a perception of the canine (or subhuman) or whether it reflects the highest naturalistic wisdom of human understanding would be hard to say. Henry Adams might have claimed the latter.

The law of competition and strength, London came to feel, was true even in the social development of nations and races. He told his cor-respondent Cloudsley Johns in 1899 that "the Teutonic is the dominant race of the world there is no question. . . ." Airily contributing to the ugly Social Darwinism of his time, he provided a clear rationalization for the domination of the strong. He said there was even a kind of biological equity in the supremacy of the white race. He believed that "The negro races, the mongrel races, the slavish [slavic] races, the un-progressive races, are of bad blood—that is, of blood which is not qualified to permit them to successfully survive the selection by which the fittest survive, and which the next centuries, in my opinion, will see terribly intensified" (*L*, I, 87). At times he seemed to think that there was indeed something progressive (rather than atavistic) in the processes of natural selection. He claimed that there was no point in

---

37 Jack London, *Before Adam* (1907; reprinted New York: Bantam, 1970), p. 47.
38 Jack London, *A Daughter of the Snows* (Philadelphia: Lippincott, 1902), p. 58;
39 *Jack London: Novels and Stories*, ed. Donald Pizer (New York: Library of America, 1982), p. 153.

trying to rein in the dominant Saxons, who ruled over the world as by a natural right:

> Evolution does not hold to leash its mighty forces till pigmy man has determined the right and wrong of the next step. Nor has it a chosen people. . . . In the struggles of type with type, it is ethnics which determines, not ethics. . . . Heart reasoners and idealizers do not retard one jot or tittle the passing of the Alaskan Indian—an erstwhile mighty race now crooning its deathsong over the cold ashes of dead fires. . . . The Anglo-Saxon stands forth the most prominent figure among the races and the highest bidder for the world.[40]

An unembarrassed racist, he dismissed Mexicans, Indians, blacks, Koreans, Melanesians, and half-breeds as marginal or even retrograde races in the evolutionary ascent of mankind. To Cloudesley Johns he wrote: "I do not believe in the universal brotherhood of man" (*L*, I, 133). Socialism was devised "to give more strength to those certain kindred favored races so that they may survive and inherit the earth to the extinction of the lesser weaker races. The very men who advocate socialism may tell you of the brotherhood of all man, and I know they are sincere but that does not alter the law. . ." (*L*, I, 89). Not only was socialism just for the white race but Anglo-Saxon imperial conquests were, for London, a reflection of the Nietzschean strength of the white race. And since he had a fantasy that he himself was the blond beast of that race, he took to calling himself Wolf. His wife Charmian he called "Wild-Mate" and the "Mate-Woman." The Third Reich would have loved London if he had not—to everyone's stupefaction—called himself socialist.

III

London did not attain the highest level of the narrative art—the level of Hawthorne, James, Chekhov, Joyce, Fitzgerald, Faulkner, and Hemingway. The journalist and writer who published forty-four volumes in sixteen years—another six appeared posthumously—was, frankly, batting it out most of the time. He wrote so much that he depleted his imagination and had to pay Sinclair Lewis and others for short story ideas. And much of the time he was merely potboiling—what Lewis has inimitably described as "turning out a swell piece of cheese to grab off some easy gravy." It would be wrong to ascribe London's defects of style to hurried composition and inadequate revision. London wrote only a thousand words a day, day in and day out, for sixteen years. He claimed

---

40 Jack London, "The Salt of the Earth"; quoted in Johnston, *Jack London*, p. 106n.

that he wrote slowly so that revision was not really necessary.

> Mr. Gilder [editor of *The Century* magazine] speaks of rough drafts. I do not make any. I compose very slowly, in long hand, and each day type what I have written. My main revision is done each day in the course of typewriting the manuscript. This manuscript is the final one, and as much time is spent on it as is spent by many a man making two or three rough drafts. My revisions of proof-sheets are very infrequent, chopping a word or a phrase out here, putting in the other there, and that is all (*L*, I, 383).

In fact London revised very little because he was always more interested in the matter of his tale than in the manner of it. When his inundating novels and stories were criticized as shapeless and self-indulgent, he exploded in indignation. "What is form?" he demanded of Elwyn Hoffman. "What intrinsic value resides in it? None, none, none—unless it clothe pregnant substance, great substance." He said he would "sacrifice form *every time*, when it boils down to a final question of choice between form and matter. The thought is the thing." He claimed that "what the world wants is strength of utterance, not precision of utterance. . . . The person who would be precise is merely an echo of all the precise people who have gone before, and such a person's work is bound to be colorless and insipid."[41] These expostulations ring hollow because in fact, in the literary art, there never is a choice between form and content. In art there can be no great substance without a great formal design, no strength of utterance without precision of style. And, so far as an *ars poetica* is concerned, "The thought is the thing" is an illustration of the slovenliness of sentence style that too often diminishes London's fifty volumes of prose.

Still, tales like "The Chinago," "A Piece of Steak," *The Star Rover,* and "The Red One" have a kind of energy and vitality, and a voice and atmosphere, that made it natural for his contemporaries to have compared him with Bret Harte and Rudyard Kipling.[42] "Hunks of raw life" cut from the still-living body of experience London aspired to give us, filtered withal through Herbert Spencer's *Philosophy of Style*. At his best he was, like Poe, expert in attaining a unity of effect. This talent demands the rigorous exclusion of whatever does not contribute to the effect aimed for. Hence London adjured himself to "mercilessly omit all

---

41 Quoted in Labor's *Jack London*, pp. 86, 69, 85–86.
42 King Hendricks has rightly called "The Chinago" "the greatest story of London's career and one of the great stories of all time." See "Jack London: Master Craftsman of the Short Story," in *Jack London: Essays in Criticism*, ed. Ray Wilson Ownbey (Santa Barbara, Calif.: Peregrine Smith, 1978), p. 27.

interesting notes that fuddle your *key.* Insist on your *key.*"[43] If the invention of plots was not London's gift, he had a ready mastery of point-of-view technique. He could even make plausible the the point of view of an animal like Buck in *The Call of the Wild.* However didactic and essayistic were his own stories, he insisted at least in theory on authorial self-effacement. He told a young writer who had sent him a story that

> on page 3 of your manuscript you stop and tell the reader how awful it is for a woman to live with a man outside of wedlock. I am perfectly willing to grant that it is awful for a woman to live with a man outside of wedlock, but as an artist I am compelled to tell you for heaven's sake, don't stop your story in order to tell your reader how awful it is. Let your reader get this sense of awfulness from your story as your story goes on.[44]

He was also accomplished in landscape description, the realization of setting and atmosphere, and the creation of primitive but at times richly complex characters such as Sitka Charley, Naass, and Baptiste the Red. His code hero, the Malamute Kid, has a mythic vitality like that of Cooper's Leatherstocking. And truly original and memorable are some of those tough Innuit or half-breed women such as Labiskwee in "The Wonder of Woman" or Killisnoo in "Siwash." How different they are from the American girls of Howells and Henry James. London called these Northern women the "daughters of the wolf who have bred and suckled a race of men," and to them he dedicated *The God of His Fathers* (1901).

IV

Jack London died at forty, perhaps of renal failure, perhaps of a deliberate overdose of morphine. Despite the narcissistic body worship I have mentioned, he had abused his health through drugs, alcohol, raw meat, and bizarre diets. Toward the end of his life he was a bloated physical wreck who had to inject himself with morphine to dull the pain of syphilis and kidney disease. For reasons rather obscure to me, some of his keenest admirers have made a spirited attempt to absolve London of the charge of suicide. In the view of Alfred S. Shivers, London's death "could easily have resulted from the severe case of uraemic poisoning which he was known to have had and which the death certificate duly

---

43 Jack London, "10 South Seas," in *Critical Essays on Jack London,* ed. Jacqueline Tavernier-Courbin (Boston: G. K. Hall, 1983), p. 271.

44 *Letters from Jack London,* eds. King Hendricks and Irving Shepard (New York: Odyssey Press, 1965), pp. 448–449.

records."[45] And Jacqueline Tavernier-Courbin has undertaken to discredit Joan London's claim that her father "had taken his own life."[46] But since empty vials of morphine were found in London's bedroom, together with his handwritten note calculating the size of a lethal dose, the matter seems not worth arguing. The fact is that London's suicide was a slow and prolonged affair that took many years to complete.

For a half-century after his death, despite his squabbles with the party, London was the darling of the American political left, which undertook to transform ordinary American sympathy for the disadvantaged into a virtue to be found only in socialists. And for the past half-century London has been advanced as proof that artistic genius and socialist humanitarianism are indistinguishable from each other.[47] Socialists were fond of pointing out, during this period, that London was the most popular American author in the world. His standing in the Soviet Union, Poland, and Hungary was invariably mentioned as a sign of his international distinction. But when we remember that the Kremlin and its satellites flooded Eastern Europe with huge reprints of every ideologically correct proletarian hack, the numbers alone mean little. Aesthetic distinction cannot be dictated by party hacks, though for decades the *apparat* did succeed in controlling what their populations could read.

Those who worked in the London papers after his death came to know a dark Jack London not so evident in the interviews and celebrity releases. The recent biographies and the 1988 publication of his letters have, however, served to bring out into the open this darker personality. This London has been a remarkable disappointment to the American political left. In consequence, the left's estimate of London is now being reconfigured. It is now commonly said that he was not an appropriate representative of the cause, not a sufficiently "pure" socialist: his values were "tainted" with sexism, racism, and (what is worse) "bourgeois aspirations." Carolyn Johnston complains that even after London "became a socialist, he remained so strongly individualistic that he could not join in genuine collective struggle."[48] What this "joining in" might have meant in London's case is not spelled out. But Joan Hedrick likewise complains in *Solitary Comrade: Jack London and His Work* that London was a loner locked into a "bourgeois consciousness" and was

---

45 Alfred S. Shivers, "Jack London: Not a Suicide," in *Critical Essays on Jack London*, p. 66.

46 See Joan London's *Jack London and His Daughters* (Berkeley: Heyday Books, 1990), p. 178; and Jacqueline Tavernier-Courbin's "A Daughter's Last Message," *Thalia*, 12 (1992), 98–99.

47 A nostalgic effort to preserve this sentimental view of the humanitarian Jack, despite his appalling racism, is to be found in E. L. Doctorow's *Jack London, Hemingway, and the Constitution: Selected Essays, 1977–1992* (New York: Random House, 1993).

48 Carolyn Johnston, *Jack London*, p. 14.

"never to know release from the burden of self" until it came "through death."[49] William E. Cain likewise admits to a "baffled disgust" with the London we see in his correspondence, which makes inescapably plain his cruelty, racism, and avidity for money. The publication of London's letters will "damage London's image as a stalwart socialist." Of course, in a typical left-wing effort at damage control, Cain blames America for London's ugly personal characteristics and transforms him into a victim: "The culture of capitalism propelled, rewarded, and killed him." [50] Hardly a victim, London was responsible for his own excesses, but the moral is plain. London is no longer politically correct and must now be treated as an embarrassment to contemporary left-wing academics.

V

One of the main reasons why radical literary critics have become disillusioned with Jack London is that shortly before his death he resigned from the Socialist party, which he saw as weak-kneed and lacking in the instinct for blood. He also abandoned his materialistic monism for the mysticism of Carl Jung and the "collective unconscious." This turn toward a philosophy of dualism and a religion of intangible spiritual concern—evident in tales like "The Bones of Kahekili" and "The Water Baby"—might have been predicted, for London had a lifelong attraction to the supernatural which his avowed atheism (and his mother's weird spiritualism) obliged him consciously to repress. Even so, at any point in London's writing the world of the spirit can suddenly and unexpectedly intervene in the affairs of men. Here is a passage from "The White Silence" which represents the visionary London at his contradictory best:

> The afternoon wore on, and with the awe, born of the White Silence, the voiceless travelers bent to their work. Nature has many tricks wherewith she convinces man of his finity,—the ceaseless flow of the tides, the fury of the storm, the shock of the earthquake, the long roll of heaven's artillery,—but the most tremendous, the most stupefying of all, is the passive phase of the White Silence. All movement ceases, the sky clears, the heavens are as brass; the slightest whisper seems sacrilege, and man becomes timid, affrighted at the sound of his own voice. Sole speck of life journeying across the ghostly wastes of a dead world, he

---

49 Joan D. Hedrick, *Solitary Comrade: Jack London and His Work* (Chapel Hill: University of North Carolina Press, 1982), p. 236.
50 William E. Cain, "Socialism, Power, and the Fate of Style: Jack London in His Letters," *American Literary History*, 3 (1991), 609, 604.

trembles at his audacity, realizes that his is a maggot's life, nothing more. Strange thoughts arise unsummoned, and the mystery of the universe comes over him,—the hope of the Resurrection and the Life, the yearning for immortality, the vain striving of the imprisoned essence,—it is then, if ever, man walks alone with God (*SS,* I, 143–144).

The passage is a *locus classicus* in London's fiction, a masterpiece of atmosphere and evocation. In a recent issue of a writer's magazine it was singled out for tyros as the right way to compose.[51] But if we take a close look at it, the passage contains a very curious movement. It begins with the blankness of nature, the meaningless of human life, and a kind of naturalistic atheism. Man is a speck, mere meat, or less—a maggot. But before we reach the end of the paragraph, a rather Kierkegaardian intuition of the existential reality of the supernatural world has replaced it. London has looked into the heart of light, the silence; and, in sounding it, he suggests that man is no longer a mere animal struggling across the frozen landscape. Instead, a spiritual consciousness has been stirred by the eloquent silence of nature, and there is now a dawning perception of the mystery of divinity. London's deity is the *Deus absconditus,* whose presence is registered as an absence in nature. If it was Pascal who said that "*Le silence éternel de ces espaces infinis m'effraie,*" perhaps no one caught that feeling better than London in his description of the vast blank white desolation of the Klondike snow. And what are we to make of it if, like Pascal, he was led to contemplate the nature of the soul and its relation to the Creator?

Anyone who probes London's fiction sees soon enough that London's realism is frankly superficial and his naturalistic determinism is merely an overlay of the scientific Zeitgeist. Earle Labor, who has rigorously analyzed every aspect of London's career, has persuasively concluded that, although London considered himself a realist and a rationalist, he was "a blatant Romantic" whose "most enduring work was generated from psychological depths beyond his logical understanding." His imagination was "permeated by poetry and myth" and was "the artistic modulation of universal dreams—i.e., of myths and archetypes."[52] Robert Barltrop concurs in observing that "Jack London's stories have their persistent appeal because, ultimately, they are not realistic at all; they are romantic fantasy."[53] Perhaps Fred Pattee said it best many years ago:

---

51 Dennis E. Hensley, "Chronicle: With His Eyes Wide Open," *The Writer's Digest* (February 1994), 79–80.
52 Earle Labor, *Jack London,* preface, pp. 9, 21, 57, 60.
53 Robert Barltrop, *Jack London: The Man, the Writer, the Rebel* (London: Pluto Press, 1976), p. 182.

Contrary to his own belief, he was not a realist at all. His tales of the Klondike were not written on the spot, but after they had mellowed for years in his imagination. Everywhere exaggerations, poetizations, utter marvels described as commonplaces, superlatives in every sentence. It is not the actual North; it is an epic dream of the North, colored by an imagination adolescent in its love of the marvelous, of fighting and action, and of headlong movement.[54]

Not the actual North, it goes without saying, but what an epic dream! Taken singly, the best of London's Klondike tales are compelling instances of literary vividness and power that can make—for the moment —ideology seem irrelevant and logical contradiction a petty concern.

Unfortunately, London's romantic imagination did not always work at the top of its form, and even when it did, he could become quite dissatisfied with the result. Although he had always been content to see fiction as a tool of radical social change, toward the end he came to regard the masses as sunk in ignorance and writing for them as a totally futile pastime. He told a reporter from the *Western Comrade:*

I no longer think of the world or the movement (the social revolution) or of writing as an art. I am a great dreamer, but I dream of my ranch, of my wife. I dream of beautiful horses and fine soil in Sonoma County. And I write for no other purpose than to add to the beauty that now belongs to me. I write a book for no other reason than to add three or four hundred acres to my magnificent estate. I write a story with no other purpose than to buy a stallion. To me, my cattle are far more interesting than my profession.[55]

Oppressed by feelings about the futility of art, or at least his own writing, he could see it only as a flimflam and a con game that deceived not only its devotees but its practitioners. London's loss of faith in art reflects a loss of faith in himself and helps to account for the despair, at the end, that led him to suicide. Even so, we have in *The Complete Short Stories* a dozen or so very nearly perfect tales and a handful of impressive novels—*The Call of the Wild, The Sea Wolf,* and *Martin Eden.* These can still amaze the troubled midnight and the noon's repose.

---

54 Fred Lewis Pattee, *The Development of the American Short Story: An Historical Survey* (New York: Harper and Brothers, 1923), p. 352.
55 Quoted in Foner, *Jack London,* p. 119.

Edith Wharton:
The Archaeological
Motive

In "Tradition and the Individual Talent," T. S. Eliot observed that the word "tradition" seldom appears except in a phrase of censure: "If otherwise, it is vaguely approbative, with the implication, as to the work approved, of some pleasing archaeological reconstruction. You can hardly make the word agreeable to English ears without this comfortable reference to the reassuring science of archaeology."[1] Eliot's reference to the science of archaeology is pleasantly facetious, but to anyone familiar with his thought it does not in any way obscure his profound respect for the significance of tradition—in art, religion, politics, and society. I wish to invoke this "censurable" term *tradition*, in relation to the science of archaeology, as a means of exploring the fiction of Edith Wharton. Paradoxically, it provides one of the most meaningful approaches to her mind and art.

Edith Wharton conceived of the Western cultural tradition as a complex interrelation of legal, political, economic, and social structures, of art, morals, and religion. She thought of it as organic rather than as atomic and as fundamentally dynamic, in the evolutionary sense, rather than as static. She grew up with the first generation of American writers to experience the impact of evolutionary thought, and for her—as for many of her contemporaries—the figure of Darwin loomed large. In her autobiography, *A Backward Glance* (1934), she identified Darwin as one of her intellectual "awakeners." She also spoke of her excitement at

---

1 T. S. Eliot, "Tradition and the Individual Talent," in *The Sacred Wood: Essays on Poetry and Criticism* (1920; reprinted New York: Barnes and Noble, 1960), p. 47.

reading the physicist John Tyndall; the biologists T. H. Huxley, Alfred Russel Wallace, George John Romanes, and Ernst Haeckel; the evolutionary social philosopher Herbert Spencer; the Finnish sociologist Edvard Westermarck; and the archaeologist Heinrich Schliemann. It is not my purpose to document the specific influence of these scientists on Edith Wharton—though she was a scientific horticulturalist, of sorts, herself, composed technical treatises on the development of landscape gardening styles in Italy, wrote a number of broadly sociological works, and went on numerous archaeological expeditions in the Mediterranean area.[2] Rather it is my intention to suggest that the notion of evolutionary development, advanced or implied in the work of these scientists, profoundly influenced Mrs. Wharton's general conception of individual human identity and of the cultural tradition that shapes it, deepened her sense of the meaning of the past for the present, and profoundly affected some of the thematic and technical choices she made in her own fiction.

I

In approaching her conception of human identity—in terms of how she believed character could be represented in fiction—it is instructive to recall her response to the argument between Howells and Henry James on American society as a field for fiction. James complained that the American novelist lacked those social forms and institutions available in Europe which help the European novelist to characterize his people and their manners—no state, barely a specific national name, no sovereign, no court, no aristocracy, no church, no clergy, no army, no diplomatic service, no country gentlemen, no palaces, parsonages, thatched cottages, ivied ruins, cathedrals, universities, no public schools, political society, no sporting class, no Epsom, no Ascot! All these phenomena, he argued, help the novelist to locate and materialize his people and to recreate exterior reality. The American novelist—Hawthorne is James's prime example—lacking a social field, is driven inward, forced to focus on the complexities of human psychology and to express interior reality through the mode of romance.[3] Howells reviewed James's biography of Hawthorne in 1880 and attacked James's view of the deficiencies of American society. Dispose of these social institutions, he argued, and the novelist still has the whole of human nature as his subject.

---

2 Mrs. Wharton's gardens are usefully illustrated in Eleanor Dwight's recent biography *Edith Wharton: An Extraordinary Life* (New York: Harry N. Abrams, 1994), as well as in Dwight's "Edith Wharton's French Landscapes," *Architectural Digest*, 51 (March 1994), 84–93.

3 Henry James, *Hawthorne* (1879; reprinted New York: Macmillan, 1966), pp. 48–49.

In this controversy Edith Wharton, many years later, came to side with Henry James and rebuked Van Wyck Brooks for taking the position Howells had espoused. For her, human nature consisted precisely *in* those forms and institutions which surround, enclose, and structure human life. Desmond Morris, the anthropologist, has claimed that, for all our cultural overlay, man is basically a human animal, a "naked ape." Mrs. Wharton, as a student of Darwin, would have agreed. But despite the primacy of our biological existence, human life for her was principally a social phenomenon, and it was life as a social phenomenon that mattered for the writer. In an essay entitled "The Great American Novel," Mrs. Wharton asked what human nature does consist in if it is denuded of "the web of custom, manners, culture it has elaborately spun about itself." Her point was that very little of distinctively human nature can exist independent of society and its forms. If you strip away the web of custom and manners, she argued, the only thing left is "that hollow unreality, 'Man,' an evocation of the eighteenth-century demagogues who were the first inventors of 'standardization.'" She went on to assert that "human nature" and "man" are mere intellectual abstractions, whereas real men are bound up with the effects of climate, soil, laws, religion, wealth, and leisure.[4]

In her best, most representative works, Mrs. Wharton continually returned to the idea of tradition and the need of viable modes of cultural transmission as important factors affecting the character of man's social history. She continually argued the necessity of the individual's commitment to the cultural tradition; the danger of alienation from it; the catastrophe that ensues when social upheavals like anarchy, revolution, and war destroy the slowly and delicately spun web of that tradition; and the necessity of imaginatively preserving—if necessary even reconstructing—the precious values of the past. Her artistic treatment of the theme of tradition usually involved two methods. The first was to dramatize the importance for men of the web of culture, manners, and mores that interlinks them and to warn of the disaster in store for those who become culturally deracinated or alienated and for those who destroy the delicate web in a radical obsession to replace or reform it. And the other method, evident in the final years of her life, was an impulse to reconstruct—archaeologically, as it were—the social world of her youth: the traditions that vitalized the culture of old New York in the period from about 1840 to 1880. She hoped to revive the memory of a set of slowly evolved cultural values suddenly wiped out by a succession of destructive changes in American life beginning in the 1880s.

---

4 Edith Wharton, "The Great American Novel," *Yale Review*, n.s., 16 (1927), 652.

These included the rise of the industrial plutocracy (the "lords of Pittsburgh," as she called them); the massive immigration that totally altered the ethnic character of New York City; the First World War, the depression, and the New Deal; and the nationalistic hatreds, at the close of her life in 1937, building toward the Second World War.

II

Her philosophical conservatism was expressed most aggressively in her first novel, *The Valley of Decision* (1902). This historical novel, set in eighteenth-century Italy on the eve of the Napoleonic invasion, dramatized the collapse of social order in a small Italian duchy near the French border. The "eighteenth-century demagogues," in this case, were utopians of the French perfectibilitarian school who preached political revolution as the only means of correcting the economic injustices of Pianura. The effect of the doctrines of these impractical "city demagogues theorizing in Parisian coffee-houses on the Rights of Man and the Code of Nature"[5] is twofold: the destruction of the relation of the social classes to each other and to the church; and the destruction of those social institutions that had historically organized, delicately balanced, and harmonized the conflicting claims of members of society. Their visionary schemes divide families, wreck commerce, and plunge the country into famine and anarchy as the balance of need and agricultural supply is destroyed. *The Valley of Decision* ends with the collapse of the duchy of Pianura. The implication of the novel is clear that the institutions of society—law, religion, government—are necessary restraints to what T. S. Eliot once called, in another connection, "disorderly minds and unruly passions."[6] Without the checks provided by the social tradition, freedom—Mrs. Wharton suggests—denotes only license, license to act in a state of nature, like a beast, the naked ape.

Edith Wharton planned a sequel to *The Valley of Decision* which she tentatively named *The New Day*. Set in 1835, after Napoleon's defeat at Waterloo, in a Pianura which is now "The Land of the Dead," the novel was to have dramatized the more violent counterrevolution which restored the *status quo ante* in the Italian duchies, from the reintroduction of minute court punctilio to the revival of feudal class distinctions. The sequel was to demonstrate that tearing apart the social order brought on evils unimagined by the good-intentioned and provoked violent social reactions more horrible than the original situation, so that the last con-

---

5 Edith Wharton, *The Valley of Decision* (New York: Scribner's, 1902), II, 166.
6 T. S. Eliot, "Thoughts After Lambeth," in *Selected Essays* (New York: Harcourt, Brace and World, 1964), p. 329.

dition was worse than the first. And of course she had a wealth of historical data on the political history of the Italian duchies after the Napoleonic wars to present as evidence that the perfectibilitarianism of the *philosophes* and the radicalism of their followers had, in history, backfired. But even though she had the historical evidence to document her views, writing *The Valley of Decision* and its incomplete sequel taught her that there are only two rules for a writer and that she had violated them both: one was that "the novelist should deal only with what is within his reach, literally or figuratively, . . . and the other was that the value of a subject depends almost wholly on what the author sees in it, and how deeply he is able to see *into* it."[7]

The House of Mirth (1905), set in contemporary New York high society, satisfied both rules and turned out to be one of Edith Wharton's finest novels and a best-seller. Fundamentally, it is the story of missed connections, of Lily Bart's failure to get into relation with an order of cultural and social values superior to the goal of worldly pleasure pursued by the fashionable *haut monde*. Lily rejects Lawrence Selden, the cultivated but poor young man who loves her, pursues a rich husband, fails to find one because of her fastidious tastes, and dies in a cheap boardinghouse of an overdose of chloral. The novel thus dramatizes what Mrs. Wharton called the triumph of "the house of mirth," or mindless pleasure-seeking, over "the republic of the spirit," a concept signifying psychological freedom from the accidents of material existence. Lily Bart is not a tragic heroine, but her fate is full of pathos because it is as much caused by the materialism of her social world as by her own whims. Balancing the social forces against Lily's personal vacillations, Mrs. Wharton showed that Lily fell from her high station, after her family's money was gone, because "there was no center of early pieties, of grave endearing traditions, to which her heart could revert and from which it could draw strength for herself and tenderness for others."[8] Again, the source for the title, Ecclesiastes 7:4, implies the thematic significance of the action: "The heart of the wise is in the house of mourning; but the heart of fools is in the house of mirth." As Mrs. Wharton told her correspondent Erskine Steele shortly after she published the book, the central meaning of the action is expressed in the idea that "In whatever form a slowly-accumulated past lives in the blood—whether in the concrete image of the old house stored with

---

7 Edith Wharton, *A Backward Glance* (New York: Scribner's, 1934), p. 206. Quotations from this work will hereafter be given as *ABG*, in parentheses, in the text.

8 Edith Wharton, *The House of Mirth*, ed. R. W. B. Lewis (1905; reprinted New York: New York University Press, 1977), p. 313. Citations from this work will hereafter be given as *HM*, in parentheses, in the text.

visual memories, or in the conception of the house not built with hands, but made up of inherited passions and loyalties—it has the same power of broadening and deepening the individual existence, of attaching it by mysterious links of kinship to all the mighty sum of human striving" (*HM*, 313).[9]

Hudson River Bracketed (1929) and a sequel entitled *The Gods Arrive* (1932), written toward the close of Edith Wharton's career, dramatize the disastrous consequences of cultural deprivation for the American who aspires to become an artist. Born in the culturally barren Midwest, where innovation and continuous change have eclipsed the values of tradition and continuity, Vance Weston (her would-be writer) gets his first glimmering of the values of tradition in New York state, where he has been sent to recuperate from an obviously symbolic illness. There he discovers a cultured Eastern girl, Halo Spear, and an old house, The Willows, built in the 1830s by A. J. Downing in the style of Hudson River Bracketed. The house comes to symbolize for Vance "that sense of continuity that we folks have missed out of our lives—out where I live, anyway"—and it gave him "the idea of a different rhythm, a different time-beat: a movement without jerks and breaks, flowing down from ever so far off in the hills, bearing to the sea."[10] (This rhythm without jerks and breaks, incidentally, is a fair approximation of what Edith Wharton was trying for in her prose—the style complementing and itself expressing the theme of continuity.)

Vance Weston tries to write novels embodying his new insight into the interrelatedness of the past and the present, expressing the way, for example, an old house like The Willows, by putting us in touch with the lives that have gone before us, can enrich and deepen individual existence. But because Vance has not yet sufficiently implanted himself in the deep soil of the past (the house is only about a hundred years old), his books are comparative failures. In *The Gods Arrive*, Mrs. Wharton takes Vance to Europe on a further search for his cultural roots, on a deeper descent into himself to engage his artistic energies. From this old house in New York, he passes on, in the footsteps of Henry Adams, to monuments witnessing more significantly to the continuity of the Western cultural tradition—the medieval cathedrals of Chartres and Cordova. These provide him with an even fuller realization of that "historical sense" which involves, as Eliot pointed out, a perception "not only of the pastness of the past, but of its presence," that awareness that makes a writer "traditional," makes him "most acutely conscious of his place in

9 Erskine Steele, "Fiction and Social Ethics," *South Atlantic Quarterly,* 5 (July 1906), 262.
10 Edith Wharton, *Hudson River Bracketed,* ed. Louis Auchincloss (1929; reprinted New York: New American Library, 1962), p. 263.

time, of his contemporaneity."[11] Eventually, with this germinal experience of the European founts of culture, Vance returns to America, ready
to attempt the great American novel. *The Gods Arrive* ends with the
marriage of Vance Weston and Halo Spear, an Eastern girl of an old established New York family. This union suggests, as E. K. Brown rightly
observed, that "only when the energies of the west and the traditions of
the old east are brought together can an adequate civilization develop."[12]
Only then can the gods arrive.

III

The failure of American society to preserve any kind of traditional system of values led Mrs. Wharton to observe that the really "vital change"
between the prewar and postwar worlds was that in her youth "the
Americans of the original States, who in moments of crisis still shaped
the national view, were the heirs of an old tradition of European culture
which the country has now totally rejected" (*ABG*, 7). Her postwar
novels, *The Glimpses of the Moon* (1922), *The Mother's Recompense*
(1925), *Twilight Sleep* (1927), and *The Children* (1928), though artisti-
cally weak, vividly portray the plight of rootless and ephemeral people
in the postwar world, cut adrift from their moral moorings, ignorant of
the social connections that enrich life, falling back finally on the frantic,
meaningless pleasures of the moment.

As she witnessed the Jazz Age spectacle after the war, Edith Wharton
was moved to try to recover and imaginatively project some of the
values expressed in the social and moral traditions of her youth in the
1870s. If the first method of her two approaches to the theme of tradition in her fiction was to portray (in the fate of Prince Odo's Pianura, in
Lily Bart, in Vance Weston) the ominous consequences of cultural de-
racination, the second was to provide a quite positive example of what a
continuous social tradition could do for the lives of people who were
fortunate enough to experience it. But none was conspicuous in the aftermath of the First World War and to provide the right example she
had to turn to the past, to produce the archaeological reconstruction.
The Age of Innocence (1920) and *Old New York* (1924) were in large part
an attempt to recapture from forgetfulness a social world swept away by
the acceleration of historical forces which only Henry Adams, of her
generation, had adequately foreseen. In these works she wished to show
that old New York in the age of innocence provided a certain kind of

---

11 T. S. Eliot, "Tradition and the Individual Talent," p. 49.
12 E. K. Brown, "Edith Wharton," *Études anglaises*, 2 (1938), 19.

social norm for the modern world. There is no question, from her portrait of it, that old New York was an imperfectly developed culture; indeed, it was marked by sexual hypocrisy, intellectual narrowness, civic irresponsibility, and class snobbery at its worst. But at its best it preserved the values of private dignity and personal decorum; a sensitivity to feeling and emotion, however bound in expression by conventional restraints; an appreciation for pictorial beauty and a feeling for the grandeur and sublimity of the English language; an unshakable belief in the civilizing power of education; a flair for the elegant (but not gaudy) social style; and a commitment to the obligations of honor in public life—all these qualities seemingly inconceivable in the age of flappers, jazz babies, flagpole sitters, and bathtub gin.

At the end of *The Age of Innocence*, Newland Archer marvels at the greater openness and spontaneity, at the greater freedom in manners possible in turn-of-the-century New York society. But he also reaffirms the goodness of the old established social and moral traditions of the 1870s which have already begun to disappear in New York. Mrs. Wharton characterized the quaintness of old New York moral standards in the age of innocence by an expert use of the symbolic setting: Archer's last interview with Ellen Olenska takes place in the Metropolitan Museum of Art. His struggle with his conscience—over whether or not to leave his wife—takes place in the room exhibiting the moldering Cesnola antiquities. As Archer and Ellen explore this moral dilemma in the presence of the glass cabinets displaying "the recovered fragments of Ilium" and the "small broken objects—hardly recognizable utensils, ornaments and personal trifles," it grows upon the reader that the scruples of conscience which marked the 1870s are as meaningless to the generation of the 1920s as the archaeological antiquities Archer stares at—so rapidly and totally have the foundations of the moral life changed in the modern age.[13]

Archer remains with his wife, May, and Ellen returns to Paris alone. The novel affirms Archer's decision—though Mrs. Wharton frankly acknowledges that in giving up romantic love Newland Archer missed "the flower of life" (*AI*, 350). His decision to stay is affirmed because it constitutes a recognition that a man has institutional, familial, and social responsibilities which cannot be abandoned simply for the gratification of romantic passion. Archer's piety for the values of the past Mrs. Wharton later called "the memorial manner," the conservative's sense of the past and the commitment to traditions which—however short-lived

---

13 Edith Wharton, *The Age of Innocence* (1920; reprinted New York: Random House, 1948), p. 312. Hereafter, quotations from this work will be given as *AI*, in parentheses, in the text.

in a long Darwinian perspective of man's social history—still enrich, deepen, and intensify the value of human life.

Mrs. Wharton's emphasis on the memorial manner, on preserving enduring institutions and values amidst evolutionary social change, because they satisfy age-old human needs, testifies to the sociological character of her imagination. Some of her fictional characters embody her own interest in the newer sciences of man and society. At the end of *The Age of Innocence,* emancipated New Yorkers are rejecting the frivolous pastimes of the idle rich and studying architecture and archaeology. Paul Marvell, in *The Custom of the Country,* studies sociology and is therefore well equipped to understand the disintegration of old New York as the plutocracy emerges in society. But he cannot cope with the effect of these changes on his personal life, and he commits suicide. Mrs. Wharton personally knew sociologists like Jean du Breuil de Saint-Germain, and she wrote one broadly sociological study herself, *French Ways and Their Meaning* (1919). Ostensibly a manual for American soldiers and tourists in France, *French Ways* in fact expressed a profound social conservatism that developed out of her study of the evolution of human societies. The quality and character of her sociological observation are evident in the emphasis she gives to continuity as a value particularly appropriate and necessary to American society.

> In all this, France has a lesson to teach and a warning to give. It was our English forebears who taught us to flout tradition and break away from their own great inheritance; France may teach us that, side by side with the qualities of enterprise and innovation that English blood has put in us, we should cultivate the sense of continuity, that "sense of the past" which enriches the present and binds us up with the world's great stabilizing traditions of art and poetry and knowledge.[14]

It may rightly be objected here that Mrs. Wharton is wildly idealizing French thought, which is, of course, the very source of those disastrous Jacobin ideas that she had dramatized in *The Valley of Decision* nearly two decades before. But in 1902 she had not yet left New York for permanent expatriation in Paris. She had not yet steeped herself in the antiquity and complexity of French society. It was not yet hers. By 1914, however, it was. If she idealized France in this postwar book, it was because she had been appalled at the German atrocities in World War I. She read the German action as an assault on civilization itself. At the head of civilization, as she saw it, was her adopted country, France. And the wholesale deaths of civilians and armies, and the manifest destruc-

---

14 Edith Wharton, *French Ways and Their Meaning* (New York: D. Appleton, 1919), p. 97.

tion of French towns and villages—which she had personally witnessed and reported on in *Fighting France: From Dunkirk to Belfort* (1915)—as well as the devastation of the displaced peoples of the Low Countries, whom her charities in Paris undertook to assist, made her acutely sensitive to everything that war could destroy.

A Backward Glance was published in 1934. In 1937, as she looked back over the radical social changes that had occurred in the three years since she had published her autobiography, it seemed to her as if the childhood world she had described in *A Backward* Glance was no longer memorable or even imaginable. In an essay entitled "A Further Glance" (posthumously published in 1938 in *Harper's* as "A Little Girl's New York"), she lamented that

> Everything that used to form the fabric of our daily life has been torn in shreds, trampled on, destroyed, and hundreds of little incidents, habits, traditions which, when I began to record my past, seemed too insignificant to set down, have acquired the historical importance of dress and furniture dug up in a Babylonian tomb.[15]

In this little essay she sought to unearth buried relics of that childhood world forever gone which *A Backward Glance* had failed to include—the architecture of the brownstones on Fifth Avenue, the bejeweled arbiters of old New York society, the balls at Delmonico's, long-forgotten dramatic performances at Lester Wallack's theatre, the old Academy of Music where Nilsson sang, the rhapsodic revivals of Moody and Sankey which alternated with the prizefights at Madison Square Garden, and the memorable rhetorical style of the Reverend Dr. Washburn at the Calvary Church off Gramercy Park.

At the time of her death she was working on the posthumously published novel *The Buccaneers* (1938). This novel also sought to reconstruct the habits, customs, and traditions of a genteel era which, in the age of the New Deal, seemed "as quaintly arbitrary as the domestic rites of the Pharaohs" (*ABG*, 6). The book also contained her final declaration of the significance of tradition for full individual human development. The parvenu American heroine Nan St. George, who marries an English duke, becomes disillusioned with the materialism and mindless social ambition of her circle. Renouncing the life of fashionable society, she seeks to root herself in the deep soil of English culture, in "the layers and layers of rich deep background, of history, poetry, old traditional observances, beautiful houses, beautiful landscapes, beautiful ancient buildings, palaces, churches, cathedrals."

15 Edith Wharton, "A Little Girl's New York," *Harper's Magazine*, 176 (March 1938), 356.

Would it not be possible, this provincial American girl asks herself, "to create for one's self a life out of all this richness, a life which should somehow make up for the poverty of one's lot?"[16] The question is largely unintelligible in the age of Meet-My-Needs and Dr. Ruth. It *was* possible, and Mrs. Wharton's expatriation suggests the extent to which this daughter of old New York was willing to go to relate *herself* to European culture. By establishing herself in relation to the cultural traditions of Europe, Nan St. George unifies her own life (as Lily Bart could not) with "all the mighty sum of human striving." Nan thereby becomes, even more so than James's Milly Theale, "the heiress of all the ages."

The important social values affirmed in *The Buccaneers* had to be identified with the continuity of European (particularly French and English) social history because Mrs. Wharton could find no continuity in the social history of America. Old New York offered the most appealing possibility, but by the 1930s it was as utterly obliterated as the lost cities of the Dead Sea. As a young woman she had deplored the physical ugliness of New York, with its gridirons of chocolate-colored houses. But what she could not guess then was that her old New York "would fifty years later be as much a vanished city as Atlantis or the lowest layer of Schliemann's Troy." Nor could she know that "the social organization which that prosaic setting had slowly secreted would have been swept to oblivion with the rest." She knew that old New York was of little national or historical importance in the development of the republic. But she felt that "the Atlantis-fate of old New York, the New York which had slowly but continuously developed from the early seventeenth century," had a sociological interest which made her childhood worth remembering. And toward the end of her life, in the disorder of the depression years, she came to believe that "the value of duration was slowly asserting itself against the welter of change," and that "sociologists without a drop of American blood in them" were beginning "to recognize what the traditions of three centuries have contributed to the moral wealth of our country" (*ABG*, 5). In dozens of short stories, therefore, and in several longer works of fiction (as well as in her autobiographical writings), Mrs. Wharton sought to reconstruct, like Schliemann, the buried city of old New York—its people and places, its vanished buildings and institutions, its manners and mores, its symbolic value for American social experience. "The compact world of my youth," Mrs. Wharton wrote, "has receded into a past from which it can only be dug up in bits by the as-

---

16 Edith Wharton, *The Buccaneers* (New York: D. Appleton-Century, 1938), p. 305. Recently Marion Mainwaring has had the effrontery to try to "complete" Mrs. Wharton's unfinished novel. An unmitigated disaster, the badly written Mainwaring version of *The Buccaneers* deserves to be permanently consigned to the *oubliette*.

siduous relic hunter; and its smallest fragments begin to be worth collecting and putting together before the last of those who knew the live structure are swept away" (*ABG*, 7).

I have not said much here about Edith Wharton as a literary artist, but let me just note an aspect of her precise and suggestive imagery: the *spun web* of society which she speaks of in "The Great American Novel"; the *secretion* of energies that *flower* into great art; the *seed* of perfectibilitarianism in *The Valley of Decision* which produces a great *harvest* of anarchy; *the past alive in the blood* linking us to all the mighty sum of human striving; characters like Lily Bart conceived as *stray uprooted growths* swept down the heedless current of the years; individuals imagined as mere spindrift of the whirling surface of existence without anything to which *the tentacles of self* can cling; the customs and manners of Newland Archer's world as *relics* or *fossils* testifying to *live social structures* heedlessly swept away;—all of this imagery, all of the metaphors are not merely decorative. They are also distinctively evolutionary in theme and imply a reasoned view of the existence of (and indeed the necessity of) acknowledging continuity as a preeminent value in man's social experience.

Hamlin Garland had argued in *Crumbling Idols* (1894) that "the study of evolution" had so "liberated the thought of the individual" that "the power of tradition" was growing "fainter year by year."[17] For Edith Wharton, however, "liberation" from tradition was no cause for rejoicing. For her the study of evolution provided precisely those sanctions for tradition which Garland had repudiated. In a world without absolutes, the traditional provided the only real possibility of stability and civilized living. Steeped in the literature of the biological, archaeological, and sociological sciences, passionately committed to a sense of the past, to the value of continuity and tradition (this is, after all, *her* figure in the carpet), Edith Wharton is especially relevant today. Her literary conservatism soured some older leftist critics of the 1930s who regarded her as hopelessly out of touch with the dynamics of social change. But perhaps a half-century after her death—in light of the collapse of so many liberal illusions, in the context of the end of revolutionary socialism and communism in Eastern Europe and the former Soviet Union—we have enough perspective to see her in relation to her own changing times and to appreciate the quality of the fiction evoked by her historically and sociologically oriented imagination. In the contemporary atmosphere of restless innovation and experiment in arts and society, of existential

---

17 Hamlin Garland, *Crumbling Idols: Twelve Essays on Art Dealing Chiefly with Literature, Painting, and the Drama,* ed. Jane Johnson (1894; reprinted Cambridge: Harvard University Press, 1960), pp. 37–38.

freedom eagerly invoked to create situational ethics and ad hoc manners and morals, Edith Wharton's emphasis on the web of cultural connections that defines and enriches the self reminds us that we do not create ourselves *ex nihilo* and that the possible good still embedded in some of "the old ways" may deserve, like an archaeological find, to be exhumed, inspected, renovated, and put to creative use.

Emasculating Papa: Hemingway at Bay

"It's a hell of a nuisance once they've had you cer-
tified as nutty," Nick said. "No one ever has any
confidence in you again."
   —Ernest Hemingway, "A Way You'll Never Be"

If strange things are happening in the academy today, perhaps
none is stranger than the crisis over the tales of Ernest Hemingway. Recently Professor Lawrence Buell of Harvard demanded a new
nonsexist literary criticism that will "foment reorderings in the pre-
feminist canon (the demotion of Hemingway, for instance.)" [1] Papa
demoted? Is Hemingway now *out*? So it seems—at least with some academic ideologists for whom purity of style, clarity of image, and vividly
rendered dramatic action are no longer as important to fiction as holding the politically correct position on contemporary feminism.

The call for the demotion of Hemingway comes down to two complaints. First, his subject matter is too masculine (warfare, safaris, deep-
sea fishing, fighting, drinking, and making the earth move). His portraits
of men, it is said, reflect mere sexism and violence. Not long ago, in *The*

---

1 Lawrence Buell, "Literary History Without Sexism: Feminist Studies and Canonical
   Reconception," *American Literature*, 59 (March 1987), 114.

Great American Adventure, Professor Martin Green attacked Hemingway for writing stories that—in celebrating the virtues of courage, fortitude, cunning, strength, leadership, and persistence—brainwash young men (or so he said) into serving the ideological purposes of a capitalist, anti-Christian, and antidemocratic society. We will never attain an androgynous utopia, Green argued, unless we stop glorifying writers like Hemingway.[2] The second complaint involves Hemingway's characterization of women. Let us have no fictional women, the professors are saying, who are like Catherine Barkley in *A Farewell to Arms* or Maria in *For Whom the Bell Tolls*—that is, womanly women, tender, loving, and self-sacrificing heroines. Women of this kind are an embarrassment, even an outrage, to the academic feminist power bloc, which is intent on training up young women to seethe "I am angry, I am angry, I am angry. . . ." Hemingway's heroines are old-fashioned, self-sacrificing, and totally involved in and devoted to fulfilling the needs (sexual, physical, and emotional) of the men in their lives, in these cases Frederic Henry and Robert Jordan. Catherine says, "There isn't any me. I'm you. Don't make up a separate me. . . . You're my religion. You're all I've got." And Robert Jordan assures Maria, "You are me now. . . . Surely thou must feel it, rabbit."[3] The feminist attack on Hemingway for creating Catherine and Maria reminds us how far we have come from the nineteenth century, when women (including women writers) cherished lovingkindness, even toward men, as a virtue. So women characters (and novelists) with a vision of the redemptive value of self-sacrifice are out—and so is Hemingway, whose most positive images of women were based upon this now-discredited view.

To be fair, some canon-busters seem willing to tolerate Hemingway for the sake of Brett Ashley in *The Sun Also Rises.* But this appears to be because she takes her pleasure wherever she finds it and, for most of the novel, seems intent on being a bitch to every man who crosses her path. And why not? The men are all either fumbling boys (like Romero), disgusting drunks (like Mike), *hombres falto cojones* (like Robert Cohn), or penile incompetents (like Jake Barnes). What's a girl to do? Whatever the answer to that question may be, another reason why Brett appeals has been officially endorsed by the Modern Language Association, which has embraced sexual deviancy with all the fervor of a new religion. Brett's alleged lesbianism or bisexuality is shown in her being an attractive "cross-dresser" who wears her hair short, sports a man's hat, dances with the Parisian fairies, and continually thinks of herself as one of the

---

2 See Green's *The Great Adventure* (Boston: Beacon Press, 1984) and Chapter 2.
3 Ernest Hemingway, *A Farewell to Arms* (New York: Scribner's, 1929), p. 120; *For Whom the Bell Tolls* (New York: Scribner's, 1940), p. 463.

"chaps." Of course Hemingway meant her to be one of the walking wounded, a victim (like the others) of the "dirty war" of 1914–1918, a woman whose emotional suffering is manifest in psychosexual confusion. But we live in the 1990s when the gay American Psychiatric Association and Dr. Ruth have informed the nation that a deviancy such as homosexuality or transvestitism is merely a wholesome alternative lifestyle.

I

Even so, the radical feminist call for the demotion or ejection of Hemingway from the canon of classic American writers does not seem to have had an effect on American book publishing. Studies of Papa's fiction continue to proliferate: more than twenty-five new books have been published in the last decade, and there seems to be no end of them in sight. Moreover, despite Carlos Baker's apparently definitive biography of 1969, there has been a steady stream of Hemingway lives that testifies to the ongoing public fascination with the man and writer. Lesbian ideologists in the academy—intent on transmogrifying Hemingway into a "chainsaw sexist"[4]—may complain that Hemingway was a macho fake and a sexist pig whose simplistic stories of sex and safaris degrade women. But as new facts about Hemingway's life and his relationships have emerged, fact by fact, the image of a complex, deeper, and more difficult writer has come into focus, a writer who simply cannot be tied down in any gender-obsessed straitjacket.

Partly this new interest has arisen from the publication of Hemingway's *The Garden of Eden*—a novel based on unfinished manuscripts that lay in the vault for more than twenty-five years after his death. This work, when it was published in 1986, created something of a double sensation in literary circles. Begun in 1946, the novel was intended by Hemingway to be a major treatment of the themes of good and evil, innocence and corruption, and sex in its relation to the literary art. But the size and complexity of his imaginative task and Hemingway's physical injuries and illnesses, culminating finally in a full-blown case of depressive paranoia and his suicide in 1961, prevented him from completing the work, though it deeply absorbed him for nearly two decades.

The manuscript of *The Garden of Eden* exists in three irreconcilable drafts of varying lengths. To jerry-build a story in publishable form, Tom Jenks, a Scribner's editor, did a cut-and-paste job on the longest of these

---

4 See Susan F. Beegel's "Fitzgerald and Hemingway," in *American Literary Scholarship: An Annual, 1990* (Durham: Duke University Press, 1992), p. 176.

manuscripts (a version of some twelve hundred pages)—deleting a great deal, changing around much else—thus producing the version that we now have. The result bears a suspicious resemblance to Thomas Wolfe's last two novels, which by common consent are now to be seen as the "compositions" of his Harper's editor, Edward Aswell. In any case, so altered and manipulated were the Hemingway manuscripts that Barbara Probst Solomon pronounced the Scribner's version of *The Garden of Eden* a "travesty" and even worse: "I can report that Hemingway's publisher has committed a literary crime."[5]

Setting aside the literary ethics of publishing unfinished and incoherent manuscripts, much less altering them as Jenks had done, *The Garden of Eden* was no less sensational in its revelation of Hemingway's unexpected preoccupation with transsexual fantasies, androgyny, and gender-merging. While no adequate précis of *The Garden of Eden* texts can be given here, suffice it to say that the story involves a rather passive writer named David Bourne and his wife, Catherine, who cuts off her hair and begins to insist on playing the role of a boy while making love. Into their world arrives a rather shadowy young woman named Marita, who at first sleeps with Catherine but comes to be sexually shared by David as well. Hemingway once referred to the novel's theme as "the happiness of the Garden that a man must lose."[6]

The introduction of sexual evil into the writer's world, the loss of youthful innocence, and the relation of this experience to the writer David's struggle to create his art clearly suggest Hemingway's *ménage à trois* with his wife Hadley and Pauline Pfeiffer (who, after living with the Hemingways for a while, and sleeping in their bed, eventually became his second wife). The novel also intimates the 1920s Left Bank lesbian underworld of Natalie Barney, Gertrude Stein, Alice B. Toklas, Solita Solano, and Jinny Pfeiffer (Pauline's lesbian sister). Further, the book is not without its connection to Fitzgerald and his difficulties as a writer. For Zelda Fitzgerald at one point told her husband that he was sexually inadequate, insinuated that he was Hemingway's homosexual lover, had an affair with Edouard Jozan, and, as she came unhinged, herself took up with other women. In any case, the sexually passive novelist and the sexual perversities pictured in *The Garden of Eden* appear to have destroyed in one blow the last vestiges of the myth of Hemingway as The Man's Man, the stoic soldier, the virile boxer, the macho big-game hunter and lover of women *par excellence.*

The myth of Hemingway's absolute masculinity was no doubt his

---

5 Barbara Probst Solomon, "Where's Papa?" *New Republic,* March 9, 1987, p. 31.
6 Carlos Baker, *Ernest Hemingway: A Life Story* (New York: Scribner's, 1969), p. 460.

supreme fiction, and he wrote and rewrote the story of it throughout the whole of his lifetime. Yet the myth rested on a bedrock of fact—those flamboyant masculine experiences that set him apart from most writers, whose lives are spent largely in the study. Hemingway's combat injuries at Fossalta di Piave in World War I, his Greco-Turkish war correspondence, his expatriate life in Paris in the twenties, his wild adventures in the world of Spanish bullfighting, his daredevil journalism in the Spanish Civil War and World War II, the airplane crashes and jeep collisions, the African safaris, the big-game hunts in Wyoming, the deep-sea fishing in the Caribbean, his four marriages and many affairs, his hard drinking, hard fighting, and hard loving—all of these made good copy, and contributed to the legend of The Man's Man.

Of course, Hemingway's virility began to come under heavy bombardment even during the author's lifetime. Women writers, gay victims of Hemingway satire, and plain literary wimps were always ready to invent gossip about his manliness, and occasionally it reached the press. Stein publicly called him "yellow" in *The Autobiography of Alice B. Toklas,* and in 1933 Max Eastman remarked in "Bull in the Afternoon" that

> some circumstance seems to have laid upon Hemingway a continual sense of the obligation to put forth evidences of red-blooded masculinity. It must be made obvious not only in the swing of the big shoulders and the clothes he puts on, but in the stride of his prose style and the emotions he permits to come to the surface there. This trait of his character has . . . begotten a veritable school of fiction-writers—a literary style, you might say, of wearing false hair on his chest.

For Eastman it was "of course a commonplace that Hemingway lacks the serene confidence that he *is* a full-sized man."[7] Frederic Prokosch has suggested that Lady Emerald Cunard was also on to Hemingway. As he recounts it, when she met Hemingway in 1944, she told Cyril Connolly:

> "I was startled. . . . Not a bit of what I expected. You may think it bizarre of me but he struck me as androgynous." Connolly replied that that was a very peculiar word to apply to Hemingway. "I am sure that it is," she said. "It is not the *mot juste,* perhaps. But that's how he struck me. Distinctly emasculated."[8]

But despite the jealous sniping, Hemingway could usually be counted on, during his lifetime, to defend his virility—sometimes by punching out his detractor or by paying him (or her) back, in print.

---

7 Max Eastman, "Bull in the Afternoon," *New Republic,* 75 (June 7, 1933), 94-97.
8 Frederic Prokosch, "Voices: A Memoir," *The New Criterion,* 1 (March 1983), p. 25.

(Without question he was one of the nastier literary pugilists of his time.) His death by suicide, however, seemed to give his detractors the last word. Evidently he took, like his suicide-father, the cowardly way out. Missing throughout the writer's lifetime, in any case, was an adequate explanation of *why* the masculine pose was so important to Ernest Hemingway. Zelda Fitzgerald might aver that Scott's friend was "as phony as a rubber check" and "a pansy with hair on his chest,"[9] but such insinuations about Hemingway's virility never rang true or proved out from any evidence. And none of his contemporaries could account for his macho behavior except with the limp Freudian formula of repressed homosexuality.

II

Life—anyone's life—is a messy affair, with those invariable false starts, unexpected contingencies, and roads taken or not. But the art of the biographer is the art of discovering an order latent in the mess, a key to the life, the figure in the carpet. Various biographers have seen various figures in the carpet of Hemingway's life and work. In 1952 Philip Young argued that the key to understanding Hemingway was the trauma of his World War I wounding, at Fossalta di Piave on July 8, 1918, when 227 fragments of Austrian trench-mortar shrapnel riddled his body and nearly killed him. Hemingway said that the concussion of the shell made him feel that his soul was momentarily sucked out of his body, like a silk handkerchief slipped out of a breast pocket by its corner. Then it came rushing back into him. A number of the stories meditate darkly on this experience of nearly dying, of which the following passage in "Now I Lay Me" is representative. Hemingway has Nick Adams think:

> I myself did not want to sleep because I had been living for a long time with the knowledge that if I ever shut my eyes in the dark and let myself go, my soul would go out of my body. I had been that way for a long time, ever since I had been blown up at night and felt it go out of me and go off and then come back. I tried never to think about it, but it had started to go since, in the nights, just at the moment of going off to sleep, and I could only stop it by a very great effort.[10]

The chronic insomnia of Hemingway's characters and their *pavor nocturnus;* their repression of cerebral thought and their indulgence in

---

9 Quoted in Sara Mayfield, *Exiles from Paradise* (New York: Delacorte, 1971), pp. 112, 141.
10 Ernest Hemingway, "Now I Lay Me," in *The Short Stories of Ernest Hemingway* (New York: Scribner's, 1953), p. 363. Hereafter, citations from this volume will be given as *SS*, in parentheses, in the text.

the senses (especially in the "giant killers," sex and drink); their existential nihilism; their need to create a clean, well-lighted place, a place of order and self-imposed meaning in the dark abyss of the cosmic *nada;* their brave (or even foolhardy) solicitation of physical danger, amounting almost to a suicidal attraction—all these are to be understood, Philip Young told us, as Hemingway's response to a psychic trauma so profound as to portend his eventual suicide. Although he hated Young's book, Hemingway seemed to prove Young prescient when he later took his own life.[11]

Other biographer-critics have woven a different figure in the carpet. Jeffrey Meyers's pathographic *Hemingway: A Biography* (1985) presents the novelist as a nasty piece of work, in contrast to Peter Griffin's multivolume *Along with Youth: Hemingway: The Early Years* (1985) and *Less Than a Treason: Hemingway in Paris* (1990), which simply admire the novelist without understanding him. Many readers have agreed with Michael S. Reynolds, who criticized Griffin for reflecting the erroneous idea that whatever Hemingway wrote was really biography and that anything Hemingway put to paper, in letters, in journalism, or fiction, was true. Reynolds may overstate the case, but Griffin does skirt serious analysis: ". . . I do not analyze this well-examined life; I try instead to recreate it."[12]

Yet Hemingway's stories so often advert to specific events that demonstrably mirror his own life that the temptation to biographical interpretation is well nigh irresistible. What are we to do with the many instances, in the fiction, where Hemingway protagonists ruminate in virtually identical terms on their war wounds? where they excoriate the mother? where they reflect contemptuously on the suicide of the father? or where the real-life names of Hemingway's models have not even been changed? Reynolds himself is also one of Hemingway's biographers and thus is, by his own admission, hardly disinterested in his assessment of Griffin's volumes. While Lawrence Buell and the feminists are undertaking to drum Hemingway out of the canon, Reynolds has proposed that Hemingway is so important that no less than five volumes are required to do him justice. Of this projected life, only three volumes have so far appeared: *The Young Hemingway* (1986), *Hemingway: The Paris Years* (1989), and *Hemingway: The American Homecoming* (1992). It may perhaps be unfair to judge an incomplete biography. But some sense of this work can be gathered from Reynolds' proposal that the key

---

11 See Philip Young, *Ernest Hemingway: A Reconsideration* (1952; rev. ed. University Park: Pennsylvania State University, 1966).
12 Peter Griffin, *Less Than a Treason: Hemingway in Paris* (New York: Oxford University Press, 1990) p. viii.

to understanding Hemingway is to *feel and think* what *Hemingway* felt and thought. Reynolds thus provides us with an "inside narrative" marked by a stream-of-consciousness technique, in which the biographer moves into and out of Hemingway's consciousness. Reynolds's "mind-reading," however, even if based on authentic documents, does not always produce a pleasant experience, since, for Reynolds, Hemingway had "a mean, bullying streak that some people brought to the surface without even trying." [13] But if appropriating the consciousness of your biographical subject is a fictional technique, hasn't Papa always brought out the mythmaking propensities of his critics? And in any event there has been so much written about him that biographers are now hard pressed to find a new angle.

III

Kenneth Lynn, however, has found one. The perverse sexual implications of *The Garden of Eden* were not, for Lynn, a novelty. For him, many of Hemingway's previous works disclosed similar transsexual fantasies, motifs of twinning, and incestuous overtones. The source of these, according to Lynn, was Hemingway's relationship to his mother, Grace Hemingway, "the dark queen of Hemingway's world." [14] Charles T. Lanham, a Hemingway friend, described that relationship: "he always referred to his mother as 'that bitch.' He must have told me a thousand times how much he hated her and in how many ways." [15] But *why* Hemingway hated his mother was never clear. "The Doctor and the Doctor's Wife" and "Soldier's Home"—in their savage treatment of the mother figure—suggest that Grace was a possessive, dominant, and overbearing woman who had emasculated her husband. And since Hemingway clearly identified in youth with his father, who taught him everything there was to know about hunting and fishing, it was reasonable to infer that Hemingway thought his mother guilty of driving his father to suicide, a tragic event the novelist came to see as an act of cowardice. But, according to Lynn, the reason for Ernest's hatred of his mother goes deeper.

As Lynn recounts it, Hemingway suffered a deep sexual wound originating from his mother's treatment of him as a child. Grace Hemingway dressed young Ernest and his slightly older sister, Mar-

---

13 Michael Reynolds, *Hemingway: The Paris Years* (Oxford: Basil Blackwell, 1989), p. 128.
14 Kenneth Lynn, *Hemingway* (New York: Simon and Schuster, 1987), p. 65. Hereafter, quotations from this work will be cited as *L*, in the text, in parentheses.
15 Quoted in Bernice Kert, *The Hemingway Women: Those Who Loved Him—The Wives and Others* (New York: W. W. Norton, 1983), p. 21.

celline, in identical outfits—as twins of the same sex (sometimes dressed as little boys, sometimes as little girls). On a scrapbook photograph of Ernest at age two, she wrote "summer girl," suggesting that she regarded him as female (*L*, 41). Further, long after he ought to have been shorn, she insisted on keeping his hair the length of a girl's. Paradoxically, she played up his masculinity and encouraged him to be a little man. Thus the seeds of an androgynous personality were planted: "Caught between his mother's wish to conceal his masculinity and her eagerness to encourage it, was it any wonder that he was anxious and insecure?" (*L*, 45). According to Lynn, much of Hemingway's plain meanness to friends and lovers can be accounted for by an insecurity arising out of Grace Hemingway's betrayal of his masculine sexual identity. At some point "in his edenic infancy he awakened to an understanding of the situation in which his mother had placed him. . . . If he was [treacherous to friends and acquaintances], perhaps it was because he thought of himself as a victim of treachery long before he knew what to call it" (*L*, 43). The relationship between Ernest and his "twin" sister Marcelline was a highly complicated one. Besides gender confusion, both children experienced confused ego boundaries and felt not merely twinned but androgynously and incestuously intimate. In adolescence, the tomboy Marcelline had a clear crush, at the very least, on her brother. He evidently repulsed this; offended, she refused to go to his wedding to Hadley Richardson, a woman eight years his senior.

Hemingway may have turned away from his problematic "twin," Marcelline, to their younger sister, Ursula. The incestuous overtones of the story "The Last Good Country" suggest that they may have been intimate. Certainly in 1950 Hemingway wrote to Arthur Mizener that when he came back from the war in 1919, his seventeen-year-old sister Ursula

> always used to wait, sleeping, on the stairway of the third floor stair-case to my room. She wanted to wake when I came in because she had been told it was bad for a man to drink alone. She would drink something light with me until I went to sleep and then she would sleep with me so I would not be lonely in the night. We always slept with the light on except she would sometimes turn it off if she saw I was asleep and stay awake and turn it on if she saw I was wakeing [*sic*].[16]

In any case, there can be no doubt that Hemingway's stories are filled with love relationships where couples feel like "brother and sister,"

---

16 *Selected Letters of Ernest Hemingway, 1917–1961*, ed. Carlos Baker (New York: Scribner's, 1981), p. 697. Quotations from this work will hereafter be cited as *SL*, in parentheses, in the text.

where the *length* of the woman's hair is itself fetishized (if that is possible), where the protagonist's penis is mutilated ("God Rest You Merry,
Gentlemen," *The Sun Also Rises*), where reversals of gender or at least of
coital position are suggested, or where Hemingway seems fascinated by
the idea of sex with a lesbian. Paris was awash with lesbians in the 1920s,
and he was not oblivious to the flamboyant posturing of Natalie Barney
and Renée Vivien, Sylvia Beach and Adrienne Monnier, Gertrude Stein
and Alice B. Toklas, Djuna Barnes, Jane Heap, Winifred Ellerman, Hilda
Doolittle, Margaret Anderson, and Solita Solano. He was remarkably
close to a number of them, and, even more surprising, he claimed to
have been sexually attracted to the older and obese Gertrude Stein (who
appears to have resembled Grace Hemingway in size). In 1948 Hemingway told Stein's biographer, W. G. Rogers, that he had

> liked [Gertrude Stein] better before she cut her hair and that was sort of
> a turning point in all sorts of things. She used to talk to me about
> homosexuality and how it was fine in and for women and no good in
> men and I used to listen and learn and I always wanted to fuck her and
> she knew it and it was a good healthy feeling and made more sense than
> some of the talk (*SL*, 650).

As Lynn points out, Hemingway never directly fictionalized these lesbians. His protagonist in *The Sun Also Rises*, however, Jake Barnes, has a
name suspiciously close to that of Natalie *Barney*, who lived at 20 rue
Jacob. Does this tale—involving a hero without a penis [17] who cannot
penetrate the mannish Brett Ashley—distortedly symbolize a transsexual fantasy of lesbian love? In light of *The Garden of Eden*, Lynn
thinks it does.

Hemingway's treatment of gender-merging in *A Farewell to Arms* is
also intriguing. How are we to read the love scenes between Frederic
Henry and Catherine Barkley? Is she a submissive woman to her virile
lover? In bed, Catherine tells Frederic, "I'm you." She says, "Don't make

---

17 The precise nature of Jake's wound is somewhat ambiguous in *The Sun Also Rises*, and
some readers have concluded that he was castrated. But Jake's facetious conversation with
his friend Bill, in which he refers to "the joystick," suggests a penis injury, as well as the
airplane instrument. In 1958 George Plimpton solved this ambiguity in a conversation
with Hemingway published in *Writers at Work*. In the interview Plimpton casually
remarked at Jake's having been "emasculated precisely as is a steer." "*HEMINGWAY:* . . .
Who ever said Jake was 'emasculated precisely as is a steer'? Actually he had been wounded
in quite a different way and his testicles were intact and not damaged. Thus he was capable
of all normal feelings as a *man* but incapable of consummating them." Hemingway said
that "the important distinction is that his wound was physical and not psychological and
that he was not emasculated." The interview is reprinted in *Ernest Hemingway: Five
Decades of Criticism*, ed. Linda W. Wagner (East Lansing: Michigan State University Press,
1974), p. 31.

up a separate me." "I want us to be all mixed up." She asks Frederic to let his hair grow and proposes to cut hers off, so they will be "the same." He is reluctant because, sexually passive, he likes to lie under her, to assume the "female position," enclosed in the tent of her hair. According to Lynn, these scenes are not evidence of the Hemingway woman's abject submission to masculine domination but rather transsexual fantasies that haunted Hemingway throughout his lifetime. In deriving their names from that of his friend Barklie Henry, "he thought of them as the two halves of an androgynous whole" (*L*, 297). Likewise, in *For Whom the Bell Tolls* the real issue between the lovers Maria and Robert Jordan is not macho domination of a mindless and compliant woman but rather Hemingway's recurrent fantasies of what it would be like to merge into a woman. Maria's head has been forcibly shaved by the fascists, but Jordan wants to take her to his barber in Madrid so that their hair can be styled identically, so that they will (twinlike) resemble each other. Lynn puts it this way:

> Pilar observes of them very early, "You could be brother and sister by the look," to which Maria replies, "Now I know why I have felt as I have. Now it is clear." Jordan, too, likes to think that he and Maria are related. "Maria is my true love and my wife. I never had a true love. I never had a wife. She is also my sister, and I never had a sister, and my daughter, and I never will have a daughter." In their nights of lovemaking in his sleeping robe, these lookalike siblinglike lovers feel so much a part of one another that it is as if they have merged ("I am thee and thou art me and all of one is the other") and could switch identities if they wished ("if thou should ever wish to change I would be glad to change") (*L*, 487–488).

The important point here seems to be the recurrent and irresistible longing in some part of Hemingway's psyche to experience and recount life as it is experienced by a woman.

The effect of recent Hemingway criticism is to send us back to the novels and stories with a new and heightened sense of how intimately Hemingway longed to experience the sensibilities and sensations of a woman and how fascinatingly and disturbingly he dramatized those feelings. If Ms. Solomon is correct in thinking that *The Garden of Eden* is "a sort of summa of Hemingway's aesthetics,"[18] with sexual metamorphosis as its cornerstone, the put-down feminist critics will have to take another look at his work, for things are evidently not as they seem. Stories like "Up in Michigan" and "Cat in the Rain," viewed in light of

---

18 Solomon, "Where's Papa?" p. 31.

Hemingway's supposed androgyny, take on a new poignance and set at naught the claim that Hemingway's women characters are really nonentities. And the great novels in the Hemingway canon now require a full critical reconsideration, not as case studies of a disturbing neurosis but as dramatizations of some very old issues in male-female relationships, issues first suggested in Plato's myth about the androgynous soul in search of its twin.

This reconsideration of Hemingway's portraits of both men and women is slowly beginning to emerge. I have in mind the book by Nancy R. Comley and Robert Scholes called *Hemingway's Genders: Rereading the Hemingway Text* and Mark Spilka's *Hemingway's Quarrel with Androgyny*. These writers seriously address the reconfiguration of the psychic life provoked by Lynn and by *The Garden of Eden*. None of them has it in for Grace Hemingway or credits much what Comley and Scholes call "The Mummy's Curse" theory. In fact, for Spilka the elements of androgyny and the confusion of gender roles that we find in Hemingway's fiction have their origin less in the family romance than in the Anglo-American sexual culture of the Victorian era. For Spilka the androgynous material in Hemingway's fiction in fact permeated the literature that Hemingway read as a youth and so naturally found its way into the prose as a *Zeitgeist* element. Spilka concedes that Grace feminized her son in dress and hair style and twinned him with Marcelline. But he remarks that one can "connect such predilections historically with the way women began to define maleness in mid-nineteenth century as an expression or projection of their own wishes and desires, whether for power or recognition. . . ."[19] Spilka gives interesting readings of the literature of Dinah Craik, Emily Brontë, Captain Marryat, Rudyard Kipling, and John Masefield which illustrate a comparable blurring of male and female roles.

Thus it is useful to remember that while Hemingway's fictional interest in androgyny *may* have had an origin in Grace Hemingway's bizarre neurosis, androgyny has in fact a literary history and a cultural provenance and may at a particular time be merely a theme, like any other. The cited instances in Spilka's account of Hemingway's boyhood reading are all Victorian and Edwardian. Let me add a few others. We need to remember that Freud had dignified for Hemingway's generation the serious consideration of clinical matters that literature had mythicized and that sexologists like Krafft-Ebing had cloaked in Latin secrecy. Writers of Hemingway's own time were quick to bring to the surface of

---

19 Mark Spilka, *Hemingway's Quarrel with Androgyny* (Lincoln: University of Nebraska Press, 1990), p. 4.

literature these elements of the new "psychological science." Sherwood Anderson, whose influence on Hemingway is demonstrable, wrote about such an imaginative sexual transformation in "The Man Who Became a Woman." Pound likewise invoked the double-sexed Tiresias in Canto I and made the Ovidian metamorphosis of men and women (into beasts, into trees, into the forms of each other) a central motif of his epic poem. And T. S. Eliot in *The Waste Land* objectified in Tiresias ("Old man with wrinkled female breasts") both the genital wound that fascinated Hemingway (as he created the character of Jake Barnes) and the motif of the two sexes as merging into each other. Hemingway was not oblivious to these elements of literary modernism. Is it any wonder, then, that at the heart of *The Garden of Eden* is the symbolism of androgyny figured in Rodin's statue of the merging sexes—a statue based on the *Metamorphoses* of Ovid?[20]

All writers, if they are any good, are capable of imagining what it is like to have the body of a member of the opposite sex and to have the feelings of that sex. The cultivation of an androgynous sensibility is a necessity of the artist; certainly it is a feature of what Keats called "the chameleon poet," who, emptied of himself, can be filled with the ideas and feelings of another wholly alien to him, and so represent them. In Hemingway's case, these themes doubtless arose in part from the bizarre psychosexual character of Pauline Pfeiffer, his second wife. She identified with and loved both Hadley and Ernest, claimed their child Bumby as her own, and took Ernest away from Hadley. She induced him to act out sex scenarios in which she "became" Ernest and he was supposed to be the female, in which she was to be on top and he below, her hair was to be short, his long, and so forth. Women critics have long complained about Catherine and Maria merging their identities in those of Frederic and Robert Jordan. But Hemingway's narratives appear to have come right out of Pauline's disturbed sexual needs, to which he not only acquiesced, and explored for the purposes of his fiction, but which finally destroyed his family with Hadley and Bumby. This was the corruption in Eden, the sin that shattered his marriage and supposedly led to his expulsion from an Eden of paradisal happiness.

But the writer's imaginative taking over of another person's identity (not to speak of another person's sex) is especially problematic for the

---

20 Spilka insists on seeing the statue as representing two lesbians making love, but the sex of the two figures is really ambiguous. And Hemingway makes a point of not identifying the figures, or giving the statue a name, or describing what kind of metamorphosis is taking place. In my view, what intrigues the novelist is how, through sexual union, identities merge, so that maleness and femaleness flow into each other and are fused into the unity of one love. References to the statue are unfortunately excised in the Scribner's edition.

author who already has a weak ego or an insecure sense of his own identity and sexuality. And since the will has a force in these matters, it is always wise to decide to be clear about who and what one is. It was best for Hemingway to become patriarchal, to become a man's man, to take on the role and even the name of "Papa." And that he did and that he was. Robert McAlmon, Max Eastman, Zelda Fitzgerald, Emerald Cunard, and some other jealous or spiteful contemporaries did not like the macho style that expressed this patriarchal Hemingway and tried to insinuate that he was not as masculine as he seemed. But by every measure of action and adventure, style and substance, he was a fully virile, masculine man's man. His was a life of outdoor adventure, physical danger, and emotional risk—excitement of a kind many, if not most, men crave. Certainly they like to read about such things. But Hemingway's predilection for masculine activities does not add up to the perversions his detractors have insinuated. In this respect, biographer Jeffrey Meyers is absolutely right:

> Hemingway has been suspected and even accused of being a covert homosexual because of his aggressive masculinity, his preference for exclusively male company, his occasional impotence, his sexual boasts, and his hostility to inverts. But this suspicion is as unconvincing as the theory that Don Juan is a homosexual because of his obsessive need to prove his virility. Despite all the theorizing, there is not a shred of real evidence to suggest that Hemingway ever had any covert homosexual desires or overt homosexual relations.[21]

Yet aggressive masculinity is now so hysterically *verboten* that Hemingway has been slandered as a sexual being and his fiction has been placed on an *index expurgatorius*. Spilka even complains that in not yielding to the androgynous impulse within him (a pathology induced by his mother's craziness and his childhood reading), Hemingway was somehow betraying himself: "This, it seems to me, is the ultimate importance of Hemingway's lifelong quarrel with androgyny: that it was crucial to his creative strength throughout his life, and that he came remarkably, even heroically, close to affirming it before tragically betraying it as his life neared its grim conclusion."[22]

Now, all of us are made up of male and female genetic elements and

---

21 Jeffrey Meyers, *Hemingway: A Biography* (New York: Harper and Row, 1985), p. 202. Despite the abundant evidence of Hemingway's confirmed heterosexuality, however, the *New York Times*, which has now become the homosexual paper of record, continues its Queer Nation agenda of "outing" even heterosexual writers. See, for example, Christopher Lehmann-Haupt's "Was Hemingway Gay? There's More to His Story," *New York Times*, November 10, 1994, p. C–21.

22 Spilka, *Hemingway's Quarrel with Androgyny*, p. 336.

undergo various social and psychological influences, so that one's masculinity or feminity is a complex matter. But since when is it heroic to be androgynous rather than (if one is a man) male or (if one is a woman) female? This idea that we must deliberately incorporate the sexual characteristics of the other gender is, as Camille Paglia has wittily and rightly shown in *Sexual Personae*, a manifestation of epicene intellectual decadence and the sexual confusion of the age.

IV

If we dismiss the demand for Hemingway's ejection from the canon by lesbian, gay, or feminist critics—who evidently fear the reader's encounter with the writing of a man's man—and if we look at biographies of Hemingway (or of his wives) *by women,* one notes a curious fact: there is more sympathy for the writer than one might have gathered from reading the academic lit-crit. For Hemingway's women biographers, it is the writer's relationship with women that is the key to the life. Many of Hemingway's sisters, lovers, wives, and ex-wives (Marcelline and Carol Hemingway, Agnes von Kurowsky, Hadley Richardson, Pauline Pfeiffer, Martha Gellhorn, and Mary Welsh, among others) wrote about or talked about him in a heterosexual context; and it surprising that, whatever their personal stresses and strains, with the exception of Martha Gellhorn they all remained on fairly good terms with Hemingway while he was alive. Sometimes—as Bernice Kert notes in *The Hemingway Women: Those Who Loved Him—The Wives and Others* (1983)—these women afterward became the friends of one another; they became bound to one another, as it were, through their bond with Hemingway.

But didn't Hemingway really hate women? The question recurs in feminist criticism. Mary Welsh Hemingway, the novelist's fourth wife, was so often pitied by feminists who supposed her life with Hem was awful that she concludes *How It Was* (1976) with a bit of invented dialogue in which she answers the feminist ideologues. One of the questions involved her "submission" to her husband: "Did you feel yourself 'slaving' for Ernest in Cuba?" And she responds: "I slaved at the Finca as that lovely man, Artur Rubinstein slaves at the piano. Most blessed are they who enjoy their work, I think." Another similar question was put to her: "Do you concur that men are chauvinist pigs?"—to which she responded:

> No more than that women are chauvinist sows. I'm thankful for almost every man I've known and the mother who produced him. I've been

remarkably lucky with men friends, it seems to me. Through all these years only one fellow quote took advantage unquote of me, as I recall, and I don't include Noel's [a former husband's] heisting our joint bank account. Otherwise those sweet, various alliances ended, for whatever reasons, with our continuing to be cheerful friends.[23]

Clearly, for Mary and for many of the other women in Hemingway's life, Ernest was no antifeminine monster, a fact that biographer Bernice Kert has amply demonstrated but that feminist critics nevertheless keep denying. But the various wives and lovers of Hemingway provide, in fact, only a partial key to understanding the man and his work.

At least, in the view of James R. Mellow, "what one misses" in much of this recent attention to Hemingway's women "is a real sense that there were men who were equally as important as the women in Hemingway's personal life and certainly more important to his literary career." [24] In his own biography, *Hemingway: A Life Without Conse-quences* (1992), Mellow offers a *new* pattern in the carpet: male bond-ing. Mellow's work is to be distinguished from that of others by his focus on the rites of male camaraderie, the skiing, fishing, and hunting expeditions that were essential to his life because Hemingway needed to be the center of a gregarious group of males. Mellow's Hemingway has cut the female apron strings, and the volume is festooned with photo-graphs of Hemingway with groups of boys and then of men who formed one or another masculine circle. Some of the men (such as Morley Cal-laghan in *That Summer in Paris* [1963], Denis Brian in *The True Gen* [1988], and A. E. Hotchner in *Papa Hemingway* [1966])—wrote about what it was like to hang out with Hem. But there was also a large cast of shadowy men friends, many of them not writers, who for shorter or longer periods knew Hemingway closely and who enjoyed with him nonliterary pursuits: the bar-hopping, the fishing expeditions, the skiing and hunting trips, the swapping of war stories over brandy and cigars. Mellow adds to our knowledge of Hemingway by identifying and making plain to us what Hemingway found in the companionship of Jim Gamble, Bill Smith, Charlie Hopkins, Carl Edgar, Bill Horne, Howell Jenkins, Chink Dorman-Smith, and many others.

In his effort to create the special feeling associated with male camaraderie, Hemingway chose his men friends very carefully. Most of them were a few years older than he (as, by the way, were a number of Hemingway's wives and lovers). These men were generally less self-

---

23 Mary Welsh Hemingway, *How It Was* (New York: Alfred A. Knopf, 1976), p. 618.
24 James R. Mellow, "Reading Hemingway with One Eye Closed," *New York Times,* April 24, 1988, p. H–33.

assured than he, and sometimes there was "some weakness in their character" or "some lack of self-worth."[25] Even if older, they had to be ignorant of—or at least willing to take instruction in—hunting, fly-fishing, the cunning of a wounded lion, or the finer points of taurine behavior. It was also necessary for Hemingway to appear to them as an expert on what women want and on the sexual techniques that will satisfy them. Generally, the circle of Hemingway's male friends regarded him as a charismatic presence, a genuine hero, a brilliant talker, a great drinker, and a world-class sportsman. He flourished in such company. But he frequently dealt with his friends ironically and acerbically.

Of course a number of homosexual men were drawn to Ernest Hemingway—as his wives and lovers kept discovering. As Agnes von Kurowsky offhandedly remarked to Mary Welsh Hemingway, "You know how he was. Men loved him. You know what I mean" (*M*, 70). And Hemingway had a genuine affection (it is not too much to call it love) for a number of his heterosexual male friends. But he was frankly repelled by the homosexuals, rejected their advances, and shut off conversation about masculine friendship. In *The Sun Also Rises*, Bill Gorton says to Jake:

> "Listen. You're a hell of a good guy, and I'm fonder of you than anybody on earth. I couldn't tell you that in New York. It'd mean I was a faggot. That was what the Civil War was about. Abraham Lincoln was a faggot. He was in love with General Grant. So was Jefferson Davis. Lincoln just freed the slaves on a bet. The Dred Scott was framed by the Anti-Saloon League. Sex explains it all. The Colonel's Lady and Judy O'Grady are Lesbians under their skin."
>
> He stopped.
> "Want to hear some more?"
> "Shoot," I said.
> "I don't know any more. Tell you some more at lunch."
> "Old Bill," I said.
> "You bum!"[26]

The problem with male bonding is how to indicate friendship without its being misconstrued as a homosexual come-on; and facetious verbal horseplay is one way out of an edgy situation where affection is sensed but the expression of it will need to be repressed because the

25 James R. Mellow, *Hemingway: A Life Without Consequences* (Boston: Houghton Mifflin, 1992), p. 163. Hereafter, citations from this volume will be given as *M*, in parentheses, in the text.
26 Ernest Hemingway, *The Sun Also Rises* (New York: Scribner's, 1926), p. 116. Hereafter, citations from this novel will be given as *SAR*, in parentheses, in the text.

men are not queer. Hemingway's letters are full of this kind of horseplay. But whenever any male friend got too dependent or mawkish, Hemingway knifed him or abandoned the friendship. *Fitzgerald and Hemingway: A Dangerous Friendship* reprints this Fitzgerald notebook entry about Hemingway: "I really loved him, but of course it wore out like a love affair. The fairies have spoiled all that."[27] Here Fitzgerald is ruing the evident fact that the queer insistence on turning every male friendship into a sodomitic one destroys the capacity of men for genuine nonsexual love. In any event, in consequence, these knifed friends often lashed back at Hemingway. After one row with Bill Smith, Hemingway complained, "Isn't that a goddam hell of a letter from a guy whose been like Smith and I have been. . . . It's hell when a male knifes you—especially when you still love him" (*M*, 160).

But if homosexuality is invariably a profound evil in Hemingway's mind, it is not clear whether his objection had a moral basis. Did Papa think of homosexuality as immoral? Was it merely sterile? Was it subversive to rightly directed heterosexuality, which is procreative and life-affirming? Did he regard it as an illness or merely a filthy habit? The matter is murky. In *A Moveable Feast*, Hemingway records an episode in which Gertrude Stein instructs him that "the act male homosexuals commit is ugly and repugnant and afterwards they are disgusted with themselves. They drink and take drugs, to palliate this, but they are disgusted with the act and they are always changing partners and cannot really be happy."[28] Whether Stein really thought this, it is difficult to say. But it is clear that Hemingway regarded with contempt the male homosexuals who crossed his path.

On the other hand, Mellow believes that Hemingway was comfortable with the lesbian relationships among his women friends—including Stein and Toklas, Janet Flanner, Renata Borgatti, and Solita Solano. Intrigued Hemingway was, curious and probing in his gossip. But I am not at all convinced that he was comfortable with it. In part, his fascination with Stein and other lesbians involved trying to figure out what they might be like with him, in bed, as a sexual partner. In Stein's case, Hemingway was drawn to the older writer's "beautiful eyes and strong German-Jewish face," her "lovely, thick, alive immigrant hair," and those big breasts that—as he told Hadley—"must have weighed ten pounds apiece" (*L*, 169). If, grotesquely, Hemingway wanted to bed Gertrude Stein, I suspect that the wish came out of the commonplace heterosexual belief that one can "turn" the homosexual toward normal

---

27 See Matthew J. Bruccoli, *Fitzgerald and Hemingway: A Dangerous Friendship* (New York: Carroll and Graf, 1994), p. 227.

28 Hemingway, *A Moveable Feast* (New York: Bantam Books, 1965), p. 20.

sexuality. In the period between the 1920s and the writing of *A Moveable Feast*, however, Hemingway came to see the doubtful naiveté of his earlier sexual interest in Stein. For in the passage I have just cited he has Gertrude Stein go on to say that "in women it is the opposite. They do nothing that they are disgusted by and nothing that is repulsive and afterwards they are happy and they can lead happy lives together." [29] It seems doubtful to me that Stein would have made so fatuous a remark. In any case, *A Moveable Feast* is meant to illustrate just the opposite: it leaves us with a chilling portrait of a Stein in humiliating bondage to her lesbian partner, Alice B. Toklas.

V

Yet is androgyny—or male bonding, for that matter—really the figure in Hemingway's carpet? The fact is that Hemingway often broke off his friendships, sometimes by performing an act so rude that it required the friend to end it. It appears to be the case that Hemingway let very few people—men or women—get close to him, at least for very long. Aside from an ordinary natural desire for company, especially in rough and risky outdoor activities, Hemingway's relationships seem rooted in another desire that his biographers have sketched in very delicately. Friends are needed to recreate the Edenic world of sensuous pleasures that Hemingway had known up in Michigan during his boyhood.

Male companions were important to this task but perhaps only as adjuncts, that is, as mere participants in a scene of action and adventure that Hemingway needed to construct and complete for his own inward purposes. We know that he exploited these scenes in his fiction; but perhaps, just as certainly, he needed them for obscure psychic reasons having to do with childhood gratifications that had been lost in maturity. In the following canceled passage from "Big Two-Hearted River," Nick Adams recollects the summers he had spent with Bill Smith up in Michigan, where "all the love went into fishing and the summer":

> He had loved it more than anything. He had loved digging potatoes with Bill in the fall, the long trips in the car, fishing in the bay, reading in the hammock on hot days, swimming off the dock, playing baseball at Charlevoix and Petoskey, living at the Bay, the Madame's cooking, the way she had with servants, eating in the dining room looking out the windows across the long fields and the point to the lake, talking with her, drinking with Bill's old man, the fishing trips away from the farm, just lying around. He loved the long summer (*M*, 162).

---

29 Hemingway, *A Moveable Feast*, p. 20.

Bill Smith seems to have been important to the experience. (And certainly his importance is unquestionable in the literary recreation of that summer in "The Three-Day Blow" and "The End of Something" in *In Our Time*.) But Bill Smith as such seems less important than the Edenic *Gestalt* of which he was merely a part. In fact, one could always find any number of Bill Smiths ready to drop everything and load up the rifles or tramp into the interior where the fishing was good.

But if *men* most often served Hemingway in the recreation of these early experiences of Edenic outdoor adventure, such as he had known in his childhood in the Michigan Upper Peninsula, the problem is that there can be no Eden without an Eve. Consequently, even the women Hemingway chose had to be assimilable into this active world of male adventure. The nurse Agnes von Kurowsky dumped Hemingway before he could draw her into the outdoor life. And this rejection may have been the blow that soured Hemingway on the adequacy of *all* relationships. His first wife, Hadley, was game, but she was pretty quickly consumed by maternal responsibilities with Bumby. In "Cross-Country Snow," Nick Adams gets rather upset when his wife becomes pregnant. "Maybe we'll never go skiing again, Nick," says his friend George. "We've got to," Nick says; "It isn't worth while if you can't" (*SS*, 188). Skiing, hiking, hunting, fishing, shooting—life isn't worthwhile if you can't do them when you want to. And what is a friend for—what is a wife or lover for—if not to provide company on the trail, or to fish knee-deep in the stream with the rod and reel, or to stalk the big buffalo with the native boys and a 6.5 Mannlicher? Good sex with a woman is a Hemingway necessity: the moment of ecstasy eclipses, however momentarily, one's consciousness of the *nada* at the heart of existence. But sex enmeshes the man, as well as the woman, in the biological trap. There are always complications, circumscribing consequences, in human relationships: Nick's wife is going to have a baby.

The Hemingway we find in Mellow's biography wants to live a "life without consequences." The subtitle of the life is derived from "Soldier's Home" in *In Our Time*. Mellow identifies Hemingway with his character, the wounded Krebs, who has come home shattered by the war. Krebs is a man who wishes no longer to have any close human involvements. He is distant from, even irascible to, his mother, father, and sisters, who expect him to carry on as if the war had never devastated his life. Krebs watches the young girls of the town walking along the other side of the street, yet he keeps his distance. He would like to have a girlfriend, Hemingway writes, but "he did not want to get into the intrigue and the politics. He did not want to have to do any courting. He did not want to tell any more lies. It wasn't worth it." Hemingway writes that

Krebs "did not want any consequences. He did not want any consequences ever again. He wanted to live along without consequences" (*SS*, 147).

Immersion in the active outdoor life of adventure was a way of more or less evading people (and their ongoing messy emotional problems); it was a way of abandoning subjective transactions for more permanent and consequential matters: the direct engagement of the self with the order of nonhuman nature. Men were useful as friends in this milieu because, if carefully chosen, they did not muck things up by constantly intruding their emotions into the business at hand—angling, tracking, or bringing a lion into the cross hairs. And if they did talk too much, they were easier to shut up without wounded feelings. Men understood quicker that mouthing it up ruined any good outdoor experience. Friends and lovers—men and women—might come and go, in fact *would* come and go, but the edged encounter with a predatory lion in the tall grass or the pull of a six-hundred-pound marlin or a twenty-foot shark brought a man face to face with the existential human condition.

The direct engagement with nonhuman nature always interested Hemingway as much as people did; but natural conditions, paradoxically, were more reliable. People turned on you; they abandoned you; even if they said they loved you, they were still going to die and abandon you. "All stories, if continued far enough, end in death," Hemingway once said, "and he is no true story-teller who would keep that from you." In "In Another Country," the Italian major whose young wife has died tells Nick that a man should not marry. "If he is to lose everything, he should not place himself in a position to lose that. He should not place himself in a position to lose. He should find things he cannot lose" (*SS*, 271). *The Sun Also Rises* appears to focus on the messy lives of the "lost generation"; but Hemingway told his Scribner's editor, Max Perkins, that "the earth abiding forever" was "the hero" (*SL*, 229). People like Brett and Mike and Robert Cohn are the *ephemeridae* of existence, but what partakes of the abiding earth survives the transience of every human relationship. One of the key scenes of the novel occurs when Jake, Bill, and Cohn descend from the Spanish mountains onto a plain where "there were trees along both sides of the road, and a stream and ripe fields of grain, and the road went on, very white and straight ahead. . . ." The landscape is beautiful, permanently so, as is the Cézanne-like style with which Hemingway paints it. But the important point is the wordless reaction of Jake and Bill: "I was up in front with the driver and I turned around. Robert Cohn was asleep, but Bill looked and nodded his head" (*SAR*, 93). A vision like that, for them that have eyes to see it, cannot be lost and must not be babbled about.

Likewise, in "Big Two-Hearted River," there occurs a scene which suggests Hemingway's need to have a "room of his own," to be delivered, that is, from human entanglements.

> Nick was happy as he crawled inside the tent. He had not been unhappy all day. This was different though. Now things were done. There had been this to do. Now it was done. It had been a hard trip. He was very tired. That was done. He had made his camp. He was settled. Nothing could touch him. It was a good place to camp. He was there, in the good place. He was in his home where he had made it (*SS*, 215).

Hemingway wanted a life like Nick's—a life lived "all the way up," but with a space free of the entanglements and consequences of human relationships, free of the messy lives of companions who so often took and drained and had no serious work to do. Despite his need for these companions, male or female, Hemingway was, perhaps like every writer, a profound loner, and only his writing could finally matter.

Hemingway wanted his art to partake in that which survives the inevitable transience of human relations. Wanting to write well and truly about what really happened required him, like the matador Romero, to risk his life in holding "the purity of his line through the maximum of exposure" (*SAR*, 168). Most of the time Hemingway failed. And Mellow finds "The Snows of Kilimanjaro," with its embittered writer Harry, to be an allegory of Hemingway's sense of lost possibility and failed effort. He thought that only another writer, perhaps, would

> appreciate how close to the truth Hemingway had come to that sense of failed ambition and the terrible, fixed preoccupation, the irreducible selfishness of the writer's life; how the dogged practice of the craft takes hold—the time spent, the time wasted—with few things, other than war or marriage or a love affair, nearly as real or compelling or of more consequence than what was on the page in front of him (*M*, 3–4).

But if Hemingway's later years were, with one or two exceptions, marked by wasted experience and failed stories, there are still those surviving masterworks I have mentioned—visions of the way it was in a pure style that revolutionized modernist fiction. In "The Snows . . ." there is that perfectly preserved carcass of a leopard, up close to the western summit of Mount Kilimanjaro. It is the form of a once-living figure that nobody in the Modern Language Association seems able to explain. But the novels and stories and these several biographical portraits make a rather clear case, it seems to me, for Hemingway's having scaled a fairly high point on the slopes of Parnassus.

Vitality
and Vampirism in
Tender Is the Night

I am not nor mean to be
The Daemon they made of me.
—Hilda Doolittle, *Helen in Egypt*

The gist of this essay is a simple but lurid thesis: first, that there is a motif of female vampirism latent in *Tender Is the Night*; second, that this theme is a constant in F. Scott Fitzgerald's fiction from *This Side of Paradise* onward; and third, that while this motif expresses one of Fitzgerald's recurrent anxieties about woman's consuming power, it takes its form from a literary source—the poetry of John Keats.

We are all familiar with the image of the golden girl, the lovely woman of the romantic dreamer's illusion, the lost Ginevra King, the young, elusive Zelda Sayre—women who created "those illusions that give such color to the world," Fitzgerald wrote, "that you don't care whether things are true or false as long as they partake of the magical glory."[1] I cannot deal here with the many positive images of Fitzgerald's lovely and appealing women. I want rather to deal with another aspect of woman—also a constant in Fitzgerald's fiction—and often involving the same girl: the beautiful enchantress, the alluring and seductive but ultimately demonic and destructive woman—figured frequently and

---

1 *Correspondence of F. Scott Fitzgerald*, eds. Matthew J. Bruccoli and Margaret M. Duggan with the assistance of Susan Walker (New York: Random House, 1980), p. 145.

openly as a vampire who drains the hero of his vitality. Keats is the source of this image, and the ambivalence that made Keats recur to the image was virtually identical in Fitzgerald.[2]

I

The evidence for Fitzgerald's knowledge of Keats is extensive and cannot even be summarized here.[3] *Tender Is the Night* takes its title from Keats's "Ode to a Nightingale." And a number of books and articles have usefully linked the two works: the setting of the Riviera with Keats's Provençal sunburnt mirth, the seductive death wish in both texts, the "nights perfumed and promising, the dark gardens of an illusory world,"[4] and the people who, as Abe North puts it, are "plagued by the nightingale."[5] These and many incidental references in the novel to Keats's "Ode" are helpful. But *Tender Is the Night* was a very late title choice. The novel was not written and revised with the "Ode" principally in mind. It is my contention that a significant Keatsian source is to be found in three of Keats's narrative poems which deal with the man-woman relationship in a strikingly similar way: "Endymion," "La Belle Dame sans Merci," and "Lamia."

In all of these poems an idealistic youth, a romantic dreamer, falls in love with a beautiful creature. She may be Cynthia, the Moon Goddess, or one of her lovely female incarnations. In only one poem, "Endymion," does the protagonist, after suffering great anguish of lovesickness, attain

2 For a different treatment of Fitzgerald's women, see Sarah Beebe Fryer's *Fitzgerald's New Women: Harbingers of Change* (Ann Arbor: UMI Research Press, 1988). A more probing study is Theodora Tsimpouki's excellent *F. Scott Fitzgerald's Aestheticism* (Athens: Parousia, 1992), which sees in Pater, particularly in his troubling account of the Mona Lisa, a basis for Fitzgerald's complex view of women, art, and morality.

3 John Kuehl has rightly remarked that "John Keats was Fitzgerald's favorite author." Kuehl's account of Keats's influence is to be found in "Scott Fitzgerald's Reading," *The Princeton University Library Chronicle*, 22 (Winter 1961), 61–62; see also Kuehl's "Scott Fitzgerald: Romantic and Realist," *Texas Studies in Literature and Languages*, 1 (1959), 412–426. Sheilah Graham's *Beloved Infidel* (New York: Bantam, 1959) and *College of One* (New York: Viking, 1966) are indispensable in defining the Keats relation. For more specialized studies see also William Bysshe Stein, "Gatsby's Morgan Le Fay," *Fitzgerald Newsletter*, No. 15 (Fall 1961), 67; Dan McCall, "'The Self-Same Song That Found a Path': Keats and *The Great Gatsby*," *American Literature*, 42 (1971), 521–530; Tristram P. Coffin, "Gatsby's Fairy Lover," *Midwest Folklore*, 10 (Summer 1960), 79–85; Richard L. Schoenwald, "F. Scott Fitzgerald as John Keats," *Boston University Studies in English*, 3 (1957), 12–21; John Grube, "*Tender Is the Night*: Keats and Fitzgerald," *Dalhousie Review*, 44 (1964–1965), 433–441; and William E. Doherty, "*Tender Is the Night* and the 'Ode to a Nightingale,'" in *Explorations of Literature*, ed. Rima Drell Reck (Baton Rouge: Louisiana State University Press, 1966), pp. 100–114.

4 Doherty, "*Tender Is the Night* and the 'Ode to a Nightingale,'" p. 101.

5 F. Scott Fitzgerald, *Tender Is the Night* (New York: Scribner's, 1934), p. 55. Subsequent quotations from this work will be given as *TN*, in parentheses, in the text.

his ethereal love with the goddess. In "Endymion" the Moon Goddess, in her aspect as Cynthia, is a positive divine energy. But in her aspect as Diana or Hecate—goddess of the moon, earth, and underground realm of the dead and regarded as the goddess of sorcery and witchcraft—her allurements are sinister and work to the destruction of the male protagonist in Keats's poems. (In *The White Goddess* Robert Graves has devoted an odd but learned book to the positive and negative images of this anima of the unconscious, in its lunar, literary, and folkloric manifestations.)

In "La Belle Dame sans Merci," we recall, a knight is found alone and wandering on a cold hillside. He tells the narrator of the poem that he has encountered a lady in that wild landscape—"Full beautiful, a faery's child"—who took him to an "elfin grot" where, after their sweet moans of love, she lulled him to sleep. In this sleep he had a dream of pale kings, princes, and warriors who cried out to him "La belle dame sans merci / Thee hath in thrall." Upon awakening he is found alone, languid, *épuisé*, wandering purposelessly in the withered landscape.

This beautiful faery's child has taken the knight to her elfin grot, where an act of erotic fulfillment has occurred; she has devitalized him, sexually and psychically, leaving him, like his predecessors, pale and bloodless, enchanted and enthralled in a living death. Nothing in the poem suggests that the woman has a serpentine form; but in the folkloric and literary sources of "La Belle Dame" it is clear that the figure metamorphoses into her enchanting form out of the form of a serpent, hag, or witch. And her lethal intent is to vivify herself by sucking out of the young man his life's blood. In Keats's "Lamia" this metamorphosis is explicitly described: the vampire witch transforms herself from a hissing and coiling serpent into the form of a beautiful woman who offers fair young Lycius the dream of love, to which he capitulates, until the serpent is unmasked by the sage philosopher Apollonius—whereupon she vanishes in a scream, Lycius dying just thereafter, a victim of her debilitating enchantment and of the shock of the revelation of her poisonous betrayal of innocent love.

II

What is the relation of these poems to *Tender Is the Night?* Are they evidence of that passion for Keats that led Fitzgerald to memorize and recite the poems at length and to commend them to Sheilah Graham as essential reading? Indeed they are. We must take note, first, of Fitzgerald's lifelong fascination with the lamia figure. In *This Side of Paradise,* among his other readings, Amory Blaine reads "'Belle Dame sans

Merci': for a month was keen on naught else."[6] He becomes enchanted with Rosaline Connage (modeled on Zelda), whom the used-up and rejected Howard Gillespie calls "a vampire, that's all" (*TSOP*, 193). Amory's next girl, Eleanor Savage, is truly moon-mad: "a witch, of perhaps nineteen" (*TSOP*, 243), she puts Amory "in a trance" (*TSOP*, 245). Afterward she represented "the last time that evil crept close to Amory under the mask of beauty, the last weird mystery that held him with wild fascination and pounded his soul to flakes" (*TSOP*, 238). Somehow he knows that she is complicit in a dark evil. The following passage is of paramount importance in understanding the inner dynamics of Fitzgerald's ambivalence about women: "The problem of evil had solidified for Amory into the problem of sex. . . . Inseparably linked with evil was beauty. . . . Amory knew that every time he had reached toward it longingly it had leered out at him with the grotesque face of evil. Beauty of great art, beauty of all joy, most of all the beauty of women" (*TSOP*, 302).

The manuscript of *The Beautiful and Damned* indicates that Fitzgerald originally intended to call it "The Beautiful Lady Without Mercy," but he canceled the title; and the manuscript also has a cancelled epigraph from this Keats poem. In the novel the character Richard Caramel publishes a book called *The Demon Lover*. The ethereal beauty of the Moon Goddess in *The Beautiful and Damned* incarnates itself in the form of the 1920s: as a "susciety gurl," "a ragtime kid, a flapper, a jazz-baby and a baby vamp."[7] While "vamp" was a common slang term in the 1920s for a flirt, its deeper resonance should not be underestimated.[8] A section of Book I is called "Portrait of a Siren" (and features an erotic Geraldine, the name of Coleridge's lamia in "Christobel"), as well as a section called "The Beautiful Lady," concerning Gloria Gilbert, of whom Fitzgerald remarks, she was "beautiful—but especially she was without mercy" (*B&D*, 116). Mrs. Granby thinks that Gloria may be a vampire (*B&D*, 186), as indeed she is. And at the end of the novel, the devitalized Anthony Patch is reduced to childish impotence, playing idly with his stamp book, fully in Gloria's control, then dreaming of an escape to Italy, specifically to the Piazza de Spagna, where, not coincidentally, Keats lived and died.

---

6 Fitzgerald, *This Side of Paradise* (New York: Scribner's, 1920), p. 57. Subsequent references to this work will be given as *TSOP*, in parentheses, in the text.

7 Fitzgerald, *The Beautiful and Damned* (New York: Scribner's, 1922), p. 29. Subsequent references to this work will be given as *B&D*, in parentheses, in the text.

8 I am grateful to Theodora Tsimpouki for locating some doggerel of Fitzgerald's—in the 1916 piece "The Vampires Won't Vampire for Me"—that makes the connection specific: "Why are ladies I meet / Never more than just sweet? / Girls seem to be Vampires / But they won't Vampire for me." See *F. Scott Fitzgerald's Aestheticism*, p. 67.

This vampire role is also played by Daisy Fay in *Gatsby*. Gatsby, according to William Bysshe Stein, succumbs "to the enchantments of the reincarnation of Morgan le Fay."[9] And the figure is right in Milton R. Stern's *The Golden Moment: The Novels of F. Scott Fitzgerald*, where he writes of the desexualizing power of rich women: "As moneyed 'female' destroys energy (Daisy's killing Myrtle, her indirect destruction of Gatsby), sucking it up like a vampire and leaving corpses strewn after her, the hardening, using female becomes indistinguishable from the predatory male."[10]

The *Esquire* articles that describe Fitzgerald's complete collapse in the mid-1930s, just after the completion of *Tender Is the Night*, dwell obsessively with the theme he had developed in the novel: the loss of vitality. He remarks that of all natural forces "vitality is the incommunicable one. In the days when juice came into one as an article without duty, one tried to distribute it—but always without success; . . .vitality never 'takes.' You have it or you haven't, like health or brown eyes or honor or a baritone voice." Later he posed the question "of finding why and where I changed, where was the leak through which, unknown to myself, my enthusiasm and my vitality had been steadily and prematurely trickling away."[11] The issue was obsessive with him, though the answer was never fully grasped. Partial explanations must include Zelda's consuming need, her madness, paternal anxieties, his own alcoholism, his depression-era poverty, self-contempt at the overproduction of second-rate magazine stories, the loss of an audience for his novels in the nine years after *Gatsby*, and the marginal reception of *Tender Is the Night*. An equally compelling reason for this loss of vitality was his tendency, arising out of his fragile sense of self and intensified by the novelist's task of entering into other identities, to merge with more attractive others, resulting in the destabilization of ego boundaries and the loss of identity.

The diminution of Fitzgerald's sexual, emotional, psychic, professional, in short his creative vitality is central in *Tender Is the Night* and is dramatized as an affect that gradually overcomes Dick Diver in the process of courting, marrying, and curing Nicole Warren through psychoanalytic processes involving transference and countertransference. So central is it in Fitzgerald's imagination that every major character in the book is assessed in relation to his or her vitality, or the lack of it. The scenario of the novel notes that the actress is "simply reeking of vitality,

9 Stein, "Gatsby's Morgan Le Fay," p. 67.
10 Milton R. Stern, *The Golden Moment: The Novels of F. Scott Fitzgerald* (Urbana: University of Illinois Press, 1970), p. 326.
11 F. Scott Fitzgerald, *The Crack-Up*, ed. Edmund Wilson (New York: New Directions, 1945), pp. 74, 80.

health, sensuality."[12] And Dick tells Rosemary: "That vitality, we were sure it was professional—especially Nicole was. It'd never use itself up on any one person or group" (*TN*, 49). Throughout her illness, Nicole does not have it: ". . . she sought in [other people] the vitality that had made them independent or creative or rugged, sought in vain—for their secrets were buried deep in childhood struggles they had forgotten" (*TN*, 236–237). Abe North lacks it; in fact, all the sanitarium patients lack vitality to Lanier, Dick's son: ". . . the patients appeared to him either in their odd aspects, or else as devitalized, over-correct creatures without personality" (*TN*, 237).

But Fitzgerald focused his theme of waning vitality principally in Dick's disintegration. As the novel proceeds we become acutely conscious of his waning powers. Halfway through the action, Tommy Barban tells Dick that he doesn't look "so jaunty as you used to, so spruce, you know what I mean." Fitzgerald observes that "the remark sounded too much like one of those irritating accusations of waning vitality" (*TN*, 257). As Dick's descent continues, he comes to recognize that "He had lost himself—he could not tell the hour when, or the day or the week, the month or the year" (*TN*, 262). He reflects that at an earlier meeting with Rosemary he had "been at an emotional peak," but "since then there had been a lesion of enthusiasm" (*TN*, 271). In a later scene, after half an hour of Collis, who is pursuing Rosemary, he felt "a distinct lesion of his own vitality" (*TN*, 290). Toward the end he confesses to Rosemary that he had "gone into a process of deterioration" (*TN*, 368). And afterward, "though Nicole often paid lip service to the fact that he had led her back to the world she had forfeited, she had thought of him really as an inexhaustible energy, incapable of fatigue—she forgot the troubles she caused him at the moment when she forgot the troubles of her own that had prompted her" (*TN*, 388). Even the hack novelist McKisco "realized that he possessed more vitality than many men of superior talent," like Dick, "and he was resolved to enjoy the success he had earned" (*TN*, 268).

III

How does this motif of loss of vitality connect with the vampire motif? Is Nicole a lamia who devitalizes Dick in ways reminiscent of the Keats poems? Let me observe at first that Fitzgerald does not directly characterize Nicole in images of the serpentine woman, the lamia, or vampire. To have done so would too greatly undercut reader sympathy for Nicole.

---

12 Arthur Mizener, *The Far Side of Paradise* (New York: Vintage, 1959), p. 334.

The serpent-woman figure is displaced onto others and is later general-
ized in wider images of the battle between the sexes. Even so, the Keatsian analogues resonate powerfully. The language of faery enchantment
permeates the early part of the novel, where Dick falls under Nicole's
spell. In this novel, though, the psychoanalytic process of transference
substitutes for the older folkloric vampire imagery. Fitzgerald's understanding of transference, a complex psychoanalytic concept, is limited
and rudimentary. What it comes down to is the transference of Dick's
health to Nicole, his vitality to her. This analytic concept, which he had
discovered in talking to Zelda's doctors and in reading about mental illness, replaces in substantial measure the older folkloric images of the
vampiric woman.

Nevertheless, several significant associations in the novel make plain
the continuing undercurrent of Keatsian vampirism in *Tender Is the
Night*. The Murphys' Villa America is renamed the Villa Diana, the name
of the Moon Goddess, and Nicole is her incarnation. Fitzgerald deletes
from the title-page epigraph from the "Ode" two lines that, by their sheer
absence, call attention to the power of the Lunar Goddess: "And haply
the Queen-Moon is on her throne, / Cluster'd around by all her starry
Fays." Nicole's garden is the site of the first magical enchantment, the
feast where the fireflies dance, the table appears to levitate, and the
people are strangely made to feel "a sense of being alone with each other
in the dark universe, nourished by its only food, warmed by its only
lights" (*TN*, 44). This feast is not accidentally reminiscent of the feasting
scene in "Lamia" and the "honey wild and manna dew" of "La Belle
Dame." Yet of her garden, or elfin grot, Dick says that it is diseased:
Nicole "won't let it alone—she nags it all the time, worries about its diseases. Any day now I expect to have her come down with Powdery Mil-
dew or Fly Speck, or Late Blight" (*TN*, 36). Corruptions infest it. Yet in
that enchanted darkness Nicole is transfigured, for Rosemary, into "one
of the most beautiful people she had ever known. Her face, the face of a
saint, a viking Madonna, shone through the faint motes that snowed
across the candlelight, drew down its flush from the wine-colored lan-
terns in the pine" (*TN*, 43). Because these motes blur Rosemary's vision,
seduce her through Nicole's magic, we need not be surprised that soon
enough even Rosemary herself will become a starry Fay, will come to
possess "all the world's dark magic; the blinding belladonna, the caffeine
converting physical into nervous energy, the mandragora that imposes
harmony" (*TN*, 215). In this scene, as Rosemary watches Nicole, Abe
North is talking to Rosemary about his "moral code": "'Of course I've
got one,' he insisted, '—a man can't live without a moral code. Mine is
that I'm against the burning of witches. Whenever they burn a witch I

get all hot under the collar'" (*TN*, 43) This juxtaposition of feminine images—Madonna and Witch—coalesces the sexual attraction-repulsion affect underlying Fitzgerald's best, or at least most complex, characterizations of women. Abe can observe this because he has for years been enchanted with Nicole, is in fact "heavy, belly-frightened, with love for her. . ." (*TN*, 107).

There are, in fact, three serpent women in the novel—displacements of the lamia aspect of Nicole: ". . . a trio of young women sitting on the bench. They were all tall and slender with small heads groomed like manikins' heads, and as they talked [about the Divers and their entourage] the heads waved gracefully about above their dark tailored suits, rather like long-stemmed flowers and rather like cobras' hoods." In fact, Fitzgerald calls them "the three cobra women" (*TN*, 95–96). Another incarnation of the destructive power of the Moon Goddess occurs in Maria Wallace, with the (Viking?) "helmet-like hair" (*TN*, 109). She shoots an unnamed man right through his identification card, leaving him sprawled on the train station platform without a self.

In the sanitarium garden scene where Nicole seduces Dick, Fitzgerald describes Nicole's face as emerging from its surrounding hair "as if this were the exact moment when she was coming from a wood into clear moonlight. The unknown yielded her up; Dick wished she had no background, that she was just a girl lost with no address save the night from which she had come" (*TN*, 179). Indeed it is the night—ruled by Diana —from which Nicole has emerged, more so than from Chicago. Of her singing, Fitzgerald remarks: "On the pure parting of her lips no breath hovered" (*TN*, 180), an inescapable spondaic verbal echo of the lines in "La Belle Dame": ". . . the sedge is wither'd from the lake, / And no birds sing." But Dick can hear nothing of her real song: what song the siren sang, a ditty of no tone, enchants him utterly.

In this seduction the process of vampiric draining begins. After they kiss and she says to herself, "I've got him, he's mine," Dick "was thankful to have an existence at all, if only as a reflection in her wet eyes" (*TN*, 203). As in "La Belle Dame," Nature too is transformed at this appropriation of Dick's selfhood. A storm erupts, fierce torrents of rain fall: "Mountains and lake disappeared—the hotel crouched amid tumult, chaos and darkness" (*TN*, 204). Although Dick feebly resists being bought, afterward, that night, "Her beauty climbed the rolling slope, it came into the room, rustling ghost-like through the curtains" (*TN*, 205). Soon enough he is signing their letters "Dicole" (*TN*, 136), as his identity drains into her; later, "somehow Dick and Nicole had become one and equal, not apposite and complementary; she was Dick too, the drought in the marrow of his bones. He could not watch her disintegrations without participating in them" (*TN*, 249). He even becomes more feminized, appearing at one point, on the beach, in a pair of black lace panties Nicole has given him. "Well, if that isn't a pansy's trick" (*TN*, 26), remarks Mrs. McKisco contemptuously, reminding us of how homosexuality and lesbianism, perversions of rightly directed human sexuality, give the novel an ominous undertone.[13]

Kathe Gregorovius claims that Nicole "only cherishes her illness as an instrument of power" (*TN*, 310). In her transference to Dick, she drains him of his vitality, his inexhaustible energy, his very self. Her cure complete, she calculatedly begins an affair with Tommy Barban. The change is evident in her white crook's eyes, suggesting her complicity in the social and personal evil of her family and class. Dick, swallowed up like a gigolo, is bereft of an ego, his self transformed into a vacuum, now filled up only by the egos of others, with all their imperfections. At the end he knows that, with Nicole, "he had made his choice, chosen Ophelia, chosen the sweet poison and drunk it" (*TN*, 391).

Hamlet does not drink poison from the lips of Ophelia, although he does expire from the wound of a poison-tipped duelling sword. (Hamlet's death, moreover, occurs only after his love, Ophelia, has, like Nicole and Zelda, gone mad and driven him to distraction.) But this image of choosing the sweet poison interestingly conflates the love of Scott-Dick for the madwoman Zelda-Nicole and the love of John Keats for Fanny Brawne. "Ask yourself my love whether you are not very cruel to have so entrammeled me, so destroyed my freedom," Keats wrote to her. Keats even avoided seeing her at the end, because a visit was not so much a visit as "venturing into a fire." The phrase "sweet poison" in *Tender Is the Night* comes from one of Keats's letters to her: "I have two luxuries to brood over in my walks, your Loveliness and the hour of my death. O that I could have possession of them both in the same minute. I hate the world: it batters too much the wings of my self-will, and I could take a sweet poison from your lips to send me out of it."[14] If Keats was half in love with easeful death, as he declined so poignantly from tuberculosis (an illness from which, incidentally, Fitzgerald suffered), Dick wanted "to die violently instead of fading out sentimentally" (*TN*, 49). But it is his fate to have emerged from Nicole's elfin grot depleted, to wander purposelessly throughout upstate New York.

---

13 One of the rejected drafts of *Tender* associates the three "Cobra women," mentioned above, with that crowd of lesbian writers who so much repelled Fitzgerald—Solita Solano, Natalie Barney, Renée Vivien, Adrienne Monnier, and others.

14 John Keats, *Complete Poems and Selected Letters*, ed. Clarence DeWitt Thorpe (New York: Odyssey Press, 1935), pp. 616, 627, 621.

IV

This view of woman—as an enchanting but sinister destroyer who drains a man of his vital energies, leaving him spent and empty of a self—is of course insulting to women. But during his darkest hours Fitzgerald felt, however wrongly, the terrors of what I can only call Zelda's oral cannibalism. He wrote to Dr. Squires, apropos of the unfairness of her writing fiction about *his* themes, *his* subjects, that he could not "stand always between Zelda and the world and see her build this dubitable career of hers with morsels of living matter chipped out of my mind, my belly, my nervous system and my loins."[15] There is no doubt that Fitzgerald, like Dick, felt he had exchanged his vitality for his wife's sanity. After quarreling with Zelda about her using *Tender* material for her own fiction, he composed this note:

> As I got feeling worse Zelda got mentally better, but it seemed to me that as she did she was also coming to the conclusion that she had it on me, if I broke down it justified her whole life—not a very healthy thought to live with about your own wife. . . . Finally four days ago told her frankly and furiously that had got & was getting rotten deal trading my health for her sanity and from now on I was going to look out for myself & [their daughter] Scottie exclusively and let her go to Bedlam for all I cared.[16]

If the critic's task is to understand these feelings and their transformation into fiction, however denigrating they may have been to Zelda or may be to other women, some sympathy must arise in our conclusion that the demonic image of woman arose out of Fitzgerald's deep feelings of insecurity as a person, out of the destabilization of ego boundaries as he headed for his breakdown, out of his ambivalence over female sexuality in a newly liberated age, and out of a profound anxiety over his own manliness—castration fears, frankly, as Zelda questioned his virility and accused him of homosexuality. At the root of this fragile sense of self is of course the looming figure of Mollie McQuillan Fitzgerald, the powerful mother to whom ultimately these engulfing images refer. It is no malarkey to say that he spent his whole lifetime running away from her, even as a child fantasizing that he was not her son but rather a foundling, descended from the royal house of Stuart, a displaced prince. But his "possession" by her, and what that did to his relationship with Zelda, is the subject of another paper.

---

15 Quoted in Nancy Milford, *Zelda: A Biography* (New York: Harper and Row, 1970), p. 222.
16 Quoted in Scott Donaldson, *Fool for Love: F. Scott Fitzgerald* (New York: Congdon and Weed, 1983), p. 86.

To his credit, Fitzgerald did not abandon Zelda. "Vitality shows in not only the ability to persist but in the ability to start over,"[17] he recorded in his notebook. If, as he remarked in "The Crack-Up," "It was strange to have no self," if "there was not an 'I' any more—not a basis on which I could organize my self-respect," not even that "limitless capacity for toil that it seemed I possessed no more,"[18] still, Fitzgerald did pull himself together; he went on working, supported Scottie and Zelda, whom he deeply if ambivalently loved, pasted it together, and attained some kind of stability, thanks paradoxically to Sheilah Graham. Had he lived to complete it, *The Last Tycoon* might have reflected the kind of artistic purity he had first achieved in *The Great Gatsby*. But so deeply implanted was his insecurity and his ambivalence about women that no doubt this spoiled priest of a novelist would have recreated, again and again, The Beautiful Lady Without Mercy.

---

17 *The Notebooks of F. Scott Fitzgerald*, ed. Matthew J. Bruccoli (New York: Harcourt Brace Jovanovich, 1978), p. 57.
18 F. Scott Fitzgerald, *The Crack-Up*, p. 79.

Sherwood Anderson: A Room of His Own

In 1956, long after the death of Sherwood Anderson (1876–1941), William Faulkner called him the father of his generation of American writers and of a tradition which their successors would carry on. His moving tribute celebrated the older writer's exceptional prose style in *Winesburg, Ohio* (1919). This short-story sequence and a handful of tales such as "I Want to Know Why," "The Egg," "I'm a Fool," "The Man Who Became a Woman," and "Death in the Woods" have assured Anderson a place in the history of modern American letters. But despite Faulkner's praise, the place Anderson occupies in the development of American literary modernism is nevertheless problematic. Although he was the author of several novels—*Windy McPherson's Son* (1916), *Marching Men* (1917), *Poor White* (1920), *Many Marriages* (1923), *Dark Laughter* (1925), *Beyond Desire* (1932), and *Kit Brandon* (1936)—none of them is read any longer. And there is good reason for this neglect: Anderson simply did not attain in the novel the focus, energy, and feeling attained in his short-story collections—*Winesburg, Ohio* (1919), *The Triumph of the Egg and Other Stories* (1921), *Horses and Men* (1923), and *Death in the Woods and Other Stories* (1933). Some of his short stories are as good as any written by an American. But the fact is that his influence on the generation of Hemingway and Faulkner and his reputation for giving all to his art have come to be seen as more important than his work itself, always excepting *Winesburg* and a few tales.

In part, Anderson's fading critical reputation is to be accounted for by the fact that he was never committed to radical experimentalism in the interesting modernist vein of Stein and Faulkner. The older tradition to which Faulkner assigned him was the tradition of Mark Twain, the storyteller of a boy's adolescent awakening, the tradition of the vernacular stylist of mid-America. Furthermore, Anderson, like Willa Cather, longed for the past and resented the developing machine culture of technological America. Looking backward, he chose as his essential social theme the impact of industrialization on agrarian small-town life, and his tone was nostalgic for a lost world of displaced farmers, harness-makers, and blacksmiths, together with the wheelwrights, country doctors, and local newspapermen of the small town in America. If Anderson was modern, he was modern in the way of D. H. Lawrence—in his persistent exploration of the power of human sexuality and the inarticulate struggle of commonplace people to understand it.

These attitudes and themes come out, confusedly, in his several autobiographical writings—*A Story Teller's Story* (1924), *Tar: A Midwest Childhood* (1926), and the posthumous *Sherwood Anderson's Memoirs* (1942), edited by his friend Paul Rosenfeld. These recollections create, with fictional variations, the story Anderson wanted to tell about himself—about his parents, the world of Clyde, Ohio (the model of Winesburg), about his life in business, his decision to become a writer, his many marriages, and his failed personal relationships. Taken together, the memoirs create the myth of the artist that Anderson wanted us to know. It is not a trustworthy image that Anderson gives us. James E. Schevill tried to sort out the facts from the myth in *Sherwood Anderson: His Life and Work* (1951). But a definitive understanding of Anderson has had to await the recent publication of Ray Lewis White's compilation *Sherwood Anderson: A Reference Guide* (1977); *Sherwood Anderson: Selected Letters* (1984), edited by Charles E. Modlin; the *Letters to Bab: Sherwood Anderson to Marietta D. Finley, 1916–1933* (1985), edited by William A. Sutton; and Kim Townsend's *Sherwood Anderson* (1987). Now that we have these works other letters, together with citations to a half-century of interviews and essays in literary criticism, what can we say about the life of this complex man?

I

Sherwood Anderson was born to Emma Smith Anderson and her husband Irwin in 1876 in Camden, Ohio. In 1883 they removed to Clyde, a small town of 2,500 people, and lived a makeshift life with six children during Sherwood's youth. Of his parents, biographer Kim Townsend makes some extremely interesting observations:

> A diary that she [Anderson's mother] kept during 1872 shows her to be a hard-working and lively young woman, happy to do her chores, to churn, to clean up the yard, to wash and iron, delighted to go on the social rounds that school and church and the rituals of courtship prescribed. A diary that Irwin [Anderson's father] kept shows him to be industrious, pious, and a lover of women.[1]

Because Anderson's father was a financial failure who left it up to his wife to manage the family, the boy Sherwood was necessarily a hustler, working at a variety of odd jobs, scrabbling for nickels and dimes to help the family survive. Out of this experience arose Anderson's lifelong anger at his father. In the town of Clyde, Irwin Anderson was well liked as a storyteller of Civil War tales, a lover of parades, a performer of magic acts, and a supporter of town theatricals. But although Sherwood's storytelling gifts derived from his flamboyant father, he could not help feeling resentment about the treatment of his mother. He got his revenge in the fiction. In *Windy McPherson's Son,* he described Irwin Anderson, fictionally, as "the boasting, incompetent father," "the blustering, pretending, inefficient old one." For the son, "the realisation that his father was a confirmed liar and braggart had for years cast a shadow over his days. . . ."[2] And in *Winesburg, Ohio* it is said of George Willard's father: "He had always thought of himself as a successful man, although nothing he had ever done had turned out successfully. However, when he was out of sight of the New Willard House [their failing hotel] and had no fear of coming upon his wife, he swaggered and began to dramatize himself as one of the chief men of the town."[3] Since *Winesburg* was dedicated to Emma, "whose keen observations on the life about her first awoke in me the hunger to see beneath the surface of lives," it will come as no surprise that Anderson resented the poverty of his mother's existence. Afterward he remarked in *Tar* that "he was in love with her all his life" and that when a mother like her dies when you are eighteen, "what you do all your life afterwards is to use her as material for dreams."[4] Her death in his adolescence froze Emma Anderson, in the writer's imagination, as an ideal woman.

---

1 Kim Townsend, *Sherwood Anderson* (New York: Houghton Mifflin, 1987), p. 2. Hereafter, quotations from this work will be given as *SA,* in parentheses, in the text.

2 Anderson, *Windy McPherson's Son* (Chicago: University of Chicago Press, 1965), p. 15.

3 Anderson, *Winesburg, Ohio: Text and Criticism,* ed. John H. Ferres (New York: Viking Press, 1966), p. 44. Hereafter, quotations from this work will be given as *WO,* in parentheses, in the text.

4 Anderson, *Tar: A Midwest Childhood,* ed. Ray Lewis White (Cleveland: Press of Case Western Reserve University, 1969), p. 107.

After a stint in the army during the Spanish-American War, Anderson, as the new century dawned, went to work for an advertising agency in Chicago. His success in business was quite remarkable for someone who was later so hostile to the business life, and it led him to take other jobs in Cleveland and in Elyria, Ohio. According to Townsend, "Anderson wrote copy about everything from ditch-digging machines to canned tomatoes, from patent medicines for loose bowels and thinning hair, toothpaste and washtubs and kitchen cabinets, to a remedy for disease for hogs" (*SA*, 44). He gave speeches with titles such as "The Sales Master and the Selling Organization," and he published business-boosting articles in periodicals such as *Agricultural Advertising*. A commercial success, in 1904 he married an educated, well-to-do Clyde girl, Cornelia Platt Lane. He and Cornelia had three children by 1911. In Elyria, Anderson established himself as president of the Anderson Manufacturing Company, a firm that sold a roofing compound. For five years he plied this trade as an esteemed member of the Elyria Elks Club, the Country Club, and the Round Table Club, a town discussion group.

But he was clearly miscast in the role he was playing in the commercial and domestic life he had chosen. Gradually he became moody and eccentric. He needed and wanted isolation. In his Elyria house he created a special room where he could lock himself in. Secure in this private place, he would wash down the room, then scrub himself, preparing himself to write stories. Guilt and shame seem to have provoked an obsessive-compulsive desire for cleanliness. But about what did he feel guilty? We could, of course, take it on Anderson's word that he wanted to cleanse himself of his commercial sins, perhaps for writing mendacious ads or selling an unwanted roofing mix. Writing in his locked room was a curative, Anderson said. It delivered him from the feeling of being a "smooth son of a bitch."[5] None of this writing was immediately publishable, but vestiges of the monastic experience survive in *Windy McPherson's Son*, a novel ostensibly in revolt against money making as an end in life. Something was definitely going on in that room. In that shut-in place appeared another self, projected in *Windy* as his fictive protagonist Sam, who had "another personality, a quite different being altogether, buried away within him, long neglected, often forgotten, a timid, shy destructive Sam who had never really breathed or lived or walked before men."[6]

It would be too simple to say that the alter ego of the artist was replacing the businessman in Anderson. The destructive figure who

---

5 *Sherwood Anderson: Selected Letters*, ed. Charles E. Modlin (Knoxville: University of Tennessee Press, 1984), p. 20.
6 Anderson, *Windy McPherson's Son*, pp. 327–328.

emerged in that room had never lived or walked before women either. He was soon to do both. The crisis in Anderson's life, the eruption of that destructive personality, occurred in November 1912, when he was thirty-six. Anderson simply walked out of his office one day, said goodbye to his secretary, and left a strange note to his wife Cornelia: "There is a bridge over a river with cross-ties before it. When I come to that I'll be all right. I'll write all day in the sun and the wind will blow through my hair" (*SA*, 77). Four days later he stumbled into a pharmacy in Cleveland, filthy, dazed, and incoherent. He had no idea who he was or where he was. From an address book in his pocket, his identity was established and he was hospitalized until, as he put it later, "my mind came into my body."[7] In accounting for this episode, Anderson's biographer Kim Townsend invokes the diagnosis of the "fugue state," as defined by Harry Stack Sullivan. According to Sullivan's *The Interpersonal Theory of Psychiatry*, fugue states (common enough in adolescents) are episodes of "dreaming-while-awake." In this state "the relationship with circumambient reality and with the meanings to which things attach from one's past, is to a certain extent, fundamentally and as absolutely suspended as it is when one is asleep" (*SA*, 28, 81). This may indeed have been Anderson's affliction. But it should be noted that Anderson wrote notes to Cornelia while he was wandering around, ostensibly in a daze. In recounting the episode in *A Story Teller's Story*, Anderson left it up in the air as to whether he "merely became shrewd and crafty" or whether he "really became temporarily insane."[8]

Whatever may have been the medical diagnosis, Anderson described the event as a repudiation of the moral corruptions of philistine business and the strangulations of bourgeois domesticity in favor of a life devoted to the creation of art. So dramatic and thrilling was his account of the event that it came to stand, for younger writers, as a paradigm of the artist's sacrifice of everything for the sake of his art. Anderson was widely regarded as the American Gauguin, a painter whom he had never heard of at the time. It was an identification he did nothing to discourage.

The facts, however, are somewhat different from the account (or varied accounts) that Anderson's several memoirs and letters have provided us. After his discharge from the hospital, he and Cornelia in fact got back together. But given his state of mind, given his growing and unaccountable hatred for poor Cornelia, the marriage could not survive. After a visit to her family in Toledo in December, they went

---

7 Sherwood Anderson, *Letters to Bab: Sherwood Anderson to Marietta D. Finley, 1916–33*, ed. William A. Sutton (Urbana: University of Illinois Press, 1985), p. 28.

8 Sherwood Anderson, *A Story Teller's Story* (New York: Viking Press, 1969), p. 312.

back to Elyria, where Anderson settled with his business partners. They packed up their belongings; Cornelia was to take the children up to her sister Stella's cottage at Little Point Sable, Michigan; Anderson would try to find work to support them. They probably intended to resettle in Chicago. Far from thumbing his nose at the commercial life, Anderson immediately went back to work for the Taylor-Critchfield advertising agency, his old employer. In fact, as late as 1918 he could write in an advertising publicity essay: "I do not understand why more novelists do not go into it [advertising]. It is all quite simple. You are to write advertisements for one who puts tomatoes in cans. You imagine yourself a canner of tomatoes. You become enthusiastic about the tomato. You are an actor given a role to play and you play it" (*SA*, 46).[9] Though always complaining, he worked in advertising for a *decade* after crossing that bridge over the river.

In any case, Anderson continued in business by day and wrote in the evenings. During this period he also fell in with the bohemian avant-garde of Chicago—Floyd Dell, Susan Glaspell, Tennessee Mitchell, Ben Hecht, Carl Sandburg, and Margaret Anderson, the editor of the *Little Review*. They avidly discussed their "modern ideas" on sex and marriage, the role of the artist, and the corruption of the commercial life. Margaret Anderson said that Sherwood, no intellectual, "didn't talk ideas, he told stories." He began to costume himself with brightly colored clothes and scarves. Ben Hecht said the older writer "looked like an Italian barber but he exuded ego like a royalist" (*SA*, 91–92). Cornelia occasionally visited, but it was clear that she did not fit in. Of this period of Anderson's life, Floyd Dell later observed: "We were in love with life and willing to believe almost any modern theory which gave us a chance to live our lives more fully. We were incredibly well meaning. We were confused, miserable, gay, and robustly happy all at once."[10] But most of these young bohemians were in their early twenties; Anderson was nearly forty, married, and the father of three children. But he had found his niche. They were all united by what Anderson called their contempt for the stodgy life of middle-class domesticity.

It was his wife Cornelia's opinion that Anderson needed a mother instead of a wife. If so, the child inside of Anderson was increasingly of an indeterminate gender. Clearly Anderson's identity had a remarkable feminine component, and something like a feminine self began to manifest itself in his colorful clothes. (He even bought a sewing machine

---

9 See also Anderson's *A Story Teller's Story,* ed. Ray Lewis White (Cleveland: Press of Case Western Reserve University, 1968), pp. 346–347.

10 Floyd Dell, "Last Days in Chicago," *Homecoming: An Autobiography* (New York: Farrar and Rinehart, 1933), p. 242.

so that he could make his own flamboyant shirts.) An echo of this gender blurring is evident in "The Book of the Grotesque," the lead story in *Winesburg, Ohio*. There the old writer, a projection of the author, gets into bed to await the procession of figures who, passing before his inward eye, will become the grotesque inhabitants of Winesburg, memorialized so poignantly in the collection.

> Perfectly still he lay and his body was old and not of much use any more, but something inside him was altogether young. He was like a pregnant woman, only that the thing inside him was not a baby but a youth. No, it wasn't a youth, it was a woman, young and wearing a coat of mail like a knight. It is absurd, you see, to try to tell what was inside the old writer as he lay on his high bed and listened to the fluttering of his heart (*WO*, 24).[11]

Something like this repressed feminine sensibility also arises in the first story of the collection, "Hands." This tale deals with a former teacher, Wing Biddlebaum, who had been run out of another town for caressing his male students. Of Biddlebaum, Anderson wrote that "He was one of those rare, little-understood men who rule by a power so gentle that it passes as a lovable weakness. In their feeling for the boys under their charge such men are not unlike the finer sort of women in the love of men" (*WO*, 31). While it is clear that Anderson knew nothing about pedophilia and pederasty (hardly a lovable weakness), he evidently thought himself as delicate and sensitive, not unlike the finer sort of women. Anderson and his male friends went barhopping in Chicago, affecting the role of fairies, calling themselves "Little Eva" and "Mabel." Of this blurring of his masculinity Townsend remarks only that "His own [sexuality] was something of a mystery to him, a mystery that neither his marriage to Cornelia nor his encounters with nameless other women had done anything to clear up, but he did not set out to *solve* that mystery" (*SA*, 105–106). Unfortunately, neither does Townsend, though it seems clear that Anderson's gender confusions were more than the usual authorial exploration of what women think and feel.

In fact, Anderson felt a deep, obscure hostility to women. No doubt it had to do with his mother's abandonment of him, by dying in his impressionable adolescence. He both wanted to be like her—fine, sensitive, and caring, and yet he was full of rage at her—and targeted that rage on

---

11 This gender blurring is also evident in Anderson's strange little book *A New Testament* (New York: Boni and Liveright, 1927). The book has bizarre sexual ruminations such as this: "It would be strange if the man who just left my house . . . came over lands and seas, to impregnate me" (p. 11).

other women, whom he regarded as vampires. He had the candor to remark that "Most women simply frighten me." He said, "I feel hunger within them. It is as though they wished to feed upon me."[12] One of those he feared was Marietta (Bab) Finley, a reader for the Bobbs-Merrill Company whom he had met in 1914 at a play put on by Maurice Browne's Little Theatre group. They appear to have been lovers; it is certain in any case that she wanted to marry him. In a rather cruel rebuff he told her that she would have to settle for only an epistolary relationship with him. She was to receive his literary letters, once a week or oftener, and reply to him. They were to keep the correspondence, which would be a record of their feelings and ideas. But she should forget about his company and companionship; what he wanted in fact was a sounding board and a safe repository of his correspondence. Indeed, he wrote her 309 letters between 1916 and 1933, which she dutifully kept. He destroyed hers.

Meanwhile, at the top of his literary form, he was composing the tales that became *Winesburg, Ohio*. One dealt with Wing; another with the town doctor, who scribbled his thoughts on pieces of paper, then "stuffed them away in his pockets to become round hard balls." "Mother" is a tale of a frustrated but passionately mysterious woman very much like Emma Anderson. "Godliness" tells the story of the family of a God-intoxicated old farmer whose greed for land drives away his grandson. Another, "The Strength of God," tells the story of the Reverend Curtis Hartman, who cures himself of voyeurism by smashing the window through which he has spied on the naked teacher Kate Swift. Elmer Cowley, the title character of "Queer," irrationally beats up the young reporter George Willard, just to prove he isn't odd. In "Adventure," Alice Hindman, sexually crazed by years of awaiting the return of her faithless lover, bursts out of the house one night and runs naked in the rain, only to recover herself and return home.

> When she got into bed she buried her face in the pillow and wept brokenheartedly. "What is the matter with me? I will do something dreadful if I am not careful," she thought, and turning her face to the wall, began trying to force herself to face bravely the fact that many people must live and die alone, even in Winesburg (*WO*, 120).

Several of the stories deal with young Willard's attempt to understand these sexually repressed and emotionally deformed fellow townsmen, who think of him as alone capable of understanding them and telling their stories. *Winesburg, Ohio* is in part the story of George Wil-

---

12 Anderson, *Letters to Bab*, p. 147.

lard's initiation into the hidden motives and the obscure emotions of these inarticulate residents, as well as his discovery of the meaning of sex and love. Above all, he is meant to become the poet who knows the sweetness of the twisted apples in the orchard, the metaphor by which we know these Winesburg grotesques. As Kate Swift tells him in "The Teacher," "You must not become a mere peddler of words. The thing to learn is to know what people are thinking about, not what they say" (*WO*, 163). At the end of the book, he boards the train for Chicago, determined to become an artist. These remarkable tales fairly poured out of Anderson in 1915–1916. He told Cornelia that he felt "like a woman, having my babies, one after another, but without pain" (*SA*, 109). Without question the creation of the book, a kind of prose *Spoon River Anthology*, was a stunning achievement.

Although he was finished with Cornelia, Anderson was one of those who could not live, much less die, alone. He could not be without a woman. His next wife, Tennessee Mitchell, was not so much a mother as a playmate. After divorcing Cornelia he married Tennessee in 1916 after a summer with her at Camp Owlyout, a quasi-nudist colony for avant-garde women passionate about eurhythmic dance. Anderson was "the only faun in the camp" (*SA*, 127) and had a grand time. A sculptor and piano tuner who had been the mistress of Edgar Lee Masters (who savaged her as a congenital nymphomaniac in one of his poems), Tennessee Mitchell drew Anderson deeper into the bohemian life and loves of the Chicago art world. With advanced views on marriage, they kept separate apartments and saw other people. Even so, Tennessee soon came to invade the private space, the secret room, of Sherwood Anderson. Packing a bag, he left Chicago in 1920 for Alabama, where he wrote Whitmanesque effusions like those he had already published in the hopeless verse of *Mid-American Chants* (1918). In Alabama he also composed the perfectly awful novel *Many Marriages*. Meanwhile, Tennessee languished in Chicago. "The poor woman went and married me and is stuck to making her own living," he observed, "and it's hell."[13]

II

The success of *Winesburg* (1919), *Poor White* (1920), another attack on industrialization and "the mechanization of American life," and *The Triumph of the Egg* (1921) brought Anderson to the attention of the writers connected with *Seven Arts* in New York. For Waldo Frank, Paul

---

13 *Letters of Sherwood Anderson*, eds. Howard Mumford Jones and Walter B. Rideout (New York: Kraus Reprint, 1969), p. 64.

Rosenfeld, Van Wyck Brooks, and Edna Kenton, Anderson seemed an authentic mid-American voice, and they hailed him as a diamond in the rough, a home-grown artist who would inaugurate what Brooks had called "America's Coming-of-Age." Anderson tried to oblige Brooks by stressing his quintessential Midwesternness. In a 1917 essay called "An Apology for Crudity," Anderson advised that American writers ought to turn away from "neat slick writing," such as that produced by James and Howells, and dramatize "the crude expression" of the people's lives. "And if we are a crude and childlike people, how can our literature hope to escape the influence of that fact? Why, indeed, should we want to escape?"[14] Not recognizing in Anderson the merely warmed-over ideas of Van Wyck Brooks, Waldo Frank could observe, "To me, the young New Yorker who knew his Europe well and had scarce seen his own land beyond the Eastern seaboard, Sherwood Anderson was America" (*SA*, 120). Anderson played this role to the hilt: "I am an intensification of the spirit of my times," he immodestly admitted to Bab Finley.[15] But this equation of literary crudity with Americanness made Virginia Woolf very impatient. In her review of *A Story Teller's Story*, she complained that Anderson's constant repetitions of the line "I am the American man" were ridiculous, as indeed they were. But beneath the bogus nationalism of this iteration is an overstrenuous protestation of his own manliness—as if he were trying to convince himself that he was an American D. H. Lawrence.[16]

In 1921 Anderson packed his bag again and sailed for Europe. In France he met Joyce, Pound, and Stein; in England, Arnold Bennett, Ford Madox Ford, and John Masefield. Not likely to fall for expatriatism, he returned to New York and in the following year met Elizabeth Prall in a Doubleday bookstore and threw himself into her Greenwich Village crowd, which included Max Eastman, Edna St. Vincent Millay, Stark Young—and Susan Glaspell and Floyd Dell, who had come from Chicago. Divorcing Tennessee Mitchell, he married Elizabeth and took off for New Orleans in 1924. There he met and encouraged Faulkner, who had worked for Elizabeth at Doubleday's. At the height of the Harlem craze, Eugene O'Neill had capitalized on it with *All God's Chillun Got Wings* (1924), to be followed by DuBose Heyward's *Porgy* (1925) and Carl Van Vechten's *Nigger Heaven* (1926). Why not Anderson? In New Orleans he composed *Dark Laughter* (1925), a sentimental

---

14 Sherwood Anderson, "An Apology for Crudity," reprinted in *Letters to Bab*, p. 333.
15 Sherwood Anderson, *Letters to Bab*, p. 28.
16 Anderson's reverence for Lawrence, as the epitome of masculinity, is so adoring as to take on the coloration of a crush. See, among other admirations, Anderson's "Lawrence Again," in *No Swank* (Mamaroneck, N.Y.: Paul P. Appel, 1970), pp. 95–103.

fantasy about "the War, new sex-consciousness, niggers—a slow, fantastic dance of sounds and thought," with (in the foreground) "neuroticism, the hurry and self-consciousness of modern life" and (in the background) "the easy, strange laughter of the blacks."[17] Quite improbably Anderson thought himself "inward with the ways of blacks"; Mencken called it "one of the most profound novels of our time"; and indeed it was a best-seller (*SA*, 226–227). But in fact Fitzgerald was right it calling it "lousy."[18] Sentimental in its view of blacks, incoherent in structure, and grotesque in style, the book is an embarrassment even to dedicated Andersonians. Hemingway and Faulkner expressed their disillusionment with the father of their generation by parodying Anderson's style and subjects—Hemingway in *The Torrents of Spring* (1926) and Faulkner in *Sherwood Anderson and Other Creoles* (1926). In fact, Anderson's career as a serious writer was reaching its end.

After leaving New Orleans the Andersons settled in Marion, Virginia, where the novelist built a big house. His inspiration as a fiction writer had pretty much evaporated, and he felt guilty about accepting the $100-a-week advances that the publisher Horace Liveright kept sending him. To keep himself busy and earn his keep, Anderson bought the county's two newspapers, the Republican *Smyth County News* and the *Marion Democrat.* Anderson liked the life of the country journalist and wrote scores of columns and editorials about subjects of interest to small-town readers. But even this life was not to be permanently fulfilling. He frankly got tired of Elizabeth Prall and divorced her in 1932. When his rejected inamorata and correspondent Bab Finley sympathized, he told her he could no longer accept money or help from anyone, "least of all from any woman." He told her she had "as much right to all you feel, as woman, as I have to what I feel as artist and man." But, he warned her, "now I am separated from that. I have fought to get here in this room alone." Again the motif of the room—and the destructive personality that would keep the woman out of it. In any event he concluded: "As to me, as a man, it should be forgotten now."[19]

During the 1930s, Anderson focused on his one compelling subject: sex and what it does to men and women, especially in marriage. There is no reason to doubt that the subject was beyond his competence and that he had little understanding of what drove him as a man. In heroizing D. H. Lawrence, he developed an idea that true masculinity was sympathetic and tender, never boastful of female conquests, and—well in advance of Robert Bly—he claimed that men needed intimacy with each

---

17 *Letters of Sherwood Anderson,* pp. 130, 142.
18 *The Letters of F. Scott Fitzgerald,* ed. Andrew Turnbull (New York: Dell, 1963), p. 214.
19 *Letters to Bab,* pp. 321, 318.

other so as to draw off the elements of aggression he detected in their relationship with women. He told Dreiser in 1936 that "it is our loneliness for each other that has made most of us throw too much on woman . . . making women carry more than their load."

> Now what I have been thinking is that we need here among us some kind of new building up of a relationship between man and man. I feel so strongly on this matter that I am thinking of trying to get my thoughts and those of others who also feel this thing into form. I think even of a general letter or pamphlet that I might call "American Man to American Man."

Townsend believes that Anderson's dim, inarticulate longing here was for genuine male friendship—"not male bonding, not homosexual relations, or patriarchal domination by another name, but friendship" (*SA*, 306).[20] But whatever Anderson meant would require a poet, or psychoanalyst, to say. His preoccupation with the life of feeling carried with it a sense of the inadequacy of words to express the buried life as well as a suspicion of language itself as distorting the very feeling it is meant to communicate. An instance of his growing indifference to precision in the use of language, an instance of the corruption of his style, is this passage from *Dark Laughter:*

> The woman. Mystery. Love of women. Scorn of women. What are they like? Are they like trees? How much can a woman thrust into the mystery of life, think, feel? Love men. Take women. Drift with the drifting of days. That life goes on does not concern you. It concerns women.[21]

One might almost conclude that "It is absurd . . . to try to tell what was inside the old writer," yet this is a position that no serious student of Anderson's mind and art (much less any psychoanalyst) can possibly accept.

One key to Anderson's ambiguity may be suggested by his essay on D. H. Lawrence. Praising Lawrence's true maleness, Anderson concluded the piece with what Townsend calls "the curious image of blood" from a cut on Anderson's hand. Here is the passage:

> Little red blotches of my blood covering the sheets on which I try to write of D. H. Lawrence, dead.
> Spoiling the sheets.

---

20 *The Portable Sherwood Anderson*, ed. Horace Gregory (New York: Viking Press, 1949), pp. 607–608.
21 Sherwood Anderson, *Dark Laughter*, ed. Howard Mumford Jones (New York: Liveright, 1970), p. 95.

Blood spoiling clean white sheets of paper.
Not quite. Blood is nice on white sheets on which a man
speaks, even falteringly, of a man's man like D. H. Lawrence.

Townsend's only comment is: "At the very least, he imagined Lawrence as his blood brother."[22] No doubt this is true. But given Anderson's fear of women, his disgust at coarse sexuality, and the way he treated his wives and lovers, the menstrual and hymeneal implications of these lines require analysis. Townsend skirts the difficult work of naming, on the Andersonian principle that it is absurd to try to tell what was inside the writer, that there is some value in *not* precisely naming the experience. In any case, the mystery of woman in her physical sexuality did not prevent Anderson from marrying Eleanor Copenhaver, a YMCA worker, on July 6, 1933. "Poor as I am at marriage," he remarked, "I always need it, and I do think it is rather courageous and fine of her to tackle it" (*SA*, 290).

Anderson's other passion in the 1930s was politics—specifically the sentimental view of labor conditions. Eleanor had roused Anderson to get interested in working people, and—like Sinclair Lewis, Dreiser, Edmund Wilson, and many other writers—he toured factories, lumber camps, refineries, and mills. On the left, during the depression, it was the liberal thing to do. Although he had once remarked that "nothing in the world could ever make me a socialist" and that he had "no scheme for changing anything in the social structure,"[23] he started attacking business, the journalistic media, schools and churches, "pretty much the whole middle and professional classes" that, in his view, had disfranchised the worker. Ridding himself of guilt seemed to motivate this enterprise as well, for he remarked that "It is perhaps only when we try to bend the arts to serve our damn middle-class purposes that we become unclean. . . ."[24]

Out of these tours came his book *Perhaps Women* (1931), a complaint that "modern man is losing his ability to retain his manhood in the face of the modern way of utilizing the machine and that what hope there is for him lies in women" (*SA*, 263). Before long he was becoming "more and more a communist,"[25] and in 1932 he signed a manifesto (along with Dos Passos, Lewis Mumford, Waldo Frank, and Edmund Wilson) calling for "a temporary dictatorship of the class-conscious

---

22 Anderson, *No Swank*, p. 94; Townsend, *Sherwood Anderson*, p. 264.
23 Anderson, "A Great Factory," *Vanity Fair*, 27 (November 1926), 51–52; reprinted in *Sherwood Anderson: The Writer at His Craft*, eds. Jack Salzman, David D. Anderson, and Kichinosuke Ohashi (Mamaroneck, N.Y.: Paul P. Appel, 1979), p. 77.
24 *Letters of Sherwood Anderson*, p. 206.
25 *Sherwood Anderson: Selected Letters*, pp. 143–144.

workers." He felt that "as responsible intellectual workers, we have aligned ourselves with the frankly revolutionary Communist party." In that year he published "How I Came to Communism" in the *New Masses* and supported Foster and Ford, the Communist ticket, for the presidency. Of Anderson's political seduction by the left, Townsend remarks:

> Whether or not Dreiser or Anderson joined the Party, which neither ever did, whether or not they went to the Soviet Union, which Dreiser did and Anderson did not (though he made plans in 1932), as Anderson knew full well, the Party wasn't terribly interested in the likes of them. The Communist Party was a working-class party, and they were members of "the artist class" (*SA*, 272–273).

But the fact is that in the Kharkov Congress of Revolutionary Writers in 1930, Stalin called for American writers to produce a genuine proletarian literature in the United States, so as to hasten the revolution in America, and the Communist party regularly recruited every artist and intellectual who could be construed to have a "correct" ideological position. Given Anderson's typical fuzzy-mindedness and political naiveté, there was little chance that the party would accept him, though it should be pointed out that Dreiser in fact eventually *did* join the Communist party after Stalin had Earl Browder expelled. [26] Still, Daniel Aaron in *Writers on the Left* is probably right to describe Anderson as one of the "unclassifiable" authors who were merely attracted to communism. [27]

In any case, Anderson became a communist out of a bohemian aversion to the bourgeois life he had flamboyantly abandoned. "I am not respectable and do not desire to be," he said. Reflecting on his actions, he later said he had entered "a transition period" where he had been "reckless," signed manifestoes that were possibly "at bottom nonsense," for he was not "a politically-minded person" (*SA*, 281). He insisted he was just a storyteller. Nevertheless, for a short time, like a good many other muddleheaded American writers and critics, he loaned his name to the enemies of liberal democracy. [28] Perhaps in partial recompense he

---

26 William Z. Foster's letter of welcome told Comrade Dreiser that "We feel your joining the Party at this time is particularly appropriate, now that our organization is purging itself of the opportunism that seeped into it during recent years. . . . Welcome to the ranks of the Communist Party." See W. A. Swanberg, *Dreiser* (New York: Scribner's, 1965), p. 515.

27 Daniel Aaron, *Writers on the Left* (New York: Avon, 1961), p. 46.

28 James Schevill has devastatingly remarked that Anderson's "judgment, like that of many other liberals of the period, was based on the feverish enthusiasm of the moment, rather than any rational view." See "The Glitter of Communism" in *The Achievement of Sherwood Anderson: Essays in Criticism*, ed. Ray Lewis White (Chapel Hill: University of North Carolina Press, 1966), p. 153.

published *Home Town* in 1940, a paean to small-town life in America. In the following year he died on a cruise, as a result of swallowing a toothpick. He was hospitalized in the Canal Zone, but peritonitis had set in, and he could not be saved.

III

After 1925 Anderson's writing career was in effect over. But *Winesburg, Ohio* remains a testament to that spurt of creative genius that created it. Of these tales, "Loneliness" deserves a final mention. In this story a painter named Enoch Robinson tells George Willard his story. Abandoning his wife and children, and disgusted by the Greenwich Village painters who can talk only of technique, he had shut them all out of his life.

> In a half indignant mood he stopped inviting people into his room and presently got into the habit of locking the door. He began to think that enough people had visited him, that he did not need people any more. With quick imagination he began to invent his own people to whom he could really talk and to whom he explained the things he had been unable to explain to living people. His room began to be inhabited by the spirits of men and women among whom he went, in his turn saying words (*WO*, 170).

Then, as Anderson was vague in putting it, "something happened" that drove Enoch Robinson out of New York and into the backwater town of Winesburg. "The thing that happened was a woman." A woman musician in his boardinghouse makes Robinson's acquaintance. "She got to coming in there after there hadn't been anyone in the room for years," Enoch tells George Willard. "In she came and sat down beside me, just sat and looked about and said nothing. Anyway, she said nothing that mattered." The two simply sit and talk. "We just talked of little things, but I couldn't sit still," Robinson says. "I wanted to touch her with my fingers and to kiss her." Fear overcomes Enoch Robinson. "I had a feeling about her. She sat there in the room with me and she was too big for the room. I felt that she was driving everything else away." He becomes frantic and hysterical, trying to convince her "what a big thing I was in that room." Of course the woman cannot understand his hysterical ranting, but she knows enough from his curses to go away and never come back. "Things went to smash," Robinson tells young George. "Out she went through the door and all the life there had been in the room followed her out. She took all of my people away. They went out through the door after her. That's the way it was" (*WO*, 175–177).

George Willard cannot understand the meaning of the story: he is too young and inexperienced. Whether Anderson could is doubtful. But the tale is a paradigm of the relationship between Anderson's fiction and the shame of sexual desire, Oedipal in origin, that he felt to be unclean and disabling to his art. Revering his mother while raging at her abandonment of him, Anderson's conflict led him to abandon his wives before they could leave him, to insist on seclusion and privacy, and to brutalize them, if necessary, to have that room of his own.

I have mentioned that in "The Book of the Grotesque," Anderson's old writer, enclosed in his room, cannot begin to write until a procession of remembered figures, all of them grotesque, appears before him. The most important of them, an "almost beautiful" woman who is "all drawn out of shape," "hurt the old man by her grotesqueness. When she passed he made a noise like a small dog whimpering." It is only with the apparition of these grotesques, particularly the mother figure, that the old writer is able to creep out of bed and begin to write. None of the other women in Anderson's life could equal Emma Smith Anderson. She was the inspiration of his art and the figure he could not find in his many marriages. Anderson knew he had a perverse ability to step on women, to be "able to be a son of a bitch and pop right out of it as gay as a lark." [29] Thinking back over his treatment of various women, he remarked, "I could wreck myself forever on this shore. The whole coast is alive with the jagged rocks of my unkindness. . . . But if I began thinking of that I would go crazy." [30] Toward the end he told his daughter that if his writings proved "good and lasting," it would be "the only justification I shall ever be able to find for the inconvenience and suffering I have brought on others as well as myself" (*SA*, 65).

Whether the justification was adequate, readers of Anderson's work must decide. Kim Townsend is inclined to think that, "as a writer, he remains in Dreiser's shadow (which is exactly where he thought he belonged)." It is difficult to disagree with this judgment, or with Elizabeth Hardwick's view that Anderson is "unfailingly interesting" but largely "as *a case*" (*SA*, xii). For me, Anderson himself gave the best brief assessment of his art in calling himself the minor author of a minor masterpiece. To become this minor author cost him dearly, and those about him suffered a great deal of pain. Still, out of the process came some memorable fiction about the troubled state of the inner life.

---

29 *The Sherwood Anderson Diaries, 1936–1941*, ed. Hilbert H. Campbell (Athens: University of Georgia Press, 1987), p. 3.
30 *Sherwood Anderson: Selected Letters*, p. 109.

Hardy and Ellen Glasgow: Barren Ground

Ellen Glasgow is one of our most accomplished novelists of manners and an expert social historian. The range of her work, encompassing more than a score of books, is a testament to the energy of her imagination in telling the story of Southern society during the nineteenth and twentieth centuries, and to the acuity of her moral and psychological insight in dramatizing the private lives of her personae, against a background of social instability and accelerating change. In our literary histories she is properly represented as a signal figure in the Southern Renaissance, for she brought to life a compelling, ironic vision of the Tidewater and Piedmont regions after the Civil War.

For Miss Glasgow, as she observed in the preface to the Old Dominion edition of *Barren Ground*, "the novel is experience illumined by the imagination, and the word 'experience' conveys something more than an attitude or gesture."[1] What that "something more" suggests is a depth of philosophic understanding developed over a lifetime of reading, observation, and reflection. She felt *Barren Ground* to be her best novel, a work accurate in detail, graced by an "external verisimilitude," true to the landscape and character of Virginia, and vividly enriched by childhood memories—all of these constituting "lighter semblances folded over the heart of the book" (*BG*, viii.)

From the first, her aim, she wrote, had been to "write of the South not sentimentally, as a conquered province, but dispassionately, as a part

---

1 Ellen Glasgow, *Barren Ground* (New York: Doubleday, Doran, 1925), p. viii. Hereafter, quotations from the novel will be indicated by *BG,* in parentheses, in the text.

of the larger world." Yet so skillfully did she create a *Southern* world that her eminence as a chronicler of Virginia's social history remains unchallenged. Hers, in *Barren Ground* as elsewhere, was an American, a Southern, story; and many critics have found in her regionalism a rich ground for reflection about the actualities of her time and place. To see her fiction as a reflection of the social conditions of her time and place is altogether justified, and I have no wish to take issue with Allen Tate, Joan Foster Santas, Louise Field, Sara Haardt, C. Hugh Holman, Blair Rouse, and others who have sought the vital connection between her art and Virginia's life and history.[2] For to do so would be rash in view of the power and distinction of her critics, and in any event a violation of my own critical inclinations.

Instead I wish to take Ellen Glasgow, for the moment, on her own terms in order to emphasize anew what she herself stressed about her own work—namely, that *Barren Ground* (1925) objectified a resolve to "write not of Southern characteristics, but of human nature"; for she remarked that the "significance" of her work, its "quickening spirit, would not have varied . . . had I been born anywhere else." Clearly she was after a region more expansive than Queen Elizabeth County, or Virginia, or even the South. This locus was to be the site for the action of her best book, *Barren Ground*. Thus the "outward fidelity" of her dispassionate study of the South, "though important," was "not essential," as she remarked, to her "interpretation of life."

That interpretation of life took account of what lay beneath and beyond the Southern landscape and character. It took account of how the South, Virginia, and Queen Elizabeth County,

> apart from the human figures, possessed an added dimension, a universal rhythm deeper and more fluid than any material texture. Beneath the lights and shadows there is the brooding spirit of place, but, deeper still, beneath the spirit of the place, there is the whole movement of life (*BG*, viii).

The locus of this novel may thus be seen as an imagined world comparable to Faulkner's mythical Yoknapatawpha County or John O'Hara's Lantenengo County, "a world elsewhere," to use Richard Poirier's term, or, to use Louis Rubin's phrase, "no place on earth." Another way to define it would be to say that her landscape, though realistic, constitutes a *topos* or symbol of a metaphysical or philosophical interpretation of reality. Landscape in *Barren Ground* is thus mere repre-

---

2 For an excellent directive to Glasgow criticism, see Edgar E. MacDonald's "Ellen Glasgow" in *American Women Writers: Bibliographical Essays*, eds. Maurice Duke, Jackson R. Bryer, and M. Thomas Inge (Westport, Conn.: Greenwood Press, 1983), pp. 167–200.

sentation or objectification of spirit, spirit viewed as externalizing itself according to a cosmic rhythm she understood to be both tragic and divine.

I

In its imaginative form, though, this mythical region more properly relates to another country, to Wessex County. For in her struggle to descend through the actualities of the Virginia landscape to the brooding spirit of the place, and even deeper to the source of the whole movement of life, Miss Glasgow identifies herself with the metaphysical substratum of Thomas Hardy's best fiction. In reaching down toward the deeper rhythms of life, in *Barren Ground,* Ellen Glasgow, like Hardy, aspired to write a philosophical novel. Both writers shaped their philosophies of life out of a common stock of influences. Both were deeply read in what Miss Glasgow, in *The Woman Within,* called "the great scientists of the Victorian age"—Darwin, Huxley, Spencer, Haeckel—and in the contemporary philosophers of scientific thought.[3] Especially influential on Hardy was Schopenhauer, whose *Die Welt als Wille und Vorstellung* (*The World as Will and Idea*) was central.

Schopenhauer's idealistic philosophy posited the existence of a monistic Immanent Will—groundless and autonomous, aimless, unconscious, and indestructible—ceaselessly striving to objectify itself in phenomena, principally through the sexual urge.[4] Chance was an agency of this cosmic force, and it plays a profoundly moving part in the resolution of many of Hardy's plots. Later, Hardy discovered Eduard von Hartmann's *Die Philosophie des Unbewussten* (*The Philosophy of the Unconscious*), which posited the notion that the Unconscious Cosmic Power may eventually become conscious of Itself, just as, through an accident of evolutionary nature, the human mind had become self-conscious. Von Hartmann's ideas were engrafted onto Schopenhauer's, and in *The Dynasts* Hardy envisions a future world in which the Immanent Will—this blind, striving cosmic energy ceaselessly trying to objectify Itself—may grow self-reflective and end the cruelty and carnage manifest in the bloody imperfections of evolutionary history.

Like Hardy, Miss Glasgow was on a comparable philosophic quest. In "The Search for Truth," in *The Woman Within,* she offers a bewilder-

---

3 Ellen Glasgow, *The Woman Within* (New York: Harcourt, Brace, 1954), p. 89. Hereafter, quotations from this work will be cited as *WW,* in parentheses, in the text.

4 For an excellent discussion of Hardy's metaphysics, see Ernest Brennecke, Jr., *Thomas Hardy's Universe: A Study of a Poet's Mind* (1924; reprinted New York: Haskell House, 1966), especially pp. 13–34.

ing catalogue of books which were said to be influential on her. A full assessment of her fiction must take them all into account. Here one can only accent the significant books that formed a pattern consonant with the worldview I have linked to Thomas Hardy. Central to her development was Darwin, whose *Origin of Species* she studied "until I could have passed successfully an examination on every page." She was, she remarks, "looking for some hidden clue to experience, for some truth, or at least for some philosophy, which would help me to adjust my identity to a world I had found hostile and even malign. How could one live on without a meaning in life? Fortitude alone," she felt as a young woman, was "not enough to support life" (*WW,* 88–89).

In the early 1890s she read a great deal of German science as well as metaphysics and philosophy. The German science disappointed her, as did Pascal, because Pascal's Absolute did not combine "both spiritual yearning" and "hard bitten fact." Even the Absolute of Spinoza, whom she admired, was too impersonal and mathematical. Not until some time after the 1890s, she remarks, did it occur to her that the "German philosophers, especially Schopenhauer, would have been better reading, and that they possessed more of the hard truth I required—more, too, of that intellectual fortitude I was seeking." Of the German philosophy she studied, she remarked that "only *The World as Will and Idea* stayed with me, until, by pure accident, I discovered the great prose-poem, *Thus Spake Zarathustra*" (*WW,* 91). The importance of Schopenhauer's *The World as Will and Idea* to Miss Glasgow is developed in another passage of her autobiography, where she remarks that

> in spite of, or because of, his embittered compassion, Schopenhauer was the more human and certainly the more satisfying to the mortal seeker of wisdom. Moreover, alone among the modern philosophers, if we except the incomparable Santayana, who was then a stranger to me, Schopenhauer has a style that can survive, not only translation, but critical violence (*WW,* 173).

Both Hardy and Glasgow, then, were deeply influenced by the contemporary evolutionary theories that had eventuated in Schopenhauer's philosophy of the Immanent Will, or Cosmic Spirit, which objectifies Itself in matter. Both writers derived from him the notion of the world as idea, as mental projection, as mere representation. Both felt a natural awe at the vast, slow cosmic sweep of the evolutionary forces that had produced the world. But both were likewise dismayed at the meaningless carnage of the world, and they found in Schopenhauer a kindred pessimism about the conditions and character of life. But what about a more direct relationship between the two novelists?

II

It goes without saying that Miss Glasgow was extensively read in the fiction, poetry, and drama of the elder Hardy. There are extensive parallels between their fiction, as I shall suggest in the following pages. But the two writers also personally knew each other. In 1914 Miss Glasgow went to Dorchester expressly to see Hardy at Max Gate. Her remarks about him in *The Woman Within* and elsewhere are filled with reverence and admiration. On the occasion of that 1914 visit, Hardy told her that he considered *The Dynasts* his best work. Miss Glasgow remarks that "he was pleased when he found that I had read it all, and was able to repeat from the 'Semichorus of the Years':

O Immanence, that reasonest not
In putting forth all things begot,
Thou build'st Thy house in space—for what?"

She remarks: "Hardy smiled. 'Not many have read that'" (*WW*, 197).

That she had read it is not surprising. That she had memorized the passage testifies to the power over her of Hardy's vision of the Schopenhauerean Immanent Will, mindless, thrusting to put forth or objectify Itself in matter, but achieving its phenomenal representation to no end comprehensible to the human mind. *The Return of the Native* and *Jude the Obscure* were also favorite works of Miss Glasgow, who could "never decide" which she cared for most. She remarks of this 1914 visit that "From the beginning, it was easy to reach an understanding [with Hardy]. In our philosophy of life we soon touched a sympathetic chord; for he told me that he also had suffered all his life over the inarticulate agony of the animal world" (*WW*, 198). When Miss Glasgow visited the Wessex novelist again in 1927, she told Anne Virginia Bennett that she had found Hardy to be "attractive" and "far more advanced than most men of twenty-five"; and she remarked that old age had not "deadened his sensibility in the least." And she told Van Wyck Brooks in 1939 that Hardy "was to me the most sympathetic Englishman, and one of the most sympathetic persons I have ever known. Nothing rang hollow in his nature."[5]

The sensibility and sympathy that burned in Hardy until the end shine in the Wessex novels, which do for Dorchester what Ellen Glasgow wished to do for Richmond and its environs. Hardy was thus, for her, a "strong predecessor" (the phrase is Harold Bloom's) whose work could be imitated or contradicted, rewritten, overturned, or in some way transcended, but not ignored. In her case it was more nearly an imita-

---

5 *Letters of Ellen Glasgow*, ed. Blair Rouse (New York: Harcourt, Brace, 1958), pp. 89, 258.

tion than a contradiction, or at least an intent to share with readers a point of view they both had independently developed and that she had found and appreciated in Hardy's writings. Neither writer was in fact a philosopher. Indeed, Hardy called himself an "impressionist"; he described his speculative interpretations as "seemings." But Hardy and Glasgow organized their impressions so suggestively that a metaphysical statement about man and the world can be abstracted from the novels, tentative though it must be for each writer. The Wessex novels constitute a model for the "seemings" devised by Ellen Glasgow, for the "lighter semblances" folded over the heart of her work. To study the parallels between Hardy's novels and *Barren Ground* is to grasp the imaginative relation between the two writers, to perceive the parallel in their joint philosophic quest, and to locate the hidden map of Miss Glasgow's intriguing landscape.

III

Both novelists were absorbed by the conflict between the self and impersonal fate. In each the landscape is made to be symbolic of fate as well as an incarnation of the Life Force, or Immanent Will. *Barren Ground*, as Miss Glasgow remarks, is a novel of character "concerned with the place and tragedy of the individual in the universal scheme."[6] Like *Virginia* (1913) and *Vein of Iron* (1935), it treats of "the perpetual conflict of characters with fate, of the will with the world, of the dream with reality." One may grant that Dorinda Oakley is a powerful character. But the title of the novel throws the emphasis on the landscape. For, like Egdon Heath in *The Return of the Native*, the land in *Barren Ground* is anterior to and more powerful than the human ephemeridae who pass across its surface or transiently inhabit it.

The close resemblance between the sinister and encroaching fields of broomsedge in *Barren Ground* and the furze of Hardy's Egdon Heath in *The Return of the Native* is more than coincidental and has been remarked by critics like Frederick P. W. McDowell.[7] Most often, however, it is "explained" as an expression of the "land mystique" of Southern agrarianism. Yet Glasgow's remarks about the land resonate more urgently with the Hardyean source. Let us consider some parallels. In *The Return of the Native*, Hardy writes:

The untameable, Ishmaelitish thing that Egdon now was it always had

---

6 *Letters of Ellen Glasgow*, p. 206.
7 See McDowell's *Ellen Glasgow and the Ironic Art of Fiction* (Madison: University of Wisconsin Press, 1960.)

been. Civilization was its enemy; and ever since the beginning of
vegetation its soil had worn the same antique brown dress, the natural
and invariable garment of the particular formation. . . . [E]verything
around and underneath had been from prehistoric times as unaltered as
the stars overhead. . . . The sea changed, the fields changed, the rivers,
the villages, and the people changed, yet Egdon remained.[8]

Barren Ground likewise opens with a long description of the
"melancholy brown of the landscape" reminiscent of the heather of
Egdon. In winter "the country appeared obscure, solitary, vaguely
menacing" (*BG*, 26). It is marked by a "brooding loneliness," as if "the
landscape waited, plunged in melancholy, for the passing of a ray of
sunshine" (*BG*, 31). For Dorinda as a child, "the land contained a terrible force, whether for good or evil she could not tell, and there were
hours when the loneliness seemed to rise in a crested wave and surge
over her" (*BG*, 38). The broomsedge is lush, its growth harsh, its depths
at times "impenetrable." In summer "only the broomsedge thrived in the
furnace of the earth, and sprang up in a running fire over the waste
places" (*BG*, 118). Broomsedge is

> the one growth in the landscape that thrived on barrenness; the solitary
> life that possessed an inexhaustible vitality. To fight it was like fighting
> the wild, free principle of nature. Yet [the farmers] had always fought it.
> They had spent their force for generations in the endeavor to uproot it
> from the soil, as they had striven to uproot all that was wild and free in
> the spirit of man (*BG*, 128).

Glasgow's intentions could not be more explicit. An embodiment of
the principle of freedom and wildness, the broomsedge symbolizes the
force and energy of existence—wild, untamable, fecund and fertile,
thrusting ceaselessly and procreatively to extend itself, even over the
barren wastes. Dorinda has "a swift perception, which was less a thought
than a feeling, and less a feeling than an intuitive recognition, that she
and her parents were products of the soil as surely as were the scant
crops and the exuberant broomsedge. Had not the land entered into
their souls and shaped their moods into permanent or impermanent
forms?" (*BG*, 128). The question is rhetorical. The land, its inhabitants,
and the vegetation are phenomenal forms of an indwelling spirit, élan,
or energy, like Hardy's Immanent Will, which has materially objectified
itself, as on Egdon Heath, in an evolutionary development. Dorinda and

---

8 Thomas Hardy, *The Return of the Native*, ed. James Gindin (New York: W. W. Norton,
  1969), p. 5. Hereafter, citations from this text will be given as *RN*, in parentheses, in the
  text.

the others are "products," a term that implies naturalistic determinism. (Whether Dorinda is a creature of free will or a determined character is problematic. Elsewhere Miss Glasgow describes Dorinda as "free to grow, to change, to work out her own destiny.")[9] In any event, it is this energy which is permanent and enduring beneath the transient forms of social change, this energy which filters and flows into Dorinda's blood and brain, which strengthens and refreshes her.

"What no one has perceived," Miss Glasgow later complained, "is that the elements of Time and Space are the dominant powers. From the beginning, I tried to evoke a background of unlimited space, 'where the flatness created an illusion of immensity' and 'over the immutable landscape human lives drifted and vanished like shadows.' Behind the little destinies of men and women," she remarked—in a passage that might well be applied to Egdon (with its Roman, even prehistoric antiquities)—"I felt always that unconquerable vastness in which nothing is everything" (*ACM*, 158–159).

As in Hardy's *The Return of the Native*, the barren land of Glasgow's narrative is alive, even sentient. Hardy writes at one point that Egdon "became full of a watchful intentness now; for when other things sank brooding to sleep the heath appeared slowly to awake and listen" (*RN*, 3). "I wonder if everything has a soul?" (*BG*, 11), Dorinda wonders. And indeed the land does. In the October landscape,

> external objects lost their inanimate character and became as personal, reserved, and inscrutable as [Dorinda's] own mind. So sensitive were her perceptions, while she walked there alone, that the wall dividing her individual consciousness from the consciousness of nature vanished with the thin drift of woodsmoke over the fields (*BG*, 133–134).

The "whole landscape waited, inarticulate but alive" (*BG*, 184), for Dorinda's decision to leave the land for New York. She cannot escape the feeling that "the land thought and felt, that it possessed a secret personal life of its own" (*BG*, 37).

Earth in Glasgow's novel may be inarticulate and may never speak, as it does in Hardy's *The Dynasts*, but the spirit that animates the land, the broomsedge, the pine, and life-everlasting animates animals and people as well. Dorinda's father's hands are "gnarled, twisted, and earth-stained like the vigorous roots of a tree." His features, "browned and reddened and seamed by sun and wind, appeared as old as a rock embedded in earth." All his life, Miss Glasgow wrote, "he had been a

---

9 Ellen Glasgow, *A Certain Measure: An Interpretation of Prose Fiction* (New York: Harcourt, Brace., 1958), p. 155. Hereafter, quotations from this work will be given as *ACM*, in parentheses, in the text.

slave to the land, harnessed to the elemental forces struggling inarticulately against the blight of poverty and the barrenness of the soil. Yet Dorinda had never heard him rebel. His resignation was the earth's passive acceptance of sun or rain" (*BG*, 40–41). He has unusual sympathy with animals and speaks to his horses, Dan and Beersheba, in "the intimate language of the heart" (*BG*, 97). Mystically associated with the towering harp-shaped pine tree in the family graveyard, Mr. Oakley is closer to natural forms than to human society. That he should have a closer kinship with inhuman nature seems to Mrs. Oakley "a heathenish way to think about things, . . . but I can't help feeling there's a heap of comfort in it" (*BG*, 304). In this remark we may sense the depths of pagan, pre-Christian animism that is everywhere operative in Hardy's *The Return of the Native* and that is voiced most explicitly by his chorus of peasant characters on whom "civilization" has had little effect.

Miss Glasgow has Dorinda pick up some "biological patter" from Dr. Farraday in New York. This patter is never spelled out, and the term seems pejorative. But it nevertheless seems clear that Dorinda (and Miss Glasgow) affirm the notion, advanced in Hardy through Schopenhauer, that the world is Idea, or mental representation. Periodically throughout the novel, the "reality" of these natural phenomena to which humanity is allied is called into question; the idea is advanced that the world is a mere projection of mind, "as if the eternal world were merely a shadow thrown by the subjective processes within her soul" (*BG*, 144), as if each person were "a universe in one's self" (*BG*, 185). Again, "some natural melancholy in the scene drifted through her mind and out again into the landscape" (*BG*, 196). "Does it really look this way," Dorinda asks at one point about the landscape, "or is it only in my mind?" (*BG*, 377).

The idea that nature may be, as Emerson called it in *Nature*, an "apocalypse of the mind," a projection of consciousness, is an ancient one that T. S. Eliot had in mind in *After Strange Gods*, when he remarked of Hardy:

> In consequence of his self-absorption, he makes a great deal of landscape; for landscape is a passive creature which lends itself to an author's mood. Landscape is fitted, too, for the purposes of an author who is interested not at all in men's minds, but only in their emotions, and perhaps only in men as vehicles for emotions.[10]

Both Hardy and Glasgow, however, personify the landscape for more than affective purposes. The technique is a way of asserting idealism as

---

10 T. S. Eliot, *After Strange Gods* (1934), quoted in Katherine Anne Porter, "Some Notes on a Criticism of Thomas Hardy," *Southern Review*, 6 (Summer 1940), 150–161.

the key to philosophic understanding. In any case, Dorinda's questions about the interpenetration of mind and phenomena, posed without answer, such "as-if" constructions about the order of nature as a projection of consciousness, are signatures of Thomas Hardy, whose presence looms in the background of Dorinda's wonder.

Barren Ground is thus a study in the relation of character to the land and to the vital spirit that informs and animates all living beings. Mr. Oakley and Dorinda, like Hardy's peasants, are in pagan harmony with the deeper rhythms of existence, suggested by the passage of the seasons, the eternal return of plowing and planting, tending and harvesting. Even the names of Glasgow's characters—Matthew Fairlamb, James Ellgood, Joshua Oakley—have suggestive Hardyean sources and parallels, like Grandfer Cantle, Timothy Fairway, and Gabriel Oak. In both writers the names are thus appropriate to those inseparable from the animal and agricultural kingdom which exists far from the madding crowd.[11]

Personal problems come and go, and even a world war erupts toward the close of *Barren Ground,* but the milking must be done. Dorinda's final insight—that "while the soil endures, while the seasons bloomed and dropped, while the ancient beneficent ritual of sowing and reaping moved in the fields, she knew that she could never despair of contentment" (*BG,* 525)—is virtually indistinguishable in spirit from Hardy's observation (in "In Time of 'The Breaking of Nations'") that the plowing of farms and the burning of couch-grass "will go onward the same though dynasties pass."

To this catalogue of Hardyean parallels we might add that in *Barren Ground,* as in Hardy's fiction, chance plays a powerful role in determining a character's fate. Nathan's journey, the meeting of Jason on the road, "the failure of her aim when the gun had gone off," and "the particular place she had fallen down in Fifth Avenue," are all instances of what Hardy, in "Hap," had called "crass casualty" and Dicing Time." This agency of the cosmic process profoundly alters Dorinda's course, as she herself recognizes. "These accidents had utterly changed the course of her life. Yet none of them," Miss Glasgow remarks, "could she have foreseen and prevented; and only once, she felt, in that hospital in New York, had the accident or the device of fortune been in her favour" (*BG,* 416). Thus destiny *seems* to be malign, manipulating the self for pur-

---

11 Hardy called his peasants "the philosophic party" because they lived "in that continuity with their environment which for Hardy is the one root of life," observes John Holloway in *The Victorian Sage: Studies in Argument* (Hamden, Conn.: Archon Books, 1962), pp. 286–287. For a fuller treatment of how these peasants are organic expressions of the geography and climate, see Ruth A. Firror, *Folkways in Thomas Hardy* (1931; reprinted New York: Russell and Russell, 1968).

poses of its own, which conflict with personal desire. These "purblind Doomsters" had as readily strown blisses about her pilgrimage as pain.

Even so, in both Hardy and Glasgow, character is fate. This maxim by Novalis, which Hardy makes central to *The Mayor of Casterbridge,* is appropriated by Ellen Glasgow in *Barren Ground* as the "one dominant meaning" of the work (*BG,* ix). Like Hardy, Miss Glasgow tells here the story of the seduced heroine—another Fanny Robbins, another Tess, a Thomasin. The book was meant to be, Miss Glasgow announced, "a complete reversal of a classic situation. For once, in Southern fiction, the betrayed woman would become the victor instead of the victim" (*ACM,* 160). Young Dorinda, like Tess, is a pure girl, a mere vessel of emotion, untinctured by experience, incapable of resisting the power of sexual energy flowing into her.

Like her mother and ancestresses, she tries "to find a door in the wall, an escape from the tyranny of things as they are" (*BG,* 187). Of her namesake, the great-aunt Dorinda, Miss Glasgow writes that "When she couldn't get the man she'd set her heart on, she threw herself into the millrace," but she was fished out, dried off, sobered down, and married somebody else, "and was as sensible as anybody until the day of her death." Another, Abigail, "went deranged about her man" and was put away "in a room with barred windows" (*BG,* 104–105).

These parables in Dorinda's past testify to the irrational derangement of sexual passion from generation to generation, which leads Dorinda to succumb to Jason Greylock's amorous advances. Sexuality in this novel is a dark region, a Congo of the psyche, where impulse and anarchy reign. Dorinda's young sensuality, and her dissatisfaction with "things as they are," not to speak of her goddesslike body, are reminiscent of Eustacia Vye. And the anguish of the young woman, betrayed by a sexual passion she could neither understand nor control, is as poignant in *Barren Ground* as it is in *Tess,* where the milkmaids at Talbothays suffer a yearning for Angel Clare that they cannot even name. Abandoned by her lover, Dorinda tries to murder Jason, just as Tess murders Alex, out of a like sense of betrayal.

Jason Greylock, like Sergeant Troy, is a seducer, a man out of phase with the natural rhythms of life. He has no inner strength; he is out of touch with the land. In the end, as old Matthew predicts, the land conquers Jason (*BG,* 16). "As Dorinda conquered the land, which was, for her, the symbol of fate," Miss Glasgow later wrote, "so Jason surrendered through inherited weakness" (*ACM,* 161). Aspects of his story are reminiscent of the plot of *The Return of the Native.* But it is in fact Dorinda who most resembles Clym Yeobright, for it is she who is really the native returning to educate the ignorant in modern farming methods.

The consequences of Dorinda's seduction—loss of belief in religion and loss of belief in love—profoundly alter her. With respect to orthodox religion, Miss Glasgow shapes her experience to that of Tess Durbeyfield. If Tess is harassed by the stile painter, who threatens her with eternal damnation for her sexual sin, Dorinda encounters the "gospel rider," Brother Tyburn, with his ominous warning "Prepare to Meet Thy God." Her loss of belief in love plunges Dorinda into an abnormal sexual frigidity. Her fear of male sexuality eventually gives way to hatred, then contempt, then smug superiority. She cannot bear the thought of marriage; nor, like Hardy, can she bear to be touched (*BG*, 250). (It would be improbable to suggest that Miss Glasgow is here making fictive use of Hardy's well-known phobia of being touched. Perhaps it is enough to say that, in this frigidity, Dorinda is like the fallen Tess with Angel Clare; and in the abnormality of her sexual aversion she is like Sue Bridehead in *Jude the Obscure*. In any event, there is no doubt whatever in the reader's mind that once Dorinda sexually falls, she is through with all that.)

Dorinda's substitute for religion and romance is an attachment to the land and the development of a stoic philosophy in which love has no place. Dorinda becomes the woman farmer, like Tess; the agricultural manager, like Bathsheba Everdene. To the backwater district she, like Donald Farfrae in *The Mayor of Casterbridge*, brings modern agricultural methods. A composite of many Hardyean figures (and much more besides), Dorinda is perhaps most like the furze-cutter Clym Yeobright in that she returns from the big city to the "heath" in order to educate the superstitious and ignorant natives in how to retrieve the land from the ceaseless growth of broomsedge. Above all, she is single-minded in her agricultural pursuits.

Life, for the seduced and abandoned heroine, devolves into a continuous struggle against the spreading of broomsedge, which gives way to pine, and then to life-everlasting—the whole process threatening constantly to reclaim the acres of cultivated land, to overgrow the farms, and even to swallow up Five Oaks, Old Farm, Honeycomb Farm, the Old Haney Place (outposts of human civilization dotting the wilderness landscape). For Dorinda, "reclaiming the abandoned fields" is transformed from "a reasonable purpose" into "a devouring passion in her mind and heart" (*BG*, 409). To burn the broomsedge back, to grub up the scrub pine, to destroy the sassafras, to plow under the thistles: these constitute in her a veritable and terrifying obsession, an assertion of pure will against the order of nature. "Endurance," "the fibre of courage," "fortitude": these terms chime throughout the novel and serve to characterize the "vein of iron" in Dorinda's soul, an "essential self" superior to her folly and ignorance, "superior even to the conspiracy of circumstances that hemmed her in" (*BG*, 184). She will not be broken. In this aspect of Dorinda, Miss Glasgow created an archetypal form of Nietzschean will: Dorinda "exists wherever a human being has learned to live without joy, wherever the spirit of fortitude has triumphed over the sense of futility" (*BG*, viii). How similar this is to Hardy's conclusion that, given "the antilogy of making figments feel," life was "a thing to be put up with"; and that Sophocles was right—"not to be born is best."[12]

IV

In Dorinda's final philosophy of stoic endurance, Miss Glasgow borrowed from Hardy's general worldview and his characterization of Eustacia Vye and Elizabeth Jane in *The Mayor of Casterbridge*. For Eustacia "love was but a doleful joy" (*RN*, 56); and Elizabeth Jane's experience teaches her that life and its surroundings "were a tragical, rather than a comical thing, that though one could be gay on occasion, moments of gayety were interludes, and no part of the actual drama." Dorinda, like Elizabeth Jane, comes to understand "the persistence of the unforeseen," to accept the "lesson of renunciation," and to conclude that "happiness was but the occasional episode in the general drama of pain."[13] From such recognitions comes the serenity of each heroine.

Some recent Glasgow criticism has found commendable Dorinda's renunciation of love and marriage. Linda W. Wagner is not atypical in finding in *Barren Ground* a confirmation of Mrs. Oakley's view of marriage: "just the [woman's] struggle to get away from things as they are" (*BG*, 103). And it is no doubt true that Miss Glasgow, who never married, felt profound relief at the termination of her own engagement to Henry W. Anderson:

> Nothing, apparently, had changed—nothing, except that I was free. The obscure instinct that had warned me, in my early life, against marriage, was a sound instinct. . . . I was free from chains. I belonged to myself. . . . After more than twenty-one years, I was at last free. If falling in love could be bliss, I discovered, presently, that falling out of love could be blissful tranquillity. I had walked from a narrow overheated place out into the bracing autumnal colors. People and objects resumed their natural proportions. . . . Gradually, as this grasp weakened and relaxed,

---

12 For a discussion of Hardy's stoic fatalism, see Harvey Curtis Webster, *On a Darkling Plain: The Art and Thought of Thomas Hardy* (Chicago: University of Chicago Press, 1947), pp. 147–152.

13 Thomas Hardy, *The Mayor of Casterbridge* (New York: Harper's, 1922), pp. 384–386.

all the other parts of my nature, all that was vital and constructive, returned to life. Creative energy flooded my mind, and I felt, with some infallible intuition, that my best work was ahead of me. I wrote *Barren Ground,* and immediately I knew I had found myself (*WW,* 243).

For Linda Wagner, Dorinda's rejection of marriage and children in order to find "self-fulfilling directions for her healthy existence" in managing the farm is a veiled dramatization of Miss Glasgow's personal decision to forgo marriage and devote herself to fiction. Yet was she condemned to this either-or dilemma? Writers may of course make bad marriages. But the happy marriages of Edgar and Virginia Poe, Kate and Oscar Chopin, Vera and Vladimir Nabokov, and Raymond Smith and Joyce Carol Oates (among other writers) suggests that supreme devotion to "the high priesthood of art," as a reason for rejecting marriage, is a fairly paltry idea that actually died out with Henry James.[14] In any case, Dorinda's view of endurance differs from that of the admirable Hardy in its antihuman obsessiveness. Unlike Elizabeth Jane, for example, Dorinda lacks human compassion: for her murdering brother; for her perjured mother; for Nathan, her heroic husband; for Jason, one of nature's failures. The defense mechanisms of wounded pride in this seduced and abandoned heroine are such as to ensure that she will never achieve the happiness that most women seek. Her trauma, her grievance against Jason, is turned back against herself: How could she have been so "weak" as to love, to care, to trust! Grimly determined to resist and refuse the human rhythms of erotic and familial existence, she dismisses the reality and power of love as an illusion and thus forfeits the happiness that may attend it. In the end, "the conflict of frustrated desires" (*BG,* 524) is too much for Dorinda to cope with, though it may rightfully be called the mark and condition of our vital existence, the mark of what it means to be human. Still, Miss Glasgow found the repression of desire to be as necessary for her heroine as it was for herself: Dorinda's destiny is to work out "the implicit philosophy" of the author, which is summed up in the phrase: "one may learn to live, one may even learn to live gallantly, without delight" (*ACM,* 155). Readers may wonder whether Dorinda's renunciations are heroic and noble or merely, like those of Sue Bridehead, pathological. Nevertheless, in *Barren Ground,* Ellen Glasgow achieved a magisterial vision of human will and fortitude, a work complex in the forms of its indebtedness to the mind and art of Thomas Hardy, but a work transcendently her own.

---

14 Linda W. Wagner, *Ellen Glasgow: Beyond Convention* (Austin: University of Texas Press, 1982), p. 80.

The
Physician-Writer
and the
Cure of the Soul

I observe the physician with the same diligence
as he the disease.
                    —John Donne, *Devotions*

When a physician becomes a writer, what is the effect of his
scientific training on his vision of the world? Is there an observ-
able difference in the literature he produces, as reflected in point of view
and style as well as in content or theme? Do the years in medical school
or the period of internship and residency permanently alter the way a
man or woman might otherwise record observations and describe the
crises of life and death? These are enigmas, but as questions they are no
less puzzling than why a doctor would even want to write at all.
Medicine is so demanding a profession that it comes as a surprise to hear
that a physician might have or reserve some time for composition. And
medicine is so highly valued a profession that it is surprising to encounter doctors who have given up a practice for the contagion of the
blank page. In any case, ruminations of this kind invariably arise when
we read the work of Chekhov, Schnitzler, Arthur Conan Doyle, William
Carlos Williams, Gottfried Benn, Dannie Abse, Michael Crichton, and
other physician-writers. In fact, in view of simple numbers, we might

very well recast the question. Why are there *so many* doctors who are writers as well? One intriguing answer has been posed by Thomas Szasz: the relationship between the writer and the physician, "compounded as it is of mutual attraction and admiration, of rivalry and even hostility, and of ceaseless fascination—qualifies as a true love affair."[1]

I

Doctors are fond of saying they belong to the "healing art." But while medicine is still an art, and perhaps even an *ars amatoria*, it began to become, in the late eighteenth and nineteenth centuries, a science as well, using the term "science" in relation to clinical experimentation in diagnosis and treatment. Eighteenth-century physician-writers such as Oliver Goldsmith or Tobias Smollett, who were hardly scientifically trained, were not much better off than Rabelais in the prescientific sixteenth century. Himself a physician, Rabelais remarked that the practice of medicine "must tend to one aim and purpose," namely, to "cheer his patient without offending God."[2] (That is still a central medical function and, in many intractable or terminal cases, it is probably the most important.) But since about 1850 physician-writers have been commonly more clinical, in so far as observation of human subjects is concerned, though clarity of observation of human phenomena is the hallmark of every *great* novelist. It was about 1852 that Flaubert, the son of a physician, remarked that "As time goes on, art will be scientific, just as science will become artistic."[3]

In retrospect, Flaubert's scientism was an historical blip, but an instance of his viewpoint is the profound effect on the novel of Dr. Claude Bernard's *Lessons in Experimental Physiology,* which, through its influence on Zola, resulted in the transformation of the novel into a naturalistic clinical experiment—an experiment *pour voir,* for the sake of seeing. In this paradigm, the novel tested out an hypothesis, often in connection with what used to be seen as moral imperfection—a vice such as alcoholism, venereal disease, unregenerate criminality, and so on. In *McTeague* (1899), Frank Norris accounts for his homicidal dentist with the genetic explanation—if his veins were a "sewer of vice" we ought to feel some sympathy, for McTeague is the helpless product of a biological inheritance of several generations of alcoholism and syphilis.

---

1 Thomas Szasz, "Literature and Medicine," *Literature and Medicine,* 1 (1982), 36.

2 François Rabelais, *Gargantua and Pantagruel,* trans. Jacques LeClercq (New York: Heritage Press, 1936), preface to Book IV, 3.

3 Gustave Flaubert, *Oeuvres,* ed. Maurice Nadeau (Lausanne: Editions Recontre, 1965), VI, 260.

Of course, daily exposure to the corruptions of the flesh may sour the doctor-writer and lead him to respond as Gottfried Benn did: "Die Krone der Schopfung, das Schwein, der Mensch" ["The crown of creation, the pig, man"].[4] But, on the whole, as Joanne Trautmann has observed, the physician-writer's medical training has been more often put to the service of expressing, and generating in the reader, a more compassionate understanding of frailty and human weakness.[5]

Chekhov said of his medical training: "I don't doubt that the study of the medical sciences seriously affected my literary work; they significantly enlarged the field of my observations, enriched me with knowledge, the true value of which for me as a writer can be understood only by one who is himself a physician."[6] And another doctor, Somerset Maugham, remarked that his medical training "was a valuable experience to me. I do not know a better training for a writer than to spend some years in the medical profession." It was useful, he thought, because the seriously ill drop the mask they wear in health, so that the doctor can see them as they are—both selfish and hard, grasping and cowardly, but brave and courageous as well. The doctor-writer thus sees character in its authenticity; thereby he comes to be tolerant of human weaknesses but impressed and awed by our virtues as well.[7]

Keats (trained in the apothecary's science) wrote in "The Fall of Hyperion" that "a poet is a sage; / A humanist, Physician to all men."[8] The physician's desire to write poetry, plays, and fiction may thus be seen as this aspiration to wisdom, to the condition of the sage. But as Cousins, Ceccio, and Meyers have shown, it is also founded on the desire to alleviate human suffering through dramatizing the dynamics of pain, suffering, and transcendence as only imaginative work of a high order can do.[9]

Something of this aspiration clearly underlay the work of Oliver Wendell Holmes, a physician whose "medicated novels" tried, through the medium of the psychological romance, to undermine theological notions that caused, in his view, needless suffering. This suffering, he thought, could be ameliorated through a proper understanding of how

---

4 From Stanza 2 of "Der Arzt" in Gottfried Benn's *Samtliche Werke* (Stuttgart: Klett-Cotta, 1986), I, 14.

5 Joanne Trautmann, *Healing Arts in Dialogue: Medicine and Literature* (Carbondale: Southern Illinois University Press, 1981).

6 *Letters of Anton Chekhov*, ed. Avrahm Yarmolinsky (New York: Viking Press, 1973), p. 352.

7 Somerset Maugham, *The Summing Up* (Garden City, N.Y.: Doubleday, 1938), p. 64.

8 For a treatment of Keats and medicine, see Donald C. Goellnicht, *The Poet-Physician: Keats and Medical Science* (Pittsburgh: University of Pittsburgh Press, 1984).

9 See Norman Cousins, ed., *The Physician in Literature* (Philadelphia: W. B. Saunders, 1982); Joseph Ceccio, *Medicine in Literature* (New York: Longmans, 1978); and Jeffrey Meyers, *Disease and the Novel, 1880–1960* (New York: St. Martin's Press, 1985).

character is shaped by external forces over which the individual may have no control. His heroine in *Elsie Venner: A Romance of Destiny* is a sinister creature with mesmerizing serpentine movements, glittering diamond eyes, and a poisonous tongue. It would be easy to call Elsie Venner "evil," for she exhibits qualities we customary define as such. Yet she is in fact a sister of Keats's Lamia and Coleridge's Christabel. About her one character remarks: something was "infused into her soul—it was cruel to call it malice—which was still and watchful and dangerous, which waited its opportunity, and then shot like an arrow from its bow out of the coil of brooding premeditation." If today we might call Elsie's serpent complex schizophrenic, Holmes, writing in 1861, intended to test the hypothesis that she might have been poisoned *in utero* when her pregnant mother was bitten by the crotalus snake:

> The real aim of the story was to test the doctrine of "original sin" and human responsibility for the disordered volition coming under that technical denomination. Was Elsie Venner, poisoned by the venom of a crotalus before she was born, responsible for the "volitional" aberrations, which translated into acts become what is known as sin and, it may be, what is punished as crime? If, on presentation of the evidence, she becomes by the verdict of the human conscience a proper object of divine pity and not of divine wrath, as a subject of moral poisoning, wherein lies the difference between her position at the bar of judgment, human or divine, and that of the unfortunate victim who received a moral poison from a remote ancestor before he drew his breath?[10]

In such remarks we see the scientific materialism of the Victorians busily at work trying to destroy the age-old association between disease and sin, with a concomitant social self-righteousness, moral judgment, and ostracism. It did not work, as any survey of the public response to the AIDS crisis will suggest. Once "moral poison" is seen as a material effect of biological inheritance, ethical chaos must ensue.

II

In Somerset Maugham's engaging novel *Of Human Bondage* (1915), the protagonist Philip Cary undergoes the medical training that Maugham had had at St. Thomas's medical school. In the outpatient clinic and emergency room, Philip eventually formulates the author's view of the meaning of human life:

---

10 Oliver Wendell Holmes, *Elsie Venner: A Romance of Destiny* (New York: New American Library, 1961), pp. xii–xiii.

But on the whole the impression was neither of tragedy nor of comedy. There was no describing it. It was manifold and various; there were tears and laughter, happiness and woe; it was tedious and interesting and indifferent; it was as you saw it: it was tumultuous and passionate; it was grave; it was sad and comic; it was trivial; it was simple and complex. . . . There was neither good nor bad there. There were just facts. It was life.[11]

Philip's medical experience is meant to teach him that life is basically amoral and that it has no transcendental spiritual meaning. Life, for the materialist physician-writer, is summed up in the parable of the Eastern King, which concludes of man: "he was born, he suffered, and he died" (*OHB*, 655). By giving him this perception Maugham means to free Philip Cary from the last of his bondages, the bondage of the illusion that life has intrinsic meaning, a comprehensible pattern; it is intended to free him to create his own pattern of a life. Toward the end Maugham writes of Philip:

He thought of his desire to make a design [of his life], intricate and beautiful, out of the myriad, meaningless facts of life; had he not seen also that the simplest pattern, that in which a man was born, worked, married, had children, and died, was likewise the most perfect? It might be that to surrender to happiness was to accept defeat, but it was a defeat better than many victories (*OFB*, 759).

And this is the design for living that Philip chooses, and, in marrying Sally Athelny, completes.

Maugham's vision in *Of Human Bondage* reflects much of the Zola-esque scientism that disfigured the *fin de siècle*, in particular the view that the soul is a superstition rendered null by the advance of scientific knowledge. And we are reminded that a great many scientists devised unsuccessful tests for locating the soul (weighing the human body, down to the last gram, both before and after death, and finding no difference). Late in his life, when he was in his seventies, Maugham asked in *A Writer's Notebook*, "What is the soul?"—by which he specified "my consciousness of myself" and the "personality compounded of my thoughts, my feelings, my experiences and accidents of my body":

My soul would have been quite different if I had not stammered, or if I had been four or five inches taller; I am slightly prognathous; in my childhood they did not know that this could be remedied by a gold

---

11 Somerset Maugham, *Of Human Bondage* (New York: Modern Library, 1942), pp. 500–501. Quotations from this work will hereafter be given as *OHB*, in parentheses, in the text.

band . . . ; if they had my countenance would have borne a different cast, the reaction toward me of my fellows would have been different and therefore my disposition. . . . But what sort of thing is this soul that can be modified by a dental apparatus?[12]

Maugham was, in fact, a materialist whose view of human nature, science, and the scientific method he gained in medical school. "I was glad to learn," he later wrote, "that the mind of man (himself the product of natural causes) was a function of the brain subject like the rest of the body to the laws of cause and effect, and that these laws were the same as those that governed the movement of star and atom."[13] Science, he said in another context, "is the consoler and healer of troubles, for it teaches how little things matter and how unimportant is life with all its failures."[14] *Of Human Bondage* suggests that the only happiness in life is to be found in perceiving that life is meaningless in terms of transcendental values and that, while a pattern may be woven out of the myriad strands of experience, the beauty, order, and significance of the pattern has meaning only for the individual, subjectively. Many will find this little consolation indeed!

III

But the manifest failure of scientism as a view of life, in the twentieth century, has meant that scientific training in medicine may not invariably lead the physician to conclusions so naturalistic as those of Holmes and Maugham. These reflections are suggested by the Ingersoll Foundation grant of the 1988 T. S. Eliot Award for Creative Writing to Dr. Walker Percy. Percy, author of several well-respected novels, including *The Moviegoer* (1961), *The Last Gentleman* (1966), *Love in the Ruins* (1971), *The Second Coming* (1980), and *The Thanatos Syndrome* (1987), received his medical training at Columbia University College of Physicians and Surgeons. He would doubtless have been content to practice medicine throughout his lifetime, with a special interest in pathology, had not he himself been immediately felled by disease. During his internship at Bellevue Hospital in New York City, where he performed some seventy-five autopsies on derelicts who had died of chronic diseases, he contracted pulmonary tuberculosis and was admitted to the Trudeau Sanitarium in the Adirondacks for a two-year convalescence. During this period of recovery he read widely, reflected deeply, and

---

12 Somerset Maugham, *A Writer's Notebook* (Garden City, N.Y.: Doubleday, 1949), p. 362.
13 Maugham, *The Summing Up*, p. 72.
14 Maugham, *A Writer's Notebook*, p. 24.

reconsidered his calling. If science had been his first intellectual discovery, his illness opened up to him the human predicament created by the world as transformed by contemporary science. What science could not address, he concluded, was the precise nature of the individual's life in this scientifically transformed world.

To describe what it is like for the living individual in our time was his lifelong project as a novelist. The abandonment of medicine for fiction was not, in his view, a particularly significant change. While he was deeply convinced of the seriousness of the study of medicine, he always contended that novel writing is a cognitive activity that discovers and interprets reality just as much as a physics experiment. As Lewis Lawson has rightly observed, for Percy "scientific research, medical diagnosis, and fiction writing are essentially identical activities."[15] Percy turned to fiction precisely because it offered a special opportunity for understanding and a great clinical responsibility: the diagnosis of the soul's ill. In his several novels Percy was absorbed by the question of why the average middle-class American, who is customarily well-fed, -clothed, -housed, and in other material ways provided for, suffers such a malaise, such unhappiness: a despair that has no name. This existential dread he found evident in American fiction as well as in American life. "What happens to Sinclair Lewis's Dodsworth after he settles down in Capri?" he asked. What happens to the Midwesterners of Sinclair Lewis or "to the Okie [of John Steinbeck] who succeeds in Pomona and now spends his time watching Art Linkletter? Is all well with them or are they in deeper trouble than they were on Main Street and in the dust bowl? If so, what is the nature of the trouble?"[16]

The nature of the trouble, as *Love in the Ruins* and *The Thanatos Syndrome* make plain, is that men in our time, like their predecessors, have a sense of themselves as pilgrims in transit, but, having lost the direction provided by traditional religion and having embraced a secular scientism, they have a sickness of soul that none of the institutions of contemporary society can heal. Setting aside the physiological and pathological processes of the human body, what came to interest Percy was the larger problem of man's nature and destiny as problematized by his modern technological society. For Percy, the current human problem was not one that a psychiatrist could cure. Percy wrote from the vantage

---

15 Lewis Lawson, *Following Percy: Essays on Walker Percy's Work* (Troy, N.Y.: Whitson, 1988), p. 237. Percy elaborated on the diagnostic function of the novelist in *Diagnosing the Modern Malaise* (New Orleans: Faust Publishing, 1985) and in "Physician as Novelist," *Chronicles: A Magazine of American Culture,* (May 1989), 10–12.

16 Walker Percy, "Notes for a Novel About the End of the World," in *The Message in the Bottle* (New York: Farrar, Straus and Giroux, 1975), p. 103.

point of Christian existentialism. This view assumed that the vital principle in the material body is in fact a soul but that technological society
has deprived us of access to understanding what it is. And to the extent
that one stakes his well-being on the "objective-empirical" view of life,
to that extent he is alienated from his own existence and suffers what
Kierkegaard called dread and anxiety, fear and trembling, and the sickness unto death.

For Percy it was Christianity, filtered through the existentialism of
Kierkegaard, Jaspers, Heidegger, and Marcel that offered the antidote to
the modern malaise. In this respect, as one critic has observed, Percy
"tends to move in on the territory once held by the theologian."[17] Percy,
however, was never evangelical in proposing a remedy: he was clinical in
acting the diagnostician and pathologist who identifies the symptoms so
as to lead the reader into a fuller consciousness of the nature of modern
suffering. Even his own protagonist in *Love in the Ruins* (1971) and *The
Thanatos Syndrome* (1987), Dr. Thomas More (a psychiatrist and a col-
lateral descendant of the saint), cannot understand what the cure of soul
involves, for he tries with a mechanical invention called the lapsometer
"to treat a spiritual disease with a scientific device," only to acknowledge
finally the therapy of faith. In such ways Percy's novels are "healthy
texts"—as opposed to much of the diseased and pornographic work that
pollutes the literary stream—and are thus iatric and meliorative in their
effect.

In the long run, Percy's view is like that of Karl Jaspers, the existential philosopher who was also a doctor. In "The Doctor and Patient,"
published in *Philosophy and the World,* Jaspers wrote:

> Today the need is once again for a conscious distinction of medical cure
> from the cure of souls, of the physician from the minister of religion.
> With the blurring of the physician's role we lose the seriousness of
> religion, and at the same time the purity of a medical skill based on
> science. The doctor must not come to be a substitute. He cannot
> provide what people secretly expect of him. . . . In the wish to entrust
> themselves to the doctor as a guide to the conduct of their lives, many
> moderns find an escape from seriousness into convenience. It is their
> lack of faith which leads them to confuse the doctor with the priest.[18]

The failure of science and medical technology, along with other
secular institutions, to assuage modern alienation and to create a utopia

---

17 Martin Luschei, *The Sovereign Wayfarer: Walker Percy's Diagnosis of the Malaise* (Baton
Rouge: Louisiana State University Press, 1972), p. 239.
18 Karl Jaspers, "The Doctor and Patient," *Philosophy and the World,* trans. E. B. Ashton
(Chicago: Henry Regnery, 1963), pp. 190–191.

in the *old* Sir Thomas More's sense of the word, gives Percy, among others, a ground for exploring afresh the nature of the human spirit and its maladies. In the case of a skeptic like Maugham, both the individual's life-style and the novelist's art were posed as substitutes for religion, in the sense that the creation of the work of art (and of a life) involved the interweaving of the multiple and varicolored strands of observed human experience into an intricate design, a pattern, that made sense of the world. Despite Maugham's strictures on Pater's defects of style, this is the Paterian aesthete's response to the felt amorality of existence. But for a writer like Percy, art, in spite of its acclaimed dignity and majesty, can never substitute for the Judeo-Christian religious conception of the soul. For Percy the soul is not something that a gold band can heal, along with a prognathous bite, but rather a central and continuing mystery, beyond the reach even of psychiatry. But if the medical doctor cannot cure souls, his imaginative vision of our deeper spiritual experience may help to define what is making this era the Age of Death, Thanatos.

These two doctor-novelists, Maugham and Percy, I have presented as twentieth-century extremes of a sort, within the outer limits of which certainly lie other visions of the relationship between medicine and literature. At the extremes it appears still to come down to body and soul, the flesh and the spirit, heaven and earth, the old familiar dualisms. After the original presentation of these remarks in 1988, at the Twentieth-Century Literature Conference in Louisville, Kentucky, a hitherto unknown, undated essay by Percy, entitled "Is a Theory of Man Possible?," was posthumously published.[19] In the essay Percy traced the mind-body split to Descartes, dismissed it as out of date, complained that "there does not presently exist a coherent theory of man in the scientific sense," and undertook to invent a theory and to resolve the "angel-beast" dichotomy through, of all things, a system of semiotics. Far from healing the split, though it nobly undertook to do so, Percy's reflections on the subject only confirmed for me the conclusion arrived at so elegantly so long ago by Sir Thomas Browne, himself a doctor, who remarked in *Religio Medici* [*The Religion of a Doctor*] (1643) that man is "that great and true *Amphibium* whose nature is disposed to live not onely like other creatures in divers elements, but in divided and distinguished worlds."[20] That observation still serves rather well to define our present situation.

---

19 Walker Percy, "Is a Theory of Man Possible?" in *Signposts in a Strange Land,* ed. Patrick Samway (New York: Farrar, Straus and Giroux, 1991), pp. 111–129.
20 Sir Thomas Browne, Part I, Section 34 of *Religio Medici,* ed. Jean-Jacques Denonain (Cambridge: Cambridge University Press, 1953), p. 5.

Jacques et moi

Understanding is a special case of
misunderstanding.
—Jonathan Culler, *On Deconstruction*

Sitting here in my university office, looking out of the window toward Washington Square Park in New York City, I observe a rather peaceful scene at the moment. The noise of the city traffic has hushed, the flags of the university drift lazily above the buildings, and the students are standing about in groups or strolling across the park. All these snapshots are surprising evocations, of a sort, of the square as it used to be—that "ideal of genteel retirement" that Henry James remembered from his youth and tried realistically to represent a century ago in that splendid little tale *Washington Square* (1881). James is always worth thinking about, especially in relation to the theory of art (as expressed in, say, "The Art of Fiction" or "The Real Thing"). But James and the distant horizon of the square now fade in my memory and are replaced with a sharper and more immediate consideration: Jacques Derrida, the father of French deconstructionism, has joined the faculty of New York University, at least on a part-time basis. He is to teach a course, every fall, for the next few years. This appointment, it is fair to say, has put me to reconsidering some writers whom I regularly teach, writers whose aesthetic intention was manifest as a call to represent life as they had seen it—the young James, the young Howells, Mark Twain, Hamlin Garland, Edward Eggleston, Edgar Watson Howe, John William DeForest, the local colorists such as Mary Wilkins Freeman, Kate Chopin, Sarah Orne Jewett, and others of that time.

The writing of these American literary realists after the Civil War has always appealed to me because (however inconsistent they were in practice) their intent was admirable—to rescue American literature from the domestic sentimentalism and defunct romantic symbolism of the antebellum popular writers and to sweep away the vestigial remnants of a saccharine worldview and a literary aesthetic that had outlived its usefulness but had survived in vestigial form into the 1870s. Much of what these realists believed about the capacity of literature to represent reality survived into the literary program of the naturalists, who, in a qualified way, are included in the vexed ruminations that follow.[1] In any case, these thoughts are occasioned by the convergence in my mind of M. Derrida and the theory of American literary realism. Not only is he to give a course each fall to our students; he has also been assigned the office next door to mine. The hallway has therefore been busier than usual. I hear the hurried footfalls of those who cannot defer knowing the difference between *différence* and *différance* and hope, by learning it, to be granted a glimpse into the abyss. Here I sit wondering what he will tell my students, who have just begun to grasp with full understanding Howells's call for a literature that faithfully represents reality.

If my ruminations are vexed, it is not, in any case, with the man himself—whom I have welcomed with all collegiality and who, personally, has been very charming at the informal parties where this faculty invariably avoid discussing their work. On such occasions I have always found M. Derrida quite congenial, though rather enigmatic—perhaps because my French cannot not be risked in serious conversation, perhaps because his English offers a barrier to intrusive ontotheological personalities like myself. In any case, the other day I asked him what was the topic of his graduate seminar. "Secrets," he answered, and it seemed clear that I would get nothing more from him about *that.*

I afterward reflected that there were many secrets in Henry James, and even more in Derrida's premier disciple, Paul de Man. But it also came to me that James and like-minded realists loved secrets as engaging elements of human psychology—in the literary representation of life. But the covert or the overt—it hardly mattered to them: the novel was to show us as we were. Viewed theoretically, the realists' implicit (and sometimes explicit) notion of literature was allied to the great Platonic-Aristotelian tradition that viewed art as an imitation of the external world of nature. This grand tradition—emphasizing *mimesis*, verisim-

---

1 As a critical term, the polysemous "realism" is of course a lexicographer's mare's nest. But for some precision in understanding the meaning of the term as I use it here, see René Wellek's essay "The Concept of Realism in Literary Scholarship," in *Concepts of Criticism,* ed. Stephen G. Nichols, Jr. (New Haven: Yale University Press, 1963), pp. 222–255.

ilitude, *vraisemblance*—had been given a great injection of theoretical support in the Renaissance (Hamlet's line about holding a mirror up to nature is an instance of it, as is Sidney's "Apology"). Further, in the eighteenth century the mimetic view of literature was proclaimed anew in the neoclassical aesthetic of Dr. Johnson, Joshua Reynolds, Dryden, Pope, and others. These were the masters of theory in that era. But theory in that time was also matched by impressive practice. In the novel the great realistic narratives of Fielding, Smollett, and Austen constituted a model that was felt by Howells and other realists to be superior to the novel of sentimentality, the novel of seduction, the Gothic extravaganza, the symbolic romances of Monk Lewis, Radcliffe, Walpole, Poe, Hawthorne, Melville, and Simms. (Hawthorne in the post–Civil War period was the only American romancer to be accorded continuing respect, largely—I have always felt—because of the Christian morality explicit in his allegorical romances.)

Nowadays, it would seem, Plato, Socrates, and Aristotle—as expositors of *mimesis*—are out. The metaphysics founded in their thinking, the doctrines of the real and the represented, are said to be passé. Wouldn't it have been better, I was recently asked by an earnest graduate student, if our conception of reality had instead derived from the Presocratics? I had thought it better to get our concepts of reality from the real itself, but, no doubt, the obscure fragments of Anaximander, Heraclitus, and Parmenides have their ongoing fascinations. They do not strike me, however, as sufficiently developed to reground one's thinking about the real. Of course there were the Sophists. I regard them as sufficiently eviscerated in the great dialogues of Plato, in Socrates' innocent questions, and in the stunning *Metaphysics* of Aristotle. But Error has a thousand heads, and most of them are engaged in planning papers and panels for the Modern Language Association convention.

I have been a student of the American literary realists for most of my life, but M. Derrida's writings have led me to wonder whether it has been a waste of time: he dismisses the conviction that the literary art can reflect reality. But for the realists, it was precisely art's capacity to represent reality, in more or less comprehensive detail, that made the novel a moral and social agent in the contingencies of real life. They saw the mimetic function as offering a means of showing us to ourselves in our social, political, psychological, and moral dimensions; and art's very capacity to be truthful (with or without overt preaching) meant that it had, implicitly, the power to effect a social transformation and to promote useful private moral growth. Intermixed with the mimetic intent of Howells, Garland, James, and other realists was the ancient doctrine of the utilitarianism of art. In defending art's pragmatic and functional use, realists were likely to cite Sidney and other moralists who invoke the classical doctrine that poetry has the true end of teaching and delighting, in fact teaching by means of the lure of aesthetic pleasure. The late nineteenth century was a time of great moralizing in literature, precisely because the moral foundations of Western culture were undergoing great stresses—principally owing to the increasing scientism of the age, biblical higher criticism, the decline of the Judeo-Christian worldview, the image of man as an evolutionary animal, the transition from an agricultural to an industrial economy, and so on. The Victorians clung desperately to their Judeo-Christian morality even as the ontology that founded it seemed to them to slide away. It follows from M. Derrida's thinking that since the old ontology and its morality are defunct, any discussion of the moral effect of art is nonsense, should be demystified, must be exposed as merely ideological.

The twentieth century has substantially reacted against both realism as a literary-critical premise and the classical utilitarian view that art delights in order to teach us. M. Derrida is innocent of inventing this attack, however much he still prosecutes it. We can see it begin early in the century in the rise of the claim that the literary work is a self-contained heterocosm, an arrangement of language self-sufficient unto itself, constituted by its internal elements of structure, tension, imagery, irony, paradox, symbolism, and the like. The New Criticism—as practiced by John Crowe Ransom, Allen Tate, Cleanth Brooks, Robert Penn Warren, and others—was a text-centered reaction to the pedantic historicism of contemporary academic scholars, to the genteel moralism that had guided critical practice in the preceding half-century, and to the heavy-handed sociology of literature by Marxist critics who appeared during the depression years with the intent of destroying the country. I have never believed it true that the New Critics were utterly ahistorical, nor did they regard the artwork as utterly autonomous. But the force of their arguments led in that direction, especially for their followers who extended the doctrine to a general view that the poem or novel is a linguistic entity, artfully arranged, which should be aesthetically contemplated and not tested by any so-called similarity to reality as such, should not be ransacked for moral principles, and should not be enlisted in programs for social change: "A poem should not mean but be," Archibald MacLeish intones in "Ars Poetica." *Ah, but what is the being of the poem?* I am moved to ask, and it occurs to me to pose this question as the topic of *discours* when next I meet M. Derrida at the water cooler in the hall. *What, M. Derrida, is the being of Wallace Stevens's poem "Not Ideas About the Thing but the Thing Itself?"* (Of course I shall ask it in perfect French.)

I

In all the critical battles of the earlier twentieth century—the conflicts among the New Critics, the historical scholars in the academy, the New Humanists, the vulgar Marxists, and so on—there was not much in the way of an attack on representation itself. That is, the capacity of art to represent reality, more or less accurately, if it undertook to do so, was never much in question. And Dreiser, Wharton, Steinbeck, Wright, Bellow, and others continued to ply a realist art. What happened in criticism was principally an argument about where to put the stress. In effect, the great metaphysical doctrines underlying the theory of representation—derived from Plato and Aristotle and sustained through centuries of criticism—were more or less left untouched, while arguments proliferated about what we read a work of art for, and where in our criticism the emphasis should be placed.

But while I have been sitting in this office—thinking about books like *Washington Square* and *The Age of Innocence,* the poems of Wallace Stevens, and the social criticism of T. S. Eliot—there has developed this new attack on the theory of representation itself, M. Derrida's. It is an attack with the greatest implication for the work of James, Twain, Howells, and the other self-described realists of the post–Civil War era, as well as for any modern realist like Cheever, Cozzens, Bellow, Auchincloss, or Updike (not to speak of any dramatist or poet who wants an audience and who believes that he has something to say). I am moved to get up, open the office door, and announce to the bustling hallway that M. Derrida will have to take the blame for this new attack on representation.

Of course it seems inhospitable to pin the rap on the distinguished guest in the office next door, whose unintelligble hum of mellifluous French evokes a student conference full of *structure, signe, et jeu.* There are, after all, others to pin the rap on—his disciples, for instance, who have disseminated the word, people like Paul de Man, J. Hillis Miller, and Jonathan Culler, not to speak of the horde of epigones at the annual MLA convention who have found in skepticism a ladder to tenure. Some of them declaim every conceivable inanity under the banner of deconstructionism. Probably the English teacher should stick to his last, to poems and novels, and not poach on the domain of Kant, Hegel, & Co. But lit-crit has invaded the domain of philosophy with a wild abandon, largely to the discredit of our profession. M. Derrida, I understand, has had to disown quite a number of the faithful for transmogrifying deconstructionism into a hideous child the father finds now unrecognizable. I wonder whether—among the raft of disowned literary disciples—M.

Derrida still claims the celebrity professor Jonathan Culler, whose astonishing enunciation ("understanding is a special case of misunderstanding") constitutes my epigraph?[2]

So here I am, sitting in my office, thinking that if the Derridean attack on representation as such has any merit, nearly everything that Howells, James, Twain, Garland, and others were trying to do, or thought they were doing, will be seen as utterly useless, misguided, and naive. As J. Hillis Miller has boldly asserted,

> The study of literature should certainly cease to take the mimetic referentiality of literature for granted. Such a properly literary discipline would cease to be exclusively a repertoire of ideas, of themes, and of the varieties of human psychology. It would become once more philology, rhetoric, an investigation of the epistemology of tropes.[3]

I suppose that I shall have to give up Eliot and Stevens too, for laboring under a delusion that poetry makes meaning and can communicate it. Willa Cather, Edith Wharton, and Tom Wolfe will have to be seen as self-deceived. Certainly some of the postmodernist fictionists—John Barth, John Hawkes, Donald Barthelme, Ronald Sukenick, and Raymond Federman—assume that the realists were misguided; and the recent postmodern aesthetic of self-referential work, emphasizing the artifice of art and the uselessness of *mimesis,* does suggest a change in the history of taste. I have no objection in principle to antirealist art as such, though I am highly critical of the antihumanism in much modern fabulation, metafiction, surfiction, or whatever one wants to call the modern mode of the romance form.[4] But more than taste is involved; for what is at stake here is an argument over the very capacity of language to articulate truth. And I am sure that—if I stuck my head out the door and yelled as much into the hallway—the voice of M. Derrida might very well be heard exclaiming *Oui! C'est vrai!*

Let me say at the outset that I believe there is such a thing as truth and that language can (though not perfectly) represent it. I realize that this admission disqualifies me for membership in the intellectual avant-garde of our time. And it may be enough to banish me from the national literary conventions. But as I reflect on this matter, the suspicion

---

2 See Jonathan Culler's *On Deconstruction: Theory and Criticism After Structuralism* (Ithaca: Cornell University Press, 1982), p. 176.

3 See J. Hillis Miller's essay "Nature and the Linguistic Moment," in *Nature and the Victorian Imagination,* eds. U. C. Knoepflmacher and G. B. Tennyson (Berkeley: University of California Press, 1977), p. 451.

4 John Kuehl and I discuss these matters at some length in the epilogue to his excellent book *Alternate Worlds: A Study of Postmodern Antirealistic American Fiction* (New York: New York University Press, 1989).

arises in me that deep down, after all, M. Derrida believes in truth too; for he has expended a great deal of verbal energy in explaining how various people have misunderstood him.[5] It naturally follows that I regard the current attack on representation as the latest form of nihilism. The intent of these ruminations is therefore to turn for a moment to the ancient philosophical ground for understanding reality and representation the better to articulate it. I confess to inadequacy before this task. I would rather stick to my last and let James's "The Real Thing" or Stevens's "Not Ideas About the Thing but the Thing Itself," guide me into an understanding of their meanings. Yet I. A. Richards has nailed me cold:

> The teacher of English, at whatever level, is oddly reluctant to discuss his principles. He takes them for granted. Whether they could be granted, were they available for inspection, must be doubted until they are set forth. This shyness may indicate the presence of beliefs too deep to be confessed. It may result, on the other hand, from a felt absence of any notion as to why, in any philosophic sense, he should be doing as he does—or be teaching English at all.[6]

What follows is a reluctant expression of the principles implicit in my own practice of reading and writing literary criticism.

II

M. Derrida's attack on the theory of representation begins with a consideration of the nature of language as described in Ferdinand de Saussure's *Course in General Linguistics*. The gist of the argument lies in Saussure's positing language as a system of signs, phonological and graphological, that operates by means of structural differences. Whether oral or written, the signs for *mat* and *cat* may be distinguished simply by the difference between the initial phoneme or grapheme. These phonemic or graphemic differences are, in Saussure's view, utterly arbitrary. In fact, his theory of semiology, or signs, posits that there is no natural, inevitable, or necessary connection between the object in reality (the mat or cat) and the sign devised to designate it or distinguish it from other signs. Language, viewed as the system of such phonemic and

---

5 I find paradoxical the deconstructionists' insistence on the unambiguous truths that they themselves enunciate, even as they champion the idea of the undecidability of the texts of others. In this regard readers may wish to consult Michael Fisher's *Does Deconstruction Make Any Difference? Poststructuralism and the Defense of Poetry in Modern Criticism* (Bloomington: Indiana University Press, 1985).

6 I. A. Richards, "Responsibilities in the Teaching of English," in *Speculative Instruments* (New York: Harcourt, Brace, and World, 1955), p. 91.

graphemic differences, is (at least in Saussure's view) an arbitrary construction of human invention which stands apart from the reality of objects and experiences. It may point to them, but there is a profound gap or fissure between the thing itself and the sign designating it. Saussure is, I am convinced, right about the matter. But the argument that the word *is* the thing is a naive linguistic conception that has no standing, and one is surprised to see the straw man brought up. All languages are artificial and unequal to expressing what happened or what we think and feel. As children we had, of old, more thoughts and feelings than we had words for—and it is no different now. And those who have had a mystical experience or felt a theophanic reality have been unable, despite desperate efforts, to find adequate words. No language, moreover, has enough words for all the objects and experiences that need to be brought into discourse. New words are therefore always being formed and old ones dropped.

Can *anything* be expressed or grasped when we do not even know all the words of *our own* language? But it gets even worse. Can we ever understand someone who speaks another tongue? *Bar-bar-bar* was the sound of another language to the ancient Greeks—the gibberish of the barbarian. I myself think that it would be a lot simpler if Jacques Derrida stopped the nonsense and spoke and wrote like a man—in English. But, perversely, he declines, and I must translate his French or find someone else to do it for me. It is not easy to understand deconstructionism when one doesn't think in French, but then I understand that even the French have stopped thinking about it. (I am reluctant to call this to the attention of the complacent administrators, who have once again leaped onto a trendy bandwagon a tad too late.)

But thinking about M. Derrida makes me remember that even when we are listening to others in our own language we must translate what they say—we must turn what we hear and read into the meaning they intended. People are not very precise in saying what they mean, so we are obliged to translate, to recover their intention. And don't we do rather well at it? The apparent gibberish of Faulkner's idiot Benjy in *The Sound and the Fury*, the verbal displacements of the analysand's speech (in Roth's *Portnoy's Complaint*), and the countless variations in phonemes and allophones that we encounter in dialect speech (in Twain and Ellison) can seem quite confusing. But somehow we do make out the meaning, even as the bumblebee flies.[7]

---

7 Jenny Teichman has shown with wry analogical wit that human communication through language—though said to be theoretically impossible—nevertheless works, just as the bumblebee, despite its defiance of aerodynamic theory, manages to fly. See her essay "Deconstruction and Aerodynamics," *Philosophy*, 68 (1993), 53–62.

I have a fantasy that I meet M. Derrida at the water cooler to discuss Stevens's poem "Not Ideas About the Thing but the Thing Itself." It opens:

> At the earliest ending of winter,
> In March, a scrawny cry from outside
> Seemed like a sound in his mind.
>
> He knew that he heard it,
> A bird's cry, at daylight or before,
> In the early March wind.
>
> The sun was rising at six,
> No longer a battered panache above snow . . .
> It would have been outside.

The cry of the bird is, I protest to our Gallic friend, like language itself: something that echoes in the inner ear but whose meaning is not merely subjective. The phrase "would have been" suggests a Stevens wish for something that is never available to cognitive reason—absolute certitude. But through some other faculty, here unnamed, the poet seems rather confident. Language is partly external to us, as is the intentionality that in Stevens's case called the poem into being. M. Derrida's perfect English permits him to grasp my point that the birdsong announces the dawning of the light and is a part of the Reality Itself that illumines. Even as the birdcry proclaims the emerging of "the colossal sun," so linguistic utterance (however scrawny and imperfect) announces *das ding an sich,* uncovers the reality and discloses the essence of what the utterance is all about. Stevens's poem is about an epiphany, a momentary recognition that the Thing Itself can be apprehended in the choiring forms of Its expression.

> That scrawny cry—it was
> A chorister whose c preceded the choir.
> It was part of the colossal sun,
>
> Surrounded by its choral rings,
> Still far away. It was like
> A new knowledge of reality.

To discern, in the expression, the Thing Itself, to know that it exists and that it can be apprehended, to grasp the essence of what expression articulates—all this is indeed to have a new knowledge of reality. It is a knowledge obtained through analogous perception, derived through a similitude, comparison, or trope; but it is nonetheless epiphanic, and for this reason Stevens concluded his *Collected Poems* with this revelation. But it is likelier that my fantasy will dissolve in M. Derrida's taking an impatient line and disposing of all this certainty of understanding by posing a question to me: *"Polly-voo-franzy?"*

If a Frenchman is a man, as Jim says in *Huckleberry Finn*, "Well, den! Dad blame it, why doan' he *talk* like a man? You answer me *dat!*"[8] Most of us have felt Jim's frustration at the incomprehension produced in us by an unknown foreign language. How do we translate Jim's English speech? Most of us have some skill in translating into *our* English dialect what Jim means—or what other dialect speakers may mean (Synge's Irish, the Creoles of G. W. Cable, or Burns's bonny Scots). We are ingenious in running a set of rapid mental routines on phonemic and allophonic variations on the English code, mentally combining and recombining sounds, asking for repetitions and variations, testing logical probabilities, and eliminating the nonsense sounds until we fix rightly on what was meant in the dialect speech. *Ah, I see. I know what Jim means.* And most of us can carry this process even further and learn enough French to understand what Derrida means, and perhaps even enough Greek for Aristotle, Latin for Horace, or Italian for Dante. *Un homme qui parle deux langues vaut deux hommes.*

Our ingenuity in translating extends, of course, even to the extra-verbal sign—the shoulder shrug, the blush, the rolled or downcast eyes, the melody of speech, its pitch and volume. In grasping the meaning of written texts, we look at grammar, syntax, diction, figures, at anything that opens up the author's intention. We derive meaning from the ink and paper, the chain- and watermarks, the holographic hand, the scribal idiosyncrasy, the compositor's habits, printinghouse practices, and so forth. Worn or broken fonts can tell us a great deal. We are so good at reading signs that we can usually tell when a statement means the opposite of what it says—as in the case of *A Modest Proposal.*

But, unfortunately, we are not intelligent enough. We do not always get it. We cannot always understand what another has said or written. And the speaker, mind, may not be intelligent enough either, intelligent enough to say, without the possibility of misinterpretation, what he means. Poe, in his *Marginalia,* remarked that he did not believe that any thought, properly so called, was out of the reach of language, which may account for his rhetorical straining; and even Wittgenstein expressed the view that anything that could be thought at all could be expressed clearly. But their own prose is proof enough against the claim.

---

8 Mark Twain, *Adventures of Huckleberry Finn,* ed. Henry Nash Smith (Boston: Houghton Mifflin, 1958), p. 68.

We must add that in literary works the great author is, after all, too subtle for us. He may pile on the meaning, superimpose it, embed it, interweave it, imagize and symbolize it, compact and condense it to the point of breathtakingly wonderful but bewildering plurisignification. Even so, he cannot escape *his* problem—that all-too-imperfect tool, language. Between the inadequacy of language and human imperfection, it is surprising that anything gets communicated. Still, the writer does the best he can, and so do we, which is ordinarily good enough; and, from time to time and with the help of a good interpreter, literary communication is sheer pleasure for both reader and writer. Wherever, in the past, a language has been most complexly developed and deployed in art and criticism, there a complex and interesting civilization has developed. The existence of civilization in fact presupposes that the truths of reality can be known, more or less expressed, by and large understood, and communicated as meaning.

The contemporary Sophists, however, have it that the inevitable gap between the word and the thing itself, between the signifier and the signified, proves that reality is inaccessible through language. M. Derrida has called attention to our penchant for binary oppositions and our readiness to assert them in a hierarchy of oppositions. The hierarchies would include such pairs as presence/absence, speech/writing, good/evil, inner/outer, form/content, and so forth. M. Derrida wishes to reverse the hierarchy by which we normally rank binaries. As he remarks, "To deconstruct the opposition is above all, at a particular moment, to reverse the hierarchy."[9] Deconstruction, Derrida argues, must "through a double gesture, a double science, a double writing, put into practice a *reversal* of the classical opposition *and* a general *displacement* of the system. It is in that condition alone that deconstruction will provide the means of *intervening* in the field of oppositions it criticizes and which is also a field of non-discursive forces."[10]

In the murmuring, as it were, of innumerable bees next door, I listen for echoes of "logocentrism." (M. Derrida is against it and longs for its displacement.) If anyone wants to know what logocentrism is, I might as well call it the fundamental metaphysical system in the West which finds truth to be articulated in language, in the syntactic formation, in the word, a metaphysical system that "privileges" language as the expression of reality itself. Implicit in the idea of logocentrism is speech, writing, the *logos* or word. That is, in the word, in the logos, in discourse is to be located the ontological foundation—being itself as the expression of

---

9 Derrida, *Positions* (Chicago: University of Chicago Press, 1981), p. 41.
10 Derrida, *Marges de philosophie* (Paris: Minuit, 1972), p. 392.

truth and reality. Phonocentrism and logocentrism, the privileging of voice and of the word, Derrida remarks,

> merges with the determination through history of the meaning of being in general as *presence*, with all the sub-determinations that depend on this general form and organize within it their system and their historical linkage (presence of the object to sight as *eidos*, presence as substance/essence/existence (οὐσία), temporal presence as the point (*stigmè*) of the now or the instant (*nun*), self-presence of the cogito, consciousness, subjectivity, co-presence of the self and the other, intersubjectivity as an intentional phenomenon of the ego, etc.). Logocentrism would thus be bound up in the determination of the being of the existent as presence.[11]

Finally, he observes, "what inaugurates meaning and language is writing as the disappearance of natural presence."[12]

III

What is the effect of the severing of the philosophical connection and the historical linkage between writing and the presence of the object to sight, presence as substance, essence, and existence, temporal presence as the moment of now, presence as the self-presence of consciousness to itself? Clearly, M. Derrida's views have immense implications for the theory of representation and surprising effects on hermeneutic theory as the attempt to explain how meaning means or how language may be said to express meaning and understanding. Paul de Man has formalized the deconstructionist effect in insisting that "the paradigmatic structure of language is rhetorical rather than representational or expressive of a referential, proper meaning. . . ." This, in his view, authorized him to make "a full reversal of the established priorities which traditionally root the authority of the language in its adequation to an extralinguistic referent or meaning, rather than in the intralinguistic resources of figures."[13] This reduction of language to rhetoric, of meaning to an interplay of intralinguistic elements, was intended to destroy the metaphysics of presence, by which, over the past three thousand years, the Western mind has explored reality through the *logos* that represents it. Sitting here, it comes to me that, in conducting this assault on presence, M. Derrida has posited two theories of interpretation.

---

11 Derrida, *De la grammatologie* (Paris: Minuit, 1967), p. 23.
12 Derrida, *De la grammatologie*, pp. 158–159.
13 Paul de Man, *Allegories of Reading: Figural Language in Rousseau, Nietzsche, and Proust* (New Haven: Yale University Press, 1979), p. 106.

The one seeks to decipher, dreams of deciphering, a truth or an origin which escapes play and the order of the sign and which is free from freeplay and from the order of the sign, and lives like an exile the necessity of interpretation. The other, which is no longer turned toward the origin, affirms freeplay and tries to pass beyond man and humanism, the name man being the name of that being who, throughout the history of metaphysics or of ontotheology—in other words, through the history of all of his history—has dreamed of full presence, the reassuring foundation, the origin and the end of the game. . . .

There are more than enough indications today to suggest we might perceive that these two interpretations of interpretation—which are absolutely irreconcilable even if we live them simultaneously and reconcile them in an obscure economy—together share the field which we call, in such a problematic fashion, the human sciences.[14]

My students, then, will learn from deconstructionism that the text has no unity, that it is not governed by presence, by an "original" assertion that organizes and authorizes a single system of meaning. Indeed, another favorite of the contemporary Sophists, M. Jacques Lacan, warns me in *Écrits* that "we cannot cling to the illusion that the signifier answers to the function of representing the signified, or better, that the signifier has to answer for its existence in the name of any signification whatever."[15] An extension of this *énonciation* is the claim that there is therefore no "naturally" privileged center of meaning in a text. Instead there are various elements that, as interwoven, create a "play" of meanings that is not constrained by the avowed intention of the author or the text itself. The signs constituting the text, in their freeplay of meaning, have no reference to any extralinguistic reality, indeed can have none. For "there is no single 'referent' or 'transcendental signified' which would regulate all of the text's movements.'"[16]

Ideas, for me, have consequences. I have always acted on them and so, I believe, do most critics. What is the consequence of this argument banishing presence from the word, reality from discourse? What is the effect of asserting that the decentered text lacks a single referent, a unified aesthetic intention, or a tie to the transcendental signified—that, in short, there is nothing outside the text and the text is a freeplay of

---

14 Derrida, "Structure, Sign and Play in the Discourse of the Human Sciences," in *Contexts for Criticism*, ed. Donald Keesey (Palo Alto, Calif.: Mayfield, 1987), p. 333.

15 Jacques Lacan, *Écrits*, trans. Alan Sheridan (New York: W. W. Norton, 1977), p. 150. The complete separation of language from sense may seem more plausible to one who spends the day, presumably like psychoanalyst Lacan, listening to the verbal flow of mental patients.

16 Derrida, *Positions*, p. 37.

diversities wherein authorial intention and coherence of meaning cannot be discovered? The effect is that the reader, or literary critic, is freed from the task of thinking that the text means something. He is freed from trying to discover what the text means. Meaning is not inherent in the text but is rather created by the reader. Interpretation is thus a free-for-all.

IV

For many commonsense teachers like me, there is a tendency to want to ignore M. Derrida's ideas, to pass by the challenge posed by this new subjectivism in the hope that its manifest irrationality will lead it to collapse from its own inanity, that it will evaporate in its own gases and waft away. But that is very hard to do if one recurs very often to the water cooler, where M. Derrida is palpable, or to the academic journals, where all is privileged except stylistic lucidity. Some have given up. William E. Cain wants to throw in the towel. He voices the position, shared by many other teachers, that

> it is time to shift the focus of the discussion away from the deconstructive assault on categories such as reality and reference. This may look like an admission that deconstruction has triumphed, and in a sense it is. But I think that it might be more constructive simply to say that we do not seem to be making such progress in our efforts to unite the discoveries of post-structuralism with our determination to address "the real." Deconstruction has taught us much, but it has assumed an unnatural prominence in current debates in theory and criticism and threatens to exclude the asking of other questions. . . .[17]

In my view it is pusillanimous to assume that deconstructionism has triumphed. There is no doubt it has troubled a great many literary critics, but that is essentially because most of us do not have the philosophical equipment, the training in conceptual or reflective thought, to provide us with a way of responding to radical skepticism. Those in the field of philosophy, it is worth remembering, have been rather ho-hum about deconstructionism; and Meyer H. Abrams rightly remarks that "Derrida has attracted little sustained comment from English and American philosophers, and that comment has been, with few exceptions, dismissive."[18]

---

17 William E. Cain, *The Crisis in Criticism: Theory, Literature, and Reform in English Studies* (Baltimore: Johns Hopkins University Press, 1984), pp. 245–246.
18 Meyer H. Abrams, *Doing Things with Texts: Essays in Criticism and Critical Theory* (New York: W. W. Norton, 1989), p. 312.

Still, I for one cannot be dismissive of so visible a presence in our critical journals and so audible an absence in the office next door. M. Derrida's radical skepticism requires me to keep reminding myself of how some very great minds have understood language's capacity to mediate between the self and the world and to disclose and communicate truth. I need therefore to reestablish—however briefly and inadequately and only for myself—the central argument, if I have understood it, for the referential function of language and its capacity to communicate meaning and truth. Of course such a task involves one in metaphysical thinking, and deconstructionism wishes to abolish Western metaphysical thought. But as M. Derrida has himself admitted, metaphysical thought cannot be deconstructed except by recourse to the concepts and the language of metaphysical thought: "We have no language—no syntax and no lexicon—which is alien to this history [of metaphysics]; we cannot utter a single destructive proposition which has not already slipped into the form, the logic, and the implicit postulations of precisely what it seems to contest."[19] Since M. Derrida himself acknowledges that the deconstruction of metaphysical thought involves one in metaphysical thinking and cannot be expressed except in the language of metaphysics itself, let us proceed to what I openly confess will be an ontotheology of meaning in criticism.

(The auditory hum from next door, punctuated by an occasional and intelligible "*Mais, non, non,*" has diminished.) As I sit here it comes to me that the circle begins and ends with the ancient analysis of the nature of truth and how it can be linguistically represented. Quite simply, there is no better account available than that in Plato and the *Metaphysics*, the *Posterior Analytics*, and the *Peri Hermeneias (On Interpretation)* of Aristotle. There are also a number of brilliant analytical commentaries on these works commencing with Boethius, Averroës, and Aquinas and coming down into our own time.[20]

In the Aristotelian reading, truth is that which is the case in virtue of its being. It is reality; it is the constituted essence of what is. As Aristotle remarks in the *Metaphysics*, "The essence of each thing is that which it is

---

19 Derrida, "Structure, Sign, and Play . . . ," p. 326.

20 Plato of course might very well have launched such a discussion. And I would ordinarily have no objection to considering Plato's stipulation—as Aristotle puts it—that "the Forms are the cause of the essence in everything else, and the One is the cause of it in the Forms." Nor have I an objection to the even more telling Christian exegesis that accounts for meaning in terms of the divine *Logos*. But for the purposes of the following discussion, reliance on the Platonic theory of Forms or Christian doctrine is not essential. See the *Metaphysics*, in *Aristotle in Twenty-three Volumes*, trans. Hugh Tredennick (1933; reprinted Cambridge: Harvard University Press, 1989), XVII, 47. For a Christian perspective on deconstructionism, see R. V. Young's excellent "Deconstruction and the Fear and Loathing of Logos," *Modern Age*, 34 (Winter 1992), 143–154.

said to be *per se.*"²¹ It is *quod quid erat esse,* that by virtue of which a thing has to be what in fact it is. M. Derrida has put the idea of *essence* in bad odor nowadays, but what in fact a thing is is its essence or quiddity. Being, Aristotle persuades me, is "that which exists by itself and in itself. Whatever can be predicated of things (in the order of existence), is consequent upon their οὐσία."²² In accounting for the relationship between ἀλήθεια, or truth, and οὐσία, or being, most analysts have made ontology the heart of the enterprise, for as Aquinas quite properly remarks in *De Ente et Essentia,* "a thing is not intelligible except by virtue of its definition and essence."²³ To know a thing is to apprehend the essence of that thing as existing by virtue of its own nature, through its matter, form, and function.

Since the hallway is still fairly quiet, I shall continue by remarking that we come to know the essence of a thing in various ways, depending upon the mode of its being. In the case of a literary work, we are dealing not with a thing like a hammer, a material object with a specific use, but with words. The reduction to discourse is necessary in this case because, as Aristotle remarks in *Sophistical Refutations,* "It is impossible in a discussion to bring in the actual things discussed; we use their names as signs instead of them."²⁴ Thus we have to use language. And, for this reason, in the case of verbal expression, we are obliged to grasp the essence of meaning through names, signs, and predication. Meaningful linguistic utterance is always a unity of signs created by the predicate combination. But let's keep it simple. The simplest meaningful linguistic combination is the noun and its verb, the subject and its predicate. The simple noun and verb may of course be qualified by adjectives, adverbs, and any array of modifying phrases and clauses. And, as Aristotle remarks in *Posterior Analytics,* "a statement may be a unity in either of two ways, by conjunction, like the *Iliad,* or because it exhibits a single predicate as inhering not accidentally in a single subject." What this means for the English teacher like me is that the literary work—though constituted of many conjoined predications—is nevertheless a unity of utterance, a single discourse.²⁵

21 Aristotle, *Metaphysics,* VII, iv, 4, p. 321.

22 Leo Elders, *Aristotle's Theology: A Commentary of Book Δ* (Assen: Van Gorcum, 1972), p. 114.

23 St. Thomas Aquinas, *Concerning Being and Essence (De Ente et Essentia),* trans. George G. Leckie (New York: D. Appleton-Century, 1937), p. 5.

24 Aristotle, *Sophistical Refutations,* 165a5; in *Aristotle: On Interpretation—Commentary by St. Thomas and Cajetan,* trans. Jean T. Oesterle (Milwaukee: Marquette University Press, 1962), p. 6.

25 See the *Posterior Analytics,* trans. G. R. G. Mure, in *The Works of Aristotle,* ed. W. D. Ross (Oxford: Clarendon Press, 1928), I, 93b35.

But back to the simple utterance. Truth inheres not in the noun, which names, but in what is semantically conjoined with it to complete the utterance, the predicate that asserts something about the noun. As Aristotle remarks, "It is only when other words are added that the whole will form an affirmation or denial."[26] The added words thus combine to produce propositions or declarations that may be premises in syllogistic thought or eventually the logical conclusions that derive from syllogistic reasoning. Some typical propositions: *Deconstructionism produces unintelligible jargon.* Another: *Culler missed the mark.* Or another: *The MLA is a national joke.* In such declarative sentences a state of affairs that already exists prior to language has come to be verbalized; an object is named and something is asserted about it. The utterance says something about the noun, the name that is the subject of the utterance. Only in the declarative formulation is it possible to assert something truthful about a state of affairs. Truth is not communicated in the imperative sentence (*Transcend your subjectivity!*). Truth does not inhere in the question *(What's the différance?)* You won't find truth in the subjunctive syntactical combination *(Let us now give up sane literary criticism).* Truth is only to be found in declarative predications. To predicate is to make a judgment, the reference of which is something outside of it, the truth we wish to express.

I feel distinctly not trendy in brooding upon this ancient ontological analysis, especially since it is so inexorably grounded in the whole long tradition of thinking about thought in the West. The West has recently come in for a great deal of self-righteous condemnation, moral and social, and the history of the West is, like that of the Orient, an appalling record of carnage. But the strangest of all contemporary responses to the ubiquity of evil is to attribute it to our method of thought in relation to modes of representation. M. Derrida and his followers would like to change the West by draining out of language its representational function and so changing the way we think. Once we verbally invert everything—by saying that black is white, up down, central marginal, aberrational normative, and so on—perfection will arrive. This seems hopeless and a desperate counsel. In fact, the ancient mode of understanding the relation of language and reality, now, in the looming silence, seems as true today as when it was first formulated.

All right, we will begin with this axiom: truth is expressed in enunciative speech, in the proposition, in the *logos*. What then? *Logos* is Greek for the *word.* It also serves for utterance or discourse. One of the

---

26 See the *Categoriae and De Interpretatione*, trans. E. M. Edghill, in *The Works of Aristotle*, ed. W. D. Ross, I, iv, 30.

clearest expositors of Aristotelian metaphysics (however opaque and divergent his own brand of phenomenology may be), Heidegger is right in observing, in *Being and Time,* that *logos*

> as "discourse" means rather the same as δηλοῦν: to make manifest what one is "talking about" in one's discourse. Aristotle has explicated this function of discourse more precisely as ἀπόφαίνεσθαι. The λόγος lets something be seen (φαίνεσθαι), namely, what the discourse is about; and it does so either *for* the one who is doing the talking (the *medium*) or for persons who are talking with one another, as the case may be.[27]

Too enamored of Greek etymology, especially when it can improbably be linked to the *Muttersprache,* Heidegger is still right to note:

> When considered philosophically, the λόγος itself is an entity, and, according to the orientation of ancient ontology, it is something present-at-hand. Words are proximally present-at-hand; that is to say, we come across them just as we come across Things; and this holds for any sequence of words, as that in which the λόγος expresses itself. In this first search for the structure of the λόγος as thus present-at-hand, what was found was the *Being-present-at-hand-together* of several words. What establishes the unity of this "together"? As Plato knew, this unity lies in the fact that the λόγος is always λόγος τινός. In the λόγος an entity is manifest, and with a view to this entity, the words are put together in *one* verbal whole (*B&T,* 201).

As I listen for echoes of M. Derrida, what this adds up to is that the truthful utterance—through the phenomenon of language, through the semiotics of phonemics and graphemics—undertakes to reveal this entity, to disclose it in its character, structure, and form in the fullness of its truth. Language is merely the manifest, the phenomenological appearing of the hidden entity (the truth of the object or state of affairs, prior to language) that the speaker or writer is seeking to disclose. As Heidegger remarks,

> Thus φαινόμενον means that which shows itself, the manifest. . . . Φαίνεσθαι itself is a *middle-voiced* form which comes from φαίνω—to bring to the light of day, to put in the light. Φαίνω comes from the stem φα–, like φῶς, the light, that which is bright—in other words, that wherein something can become manifest, visible in itself. Thus we must *keep in mind* that the expression *"phenomenon"* signifies *that which*

---

27 Martin Heidegger, *Being and Time,* trans. John Macquarrie and Edward Robinson (New York: Harper and Row, 1962), p. 56. Citations from this work will hereafter be given as *B&T,* in parentheses, in the text.

shows itself in itself, the manifest. Accordingly the φαινόμενα or "phenomena" are the totality of what lies in the light of day or can be brought to the light—what the Greeks sometimes identified simply with τὰ ὄντα (entities) (*B&T*, 51).

The entities, ah, the intractible persistence of the idea of entities! How modern radical skepticism would like to dismiss entities and relativize essence, thus reducing the solid world to a social construct of (what else?) language, mere discourse.

But the assertion of something about something—say, *M. Derrida's theory produces interpretive anarchy*—may be true or false. The truth of the utterance does not inhere in predication as such. If that were the case, any predication would be truthful. If a predication is false, as Aristotle observes, the reason is twofold: it may be either that of epistemological error (Derrida's theory really produces order, but I failed to perceive it) or the moral defect of lying (I know that Derrida's theory produces order but call its effect interpretive anarchy so as to deceive the hearer of the utterance). But if Derrida's thinking *does* produce anarchy in interpretation, the truth of my utterance as an accurate representation of the entity is ascertainable by the hearer, who has his own perceptual and cognitive equipment for the verification of the assertion. There is of course a conviction in this ancient ontology that truth is something that objectively exists, prior to verbalization, and can be communicated and known by others despite their subjectivity. Otherwise, all is chaos.

In any event, and by way of a summation, for these ancient Greeks the term for "truth" was αλήθεια, or the unhidden. Truth is an uncovering of what has been hidden; it is the letting of something be seen, a letting of the entity (which is the subject of the discourse) be perceived. "To say that an assertion 'is *true,*'" Heidegger explains, "signifies that it uncovers the entity as it is in itself. Such an assertion asserts, points out, 'lets' the entity 'be seen' in its uncoveredness" (*B&T*, 261). But, as he rightly remarks, "Assertion is not the primary 'locus' of truth." On the contrary, "the most primordial 'truth' is the 'locus' of 'assertion'; it is the ontological condition for the possibility that assertions can be either true or false—that they may uncover or cover things up." This is a rather elaborate way (complete with self-protective ironical quotation marks) of saying what Aquinas puts with total conviction and conclusive simplicity: ". . . for it is from the facts of the case, i.e., from a thing's being so or not being so, that speech is true or false" (*B&T*, 269).[28]

Hoping for a trace of the absence next door, I come back to the

---

28 See *Aristotle: On Interpretation—Commentary by St. Thomas and Cajetan,* p. 61.

conviction that it is by means of signs, phonemic or graphemic, that we construct assertions about the poem that bring to light or disclose the poem's entities in their essence. Signs do not merely stand in contiguous relation to entities; they refer to entities in their hiddenness, prior to language, and by doing so disclose them to us. In interpreting, we do not create the meaning, we disclose it; we do not generate the sense, we reveal it. This is a galling fact to some critics more devoted to ideology than to literary works—and there are many of them in the profession. But I have a conviction of the logic of another view:

> In interpreting, we do not, so to speak, throw a "signification" over some naked thing which is present-at-hand, we do not stick a value on it; but when something within-the-world is encountered as such, the thing in question already has an involvement which is disclosed in our understanding of the world, and this involvement is one which gets laid out by the interpretation (*B&T*, 190).

In the language of a literary work we encounter words brought together with the intent of expressing an entity that we are drawn to comprehend; and the English teacher's task as an interpreter of literature is to disclose for understanding both the manifest and the hiddenness of that which is articulated, to bring to light and to let be seen in its essence the meaning of the utterance in the unity of its literary form.

V

What, we are entitled to ask, is the connection between the kinds of utterances encountered in a poem or a novel and utterances made in ostensive speech or propositional utterances encountered in literary criticism? Does a literary work, like an accurate declarative utterance, disclose truth? If so, what, broadly speaking, are τὰ ὄντα, the entities, brought to light in the novel, the poem, or in a critical discourse about a literary work? Here an observation of Paul Ricoeur may be helpful in understanding how dramatic speech or imaginative literature stands in relation to ostensive utterances that directly communicate truth. In *Hermeneutics and the Human Sciences* (1981), M. Ricoeur has argued that the hermeneutical task is to discover the "matter" of the text—its being. The essence of the text is to its structure, in M. Ricoeur's view, as, in the proposition, the reference is to the sense. He remarks that when we encounter a proposition or declarative statement we are never content just to register its syntactic form. Rather we wish to "inquire further into its reference, that is, into its claim to truth." The process is the same when we encounter the verbal codes, tropes, and figurations of a literary text: "we cannot stop at the immanent structure, at the "codes" which the text employs; we wish moreover to explicate the world which the text projects." Of course M. Ricoeur is perfectly aware—as we all must be—that imaginative literature does not refer to reality in the same way that propositional language does. But he is right to observe that

> it is precisely insofar as fictional discourse "suspends" its first order referential function that it releases a second order reference, where the world is manifested no longer as the totality of manipulable objects but as the horizon of our life and our project, in short as *Lebenswelt* [life-world], as being-in-the-world. It is this referential dimension, attaining its full development only with works of fiction and poetry, which raises the fundamental hermeneutical problem. Hermeneutics can be defined no longer as an inquiry into the psychological intentions which are hidden beneath the text, but rather as the explication of the being-in-the-world displayed by the text. What is to be interpreted in the text is a proposed world which I could inhabit and in which I could project my ownmost possibilities. . . . Reality is, in this way, metamorphosed by means of what I shall call the "imaginative variations" which literature carries out on the real.[29]

M. Ricoeur's observation draws into the general problem of hermeneutic understanding the discourse of literature as a projection of a possible world, a world that proposes an existence that I might live, a mode of being that might be mine, variations on the real customarily enunciated by the propositional language of ordinary discourse. Such variations are potentially infinite in number. And it is for this reason that "realistic fiction remains the great unfinished aesthetic adventure."[30] The world I might inhabit, the alternative life I might live, is, on the deepest level, not less "real" than the life I do live. The imagined world I encounter—in James's Washington Square or perhaps during Stevens's ordinary evening in New Haven—lives alongside, or rather in the metaphysical presence of, the world I do inhabit. That imagined world also has as its ontological *situs* the domain of the primordial truth—where what is, what was, what has been, what might have been, what might yet be, and what will inevitably be coexist, as inseparably and inextricably one. Hidden in the silence that precedes the utterance of the novel or poem are the concealed entities that the work comes into being to contain and express and that intelligent criticism can meaningfully (if imperfectly and inexhaustively) explicate.

---

29 Paul Ricoeur, *Hermeneutics and the Human Sciences,* trans. John B. Thompson (Cambridge: Cambridge University Press, 1981), pp. 111–112.
30 Raymond Tallis, *In Defence of Realism* (London: Edward Arnold, 1988), p. [189].

For most of us, I think, the appeal of literature lies precisely in this capacity of the aesthetic to call into being credible worlds alternative to our own. If literature were merely a language game, as deconstructionism suggests, we would tire of it very quickly. And, indeed, many of our students have, alas, been turned away from literature by the mind-numbing repetitive deconstruction of it. But insofar as literary language discloses a truth about worlds alternative to our own, and insofar as authentic criticism brings into the light the meanings concealed therein, consciousness is enlarged, our capacity for experience is broadened, and understanding is increased. I listen for sounds next door and give a Johnsonian *coup de pied* to the wall, as if to say *The Center Holds.* But the echoes of Gallic skepticism have already faded without a ~~trace~~ into the morning air, have already vanished as if *"sous rature,"* yes, as if under erasure, and I make my way out into the park where Henry James played as a boy. There, warmed by the colossal sun and attentive to the choral rings, I am assured of my ground by the cry of the chorister whose *c* has preceded the choir.

Some Modern Sophists

Sophists: (5th Cent. B.C.) Wandering teachers who came to Athens from foreign cities and sought to popularize knowledge. . . . The Sophists came to Athens to assist young men in achieving political success. Before long, this brought with it the subordination of purely theoretical learning to its practical usefulness, and the Sophists, far from teaching what is most likely to be true, instructed the youth in what is most likely to bear political fruit. Thus eloquent public appeal and the art of rhetoric soon took the place of pure science and philosophy. In this very desire, however, to persuade and refute, the problem presented itself as to whether among the various conflicting opinions which the Sophists had taught their pupils to defend and to oppose, there was anything of permanent value which could claim the assent of all men everywhere. This quest of the universal in knowledge and in conduct forms the basis of the Socratic Quest.
                    —Max Fishler, *Dictionary of Philosophy*

Geoffrey Hartman has protested in *Criticism in the Wilderness* that there exists a "defensive partition of the critical and the creative spirit, which recognizes the intelligence of the creative writer but refuses the obverse proposition that there may be creative force in the critical writer. . . ." Likewise Harold Bloom has complained that "I don't know what people are talking about when they think that an imaginative fiction—a poem or a novel or a story or a drama—is one thing, and a critical essay is something startlingly different." For Bloom, "as literary history lengthens, all poetry necessarily becomes verse criticism, just as all criticism becomes prose-poetry." As he puts it, "the critical event is as poetically compelling as the poetic event."[1] But is it?

I can't think of any work of criticism, by any critic, as compelling as *King Lear*, as *Moby-Dick*, as the *Four Quartets*. But these complaints are only a few of many such recent expressions of irritation at the low condition of criticism vis-à-vis creative work. Bloom and Hartman would like the critic to be called in from the hinterland of lesser distinction to an admiring Athens where the critic is freed from textual constraint in his interpretation, liberated from slavish subserviency to the text, and where his sheer inventiveness is acclaimed as on a par with Homer, Aeschylus, and Shakespeare. Vexed they are, these critics, that they are merely that—critics, and not poets or novelists or playwrights.

Claiming that the critic can be as creative as the poet is one way of getting revenge on the artist, who has often enough condemned the critic as a parasite, a bottom-feeder on original creation. Critics do not like to be thought of as parasites. In "The Critic as Host," J. Hillis Miller ruminates for several pages on the etymological origin of the term "parasite" largely for the purpose of claiming that the critic is in fact not a parasite but rather the host on which parasites feed. Then, seized by his own conceit, Miller goes on to suggest that the critic may even be the host as Eucharist.[2] This kind of delusional thinking clearly invests literature with redemptive power, as if a short story or a poem were sacred scripture. Some in the generation of Wallace Stevens believed the claim that "in an age in which disbelief is so profoundly prevalent or, if not disbelief, indifference to questions of belief, poetry and painting, and the arts in general, are, in their measure, a compensation for what has been lost. Men feel that the imagination is the reigning prince." And for a short time a few philosophically or theologically disoriented *soi disant* moderns thought that maybe poetry *would* save one's soul. This, naturally enough, led to grotesque excesses of aestheticism, a sort of arid wallowing in a sense of beauty divorced from every other aspect of life. It

---

1 Geoffrey Hartman, *Criticism in the Wilderness* (New Haven: Yale University Press, 1980), p. 253; Imre Salusinszky, "Interview with Harold Bloom," in *Criticism in Society* (London: Methuen, 1987), p. 57; Harold Bloom, *A Map of Misreading* (New York: Oxford University Press, 1975), p. 3.

2 See Harold Bloom, *et al., Deconstruction and Criticism* (New York: Continuum, 1979), pp. 218–222.

was a ridiculous enough belief,[3] but hardly less so than J. Hillis Miller's elevation of the critic to the role of host, with *its* attendant salvific implications.

But becoming "creative" in one's criticism is also a means of getting revenge on the poem. After all, a poem may be hard to grasp. It may itch at our ears till we understand it. For a great many critics, it may not merely itch but also enrage. Not instantly to comprehend what powerfully moves (other readers!) can be a vexing business. This hermeneutic task, the task of understanding the poem, can be such an irritant that a great many critics have recently announced that *there really isn't anything there to understand,* for a text has no basic idea, central theme, or unitary meaning. Far from being an aesthetic design that declares an artistic intention and communicates a formal meaning, the poem or novel is always and only a verbal ragbag from which we can pick—as a meaning (or as *the* meaning)—whatever colorful tatter or remnant may strike our fancy. Understanding a poem, however, is a more diligent and difficult business than such contemporary critical sophistry can admit. Reading well requires a large fund of general knowledge, wide experience of the world, absolute sustained attention to the text, rigor of analytic thought, the capacity for precise discriminations, common sense, sensibility, *feeling,* and (not least, dread word) *taste*—a developed capacity for the *aesthetic* evaluation of literary works. Few enough are up to the hard labor required to become good critics. It is much easier—and much more gratifying (especially to one's "creative needs")—to invent the text's meaning, to make it up out of whatever figments happen to preoccupy one at the moment.

The view that the critic makes the work of art is very popular now in the academy, thanks largely to the criticism of Jacques Derrida and its effect on several contemporary schools of critical thought. Derrida argues, among other things, that the literary text is always ruptured by a self-deconstructing *aporia,* that it therefore subverts its own manifest themes, and that the language of literature is polysemous, ambiguous, and self-contradictory to the point of undecidability. Given these "facts," all readings are misreadings, and virtually anything may confidently be said about a text.

What are the ramifications of M. Derrida's view that the poem is undecidable, has no intended or fixed meaning, and is in fact "created" by

---

3 See Wallace Stevens, "The Relations Between Poetry and Painting," in *The Necessary Angel: Essays on Reality and the Imagination* (New York: Vintage, 1951), p. 171. Stevens, it should be pointed out, spent a lifetime inveighing against Christianity and inflating the salvific power of the humanist imagination but finally abandoned the notion and, at the end of his life, was baptized into the Roman Catholic communion.

the reader who "actualizes" it? I have already ruminated on Derrida himself (in "Jacques et moi"). Here I wish simply to trace the ramifications of this view in three well-known critics who are nowadays highly acclaimed in the academy: J. Hillis Miller, sometime president of the Modern Language Association; Stanley Fish, a postmodern reader-response "theorist"; and Tony Bennett, a proponent of the new Marxism. These three critics, typical of the major modes of criticism today, are popular for a very simple reason, it seems to me: they have delivered literature teachers from the always difficult task of thinking through the poem and explaining to a class what it really means. Thanks to the new subjectivism authorized by M. Derrida, the teacher or critic is no longer the servant of the text, assisting in the explication of its themes and forms, disclosing its genius, and restoring to it the intended meaning of the writer. Since the critic is now the preeminent creative agent, *The Waste Land* or "Mending Wall" is the critic's poem and can mean anything *he* says it means. In short, the admonition to "get creative" has had the effect of leading the ordinary teacher to substitute for the text's meaning any extraliterary matter that interests him or her at the moment—feminism, racism, AIDS, homophobia, capitalism, Vietnam, anything, in other words, that is trendy, politically correct, or Uncle Toby's hobbyhorse. Let us take seriatim these three critics as illustrations of what happens to hermeneutic thought when the capacity of language to represent reality is denied.

I

J. Hillis Miller attained national recognition with a number of early works of more or less straightforward literary criticism—*Charles Dickens: The World of His Novels* (1958), *The Disappearance of God* (1963), *Thomas Hardy: Distance and Desire* (1970), *The Form of Victorian Fiction* (1979), and *Poets of Reality* (1965). These books were, in my view, responsible to the authors and texts they analyzed, and I valued them and learned from them. But in more recent works like *Fiction and Repetition: Seven English Novels* (1982), *The Linguistic Moment: From Wordsworth to Stevens* (1985), *The Ethics of Reading* (1986), *Tropes, Parables, Performatives: Essays on Twentieth-Century Literature* (1991), and *Ariadne's Thread: Story Lines* (1992), Miller has, like Derrida, claimed the illusory character of aesthetic design in the artwork. In "Ariachne's Broken Woof," he argues the idea that presence, or the self, as an entity existing in an extralinguistic reality, is not accessible through language, which cannot be used self-expressively. "The deconstructive critic," he observes, by means of "dialogical" premises, calls into question "the notions of the mind and of the self and sees them as linguistic fictions, as functions in a system of words without base in the *logos* of any substantial mind."[4] Here he is not merely echoing Nietzsche's idea of the death of God but extending it to include the death of everybody else as well.

Of course the idea of the death of the self logically entails the idea of death of the author, and this is a discovery that has educed much recent enthusiasm. If one is truly modern, there isn't supposed to be any Dickens or Keats, for how can identity or the essence of selfhood exist when the self—even yours or mine—is a verbal fiction? "Dickens" is merely a word prefixed to *Bleak House*, which is itself only a collocation of words. This Nietzschean claim has been taken up by a number of pontificating Sophists besides Miller. Heidegger, for one, assured us that "Man acts as though *he* were the shaper and master of language, while in fact *language* remains the master of man."[5] It has also been propounded by Michel Foucault in "What Is an Author?" and Roland Barthes in "The Death of the Author." For Barthes, "it is language which speaks, not the author; to write is, through a pre-requisite impersonality, to reach that point where only language acts, 'performs,' and not 'me.'"[6] Certainly language has conventions of grammar and syntax which any author must, if he wants to be understood, obey; and certainly there are preexistent literary forms (the sonnet, the villanelle) to which an author may yield in the creative moment. But do such structures absolutely control creative expression? Is the author really defunct? And did language itself write Yeats's "Sailing to Byzantium" or Eliot's "Burnt Norton"? If so, we wish that language would write a few more poems like these. The fatuity of this sophistical proposition that language speaks and not the author has been splendidly skewered by Raymond Tallis—with wonderful British drollery:

> This kind of consideration could be applied to *any* rule-governed activity. We could, for example, argue that Kevin Keegan does not play football but rather that football plays Kevin Keegan; that it is the system, the rule book, the Cannon League, that kicks the ball and scores the goals. If this seems absurd. . . .[7]

Not only seems, but is.

In the present critical climate, however, not only is the author dead but the text as written by language—the collocation of words appearing

---

4 J. Hillis Miller, "Ariachne's Broken Woof," *Georgia Review*, 31 (Spring 1976), 51.
5 See Martin Heidegger, "Building Dwelling Thinking," in *Poetry, Language, Thought*, trans. Albert Hofstadter (New York: Harper and Row, 1971), p. 146.
6 Roland Barthes, "The Death of the Author," in *Image-Music-Text*, trans. Stephen Heath (London: Fontana, 1977), p. 143.
7 Raymond Tallis, *In Defence of Realism* (London: Edward Arnold, 1988), p. 73.

in a literary work—is said to be totally arbitrary. In his review of M. H. Abrams's *Natural Supernaturalism*, J. Hillis Miller claims that "Each reader takes possession of the work for one reason or another and imposes on it a certain pattern of meaning."[8] In his view, readers intervene into the text and, without realizing that it is a mere interplay of signs and figures, they impose themes and meanings where there were none before; or else they single out one pattern while neglecting others, thus falsifying the text in an effort to find a meaning-coherence not discoverable in the text itself. All reading is thus a misreading, since there is no real, right meaning expressed anywhere in the text. Any text, in Miller's view, will itself deconstruct the false construction we put upon it, the unitary meaning we are said to impose upon it.

But do we plunge into a text just anywhere, and is it a freeplay (that is, a chaos) of conflicting meanings? Some readers may turn to the end to see how *Bleak House* concludes before commencing with Chapter 1. And others may flip through de Sade for the dog-eared pages first. But for most of us, reading is a linear, chronological experience of beginning at the beginning, going on to the middle, and ending at the end. Especially as reading sophistication grows, we observe textual similarities, our grasp of genre forms increases, and we note that beginning, middle, and end are highly important, even decisive *loci* in literary texts. Our sense of poetic wholeness may, as Aristotle shows, derive from noticing the relationships of the beginning, the middle, and the end; and this perception may lead to the formation of organizational principles like *protasis, epitasis,* and *catastasis.* We may prefer to call it Freytag's Pyramid of rising and falling action. Or we may prefer introduction and exposition, rising development and entanglement, crisis or turning point, descending action, catastrophe, and so forth. Readers have inferred or seen these structures, and playwrights have emulated them. Therefore, while it is possible to plunge into a text anywhere, or even to read it backward, the result could hardly restore an author's intention, show the aesthetic wholeness of the text, or prove instructive for hermeneutic thought.

Nevertheless, Derrida has taught the deconstructionist critic like Miller to claim that a text is a freeplay of significations, divorced from reality as such, that can never contain or express presence, the self, or reality. Various critics seize upon deconstructionism to further various personal or ideological agendas. As to Miller himself, his viewpoint expresses a simple "underlying purpose," "the eradication of truth in language, which corresponds to the *historical* disappearance of the ground

---

8 J. Hillis Miller, "Tradition and Difference," *Diacritics,* 2 (Winter 1972), 12.

of truth, of God. Post-structuralism is used to place that issue within language rather than within history, as if this might *explain* the absence of truth that a historical relativism can only describe."[9] For many readers the tendency of Miller's thought is toward interpretive chaos and is an expression of utter nihilism. Miller has recently denied that he is a nihilist, taking the Nietzschean high road of claiming that he is beyond all that, observing that criticism exists "in an uneasy joy of interpretation, beyond nihilism, always in movement, a going beyond which remains in place." [10] But the premise of his argument logically tends toward what E. D. Hirsch, in *Validity in Interpretation*, has rightly called "cognitive atheism."[11]

II

The subversion of belief in the capacity of language to refer to extra-linguistic reality, to represent it, and to express its meaning in language of common intelligibility—a subversion we owe to Nietzsche, Derrida, Barthes, Foucault, Miller, and their disciples—has also had its effect on reader-response thinking. At issue with critics in the reader-response camp is the claim that the work of art has no complete autonomous existence as a reality. In fact, for these critics it is in the reader's consciousness that the work exists. If we ask about its ontological *situs*, the locus of meaning with respect to any text, the reader-response theorist speaks of the subjectivity of the reader: it is the reader who creates the text, who brings it to life, and who provides it with its meaning. Although an excessive preoccupation with the reader will inevitably lead, as René Wellek and Austin Warren predicted in *Theory of Literature*, to "complete skepticism and anarchy" and eventually to "the definite end of all teaching of literature,"[12] critics like Stanley Fish argue the indeterminacy of literary texts and reserve for the reader powers heretofore claimed for the author or for the text itself. In fact, in "What Is Stylistics and Why Are They Saying Such Terrible Things About It?" Fish expresses his dissatisfaction with the view that the text generates literary meaning as an unworthy description of the reading experience because

---

9 Art Berman, *From the New Criticism to Deconstruction: The Reception of Structuralism and Post-Structuralism* (Urbana: University of Illinois Press, 1988), p. 234.

10 J. Hillis Miller, "The Critic as Host," *Deconstruction and Criticism* (New York: Seabury, 1979), pp. 252–253.

11 As E. D. Hirsch has correctly observed, "All valid interpretation of every sort is founded on the re-cognition of what an author meant." See Hirsch's *Validity in Interpretation* (New Haven: Yale University Press, 1967), p. 126.

12 René Wellek and Austin Warren, *Theory of Literature*, (New York: Harcourt, Brace, 1956), p. 134.

"it would deny to man the most remarkable of his abilities, the ability to give the world meaning rather than to extract the meaning that is already there."[13] I am all for giving man his due, little enough though it may be. But it is no distinction in human glory that man can attribute meanings to a text that it does not express. In any case, in "Interpreting the *Variorum*," Fish claims that interpretive strategies "are the shape of reading, and because they are the shape of reading, they give texts their shape, making them rather than, as it is usually assumed, arising from them." Instead of being a servant of the text, which has a determinate meaning that criticism can usefully characterize, Fish's ideal critic replaces the text with his own verbal inventions. To believe that all critical readings are invented, Fish remarks,

> relieves me of the obligation to be right (a standard that simply drops out) and demands only that I be interesting (a standard that can be met without any reference at all to an illusory objectivity). Rather than restoring or recovering texts, I am in the business of making texts and of teaching others to make them by adding to their repertoire of strategies.

Relieved of the obligation to be right! Here is a humanities teacher who has forsworn truth and degraded his profession to that of clown or mere entertainer. No wonder a large segment of the public currently holds the humanities in contempt. But most teachers, I submit, would rather be right than interesting. In fact, whatever is right *always* turns out to be interesting, since verity is absolutely commanding; while whatever is interesting may reflect, as we have seen in Fish, only the glib and the insincere. In another place, apropos of this subjective glibness, Fish remarks, "If we seem to be talking about 'different poems,' that is right, for each of us would be reading the poem he had made."[14] In other words, not the author and not language as such but *the reader* makes the poem. The *reductio ad absurdum* of this kind of criticism is Norman Holland's perverse, if witty, claim of "authorship" in the amusingly entitled "Hamlet—My Greatest Creation."[15]

Long ago Allen Tate asked what is for me a decisive question about the hermeneutic task—namely, "What as literary critics are we to judge?" He thought that "as literary critics we must first of all decide in

---

13 Stanley Fish, "What Is Stylistics and Why Are They Saying Such Terrible Things About It?" in *Approaches to Poetics,* ed. Seymour Chatman (New York: Columbia University Press, 1973), p. 134.

14 Stanley Fish, "Interpreting the *Variorum*," in *Contemporary Literary Criticism: Modernism Through Post-Structuralism,* ed. Robert Con Davis (New York: Longman, 1986), pp. 405–406.

15 Norman Holland, "Hamlet—My Greatest Creation," *Journal of the American Academy of Psychoanalysis,* 3 (1975), 419–427.

what respect the literary work has a specific objectivity. If we deny its specific objectivity, then not only is criticism impossible but literature also." Tate thought that "the formal qualities of a poem are the focus of the specifically critical judgment because they partake of an objectivity that the subject matter, abstracted from the form, wholly lacks."[16] And it is true that the formal properties of particular novels, poems, and plays do offer us objective matter for analyzing and assessing literary works.

But if each of us reads a poem he has "made" himself, we can never talk about the same aesthetic object. If Fish were right, there would be no common object represented by the reading experience, no common focus of study, and no escape from the atomized and fragmented subjectivities that are represented by different impressionistic readers. The fatuity of this viewpoint was immediately recognized by a great many sensible people and was hooted down in the critical quarterlies; and, in response to so much ridicule, Fish bestirred himself to find some constraint that might operate to control wildly subjective interpretation. In *Is There a Text in This Class?* he came up with the notion of an "interpretive community," a body of like-minded individuals all observing the same hermeneutical conventions who agree to agree that a text has a meaning. But it is a meaning that, as a group, they have agreed to give it. An interpretive community—like a college class, for example, agreeing about the meaning of a Wallace Stevens poem—is simply an institutionalization of a joint enterprise. Fish observes of the institutions of literature that they are "no more than the (temporary) effects of speech act agreements, and they are therefore as fragile as the decision, always capable of being revoked, to abide by them."[17] In other words, if the college class as an interpretive community agrees to change its mind and say that the Stevens poem means something else quite different from what it first said, the newest formulation is what the poem means. The class has given it a new meaning. But what kind of authority is an interpretive community once we have perceived that its interpretation is merely conventional and that it has acquired this status only by means of a temporary verbal agreement, not by virtue of the interpretation's truth to the meaning of the text itself? This is not authority in interpretation at all.

True authority in interpretation is not a matter of consensus or classroom votes as to what the meaning of a work may be. It is a derivative of knowledge and insight. The authority of the expert interpreter is

---

16 Allen Tate, "Miss Emily and the Bibliographer," in *Collected Essays of Allen Tate* (Denver: Alan Swallow, 1959), p. 57.
17 Stanley Fish, *Is There a Text in This Class? The Authority of Interpretive Communities* (Cambridge: Harvard University Press, 1980), p. 215.

immediately felt by his auditor or reader; and it arises from what Hans-Georg Gadamer has rightly called

> recognition and knowledge—knowledge, namely that the other is superior to oneself in judgment and insight and that for this reason his judgment takes precedence, ie it has priority over one's own. This is connected with the fact that authority cannot actually be bestowed, but is acquired and must be acquired, if someone is to lay claim to it. It rests on recognition and hence on an act of reason itself which, aware of its own limitations, accepts that others have a better understanding. Authority in this sense, properly understood, has nothing to do with blind obedience to a command. Indeed, authority has nothing to do with obedience, but rather with knowledge.[18]

We attain deeper levels of understanding than we are capable of when an expert reader—an interpreter of insight, judgment, and vision—shows us a latency or complexity of meaning we had not grasped before. His superior hermeneutic gift helps to define what we come to think of as the authoritative meaning of a work; and it is a matter of right-minded humility to await the text's illumination and to accept the wiser understanding of the text that can be provided by an authoritative master. This interpretive humility is far from the conceit of imposing a meaning on the text or sacrificing one's horizon of understanding to some illusory interpretive community.[19]

III

It is common to hear this complaint against M. Derrida's thinking: deconstructionism is useless in effecting politically correct social change. In other words, our current literature department reformers (the Marxists, feminists, gays, multiculturalists, and so forth) do not find deconstruction useful in transforming the political situation. This complaint presupposes that deconstructionism is merely a text-centered formalism that has no faith in the utility of the text, or its applicability to ideology, because there is an alleged gap between reality and the verbal representation of it. Indeed, J. Hillis Miller has claimed that there is a "conservative" premise to deconstructionism:

---

18 Hans-Georg Gadamer, *Truth and Method,* trans. Garrett Barden and John Cumming (New York: Crossroad, 1986), p. 248.

19 The inanity of Fish's claim is transparent to anyone who has ever conducted a free and open college classroom discussion. Open discussions stimulate a variety of viewpoints that rarely coalesce into a single interpretive consensus. But coercive teaching by a repressive and authoritarian professor will produce a temporary speech agreement. (This last, in fact, accounts for why some may think they have formed an interpretive community.)

Its difference from Marxism, which is likely to become more sharply visible as time goes on, is that it views as naive the millennial or revolutionary hopes still in one way or another present even in sophisticated Marxism. This millenarianism believes that a change in the material base or in the class structure would transform our situation in relation to language or change the human condition generally. Deconstruction, on the other hand, sees the notion of a determining material base as one element in the traditional metaphysical system it wants to put in question. . . . Deconstruction does not promise liberation from that famous prison house of language, only a different way of living within it.[20]

Certainly those who accord to history and to reality an objective status, beyond the limitation of one's consciousness and the subjectivity of the individual, are right to complain at the extent to which deconstructionism and reader-response theory enclose criticism in a web of language, what Fredric Jameson has called "the prison house of language." Jameson's reaction was to obfuscate the issues inherent in deconstructionism by a blind insistence on "late" capitalism and on an unintelligible Marxist historicism in which History with a capital H is called the Absent Cause that generates the literary work, its meaning, its reception, and its criticism. But the ideology of Marxism has failed so abysmally as a theory of economic determinism, as a theory of class relations, and as an eschatology that culminates historical development that even the Russians have abandoned it. It survives only as a tool of totalitarian repression in countries such as Cuba and China—and in a good many modern university professors who are entirely out of touch with economic and political reality. In any case, Marxism, as a monolithic theory of economic base and cultural superstructure, has totally broken down. Nobody holds to it in a consistent way anymore; and there are as many Marxisms as there are Marxists.

Still, deconstructionism has proved immensely fruitful to the political left in trying to foment that chaos in the domain of values that is said to be necessary to launch the supposed forthcoming revolution. That is largely because Derridaism is by no means the conservative agency that J. Hillis Miller has described in trying to make us all cozy and comfortable with the new nihilism. Derrida, a leftist himself, has always stressed the political character of deconstructionism, and leftists of every stripe have been quick to seize upon the political utility he accords it:

---

20 J. Hillis Miller, "Theory and Practice: Response to Vincent Leitch," *Critical Inquiry*, 6 (Summer 1980), 612–613.

According to the consequence of its logic, it [deconstructionism] attacks not only the internal construction, both semantic and formal, of philosophemes, but also what one would assign to it wrongly as its external place, its extrinsic conditions of use: the historical forms of its pedagogy, the social, economic, or political structures of this pedagogical institution. It is because it touches upon solid structures, on "material" institutions, and not only on discourses or on signifying representations, that deconstruction always distinguishes itself from an analysis or a "critique."[21]

Deconstructionism, in other words, is not merely a method for analyzing poems or providing a critique of a novel. It is a method for intervening in the field of social institutions and relations so as to alter them. The Marxist Terry Eagleton has recognized Derrida's covert intention: "Derrida is clearly out to do more than develop new techniques of reading: deconstruction is for him an ultimately *political* practice, an attempt to dismantle the logic by which a particular system of political structures and social institutions, maintains its force."[22]

This covert intention has also been identified by several other recent critics of the university. According to Paul R. Gross and Norman Levitt in *Higher Superstition: The Academic Left and Its Quarrels with Science,* deconstructionism "has come to be read as a road map for the continuation of a political struggle that seemed, by the late seventies, to have run out of steam." And John Patrick Diggins in *The Rise and Fall of the American Left,* observes of middle-aged radicals that, "Having lost the confrontation on the streets in the sixties, they could later, as English professors in the eighties, continue it in the classroom."[23] They could do this because deconstruction authorized the Marxist to view the text as indeterminate, as lacking in intentional meaning that can be ascertained through analysis. Derrida destabilized philosophemes—or our sense of the ideational conceptions and processes by which values are founded in philosophy and religion—with the effect of likewise destabilizing our sense of political reality. What better way to "intervene" and lay about in the hierarchy of social forces than to deconstruct what the reader understood as justice, morality, and truth—even the law itself? In this

---

21 Jacques Derrida, *La Vérité en peinture* (Paris: Flammarion, 1978), pp. 23–24.

22 Terry Eagleton, *Literary Theory: An Introduction* (Minneapolis: University of Minnesota Press, 1983), p. 145. On the vexed issue of deconstruction and politics, see Michael Ryan's *Marxism and Deconstruction* (Baltimore: Johns Hopkins University Press, 1982) and Christopher Butler's valuable *Interpretation, Deconstruction and Ideology* (London: Oxford University Press, 1984).

23 Paul R. Gross and Norman Levitt, *Higher Superstition: The Academic Left and Its Quarrels with Science* (Baltimore: Johns Hopkins University Press, 1994), p. 76; see also John Patrick Diggins, *The Rise and Fall of the American Left* (New York: W. W. Norton, 1992), p. 356.

respect, Gertrude Himmelfarb is quite right that Marxists have been "attracted to those aspects of [deconstructionism] that they recognize as truly subversive." And, in "the common cause of radicalism, structuralists and poststructuralists, new historicists and deconstructionists, have been able to overlook whatever logical incompatibilities there may be between their theories. . . . Like the communists and socialists of an earlier generation, they have formed a 'popular front,' marching separately to a common goal."[24]

Ruminating on what Marxists can do—indeed, have done—with the deconstructionist attack on "solid structures," one might take either Fredric Jameson or Terry Eagleton as a representative of the Marxist *trahison des clercs.*[25] But one is drawn instead to the critical writing of Tony Bennett in *Formalism and Marxism* (1979). A work like this will serve our purposes because it is much more revealing, because less rhetorically obfuscatory, of the sinister assault on liberty still manifest in the Marxist agenda. Eagleton slithers away from the political implications of almost all the viewpoints that he espouses. And insofar as Jameson is concerned, it would be difficult to extrapolate a specific praxis from his work: his views are concealed in a verbal fog. But Bennett is so transparent as wonderfully to show what happens to literary values when deconstructionist formalism provides revolutionary Marxism with a way of negating the idea that a text has an essence, a presence, and a meaning accessible to analytic thought.

If one wishes to know how deconstructionism can create political anarchy by subverting the foundations of value, how the revolutionary ideologue can capitalize on this chaos so as to attain his political goal, *Formalism and Marxism* provides us the answer. "Marxist criticism," Bennett observes,

> has hitherto proceeded on the assumption that every literary text has its politics inscribed within it and that the role of Marxist criticism is to enunciate this politics to give it voice by making it explicit. This political essentialism must be broken with. The text does not have a politics which is separable from the determinations which work upon it or the position it occupies within the disposition of the field of cultural relations. The task which faces Marxist criticism is not that of reflecting or

---

24 Gertrude Himmelfarb, *On Looking into the Abyss: Untimely Thoughts on Culture and Society* (New York: Alfred A. Knopf, 1994), pp. 157–158. Many garden-variety Marxists, however, have resisted an amalgamation with deconstructionism. A useful discussion of these points may be found in Vincent B. Leitch's *American Literary Criticism from the Thirties to the Eighties* (New York: Columbia University Press, 1988), pp. 366–407.

25 See John M. Ellis's devastating critique of Jameson, for example, in "Frederic Jameson's Marxist Criticism," *Academic Questions,* 7 (Spring 1994), 30–43.

of bringing to light the politics which is already there, as a latent presence within the text which has but to be made manifest. It is that of actively politicizing the text, of making its politics for it, by producing a new position for it within the field of cultural relations and, thereby, new forms of use and effectivity within the broader social process.[26]

For many of us, this approach would appear to be *a reading into the text* of a political dimension (favorable to Marxism, of course), an ascribing to the text of a political ideology that the text does not express itself. Can this be the case? Is it justifiable for the critic to create a political meaning for a novel that does not thematize one, or make a politics for it, independent of the novelist's political sympathies—or lack of them? Would this not result in a corruption of the text?

We know enough about Marxist criticism in history, politics, sociology, and literature—over the past seventy-five years—to know that the corruption of learning, the contamination of scholarship, by Marxist critics, has usually been justified (when exposed) on the ground of the necessity of advancing the revolutionary ideology. The revisionist rewriting of history and the exaltation of party hacks whose socialist or communist doctrine was ideologically correct (while better writers were persecuted, imprisoned, and silenced)—all this is well known in many East European countries, China, and Cuba; and comparable corruptions of the truth occurred in the United States, notoriously in the 1930s. Is it happening again, on the ground that literature has no reference to an extralinguistic reality? Evidently so, for Bennett goes on:

> The activity of criticism is itself a pre-eminently *political* exercise. For the texts on which Marxist criticism works are, in a sense, already "occupied." They are already filled with interpretations. The way in which they are appropriated is already determined by the uses to which they are put in the social process. Given this, the quest for an objective "science" of the literary text is illusory. The literary text has no single or uniquely privileged meaning, no single or uniquely privileged effect that can be abstracted from the ways in which criticism itself works upon and mediates the reception of that text. In this sense, literature is not something to be studied; it is an area to be occupied. The question is not what literature's political effects *are* but what they might be *made to be*—not in a forever and once-and-for-all sense but in a dynamic and changing way—by the operations of Marxist criticism (*F&M*, 137).

To put the text to such uses, to superimpose upon it political ideas in

---

26 See Tony Bennett's *Formalism and Marxism* (New York: Methuen, 1979), pp. 167–168. Quotations from this work will hereafter be given as *F&M*, in parentheses, in the text.

disregard of what it actually and formally thematizes, is in essence to use it in a radical effort to revolutionize social relations. That is the real agenda beneath the idea that there is no essence disclosed by the text.

Bennett's propositions sound wonderfully exciting, and it would be pleasant to believe that anything goes, but we have it on the highest authority that, if the blind lead the blind, they will both fall into the ditch. One of the more grotesque voices recently emanating from the critical ditch is that of Robert Crosman. He attacks the idea that a text has an intelligible meaning that expresses the author's intention by faulting E. D. Hirsch's argument in *Validity in Interpretation*. Crosman opines that Hirsch produces interpretive arguments and therefore "social discord." He complains of "how unsuited to a modern democracy is Hirsch's theory of meaning." It is now "totalitarian" and "fascistic" to say that a text has a right interpretation and that others may be wrong. This Sophist wants social harmony, the homogenization of all sexual, racial, and cultural differences, and perfect equality in literary criticism—even if it has to be purchased by the suppression of truth and the repression of others' freedom of speech. But if democracy thrives on the contest of ideas, on arguments about meaning, on contending interpretations that persuade us, so does criticism. In contestation, error is exposed, truth is affirmed, and there emerges an understanding of the meaning of the literary work. [27] But once the critic breaks with essentialism, anything goes. Hence, reading, Bennett goes on,

> does not restore to the text contradictions which were "always there" but hidden from view; it *reads contradictions into the text*. It does not *reflect* a work of transformation on ideological forms that literary texts can be said always to have possessed, like some secret essence which criticism has only recently discovered; it *makes* such texts effect a work of transformation on those forms of signification which are *said to be* ideological (*F&M*, 146–147).

In Bennett's view, since criticism is doomed to produce a loop of endless indeterminacies, language can mean whatever the Marxist says it does; and he ought to say that it means whatever advances the cause.

---

27 See Crosman's egregious argument "Do Readers Make Meaning?" in *The Reader in the Text: Essays on Audience and Interpretation,* eds. Susan R. Suleiman and Inge Crosman (Princeton: Princeton University Press, 1980), p. 160n. Crosman, Fish, Holland, Jane Tompkins, and other American reader-response critics have trivialized a very important area of study, the relationship of the reader and the text. For more serious discussions of the *Rezeptionsästhetik,* one must look to Europe and the work of Roman Ingarden, Wolfgang Iser, and Hans-Georg Gadamer.

IV

Derrida has said that any hermeneutic project which "postulates a true sense of the text" must be "disqualified" because reading has been "freed from the horizon of meaning or truth of being, liberated from the values of the product's production or the present's presence." Once we understand that, he remarks, "the question of style is immediately unloosed as a question of writing."[28] Now that meaning and truth are out, in other words, it is only a hop, skip, and a jump from the dismissal of language's referentiality to the reduction of language to mere rhetoric and aesthetics. And once language has been reduced (by a verbal declaration!) to mere rhetoric and aesthetics, truth itself can be dismissed as a fiction. This viewpoint merely brings up to date the sophistical query, older than Pontius Pilate, that Nietzsche posed and answered for himself in "On Truth and Falsity in Their Extramoral Sense":

> What therefore is truth? A mobile army of metaphors, metonymies, anthropomorphisms: in short, a sum of human relations which have become poetically and rhetorically intensified, metamorphosed, adorned, and after long usage seem to a nation fixed, canonic and binding; truths are illusions of which one has forgotten that they *are* illusions. . . .[29]

Against a radical skepticism this sweeping, no formal argument can succeed and no logical rebuttal can be offered—since logic has been dismissed, metaphysics outlawed, and philosophy itself reduced to tropes and illusions. Rational argumentation becomes irrelevant because, as Heidegger put it, "A skeptic can no more be refuted than the Being of truth can be 'proved.'"[30] Even so, radical skepticism of this variety always subverts its own claim to truth because its truth claims are always made in rational formulations that presuppose intentionality, logic, shared communication, linguistic decidability, and the reality of valid interpretation. Such skepticism is also subverted by the evident fact that, if knowledge is impossible, that thesis itself cannot be validated or even known by us.[31]

But most of the current academic Sophists do not, of course, believe

---

28 Jacques Derrida, "The Gaze of Oedipus," *Spurs,* quoted in Vincent B. Leitch, *Deconstructive Criticism: An Advanced Introduction* (New York: Columbia University Press, 1983), p. 167.

29 Friedrich Nietzsche, "On Truth and Falsity in Their Extramoral Sense," in *The Complete Works of Friedrich Nietzsche,* ed. Oscar Levy; trans. Maximilian A. Mügge (1873; reprinted New York: Russell and Russell, 1964), II, 180.

30 Martin Heidegger, *Being and Time,* trans. John Macquarrie and Edward Robinson (New York: Harper and Row, 1962), p. 271 [H229].

31 See Thomas M. Seebohm's "The End of Philosophy: Three Historical Aphorisms," in *Hermeneutics and Deconstruction,* eds. Hugh J. Silverman and Don Ihde (Albany: State University of New York Press, 1985), p. 16.

in the nihilism they advocate. And if we really took our three schools of criticism seriously and dismissed their claims to the truth as mere verbal inventions, as mere rhetorical constructs already subverted and undone by their own linguistic undecidability—and therefore irrelevant to any serious purpose in life, a howl of dismay would go up throughout the Modern Language Association. For these modes of radical skepticism are finally "suicidal." As M. H. Abrams has rightly put it, "as the theorist is aware, his views are self-reflexive, in that his subversive process destroys the possibility that a reader can interpret correctly either the expression of his theory or the textual interpretations to which it is applied."[32] This being the case, we are as usual free to go on reading and interpreting the texts at hand. But our reading will never hereafter be reduced to that freeplay of undecidabilities that so entrances the modern Sophist. To the exent that we are alive to questions of intellectual discovery, we will go on seeking the illumination of meaning that is always available in the magisterial forms of great literature.

---

32 M. H. Abrams, *Doing Things with Texts: Essays in Criticism and Critical Theory* (New York: W. W. Norton, 1989), p. 272.

Acknowledgments

Several individuals have played an important part in the evolution of this volume, specifically C. Hugh Holman, Leon Edel, Daniel Mark Fogel, Milton R. Stern, John Kuehl, Kenneth Cameron, and Frederick Morgan. To them I owe my thanks. But chiefly I wish to acknowledge here Hilton Kramer, editor of *The New Criterion*, whose probing criticism, fearless defense of high standards in art, and personal encouragement over the years have meant so much to me. In addition, very special thanks are due to Roger Kimball, managing editor of *The New Criterion*, whose unfailing friendship, editorial acumen, and computer wizardry made the preparation of this volume a practicable matter. The prose of a several of these essays is much more lucid thanks to the blue pencil of Erich Eichman, now book editor of the *Wall Street Journal*. To them I yield all the credit; the faults of the book are mine. Although some of the essays in *Vital Signs* first appeared elsewhere, each has been revised for this volume. Here I wish to note the place of original publication and to thank the several editors and presses for their kind permission to reprint, in revised form, the following items: "Simon Schama, Francis Parkman, and the Writing of History," *The New Criterion*, 10 (September 1991), 39–52. "The Adventures of Martin Green," *The New Criterion*, 3 (May 1985), 7–14. "The American Corinne," *The New Criterion*, 3 (December 1984), 68–71; "Margaret Fuller: The American Minerva," *The New Criterion*, 13 (February 1995), 24–29. "William Dean Howells and the Practice of Criticism," *The New Criterion*, 10 (June 1992), 28–37. "'A Runaway Dog Like Me': Stephen Crane in His Letters," *The New Criterion*, 6 (June 1988), 49–58. "A Solitary Soul: The Career of Kate Chopin," *The New Criterion*, 9 (April 1991), 12–17. "The Androgynous Papa Hemingway," *The New Criterion*, 6 (October 1987), 67–74. "Hemingway Unbound," *The New Criterion*, 11 (December 1992), 23–30. "Sherwood Anderson: A Room of His Own," *The New*

Criterion, 6 (December 1987), 67–78. "The Romance of History: Irving's Companions of Columbus," *American Transcendental Quarterly*, 14 (Fall 1974), 18–24; reprinted with the permission of AMS Press. "Jack London in His Short Stories," *Hudson Review*, 47 (Spring 1994), 291–298. "Propriety and Fine Perception: Henry James's *The Europeans*," *Modern Language Review*, 73 (1978), 481–495. "Edith Wharton: The Archaeological Motive," *Yale Review*, 61 (Summer 1972), 562–574. "Vitality and Vampirism in *Tender Is the Night*," *Critical Essays on* Tender Is the Night, ed. Milton R. Stern (Boston: G. K. Hall, 1986), pp. 238–246. "Rereading *The American*: A Century Since," *Henry James Review*, 1 (1980), 139–153; reprinted in *Critical Essays on Henry James: The Early Novels*, ed. James W. Gargano (Boston: G. K. Hall, 1987), pp. 96–116; reprinted by permission of the Johns Hopkins University Press. "Hardy and Ellen Glasgow: *Barren Ground*," *Mississippi Quarterly*, 32 (Fall 1979), 577–590. "The Physician-Writer and the Cure of the Soul," *New Orleans Review*, 16 (Winter 1989), 17–21.

Index

James W. Tuttleton is professor of English at New York University. Born in St. Louis, he studied at Harding University and the University of North Carolina. He has written on a wide range of American Literature in such periodicals as *The American Scholar, The New Criterion, The Times Literary Supplement,* and *The Yale Review.* He is also the author of *The Novel of Manners in America* and *Thomas Wentworth Higginson,* and the editor of, among other books, *The Works of Washington Irving: History, Tales and Sketches* for the Library of America. He lives in New York City.